EXECUTIVE
OPINION

Also by Herman E. Krooss

FINANCIAL HISTORY OF THE UNITED STATES
AMERICAN ECONOMIC DEVELOPMENT
THE AMERICAN ECONOMY: ITS ORIGINS, DEVELOPMENT AND
TRANSFORMATION

EXECUTIVE OPINION

*What Business Leaders Said
and Thought on Economic Issues
1920s–1960s*

HERMAN E. KROOSS

DOUBLEDAY & COMPANY, INC., GARDEN CITY, NEW YORK   1970

CONTENTS

How Articulate Are Businessmen? Business Spokes-
men Are Ordinarily Not Businessmen. The Many
Sides of Business Opinion. The Businessman's Im-
age of Himself. The Reaction to the Depression-
Induced Loss of Prestige. The Effectiveness of the
Businessman's Campaign to "Resell" Himself. The
Contemporary Image.

The Service Concept in the 1920s. The "New
Capitalism." The Resurgence of the Profit Motive
During the Depression. Business Motives in the
Post-World War II Era. The Further Depreciation
of Self-Interest. Social Responsibility. The New
View of Profits. Business Responsibility and Irre-
sponsibility.

The Postwar Boom and Collapse. Explaining
the Depression. Prescribing the Cure. The Money

Supply and the Federal Reserve.   What Businessmen
Learned from the Depression.

The Four Phases of Prosperity.   The Money Supply
and Credit.   Taxes and the Recession of 1924.   Federal Reserve Policy.   Prologue to the Bull Market.
Explaining Prosperity.   The High-Wage Doctrine.
Some Skepticism about the New Era.   The Recession of 1927.   The Federal Reserve and Speculation.
The Bull Market at High Tide.   Some Pessimism in
the Midst of Optimism.   The Business Reaction to
the Federal Reserve's Attempt to Stem Speculation.
Early Signs of a Business Depression.   The End of
the Bull Market.

The First Reaction to the Depression.   Businessmen Bewildered.   "What This Country Needs Is
a Mussolini."   The Reasons Why.   What to Do
About It.   Different Opinions About Money and
Credit.   Branch Banking and Deposit Insurance.
Overproduction, Cheap Money, and Government
Spending.   The Cures as Given by Non-banking Financiers.   The Causes and Cures According to the Industrialists.   Overproduction, a "Planned Society,"
and the Anti-trust Laws.   The Balanced Budget Panacea.   How the Non-business Community Viewed
the Depression.

The Inevitability of the Conflict Between Business
and the New Deal.   The Early Infatuation.   The
Beginnings of Disenchantment.   The AAA and the
NRA.   The Revulsion Against the NRA.   The Separation That Preceded the Divorce.   Business Aban-

"Opinion is like a pendulum and obeys the same law. If it goes past the center of gravity on one side, it must go a like distance on the other; and it is only after a certain time that it finds the true point at which it can remain at rest."

PREFACE

This is a book about business and businessmen. More specifically, it is a book about business opinion, as expressed in what businessmen said and wrote on the economic issues of the fifty years between World War I and today.

In writing this book, I have been concerned with four questions: What opinions did businessmen hold on such economic problems and issues as the business cycle, the government's relation to the economy, labor-management relations, monetary policy, the tariff, competition, price determination, and profits? Is business opinion different from what it was yesterday, and if it is, how much different is it? How much did business opinion differ from what other groups in society—academic economists, labor leaders, politicians, intellectuals, etc.—thought about economic issues? To what extent were the opinions of businessmen guided by an eye to the main chance; to what extent did they coincide with the group's self-interest?

Businessmen as here defined are those who combine labor, land, and capital in the production or exchange of goods or services with the objective of making a profit. But businessmen come in all sizes and shapes. There are young, middle-aged, and old businessmen; small businessmen and big businessmen; Eastern, Northern, Southern, and Western businessmen. There are manufacturers, bankers, merchants, utility tycoons, railroadmen, corner grocers, and butchers, bakers, and riot-stick makers.

There are owner-entrepreneurs, career managers with a large stake in their companies, and career managers with little ownership interest. There are go-getting empire builders who take big risks and who seem more interested in the power that a big business enables them to wield than in the profits it enables them to earn. But there are many more cautious businessmen who put a high marginal utility on money.

Businessmen do not think alike any more than they look alike. This is not to say that a majority, a modal opinion does not exist, but it is to say that there is no such thing as a business ideology as Webster defined ideology: "a manner or the content of thinking characteristic of an individual, group, or culture." In the 1920s and 1930s, the opinions of Henry S. Dennison on any economic issue bore little resemblance to those of the then president of the National Association of Manufacturers. In more recent times, the views of George Champion differed from those of Rudolph Peterson, even though both were bankers.

The volume of expressed business opinion, which is never very sizable, varies in direct proportion to the prominence of an issue in the public eye. Many businessmen had much to say about taxes in 1924 when the Mellon plan for tax reduction was being debated, but they had little to say on the subject in 1923 or in 1925. It is hardly necessary to add that there was almost a complete unanimity of opinion on this subject. But usually just the opposite applied. On tariffs, for example, business opinion has run the entire spectrum from fear and hope to confusion and indifference. When the 1967 Kennedy Round tariff cuts were announced, retailers were elated; airplane and motormakers were happy; tanners, steel producers, glassmakers, textile manufacturers and dyers mourned the coming of disaster. A sharp conflict was apparent in the steel industry itself. Said Crucible Steel's John C. Lobb: "Any attempt to govern free trade through quotas, tariffs, or other legislation is an invitation to government control of prices and wages." But Homer Martin of Bethlehem was reported to have commented that an import quota was "basic to the national security."

A study of business opinion presents a variety of peculiar problems for which there are no completely satisfactory solutions. Businessmen have never been very conscientious about writing down what they have thought. They have not left large collections of public papers. As Matthew Josephson, who was scarcely a champion of the business group, once said, "Businessmen spoke little and did much." The businessman's philosophy and attitudes must, therefore, be recovered mainly from bits here and pieces there of published and unpublished speeches, articles, and books. This necessarily means that the small businessman is largely omitted from the picture, for few of his opinions ever appeared in the mass media.

Even among big businessmen there is no wealth of data, for most big businessmen said as little for public consumption as they could manage. Other writers have avoided this problem by relying on the opinions of "business spokesmen"—trade association directors, periodical editors, lobbyists, and newspaper columnists. In one recent book on "business ideology," for example, there were four times as many quotes from trade association people, advertising copy writers, and columnists as from the businessmen themselves. It is assumed that these hired hands and business sympathizers accurately reflect the business leaders' opinions, but this is not true. To be sure, many, perhaps most, businessmen agree at one time or other with much of what the business scribes say, but they rarely agree with how it is said; and the how is just as important as the substance. I have relied very little on trade association statements except for comparison or contrast.

Something must be said of how the opinions cited in this study were collected. First, a universe of business leaders was constructed consisting of (a) the chairmen and presidents of the largest manufacturing, banking, merchandising, and transportation firms in the country in the last fifty years; (b) businessmen who held a number of directorships in the largest companies; (c) executives who received a substantial enough salary to be included in *Business Week*'s compendium of the high salaried; *Forbes*' list of business leaders in 1917 and 1947; Gerard's list of men who "ran America" in 1930; and those businessmen who, according to the *New York Times Index* and the *Readers' Guide to Periodical Literature,* often spoke out on economic issues.

For the opinions of business leaders of the past, I consulted the files of the *New York Times* and other newspapers, all the issues of *Vital Speeches,* and the appropriate articles listed in *Readers' Guide to Periodical Literature* and the *Industrial Arts Index.* For contemporary opinion, I consulted all the above sources and in addition wrote to the one hundred largest industrial firms, the twenty-five largest commercial banks, the ten largest life insurance companies, the ten largest merchandising firms, the ten largest utilities, and the twenty-five largest transportation companies requesting any talks, articles, speeches, or interviews on economic issues for the prior five years. The response to the direct-mail request was beyond the call of any public relations department's duty. All but forty-three of the 180 companies responded.

Of the missing forty-three, an extensive idea of the opinions of the executives of two were easily obtained from other sources. It was apparent, however, that the executives of most of these companies were not publicly expressing opinions on controversial economic issues.

Of the 137 companies that replied, twenty-six either said that their executives had not made any public statements, or sent a copy of an annual report, or a talk to a group of security analysts.

Assuming that the sample was adequate, there remains the problem of whether the expressed opinions were truly representative, that is, whether the speaker really believed the ideas contained in a given speech or interview or whether he was offering them as lip service to the prevailing prejudices of public or business opinion. But I had to assume that in most cases if a man expressed an opinion, he believed much of what he said.

Of what importance is it to know what businessmen thought? It is a commonplace today to say that America has been a business civilization, that the businessman has more than any other placed his trademark on American culture and social history. If this is true, it also answers the question of the importance of business opinion.

One final word. It seems to me only fair that an author state his biases and prejudices. I am more sympathetic to business than to its critics. Over the course of some years of thinking about business and business history I gradually became convinced, much against my earlier opinions, that the clichés about businessmen and the business world were, unlike many clichés, largely untrue. As one businessman has said:

> Business does not attract a particular type, neither the morally weak, nor the wickedly inclined, nor the knights in shining armor. It is, on the other hand, comprised of perfectly normal, reasonable human beings, subject to whatever frailties and limitations characterize man on this earth. They represent a cross section of society—the brilliant and the dull, the generous and the grasping, the expansive and the petty, the good and the bad.

Businessmen were not as much out of step with the truth as I had once thought they were. Neither they nor their opinions seemed in retrospect to be any more ridiculous than those of other groups in our society. Indeed, they sometimes were superior to the opinions offered by those who should have known better . . . or who thought they did.

H.E.K.

PART I

1. THE IMAGE OF BUSINESS, 1920–60

"A great society is a society in which men of business think greatly of their functions."

Alfred North Whitehead, *Adventures of Ideas*, 1933.

In the middle twenties, at the beginning of what was to be the most tempestuous bull market in history, the Swedish Immanuel Congregational Church in New York City offered an engraved certificate of preferred stock in the Kingdom of God to all who would contribute $100 to its building fund. In so doing, the churchmen did not mean to be blasphemous. In the mood of the day, they were recognizing the supremacy of business in the American cultural hierarchy.[1]

It is now a well-accepted truth that America has long been a business civilization. It was not always so clear, however. Earlier in history, business values had suffered some competition, especially from agrarians and intellectuals. But gradually, all other rivals succumbed to the practitioners of trade and commerce. After a long and gradual climb, business attained a position of great power in the Gay Nineties. It then survived the muckraking, progressive era, and finally emerged at the height of prestige in the 1920s when the businessman became *the* authority on matters economic, political, and even aesthetic. As one advertising man then expressed it, "Business is today the profession. It offers something of the glory that in the past was given to the crusader, the soldier, and the courtier." The publisher of a small-town newspaper, Ralph Beaver Strassburger of the *Norristown* (Pennsylvania) *Times Herald*, was quite carried away by what was occurring: "The day of the businessman has come. The hour when the businessmen of the world take actual control of the affairs of the world may be delayed by the inertia inherent in social changes, but it cannot fail to come. The present composition of society makes it inevitable. The future of society makes it an inexorable necessity."[2]

As if to prove the point, educators and churchmen, groups that had once looked upon the businessman as someone of a low order of distinction, now rushed to pay homage to business values. College deans took pride in calling themselves business executives and spoke of business as "the oldest of arts and the youngest of professions." Ministers, anxious to get straying Americans back on the path of righteousness, spread the word that it paid to pray. "Come to church," said Pastor Christian Reisner. "Going to church increases your efficency."

Almost everyone was happy with business. Intellectuals who might have contested its hegemony offered little opposition. The anti-business writers who had had such a field day in the Muckraking Era had all but disappeared. Some, like Ida Tarbell, had been converted; most of the others had sunk into obscurity. Among the academicians and lawyers, Professors Charles A. Beard and William Z. Ripley and Justice Louis Brandeis were critical but not bitterly so, and articulate though they were, they were drowned out in the general swell of business adulation. Many of the novelists of the 1920s did throw darts at the business world, but for the most part their criticisms were more an excoriation of the whole American culture rather than a condemnation of business in itself. For their part, businessmen, at the pinnacle of prestige, could afford to look upon their critics in a tolerant, patronizing way. "I'm Proud to Be Called a Babbitt" was the illuminating title of a piece by B. F. Jones which *Collier's* magazine ran in 1925. Businessmen regarded the novelists as smart alecs who were envious of those who had done better.[3] If the truth were known, many businessmen always looked with contempt upon the intellectual for being a lazy, impractical busybody who, in the words later popularly ascribed to President Eisenhower, "takes more words than are necessary to tell more than he knows."

Politicians had also in the past given the businessmen some competition. But by the twentieth century, those politicians who won national elections and who appeared to stand high in public esteem were joining business rather than combating it. To be sure, those whom Senator George Moses later called "The Sons of the Wild Jackass" were, as was often the case with Middle Westerners, anti-big business. Then too, some conservatives, such as Boston's Senator Henry Cabot Lodge and Philadelphia's Boies Penrose, thought that businessmen were politically inept. But both men knew who paid the piper even though as aristocrats they had little empathy for the business world. It was clear to them, as it was to all practical politicians, that America was a business civilization. As the *Wall Street Journal* editorialized in 1925, "Never before, here or anywhere else, has a government been so completely fused with business." Said President Coolidge, in an oft-misquoted speech to a group of businessmen:

> You gentlemen come to speak for the interest that by far surpasses any other in the American community. This is a business country . . . and it wants a business government. I do not mean a government by business nor a government for business, but I do mean a government that will understand business.[4]

Coolidge reflected the prevailing majority opinion much more accurately than did the intellectuals or the aristocrats. He was right when he told the Chamber of Commerce that its "attitude very accurately reflects that of public opinion generally." As William Allen White noted, "Coolidge took advice from American money lenders; but they led him only to where his instinct would have guided him and his instinct was probably reflected in the feeling of the American people in those days." William Feather, one of the editorial writers of *Nation's Business,* announced in 1926, "There is no doubt that the American businessman is the foremost hero of the American public today."[5]

HOW ARTICULATE ARE BUSINESSMEN?

Despite the high repute which they enjoyed in that era of prosperity, business leaders had difficulty in finding a collective mind, a collective will, and a collective voice. They were to have the same difficulty immediately after World War II, and they experienced even greater difficulty during the depression. It was only in the late 1950s and 1960s that business produced a basic set of opinions from which there were comparatively few dissents—an ideology, to use that overworked and badly misused word.

It would be a mistake to think that the mass of businessmen were at any time rushing to the press or to the lecture platform. Even though their educational level has always been higher than the average, businessmen have never been very articulate. Only a few commented on economic issues although, it must be added, the views of those few appeared over and over again in the press and in the periodicals.* Polls repeatedly showed that a large number of businessmen had no opinion at all on many major issues. Polls also revealed that like other forms of animal life businessmen were primarily interested in those things that concerned them directly and intimately. Thus, in the late 1930s, only about one quarter of those polled expressed an opinion about the Public Utility Holding Company Act; less than one fifth felt one way or the other about banking legislation; but over 90 per cent had decided opinion about social security.

There were many possible reasons for the absence of widely expressed opinion. Perhaps it was because businessmen realized that expressing one's opinions on debatable issues was a dangerous pastime to be avoided whenever possible. Perhaps it was because running a business was a full-time job which left no time for commenting on matters that were not part of the infrastructure of the firm. Or perhaps most business leaders did not think they knew enough about economic issues to comment. Or perhaps they were just not interested. The answer is probably a combination of all four with most of the emphasis on the last. Businessmen are not intellectuals. The businessman who would be successful cannot indulge much in the imaginative self-doubt that sometimes haunts the intellectual. Then, too, he is much less concerned with thinking about abstractions than with acting on practical matters.† He must, in short, be able to ignore the immediately irrelevant. Bagehot understood this very well when he wrote about the directors of the Bank of England:

> The abstract thinking of the world is never to be expected from persons in high places; the administration of first-rate current transactions is a most engrossing business, and those charged with them are usually but

* Evidence of how articulate businessmen were can be obtained by an examination of *Who Was Who*. The 1951–60 volume listed 12,829 people; 2,166 were businessmen and 167 of these were of unusual importance. Of the 167, only 61 expressed at some time or other an opinion that appeared in public print on some economic issue.

† A survey reported in the *New York Times* (July 18, 1965) found that business executives had above-average "effective intelligence," but were only "fair conceptual thinkers." What the businessman thinks about ideas, the natural resource of the intellectual's production line, is well described in the novel *The Lincoln Lords* by Cameron Hawley.

little inclined to think on points of theory, even when such thinking most nearly concerns those transactions.

Business is not a conversation piece. There is little glamour in ordinary business life. In the words of Crawford H. Greenewalt of Du-Pont, the businessman is "less romantic than the cowboy, less spectacular than the soldier, and less portentous than the statesman. There is apparently nothing in the business suit quite so glamorous as epaulets or cutaway." Business is, when one really comes down to it, a dull affair, making for anonymity in word and deed. Today's business executives are, with few exceptions, unknown to the public at large. In 1967, the magazine *Parade* asked 150 people in five large cities to identify the presidents of the ten largest companies. Only six of the respondents could name as many as three.

For many years, it was said that the eminent banker George F. Baker of the First National Bank of New York made only one speech in his entire career. According to the *Dictionary of American Biography,* he made two, but one or two, Baker's first speech, a one-paragraph affair, came at age eighty-four when he thanked a dinner group for electing him an honorary member of the Bond Club. Bankers were supposed to be strong, silent men like "Sunny Jim" Stillman, who did so much to build the National City Bank in New York. As the story has it, a friend ran into Stillman and greeted him by saying, "Oh, I see you're back from Europe." Stillman said nothing. After a long period of silence, the friend in some irritation brought the conversation to an end by remarking, "Oh, you need not confirm it."* It is commonly believed that all this has changed, that yesterday's glowering shylock has given place to the "friendly city banker," and that today's businessman is much less secretive and much more talkative than the executive of years ago. There is much evidence to deny this idea. Admittedly, the business leaders of the 1920s were not telling everything they knew to the Rotary Club, but neither are the business leaders of today. Throughout the ages, there have been some businessmen who delighted in cultivating an air of mystery. In the 1920s, this took the guise of unapologetic secrecy. In the depression years, the game was the anonymous spreading of "inside dope." The method of operation was to make a candid statement and then to

* Stillman's letters in the Stillman manuscript collection and in the Vanderlip manuscript collection at Columbia University's Special Collections lead to the impression that Stillman was not nearly so misanthropic as he has been painted.

warn the listener that the speaker must remain nameless. In a typical example, a steel executive told an author, "I'll go along with the union as long as it's top dog here," but, "If you identify me in any way when you write this up, there'll be one less economics teacher in a certain New England college."[6]

The joys of mystery-making haven't entirely disappeared. Many executives still delight in titillating the press with such statements as "If we told you what we really thought, you wouldn't be able to print it." Such crudities are, however, becoming less common. There are more sophisticated approaches. As Arjay Miller, recently of the Ford Motor Company, describes it, "The emphasis these days is on opportunism, on a more nimble response to a shifting environment."*

Looking at the picture through the other end of the glass, there were some vocal businessmen in the 1920s, probably just as many as in the 1960s. It is unlikely that any other business leader in history outdid Elbert H. Gary of United States Steel in breaking into public print. (This includes Henry Ford, who, although widely quoted, was extremely shy and regarded appearances before crowds with the same horror that he felt for bankers.) Gary held a weekly press conference until his death in 1927. He was not only a pioneer but an ardent practitioner of public relations. In other respects, he was not a great executive, and many of the curious wondered why the steel corporation paid him $400,000 a year ($225,000 salary plus bonus). It was not because he maintained U. S. Steel's dominant position in the industry, for he didn't. Nor was it because he had been a personal crony of his presumed boss, J. Pierpont Morgan, for he hadn't been. It was because the corporation's board, correctly or incorrectly, thought that without Gary, the company would fall victim to the Sherman Anti-trust Act and be broken up into pieces. Steel paid Gary for his public-relations abilities in keeping the company intact, and thought it well worth the price.

The twenties also produced Owen D. Young, another master of public relations. Trained as a lawyer, Young had superb talents in business diplomacy. Adept at both the spoken and the written word, he was probably more than anyone else responsible for creating the notion of the "new business leader," that had a vogue for a brief time in the 1920s. Although he was chairman of the board of the General Electric Company, he had little to do with making its execu-

---

* A response by no means confined to business, but common in any large organization.

tive decisions; this was the province of the autocratic Gerard Swope, president of the company, who was almost as articulate as Young. The two came to be labeled within the company as "Mr. Outside" and "Mr. Inside" and they got along splendidly, both inside and outside, although, being Democrats, they were regarded as being way out, and many of their ideas were not shared by the majority of businessmen.

Just as there were articulate businessmen in years past, so there have been inarticulate businessmen in more recent years. Some businessmen have always thought that silence was golden. George M. Humphrey, who was a very big businessman indeed, never made a public speech until he became Secretary of the Treasury. Then, ironically, he found it difficult to stop talking. In 1966, when Sebastian S. Kresge, at ninety-eight, finally retired after fifty-three years with the firm that bore his name, he said, "I never made a dime by talking." Other businesses and business spokesmen, having once been burned, are now excessively wary. The National Association of Manufacturers that once eagerly sought the public's ear has in more recent days apparently became convinced that it is easier to gain friends and influence people by being silent and mysterious. Individual companies too have found that overexpressiveness can be embarrassing. In at least two companies—one an airline and the other an insurance company—overarticulateness in the past has resulted in a "mum's the word" edict to guide the behavior of executives.

To be sure, these are not necessarily examples of "typical" behavior, but then my thesis is that there is no such thing as a "typical" businessman. There is no doubt that businessmen appear more regularly before organizational and legislative groups than they used to. There was no society of security analysts in the 1920s, and in most of the hearings before Congress in those days businessmen were noticeably missing while academic economists and spokesmen for farm and labor organizations were prominent. But few people read congressional hearings. What they do read are newspapers and magazines, and here the statistics do not show any surprising change in the degree of business articulation.

Out of a sample of big business leaders of the 1920s, 33 per cent were mentioned as subjects or as authors of articles listed in *The Readers' Guide to Periodical Literature*. The rate dropped to 24 per cent in the depression and came back to 36 per cent in the postwar years. When their names were mentioned, it was usually as subjects, not as authors. Business leaders reached their peak as authors in the 1920s. In 1925, for example, they published ninety-six magazine articles, chiefly in *The Review of Reviews,* the *American* magazine, and *Collier's* magazine.

Transportation and trade executives often appeared in the magazines, while those in banking, utilities, and insurance were usually absent. Just the opposite applied in newspapers where bankers vied with industrialists in getting coverage. In the 1920s, the opinions of bankers like Otto H. Kahn of Kuhn Loeb & Co., James A. Speyer of Speyer & Co., and Charles E. Mitchell of the National City Bank appeared regularly in the *New York Times* and the *Commercial and Financial Chronicle.* Later, Albert Wiggin, Winthrop Aldrich, Russell Leffingwell, and Melvin Traylor were widely quoted. Still later, George Champion and David Rockefeller became "good copy."

The ability or desire to obtain publicity seemed peculiarly associated with particular industries and particular firms. The executives of United States Steel, General Electric, Standard Oil of New Jersey, Ford Motor, and the Chase Bank always seemed to have been vocal.

It is frequently assumed that career executives, being less secretive, are more articulate than the owner-operators. But, here again, the evidence does not support the hypothesis. In the 1920s, professional managers, or career executives, began to outnumber the owner-managers. By the 1960s, the ratio was perhaps three to one among big business leaders. But the incidence of articulation among career managers was much lower than their proportion of the total business sample. Of the business leaders who frequently appeared in print, one half were career executives, less than 10 per cent were inheritors, and the remaining 40 per cent owned a substantial interest in the firms they managed.

BUSINESS SPOKESMEN ARE ORDINARILY NOT BUSINESSMEN

What kind of articles, speeches, and talks did business tycoons produce? In the 1920s, they wrote quantities of words on "how to"— how to succeed in business, how to run a business, how to be a good citizen, etc. They were also fascinated by the changes that were taking place in the attitudes and philosophy of business managers. There were few technical articles, so that the prevailing tone was highly subjective. Peculiarly enough, the talks and speeches were much more objective than the articles, for they were interlaced with historical and philosophical references. But this in turn made them much longer than the speeches of today.

During the depression, the "how we do it" literature seemed at best out-of-place and at worst ludicrous, and that sort of book, therefore, went out of style. It was replaced in the mainstream of business literature by a bombastic strain designed to defend the system against its many enemies, real and unreal. The success literature never made a complete comeback. Today's business leaders, with very few exceptions such as J. Paul Getty's masterpieces in *Playboy* magazine, make no effort to tell America's youth or America's middle-aged how to get ahead. An analysis of a group of speeches and articles made by the executives of 129 of the country's largest firms during the last few years shows that the majority—55 per cent—were concerned with general economic issues, that is, international economic problems, prices, profits, competition, taxes, debt, and so forth.

The out-and-out polemic is much less prevalent than it used to be. Oratory designed to convert the convinced and convince the converted, in which cries of "Hear! Hear!" greet the news that free enterprise is standing at Armageddon with both feet firmly planted in profitless prosperity, rates a poor fourth in the list of things that business leaders now talk about in public. The polemic is, however, much more quotable than the technical or the informative, for in life as in history that which is most interesting is rarely really important and the really important is rarely interesting.

Most business leaders seldom get their names in the newspapers.* As a consequence, various groups with some talents for expression—employees of trade associations, magazine writers, and newspaper columnists—have stepped into the breach and became surrogate spokesmen for business.[7]

For many years the National Association of Manufacturers and the Chamber of Commerce were assumed to be spokesmen for the business community. Shortly after World War II, the Committee for Economic Development entered the field. Indeed, it is often said

* It has been said that among old-style New England businessmen, the first admonition was don't live off capital; the second was to permit one's name to appear in the newspapers upon only three occasions: birth, marriage, and death.

that the CED speaks for the newer, more progressive, career-management wing of business opinion while NAM speaks for the older "owner-operator, classically oriented group." This is a little too neat and a good deal less than true. Not all new managers have been "progressive" in their thinking, and not all owner-operators have been "unprogressive." Then, too, no one can "speak for business." The history of the NAM clearly demonstrates that no single voice can cover the many different groups or schools of business opinion.

Far from being a spokesman for business, the NAM represented an active minority. From its founding in 1895 to the depressed year 1932, it was in the control of small businessmen and a group of bureaucrats, or professional NAMers, including John Edgerton and J. A. Emery. As a growth organization, the NAM in the 1920s was much like the American Federation of Labor. In a sea of prosperity, it hardly stayed afloat. Just as the AFL lost members, so the NAM's income and activities fell off badly. But unlike the labor union, the manufacturers' union thrived on adversity. At the bottom of the depression, a group of big businessmen, including Charles R. Hook, Tom Girdler, and Ernest Weir (all steel executives), moved in and took over control. The three citations of the NAM in the 1932–35 *Readers' Guide* jumped to eighteen in the 1935–37 volume, twenty-four in the next, and to an all-time high of thirty-two in the 1939–41 period. In the years following World War II, the NAM again ran downhill as many business leaders, both owners and managers, became disenchanted. According to William Whyte of *Fortune,* when one hundred businessmen were asked what they thought of the NAM, only twenty-seven were favorable; thirty did not answer or graded the organization mediocre; forty-three (including some who were prominent in the association) were almost "violently critical." Said Joseph Block of Inland Steel, "It has stereotyped positions that are inflexible." Other comments were more scathing. "The NAM," said one, "has the curse of death upon it." It's a "negative influence" said another. And still another marked the association as "just a bunch of top-drawer guys in an ivory tower, stewing in their own juices and issuing feudal and futile pronouncements. They do nothing but talk to themselves."

Of thirty-eight major proposals enacted into federal law between 1933 and 1941, the NAM opposed thirty-one. But polls of business-men concluded that many of the thirty-one laws were supported rather than opposed by a substantial majority of the business community.

After the war, 94 per cent of the 43 per cent who responded to a poll on price controls expressed a negative view, but 89 per cent of those polled by New York's Commerce and Industry Association favored the continuation of price controls with some modification.[8]

THE MANY SIDES OF BUSINESS OPINION

Not only are businessmen different from each other, but the ideas of different business groups have at times been sharply antagonistic, and this despite the widely held view that business is a tomb of rigid conformity. The opinions voiced by businessmen have been so diverse that they were more a mishmash than an accepted ideology. In the 1920s, E. A. Filene, Henry S. Dennison, Morris Leeds, and Samuel Fels were obvious mavericks. But some of his colleagues accused Goodyear's Paul W. Litchfield, whom most people would have classified as a far righter, of being a socialist. To be sure, such extremes were not true in the later period, but there were still differences. The waves of dissension had been replaced by ripples.

The most conspicuous antagonisms, even sharper than the differences between small and big business, and much more pertinent than the differences between owners and managers, were a function of the kind of economic activity in which businessmen were engaged. The manufacturer did not think along the same lines as the merchant and neither held the same opinions as the banker. In fact, the industrialist and the financier were as far apart in their thinking as any two members of the same genre could be. Henry Ford, the stereotyped industrialist (like Andrew Carnegie in a previous generation), would have applauded with gusto had he read what G. K. Chesterton once wrote of William Cobbett: "He would have been as ready as any merchant to face the fact that man, as God has made him, must make money. But he had a vivid sense that the money must be as solid and honest as the corn and fruit for which it stood. . . . He waged a furious war on all those intricate and sometimes imaginary processes of debts and shares and promises and percentages which make the world of wealth to-day a world at the worst unreal and at the best unseen. . . . What he was at once predicting and denouncing, like a small cloud that had not yet become a universal fog, was that vast legal fiction that we call finance."

Bankers have always emphasized the financial trimmings of business—earnings per share, dividends, financial liquidity. Industrialists have been primarily concerned with production and to a far lesser extent (sometimes not at all) with the wheels that revolve in the financial world. The financiers concentrated on corporate structure and the financing of securities and their interests were widely diversified, so much so that they had to leave the operation of the firms in which they had an interest to hired managers. Industrialists by contrast were specialists whose lives were associated with one firm; they didn't care much about capital budgets, but they were much interested in output per man hour, breakdowns on the production line, the cost of a unit of product, and such other matters associated with the inside of the plant.

Industrialists, too, differed from each other. They differed fundamentally in how they viewed money. Almost all financiers thought of money as having high marginal utility. Many industrialists agreed with them, but others placed a very low marginal utility on cash. Some, therefore, took great risks, while others played a conservative and cautious game; in the language of the poker table, they played them close to the vest.

There was a strong streak of Populism running through most industrialists. More than a few looked upon themselves as country boys who were likely to be taken advantage of by the slickers from the financial canyons of the big cities. A made-to-order example occurred in 1923 when Clarence Saunders, the brilliant and eccentric entrepreneur of self-service merchandising, caught a number of short sellers in a raid on the stock of the Piggly-Wiggly stores. His efforts to "teach the bears a lesson" were frustrated by the Stock Exchange. Whereupon, Saunders announced with some indignation and much appeal to the gallery:

> As long as I live, I will not be president of any company that has its stock traded on the New York Stock Exchange where the gambler and the speculator have such free rein to ply their trade. . . . It was strictly a question as to whether I should survive . . . or whether I should be licked and pointed to as a boob from Tennessee.[9]

Some forty years later, the president of the Wolverine Aluminum Corporation created a two-day sensation when he announced, in words that almost copied Saunders, that he was going to try to delist the stock from the American Stock Exchange. There is, he charged, "more larceny per square foot committed on the floors of stock exchanges than anywhere else in the world."

The hard-bitten, headstrong industrialist, of whom Henry Ford was one, could not speak about the financial world without becoming hysterical. A prevalent view was that bankers, financiers, and stockholders were parasites that fed at the business trough. Ford, in fact, told Clarence Barron that stockholders were an unproductive class who "bet their money on the other fellow's brains." Financiers were blamed by industrialists for most of the ills for which a more convenient scapegoat could not be found. According to E. A. Filene: "It is clear beyond need of explanation that most of the sins for which the modern revolutionists indict our social system are sins of the financial point of view, not of the administrative point of view."[10]

This was, of course, a depression point of view, but it was common. Thus, "one of the most responsible businessmen in the country" wrote to President Hoover in March 1932: "Of course, they [the bankers] are notorious for their lack of vision or common human imagination, but they are a most servile class when spoken to from authoritative power . . . too much loose talk on the part of a notably ignorant group sitting near the lodestone of public confidence."[11]

No matter how suspicious of financiers they were, few industrialists went to the extreme of Henry Ford, who blamed the bankers for war, for pestilence, and for the worst of all evils, the labor union. "Unions," said Ford, "are engineered by capitalists and leaders of finance who know that with their workers organized into units, they could be handled with twice the effectiveness that would be possible were they split into factions, unorganized and working alone." Ford thought that the strikes of 1922, of which there were many, could not be settled "so long as the moneyed interests of Wall St. continue in their efforts to dominate American industry. They are behind these walkouts."[12]

The antagonisms among businessmen, which were so easily discernible in the 1920s, dwindled considerably as career managers became more numerous. This "new breed" seemed more tolerant, polite, and self-controlled than the old-style entrepreneur. Then, too, the hired manager was certainly not as free to vent his spleen as the man who had no owner to answer to except himself. But some career managers still regarded the financier with suspicion, a suspicion that differed from the owner's hostility by recognizing that the industrialist and the banker supported the same system but did not speak the same language.

In his reflections on a busy life spent as president of Goodyear, Paul W. Litchfield remarked that Frank A. Seiberling (who had been dropped by Goodyear in one of the many banker-directed reorganizations that took place in the depression of 1920) "Like Henry Ford and many other Midwest industrialists distrusted Wall St." There was no doubt that Litchfield had considerable sympathy for Seiberling's views. Even though he had been hand picked and promoted to president of the company by Clarence Dillon, the banker, Litchfield never felt completely comfortable with financial men. Recalling the reorganization of 1921, he wrote:

> There was quite a bit of feeling between the two groups. . . . That is understandable. . . . Our differences were not personal. It was a clash between financial and industrial thinking. . . . The banking approach to business is necessarily different from that of the manufacturer. The banker thinks in terms of dollars and cents. That is his merchandise, his stock in trade. . . . He cannot take risks. It is largely other people's money he is dealing with. . . . But the manufacturer . . . is dealing primarily with people, their wants, desires, ambitions. . . . In the endeavor to meet those needs, risks must be taken.[13]

Litchfield's remarks showed that the "new businessman" was not interested in casting verbal brickbats at the banker. Gradually, the sport became part of the past, like the Charleston and flagpole sitting. In the business world of the 1960s, it is a novelty infrequently performed.

Today's business community is much more closely knit than it was a generation ago. Even the feud between small and big business, a notorious duel of the past, has diminished in the increasing homogeneity of business thinking that has taken place since World War II. A poll of the top men in forty-two small companies found twenty-seven denying that "some companies are too big" and only ten agreeing. Thirty-three opposed and only five supported putting a limit on corporate size. Still, the old suspicions and the old hostilities occasionally break out when self-interest collides with self-interest. When Robert R. Young, himself a financier, was engaged in his eventually successful campaign to take over control of the New York Central Railroad, he made a vigorous effort to arouse the anti-banker feelings of the populace by advertising that the struggle was another chapter in the age-old fight against the invidious influence of Wall Street—personified as per usual by the house of Morgan. Again when domestic steel producers were pleading in the 1960s for more rigid "anti-dumping" laws, small-business steel importers accused Roger Blough of United States Steel and others of using "scare tactics and inaccuracies in a massive effort to cajole the Administration." But excitement like this was rare in the 1960s compared to the 1920s when some businessmen seemed to disagree with others for no particular reason except the joy of disagreement.[14]

THE BUSINESSMAN'S IMAGE OF HIMSELF

One thing that a cross section of businessmen could agree upon in the 1920s was that they deserved the almost universal admiration which the public showered on them. Admittedly, they were sometimes amazed and awed at the height to which their prestige had climbed. But once having read the play, they were more than willing, indeed more than anxious, to play the role assigned to them in a business culture. Carried away by the prosperity of the era, many businessmen repainted their own image in very complimentary colors, although at times it did seem that the work was done with an amateur's brush. Many of them began to think that they had been brought into the world to cure not only its economic ills, but all other ills as well. Paul M. Mazur of Lehman Brothers thought that "while industry dominates the thought of America, there need be no fears. It will continue to write the most significant pages of American history."[15]

Nation's Business, the organ of the United States Chamber of Commerce, was especially awed by the stature that business had achieved. In 1925, it promulgated what was to become a recurrent theme: that running a business was not enough—there were more worlds to conquer:

> The American business man is today the most influential person in the nation. Because of the wealth and manpower of our nation, the American business man is today perhaps the most influential figure in the world. The American business man occupies a position of leadership which he has never held before. This means that he is on trial.

. . . Business heretofore has been permitted to concern itself exclusively with the practical details of business. . . . The question now is will and can the business man as leader concern himself with more than his business, perform his primary function of supplying the material needs of mankind and in addition make noteworthy contributions to civilization.

At about the same time, A. C. Bedford of Standard Oil told a group of the company's workers: "I have come to the conclusion that industry is the fundamental basis of civilization. The high office of civilization is to train men to productive effort. . . . If one becomes a producer, one should also become a money maker, and provided he gets wealth honestly, I think such a man has every right to be considered great. I don't believe the desire for gain is the determining principle in human action, but there is much to admire in the man who organizes and develops an industry to the point where he accumulates a fortune."[16]

People who were as successful in economic life and in building industrial firms as the American businessmen of the 1920s needed no apologist. During the decade, total production rose by 40 per cent. To be sure, 60 per cent of the families had incomes of less than $2000, but the *average* person in 1929 had the power to purchase about 25 per cent more goods and services than he had had ten years before. Most people seemed willing and even eager to give the businessman credit for this, but that apparently was not enough; the business leader wanted to think of himself in terms that had time-honored prestige. In the twenties, the word "profession" had the same grandiose aura that would later be associated with the word "science." Business leaders, therefore, sought to define business as a profession, as later they would try to define it as a science. Walter Gifford of A.T. & T. explained just how important a profession business was:

A profession is an occupation conducted on a high plane by a trained intellect having a special consideration for the public welfare. In this I class the profession of modern business management. And I would class it as the foremost American profession, for it is the profession directing the main stream of the energies of the nation; it is the profession on which the others most depend, and it is the profession on which the country most depends. I believe it to be the profession which holds the highest intellectual challenge to men of brains and a liberal education and the greatest opportunity for men of constructive capacity.[17]

Since it was the mode of the businessman that set the tone of American life, business leaders discoursed on all sorts of topics about which they knew little or nothing. Judge Gary often instructed the public on the beneficial effects of dieting. Henry Ford held forth on art, history, and the McGuffey *Reader*. But it remained for Bruce Barton, the advertising executive, to reach some sort of all-time record. In 1925, he wrote a runaway best seller, *The Man Nobody Knows*, which portrayed Christ as a great businessman who had many of the qualities which would have made Him a great success as a member of Rotary or Kiwanis. Unfortunately, Barton will probably be remembered more for that book than for his advertising abilities, which were considerable.

As long as prosperity continued there were few business leaders who did not participate in showering encomia on their fraternity. The only skeptics appeared to be in the retail business. Thus, W. T. Grant, late in the prosperity era, downgraded his colleagues. "To a surprising degree," he wrote, "business is not even intelligent. . . . Take the matter of our prosperity. True, it is the marvel of this or any other age. . . . We are quick to take credit. . . . But much of this was forced on us." Grant, along with some others whose views will be examined in more detail later, thought that prosperity could only continue if demand were constantly given another dose of vitamins in the form of higher wages.[18]

The few who had in the prosperous years some misgivings about the position of business became the many when the economy entered its long travail in 1930. As profits declined, bewilderment increased. As unemployment rose and as the price of wheat fell, the attitude of the public toward business changed from extreme to extreme. Adulated in 1929, business was condemned by 1931. The human tendency to think in black and white terms could take no middle ground toward the institution which in the public mind was responsible for everything that happened to the economy. What was most aggravating was the apparent inability of the businessman to fulfill the function of economic magician. The business philosophers had wrought better than they knew. They had been surprisingly successful in convincing the public that what business leaders chose to do, they could do. This was well illustrated by Arthur Brisbane, the widely read philosopher of the Hearst papers, when he wrote at the outset of the depression: "All the really important millionaires are planning to continue prosperity."[19]

Business was much embarrassed and upset by this naïve faith. It immediately disclaimed responsibility. But as Dwight Morrow, the banker, chided his business colleagues: "Those who take credit for the rainfall should not complain when they are blamed for the drought."

At first, the inability of business to cope with the depression bewildered the public and put an end to hero worship. Then as the depression wore on, the public treated business opinion with increasing disrespect. Bewilderment turned to hurt and then to indignation, and finally to indifference. By 1931, goaded on by many writers, the public was ready to pour scorn and condemnation on business leaders. At the height of the depression, each new pronouncement by the conventional business leader was greeted with cynical laughter. The whole attitude was well summed up by the title of Edward Angly's disrespectful little book *Oh Yeah?* The prestige of business dropped even further when, in a desperate effort to protect what they thought they were losing, a small group of businessmen joined together in a major *faux pas*—they formed the Liberty League in 1934. The league had among its most active supporters some of the ablest and most astute businessmen in the history of the nation, including Pierre du Pont, Alfred P. Sloan, and Ernest Weir. But it was a fiasco disproving again the commonly held belief that he who succeeds in business could succeed in anything to which he turned his hand.

The public was quick to make the league synonymous with business, even though most businessmen regarded the organization with indifference or misgivings. Unfortunately, for business at large, the league made the front page of the *New York Times* thirty-five times in two years. Once every three weeks was much too much for an organization which William Allen White said quite accurately was "a black beast in the public imagination," and which Stuart Chase somewhat ungenerously described as "tight-lipped, long-nosed, fanatically ungenerous, and intolerant."

THE REACTION TO THE DEPRESSION-INDUCED LOSS OF PRESTIGE

A more incongruous situation than that which developed during the height of the depression would be difficult to imagine. What should have been the principal group in a capitalistic society was almost totally without influence on public opinion. The vaunted mainspring of the enterprise system had become sprung. For the first time in American history, large numbers of people were questioning not the tenets of capitalism but the system itself.

Business leaders reacted against this downgrading of their prestige in five principal ways. Some reacted by calling for fundamental changes in the system. Said W. L. Clayton, the cotton merchant, "Private ownership of property is a permissive not an inherent right. The great majority of the American people must be made to understand the system, and its abuses must be recognized and substantially corrected." In an oft-quoted speech, Daniel Willard, president of the Baltimore & Ohio Railroad, told the students of the Wharton School:

> When I was a boy, it seemed to me that most, if not all, of our fundamental institutions had been definitely determined and fixed for all time. . . . Now all of these are under attack and all are slowly but none the less surely going through a process of questioning and of reassessment which may leave them better or worse, but will certainly mean modification. A system under which it is possible for five or six million to be out of work and unable to secure work . . . cannot be said to be perfect or even satisfactory. In such circumstances, I would steal before I would starve.[20]

Other businessmen thought that what was happening was only a return to normal. At the bottom of the depression, Fred I. Kent, the retired banker who spent most of his time thinking and speaking about the social problems of business, wrote a long letter to Owen D. Young explaining that the great prestige which business had enjoyed was a sometime thing, an abnormality. "During the life of the United States," wrote Kent, "there have been a number of short periods, usually following wars, when business interests have had the favor of the people, but in general political forces have been in the ascendancy." Kent had long since resigned himself to the conviction that business influence would remain ineffective.

> A natural and inevitable development accompanying our progress from a pioneer nation to one of great density of population is that congressional and legislative committees . . . listen to three sets of men, theorists, agitators, and representatives of business. The representatives of business are considered as being prejudiced and consequently what they have to say does not receive the same attention as statements made

by theorists and agitators. No one is to blame for this situation as it was a perfectly natural outcome of the class of human forces that so far have seemed to have to prevail.[21]

A third group, the smallest of all, demonstrated a singular lack of faith in the adequacy of their own system. The depression had produced in them a pall of defeatism, a loss of self-confidence in their ability to deal with the crisis, and a psychopathic fear of revolution. Frustration and failure drove the members of this group to seek in likely and unlikely places for an American Mussolini or Hitler to smash the revolt of the masses that was likely to break out at any moment.

Still a fourth school was composed of those few who disposed of their critics by labeling them "a bunch of Communists." Their statements made sensational reading and were, therefore, quoted at length even though they did not represent a large fraction of the big-business population. There was nothing new about this form of red baiting. Some businessmen had always answered their critics with a lazy-man's rebuttal. They continued to do so, and perhaps they always would. Edward Doheny, the oil tycoon, who is still dimly remembered for having been mixed up in the Teapot Dome scandal, delivered a typical quotable broadside immediately after World War I:

> If you believe in Democracy, you cannot believe in Socialism. . . .
> Democracy means opportunity for all. Socialism holds out the hope
> that a man can quit work and be better off . . . a majority of the college
> professors are teaching Socialism and Bolshevism. . . . President Eliot
> of Harvard is teaching Bolshevism. . . . The worst Bolshevists in the
> United States are not only the college professors . . . but capitalists and
> the wives of capitalists and neither seem to know what they are talking
> about.

Doheny then went on to name some of the Bolshevists. He included William Boyce Thompson, the mining executive; Frank Vanderlip, the banker; and Henry Ford, and labeled Thomas Lamont a fringe case.[22] Some years later, when Gerard Swope of the General Electric Company advised industry that the NAM and some notoriously anti-organized-labor trade associations had been made superfluous by Section 7(a) of the National Industrial Recovery Act, a Mr. Hinds of Crouse-Hinds, electric signal manufacturers, said,

"Swope is a dangerous man for industry; his wife, a former pal of Jane Addams of Hull House, is active in parlor pink activities."

Businessmen frequently raised the red flag either in moments of irritation or at times when they were at a loss for words. Silas S. Strawn of the U. S. Chamber of Commerce said he "was tired of attempts to Sovietize the country." Irénée du Pont, in answer to the Munitions Investigation, listed three reasons for the campaign against the gunmakers, but he especially emphasized "a subservient force instigated by the Third International."[23]

Critics of business generalized from these expressions of opinion and implied that they represented business as a whole. Typical was a statement by Elmer Davis, the newspaper and radio reporter, "Business is the most timid and the most sensitive of all creatures. It is constantly proclaiming its own lack of confidence in everything but itself, and expects that lack of confidence to be taken as final condemnation. But if anybody ventures to imply some lack of confidence in business, business is terribly hurt and calls him a crackpot and Communist."[24]

Davis was wrong. Most businessmen reacted to their declining reputation not by accusing their critics of subversion but by launching a "fighting campaign" to regain their lost position. This campaign had perforce to be badly mixed up, for the truth of the matter was that the majority, if not all, of the business leaders had no satisfactory solution or explanation for the stark problems of the depression. The program to restore business to its formerly exalted state was, therefore, often inconsistent. It was sometimes pathetic, as in the case of the Liberty League and for the most part the NAM. Occasionally, it was naïve in that it discovered things that had long been known. Lewis H. Brown of Johns Manville, one of the younger business leaders, thought that one of the changes the depression had caused was that the "secrecy which was an inevitable accompaniment of an intense competitive struggle for markets has given place to klieg lights . . . upon all business activities." But in the 1920s Henry S. Dennison had already named as "the most important contribution to economic progress the freer interchange of business knowledge and the relatively wide publicity given to internal business conditions."[25]

Occasionally, the effort to put business back in the saddle bordered on the ridiculous as when Bruce Barton told the NAM that the story of the valuable contributions of business bigness "should be told just as continuously as the people are told that Ivory Soap floats or that children cry for Castoria."

Naïve, pathetic, or ridiculous as it may have been, it was, nevertheless, an attempt, and it was launched with fanfare. Believing that business was being unjustly condemned not for that which it did but for that which it had not done, a group of business leaders, styling themselves "the Brass Hats," began in 1932 to meet occasionally to discuss the low level of esteem to which the businessman had fallen. This group planned to reorganize the National Association of Manufacturers to make it "a militant voice speaking and working in the interests of American business."[26]

From 1933 on, big business gradually replaced small business as the dominant influence in the NAM. Among the corporations that had NAM directorships and were heavy financial contributors were: International Business Machines, Standard Oil of Ohio, Eastman Kodak, Du Pont, General Motors, United States Steel, Westinghouse, National Steel, and American Rolling Mills (Armco Steel). It must be emphasized that the executives of these companies did not see eye to eye on economic issues. Their opinions ranged from those of E. T. Weir of National Steel at one end of the spectrum to Thomas Watson at the other end. But they did agree on one thing: "If we are to avoid disaster," stated the platform of the NAM, "it is essential that . . . public opinion be informed and able to discriminate between the sound and the unsound."

The first ambitious attempt by the NAM to recapture the public's affection took place at the Congress of American Industry in December 1934. President C. L. Bardo sounded the keynote by telling the delegates: "As business men, we are publicly on trial as to our ability to confederate our objectives; as organizations, we are being tested to prove our worthiness to supply leadership." The platform that came out of the meeting painstakingly denied the more familiar charges that were being used as booby traps against the American economic system. It denied that 2 per cent of the population received 80 per cent of the national income, that the workers' share of the national income had been decreasing, that corporation profits were increasing faster than wages, that industry was overexpanded, that improved machinery required limitation of hours of work in order to re-employ the millions who were unemployed, and that the economy had broken down irreparably. Sadly, in the middle of this serious and

largely respectable attempt to reconvert the American public, the
NAM characteristically indulged in a little more fun and games. The
platform asked: "Who are those who endeavor to mislead our public?" The answer was obvious: "Communists, impatient reformers,
disturbers of industrial peace, persecutors, and teacher propagandists.
. . . Abusing the privileges of academic freedom by using it as a
cloak for propaganda, a small proportion of our teachers are contributing to the spread of class prejudice. . . . Our university facul-
ties and other teaching staffs must show greater courage in safeguarding the immature minds entrusted to their care." Lewis H.
Brown was not so sure that only a small proportion of teachers
was subversive. He bluntly told the business community that "all
that three quarters of the teachers know about business was what
they read in Karl Marx and Henry George" and he placed the blame
on the heads of the businessmen.

The public relations business was one of the few growth industries in the depression. Business firms and trade associations used
public relations firms prodigiously along with college professors and
newspaper columnists. The NAM distributed movies and produced
a radio program called "American Family Robinson." Ford and General Motors sponsored radio programs which attempted to instruct
the public about the American system. The *New York Sun* inaugurated a feature called "The Voice of Business"; outdoor advertising companies donated billboard space to convince the public that
"What Hurts Business Hurts You"; the United States Steel Corporation, which had never advertised to the public, began a series of magazine advertisements combating the thesis that the American economy
had reached a state of maturity in which there was no more possibility of growth.

A few businessmen undertook to write at book length. One of the
best of these efforts was *Spirit of Enterprise* by Edgar Queeny, the
chief executive officer and son of the founder of the Monsanto Chemical Company. In explaining why he wrote the book, Queeny said:

> The majority of the friends I had made in the business world were
> taking what I thought an unjustified beating. Some were rich, but they
> were not wicked. Most were selfish, but so were many workers of my
> acquaintance. . . . My businessmen friends were not saints, nor were
> they ogres feeding upon unfortunate fellow-beings, as some high priests

of the social sciences were intimating. . . . Business did not have clean hands; but the critics and detractors were not fair nor honest toward it, either.[27]

THE EFFECTIVENESS OF THE BUSINESSMAN'S CAMPAIGN TO "RESELL" HIMSELF

It is impossible to say whether the campaign to sell business back to the public was effective. Certainly it did not arouse much enthusiasm, for the substance of its argument was out of date. The line of attack was comparable to the war between France and Austria in 1859. France planned its campaign along the lines of the tradition of 1809. Austria replied with the tactics of 1759. The attacks on American capitalism rested on the 1870 theories of Karl Marx. The defenders of the system responded by reiterating the 1776 ideas of Adam Smith. The strategy and tactics stressed the negative rather than the positive, and sometimes it seemed that this was deliberate. Indeed, the NAM seemed to take pride in this. "In opposing unsound economic and social measures," it argued, "it is unnecessary to propose alternatives." This contretemps led Milo Perkins, a Houston manufacturer, to say, "the capitalist system can be destroyed more effectively by having men of means defend it than by importing a million Reds from Moscow to attack it."[28]

The overriding objective of the campaign seemed to be to oppose change, especially change that emanated from the federal government. For this reason, most commentators thought the effort altogether ineffective. Whatever its effectiveness, it was not an adequate substitute for economic recovery. That was clearly demonstrated in the late 1930s when business indices began to inch ahead. Immediately, the status of business began to improve. At the bottom of the depression, Robert Lund, shoe manufacturing executive and chairman of the Board of the NAM, lamented, astonishingly that "the only failure of American industry has been its failure to convey to the American public a complete understanding of the fact that industry is the one and only source of the good things which everyone seeks." Just a year later, in late 1937, Lund was much more cheerful:

By some process public opinion has been shifted to the right. Now do not misunderstand me, I am not undertaking to tell you that the

NAM program has been the only factor in the change. . . . The facts are, however, that this formula, five years ago, initiated a new era . . . and that millions of our people believe today in these principles who did not five years ago.

Nation's Business was equally cheered: "After years of political experiment, the nation is again turning to business men as the only group who can give this country the $80,000,000,000 annual income it once enjoyed."[29]

Many of those who discerned the shift to the right as clearly as the NAM and the Chamber of Commerce attributed it less to the business effort and more to the improvement in the economy, the failure of the government to achieve a complete recovery, the unpopularity of some of the new labor-union tactics such as the sit-down strikes, and the hostility toward some government policies such as the attempt to reorganize the Supreme Court. Henry Dennison summed up this line of thinking by saying, "The opposition of businessmen has much less effect on the course of economic events than is commonly believed."[30]

That business prestige, if not popularity, was a function of economic prosperity was even more clearly evidenced by the rise in the stock of business that occurred when the economy entered another period of strong growth in the years after World War II. The businessman's prestige then recovered at a rapid rate, a fact which some of them were eager to recognize. Said Lynn A. Townsend of Chrysler, "Business is now occupying a higher place of respect and importance in the minds of Americans than it has in many years—and certainly a far higher place than it did in the 1930s when the American businessman was being pointed to by many as public enemy number one." Crawford H. Greenewalt of DuPont, in the McKinsey Foundation lectures, said, "Whatever he is . . . the businessman is the pilot of the system under which most of us earn our livings." Charles G. Mortimer of General Foods went further. In words that reminded one of Calvin Coolidge's cliché, he told a Columbia University audience: "This is a business country. Business is what makes the mare go in these United States."[31]

THE CONTEMPORARY IMAGE

Although a few observers* thought that business had more than regained the position of power it had held in the 1920s, business leaders and business spokesmen were under no such illusion. As *Fortune* magazine asked in a famous 1950 article entitled "Is Anybody Listening?," "Did not everyone in the 1920s agree that it was right and proper that he the businessman be entrusted with the destiny of the country? Now satirized in countless novels, politically a prophet without honor, he is ripped of the former dignities and much of the old feeling of moral contribution." Certainly, business had not regained the veneration it had received in the 1920s. Its economic successes were admired, but there was none of the awe-inspired hero worship that had prevailed in the days of Ford and Gary, Harding and Coolidge.

Nor was there the bitterness that had prevailed during the depression. The attitude now was one of indifference. A survey of public opinion conducted in the spring of 1966 showed that almost everyone thought that "free enterprise had made the country great." Almost as many thought that when business profited, the country prospered. About three out of four thought that business paid fair wages, but just as many thought that business was a dog-eat-dog proposition, and almost half of those surveyed believed that "most businessmen would do anything for a buck." In short, the public believed that business was a grimy, but necessary, affair.

This new outlook could not be explained as the result of a diminished stress on material values. A good case can be made for the argument that the emphasis that a society puts on material values varies in direct proportion to affluence and the ease with which money can be made. The present era, being the most affluent in history, puts greater stress on material values than was the case in the much-advertised materialism of the twenties. But material values are not necessarily the same as business values no matter how often the two may be confused. Thus, the paradox of a society rich enough to be indifferent to business.

In the new era of indifference, the respect once paid to the busi-

* Notably, C. Wright Mills and Robert Heilbroner.

nessmen had been transferred to the intellectuals, the group that in the 1920s had been making loud noises in the wings, while the businessmen occupied center stage. Even the businessman was awed by the intellectual, although he did not understand him any better if as well as he had understood him in the past. Businessmen hastened to hire the intellectual as a consultant, and they hastened to shower money on him through funds and foundations. Some sophisticated businessmen seemed to be adopting the strategy of if you can't lick 'em, join 'em. Donald C. Cook told an apathetic audience of graduates at a well-known school of business, "Every businessman is also an intellectual and every intellectual is also a businessman. . . . A man may live greatly in the world of business."*

For his part, the intellectual did not understand the businessman any better than the businessman understood him. The righteous indignation with which the intellectual had once regarded the business system was no longer so noticeable; most of them could not care less. To be sure, a few novelists treated some businessmen sympathetically. In plots that clung tenaciously to the same leitmotiv, the hero in the person of the career manager triumphed in Horatio Alger fashion over the old-fashioned dictatorial owner-entrepreneur. But for the most part, writers continued to voice the same banalities about business that had been expressed fifty years before. They mixed Freudian guilt complexes with generous doses of the Old Testament sins-of-the-fathers syndrome to make a hash that the public found peculiarly palatable. The sharpest barbs were always reserved for the "robber-baron," the empire-building legendary tycoon who had no friends anywhere. Even the old chestnuts about John D. Rockefeller were brought back as though they were eternal verities. In a book about how the sons of the rich had used their inherited fortunes, one writer pontificated: "Others no doubt were ridden by a sense of guilt which was translated into an enveloping sense of responsibility, as in the case of John D. Rockefeller, Jr., who devoted his life and fortune to rectify the wrongs his father had done to society."[32] Another wrote, "John D. Rockefeller, having braved the threats and hatreds of the people, had decided to restore to the people some of the benefits of the money he had made in exploitation of natural resources."

---

* The introduction given Cook at this time also illustrated indirectly the low estate to which the business world had fallen. Although Cook was getting an award for his business achievements, the presenter spent more time in recounting Cook's achievements in government.

Conservative intellectuals also left little doubt about their feeling toward business. The English historian C. Northcote Parkinson wrote in a witty satire: "The world of business is an avenue in which parasites cling to trees; a garden where weeds spring up among the flowers; an orchard in which bees carry the pollen of managerial science from one plant to another; a wood in which the branches of economic theory are strictly for the birds."* To many intellectuals, in other words, businessmen seemed to be so many bumbling oafs. But in the real world, businessmen are not the stuff of which comedies are constructed.

The intellectual apparently had considerable influence on the college student body, for in survey after survey, it was reliably reported that less than 20 per cent of college people made business careers their first choice. The businessman reacted in a way that was quite different from the reactions of the 1920s. Some were, of course, greatly alarmed and took masochistic pleasure in telling their audiences at every opportunity what the surveys had disclosed. In a sample of thirty-nine big business leaders who had something to say about general economic issues in the 1960s, fourteen were much impressed by a *Wall Street Journal* conclusion that college students thought "business was for the birds." They made just as much of a Princeton survey that uncovered the not astonishing news that most people had fantastically inaccurate notions about what business was all about. Other businessmen, however, pooh-poohed the whole thing. Said one Atlanta industrialist, "Hell, I don't blame them. That's exactly how I felt when I was young." Said a Ford executive, "This doesn't worry me. We all went through this. . . . There's nothing more conformist than a nonconformist." These men were right, for despite their efforts at rebellion, the number of the "younger generation" who went into business was much higher than the public was led to believe.†

Whatever the facts, some businessmen, although not worried, were human enough to be more than slightly irritated by the attitude expressed by the "idealists." A savings and loan executive expressed what a whole army of businessmen thought when he wrote: "What I and many other business people find hard to accept from our most

* *In-Laws and Outlaws,* New York, 1962.

† A survey taken in 1966 found that in a sample of 149 corporation presidents, 72 had no sons who could take part in business. The other 77 had 132 sons of whom 106 were in business. *Wall Street Journal,* December 14, 1966.

vociferous critics is that they are more interested in the solution to social problems. . . . One of the principal differences between businessmen and some of their noisiest critics is that the critics often confine their contribution to incessant talk, while businessmen turn out to be the doers. What are the real problems? Jobs? Housing? Education? With the possible exception of education, who but the businessman has any real chance to make any significant progress?" One Middle Western executive was far less reasonable in his reaction. He exploded, "Who the hell do they think built those buildings they're in, who pays the teachers, who pays the taxes to send them to Nigeria. Your old man who runs the laundry is the one." Some old-line, old-guard businessmen still thought in terms of meeting a payroll and held in contempt those who had rarely if ever done so. Wrote Walter Harnischfeger II to *Time* magazine: "Sir, why should college professors such as Walter Heller and his cronies advise the President on what to do? . . . Do the majority of the business leaders of our country believe in Mr. Heller's philosophy? After all, their work keeps our economy strong." Mr. Harnischfeger might have been surprised to know how many business leaders had come around to Heller's way of thinking. But in general it was still true that "the businessman looked at the intellectual as a queer kind of person who is soft in the head and best avoided," and the intellectual "looked down at the businessman as an inferior breed."[33]

Indifference may be more dangerous than outright hostility, but undoubtedly business prestige had by the early 1950s regained much of the ground that it had lost during the depression. After all, as Adlai Stevenson so wittily expressed it, President Eisenhower's first cabinet consisted of "nine millionaires and a plumber."

As they retraced their steps toward the 1920s, business leaders resurrected many of that generation's opinions about themselves, including a reaffirmation of the belief that business was primarily responsible for the economic progress that the United States had made. In all this flashback to the post-World War I world there was, however, a substantial difference; in the twenty years after World War II, opinions were more carefully qualified. Thus Logan Johnston of Armco Steel said, "In a free industrial society, the decisions of business have a more profound effect on the economic well-being of people than the decisions of any other institution, including government." Almost all businessmen would agree with this statement, but only 34 per cent of the public at large was reported as agreeing with it.

Another reminder of the twenties was the oft-repeated opinion that business was a profession. In 1950, Frank W. Abrams, chairman of Standard Oil of New Jersey, told a New York University audience, "I would like especially to impress upon you my own feeling that business management in the United States is well on its way toward achieving many of the characteristics of a profession." In 1963, Lynn Townsend came close to repeating what Walter Gifford had said a generation before: "It has not yet become clear that business management is not only a profession, but the basic profession, which provides the material foundation for all other human activities in a society." And in his *The Uncommon Man,* Crawford Greenewalt constantly referred to management as a profession. One last note to underscore the similarities in the business image of the 1920s and the 1960s: As if to prove that there was nothing new under the sun, *Reader's Digest* in 1965 brought back Bruce Barton's *The Man Nobody Knows.*[34]

But here the similarities between the two postwar periods ended, for the depression had left many scars which would take more than a generation of economic prosperity to remove. The business world had inherited a fear about the future of the system, a fear that was totally absent in the 1920s, a fear that had little substance but that only slowly diminished as the depression receded deeper into the past. Immediately after the war, the fear took on panic proportions. Charles R. Hook melodramatically warned his colleagues, "If we are realists, we will admit that despite its irreplaceable value, our private enterprise system is in the greatest danger since the tragic days of Dunkirk." Dudley Figgis of American Can echoed Hook's alarmist view:

> The intensity and duration of the great world depression did more than shake the confidence of people in the validity of the system that evolved from the industrial revolution. In many parts of the world the free market has already completely disappeared, and in this country it is being increasingly shackled. . . . A continuation of the present trend will inevitably bring the American people to the fork in the road where they will be forced to choose between the road we have been following, which made us great, and the road which leads to collectivism, where initiative will be restricted to the few.[35]

In the 1960s business leaders were still seeing boogey men but not quite so traumatically. "An image of American business has been emerging," spoke H. I. Romnes of Western Electric, "which in the absence of steps to correct it—can only lead to severe restrictions on the freedom and effectiveness with which business operates. The image I am talking about is being shaped—perhaps not consciously, certainly not conspiratorially, but with increasing force and clarity —by books, and magazines, movies, and television."

Just as they had in the depression, many leaders sought to protect business from danger by engaging in a feverish "selling" campaign. "For the past 30 years," said William C. Stolk of American Can, "American business has been on the defensive. . . . Let's face it; the politicians and the union bosses have done a better selling job and what makes it worse is that we are losing the sale by default." In a talk entitled "An Appraisal of Steel's Economic Needs," Charles M. Beeghly of Jones & Laughlin said,

> We cannot prevail in political economic differences of opinion unless we win public support for our objectives. To do so, we must compete with other interests who have demonstrated that they are politically more sophisticated than we are. We have been remarkably unsuccessful in demonstrating that our industry interests and the public interest are compatible. Some of the economic theorists will never join us. The practical politicians, however, are responsive to public opinion.

Some of the younger executives, especially those who were successful, joined in calling upon the businessman "to get off the defensive, to quit worrying and complaining about being misunderstood, and to assume that the great majority of people approved what he was doing." Walter Lippmann, at the end of the war, abjured business to get rid of its inferiority complex, to stop listening to its friends who were doing it a disservice by constantly reminding businessmen that their environment was full of people who wanted to do business in.[36]

But a number of articulate businessmen, both big and little, reacted with tepid enthusiasm to the plea to sell business. The depression had left many of them with another legacy. They were much more perceptive than their predecessors about what the public thought about them. They did not believe that they were being persecuted, nor did they believe that the basic difficulty was that business had not sold itself like some deodorant. They thought that business lacked a philosophy and a theory which adequately explained the system of

American capitalism and the businessman's place therein. They understood the paradox in the business world. As James C. Worthy of Sears, Roebuck diagnosed it, "Business in America occupies a place of unique power and prestige. Nevertheless, businessmen tend to feel uneasy about their position. Large numbers of people seem to look on the business system with skepticism, suspicion, and hostility. We need a rationale that will be a guide and a norm for businessmen, that will effectively relate business to the rest of society."[37]

Those who thought business lacked a philosophy and a clearly defined set of objectives often put the onus for this on the businessman himself. According to Theodore Houser, "The average businessman . . . in performance has run a poor third to government and labor leaders. . . . He finds himself defending a social system which he knows to be the best that ever existed, and yet he cannot find a good descriptive name for it." Logan Johnston said he knew of only a few companies that had attempted to formulate a set of answers to such basic questions as: Why they were in business? What obligations they had and to whom? What standards had they set by which to judge whether they were meeting their objectives and obligations? Such questions had occasionally suggested themselves to some businessmen during the depression, but few business leaders had had the courage to ask them, and still fewer had the courage to answer them.[38]

Many more businessmen, realizing that their institutions were not perfect, accepted criticism and sometimes offered some of their own —a state of affairs that was altogether different from the 1920s when criticism had been dismissed, or the 1930s, when criticism was salt on a raw wound. M. J. Rathbone of Standard Oil told his colleagues what everybody should have known: "Criticism there will always be, and the possession of power and influence will always attract it. Some of this criticism is justified; some of it is completely without foundation; most of it, however, has elements of both right and wrong." Theodore Houser voiced a similar sentiment, "Criticism of big business is the inevitable and useful corollary to the power it wields. At certain times the criticism has had demonstrable merit; at others it has been misdirected; and at still others its validity has faded in the wake of reforms." Robert Wood Johnson of Johnson & Johnson went much further:

Most basic ills of our business system stem from business itself; labor's power has developed too recently to have much historical importance.

For generations business has been sinking into its present muddle, and only business has the power to get itself out. In the process it must discard some long-held and deeply-cherished doctrines.[39]

So in his "philosophy" and in the way he looked at himself, the businessman had come almost full circle. He had started, in the '20s and earlier, with a naïve, egocentric, and exaggerated notion of his own importance. Then in the depression, he had sunk to utter despondency. In the post-World War II world he recovered rapidly, but with a new sense of maturity. Indeed, so thoroughly had he recovered that he came close to forgetting his main function in life— to run a business efficiently and to make a profit. Instead, he began once again to run after a vague and ill-defined will-o'-the-wisp that he thought would give him a more responsible position in the social structure. Unfortunately, his efforts at social responsibility were often ignored, which for obvious reasons mystified him.

2. CONCERNING BUSINESS MOTIVES AND OBJECTIVES

"In love, or war, or politics, or religion, or morals, it is impossible
to tell how mankind will act. . . . But once place a man's ear within
the ring of pounds, shillings, and pence, and his conduct can be
counted on to the greatest nicety."

R. Lowe, 1878.

Insiders and outsiders have written copiously about the change that
has occurred in the moral tone of business in the last fifty years. The
change which they have discerned is closely associated with the question of motivation. How idealistic is the modern businessman compared to his predecessors? What does he think of his predecessors'
behavior? What objectives did businessmen set for their firms? Were
they guided by self-interest and with an eye to the main chance? Were
they concerned with nothing more than maximizing their profits?
How important were non-profit motives such as the "service" concept
that swept through the business world in the late 1920s and the
similar "social responsibility" theme that was frequently heard in business in the 1950s and 1960s? How important was money as a motivating force for the individual business leader? These are intriguing
questions, and businessmen have talked about them at great length.

Businessmen have always thought their behavior and their motives
to be most high-minded. What is more, each succeeding generation
has not hesitated, in an unsmug way of course, to fault its predecessors. Each generation has had little difficulty in finding, in an unself-
conscious way, that it was more high-minded than its ancestors had
been. In the years after the First World War, leading businessmen
and business spokesmen liked to refer back in disapproval to the
predatory statements of the old "eat-'em-alive" entrepreneurs. They

implied that what they were quoting reflected the typical business opinion of the late nineteenth and early twentieth centuries. But what those rugged individualists had said was, like their individualism, more atypical than typical.

J. P. Morgan may have been expressing what most businessmen believed when he said in 1902, "Men owning property should do what they like with it." But very few even in 1899 could swallow Henry O. Havemeyer's frank statement: "Business is not a philanthropy. . . . I do not care two cents for your ethics. I don't know enough of them to apply them. . . . As a business proposition, it is right to get all out of a business that you possibly can." Businessmen of the next two generations condemned these ideas as brutal and in bad taste.

The tycoons of the 1920s knew that they were more idealistic than Havemeyer had been, and they did not hesitate to say so. Contrary to what most people think, the 1920s were not completely materialistic years. The decade exhibited strong strains of idealism that appeared in the form of a vision of a new era which would see the end of war on the international scene and the end of poverty on the domestic scene. The First World War, it may be remembered, was referred to as "the war to end wars." It may also be remembered that Hoover was the first President to announce the end of poverty. Touring the country during the campaign of 1928, he spoke of a "New Day," the goal of which was "to remove poverty still further from our borders." The vision of the 1920s did not come true, but it did exist, and the idealism was contagious. Business leaders could not resist its lure. According to Otto H. Kahn, in the middle twenties, "Idealism is the outstanding feature of American business." Sometimes, to be sure, the preoccupation with idealism made the businessman seem much more naïve—or more incredible—than he really was. At the height of the boom, Edward Duffield, president of the Prudential Life Insurance Company, tried to carve out the best of all possible worlds when he told a group of insurance agents: "We are living in a material age. . . . Insurance men must be leaders in preaching the gospel of unselfishness. . . . I do not mean that you should use high-pressure sales methods . . . but when you sell a man with a family a $1,000 policy you are doing him a great injustice."[1]

Yet, naïve or not, business leaders became convinced that they were participating in a revolution in which progress was taking place along three main lines: they thought that business management was becoming progressively more professional; they believed that there was a vast improvement in the way business was being conducted, including its "moral tone," its ethics, and its attitude toward labor; and they had no doubt that the motives that guided businessmen and the objectives that they wished to attain were much loftier than those that had guided the nineteenth century. What was occurring, as they saw it, was part of a broad transformation of the whole internal structure of business in a changing environment. The "Robber Baron" was dead. With slightly different overtones, this view would return in the prosperous years that followed World War II.

The introduction to the gossipy *More They Told Barron,* which was published in 1931, observed that the tone of business, as reflected in the conversations of Barron's visitors, was distinctly higher in the later years than in the earlier ones. This may have seemed a strange statement to make just after the stock market crash and at the close of a decade that had seen the Teapot Dome scandal. But what Barron had in mind was that in the 1920s there was no record of the kind of personal antagonisms among businessmen and the disregard of public interest that there had been in the 1890s. As such, Barron's statement was reasonable. As a more objective observer of the period concluded: "Business morals may be called more or less rudimentary according to the standard by which they are judged. Still he added, "they certainly exist and they seem to be evolving."[2]

The evolving concept of ethics emphasized that the business world had accepted the "end of haggling." It was now "one price for all" and "the customer is always right." Much was made of the improvement in advertising—its closer harmony with the truth, the abandonment of patent medicine advertising, and the more aesthetic appearance of highway displays. In retrospect, all of these claims are tarnished by reality. Patent medicine advertising is still with us, and highway displays are more tawdry than ever.

Commentators on the new ethics believed that the businessmen had developed a decided sense of responsibility toward their organization, to its investors, and to its customers, and some sense of responsibility toward employees. But the main achievement of the new ethics was a revised attitude toward competitors. "Cooperation rather than competition" became a watchword of the new outlook. Judge Gary, a leading advocate of the cooperation, rather than competition, school, observed that in the twenty-five years that he had been with United States Steel he had seen a radical change in the conception of moral duty in business. "When I first came to New York," said Gary, "the managers of some large institutions . . . believed that so long as they came within the strict technical rules of the law, they were immune from public and private attack . . . a corporation should be permitted to earn unlimited profit and might treat indifferently its customers, employees, competitors, and even the body politic as a whole. . . . Weaker competitors were forced to quit. . . . The financially strong grew richer and stronger. Competition was made the instrument of death."[3]

Business spokesmen saw the same thing going on. Dr. Julius Klein, commerce expert in the Hoover cabinet, observed an "amazing transformation in the soul of business. From the cynical, mercenary devotees of trickery, connivance, deceit, and general 'public-be-damned' attitude who had been so completely dominant . . . there gradually emerged a recognition that, in self-defense, business must shift its tenets. . . . Business became a thing of morals; its pursuit became a profession which took its place with equal dignity and self-respect beside the law, medicine, and the ministry."[4]

THE SERVICE CONCEPT IN THE 1920s

The strains of idealism that kept running through the twenties also brought a change in what businessmen thought their motives *should* be. As business climbed to an all-time peak of prestige, many of its leaders ceased to be satisfied with running a business and making a profit. They sought a philosophy and endeavored to create a folklore that would de-emphasize profits and produce a more appealing motivation. Businessmen became purveyors of "service." The first victim of this new trend in opinion was the doctrine of self-interest.

In the days when Adam Smith taught moral philosophy, it was held to be self-evident that self-interest motivated human action. In time, this plank in the classical platform became further simplified. Self-interest was defined in economic terms, so that it was assumed that human action, especially in business, was motivated exclusively by economic self-interest. Businessmen found this philosophical abstraction much to their liking. It provided the best of all possible worlds, for, as Adam Smith had taught, if everyone followed his own self-interest, it was axiomatic that the interest of the whole of society would be advanced. Moreover, the doctrine that people followed their own self-interest was part of the natural law. As Otto Kahn explained in 1920: "Socialists and other adherents of ultra-advanced doctrines claim that the motive of social duty and service can be substituted effectively in ordinary workaday life for the motive of self-interest, ambition, and family, but such an allegation runs counter to the general characteristics of human nature and is entirely unsupported by experience.[5]

It was not long before hordes of critics directed a devastating attack on this oversimplified theory of human behavior. They ridiculed the idea that human beings behaved in harmony with their own self-interest. Their criticism was so effective that by the late 1920s, the pendulum had swung. It became fashionable to deny that self-interest had anything at all to do with human behavior, a proposition that was more ludicrous than the classical theory.

De-emphasizing self-interest and the importance of monetary incentives, most business leaders in the 1920s welcomed the much-publicized spread of corporate ownership. Said Owen D. Young, who had a wide reputation as a liberal businessman: "Exploiters no longer own the big concerns. Bankers no longer own them. Their shares are spread from one end of the country to another. And broadly speaking the vast organizations are in skilled hands." Apparently, Young, like many other professional managers, did not fear the potential problems that were created by the separation of ownership from responsibility, and he apparently did not anticipate the questions regarding the legitimacy of management's power that would later be raised by critics of big business. Nor did most business leaders. But here and there a few clung to the notion that incentives did have something to do with performance. One of the exceptions was Alfred P. Sloan, who wrote in 1926: "There is a point beyond which diffusion of stock ownership must enfeeble the corporation by depriving it of virile interest in management upon the part of some one man or group of men to whom its success is a matter of personal and vital interest."[6]

The whole problem of self-interest was of course intermeshed with the stated objectives of the business firm and the businessman. Throughout the fifty-year period, businessmen differed sharply from one another in their concept of the fundamental objective and function of the firm. To Gerard Swope of General Electric in the 1920s, the objective of the firm was "to produce more and better goods for more people at relatively lower prices, while preserving for those who

work in the industry and those who invest in it an adequate return."
To P. W. Litchfield in 1945, "The whole beginning and end and
purpose of business was to increase the value of its output, and still
keep the price reasonable in order to reach the greatest possible
number of people." And to William G. Caples of Inland Steel in
1965: "The skill of management, whether it be considered an
art or a science, consists of the ability to combine human talents and
material resources to achieve a desired output of goods and services
at the least possible cost."[7]

Note that these quotations about the functions and objectives of
the firm either omitted the stockholder or put him last on the list. This
did not mean that the businessman was not interested in profit, although during the 1920s some of his comments led to that impression.
At all times, it was understood that business firms had to make a
profit. Any other view would have been absurd, for every businessman
knew that if a firm did not make a profit, it would die. But in the
1920s this sentiment was rarely expressed aloud, for any mention of
profits was regarded as vulgar, and any admission of a desire for
profits was regarded as anti-social. Profits were necessary, but they
should not be emphasized, and they should not be too large. As a
spokesman for the telephone company said, "It would be contrary to
sound policy for the management to earn speculative or large
profits."[8]

To be sure, A.T. & T. was a regulated industry. Many other businessmen, however, were almost as quick to explain that their firms
had objectives other than making money, objectives which, they intimated, were incompatible with the profit motive. All these non-
profit objectives were soon lumped together under the word "service."
Early in the 1920s, 1923 in fact, Samuel Vauclain of Baldwin Locomotive warned British businessmen that they could never hope to
equal the Americans unless they mended their ways and emphasized
"service." Many business leaders picked up the word, and by the
middle of the decade, it was already well worn. One of the leading
proponents of the "service" objective was Walter Gifford, who wrote
in 1926, "It is popular to smile at the notion that the idea of service,
of a job well done is an adequate substitute for mere acquisitiveness,
but I see daily more evidence that it really is." In the same year, B. C.
Forbes, the financial writer and editor, carried the concept about as
far as anybody could by telling his readers: "Providence would seem

to have ordained that the man who *serves* most shall reap most. Success is coming to be spelt service."[9]

Bankers also thought that a revolution had occurred. Charles Cason, vice-president of New York's Chemical Bank, told a group of college students: "A new type of businessman has emerged very rapidly during recent years. This new business leader is a man of vision. . . . He leads a large life. He is broad-minded. . . . This new type of business leader has inevitably created a new philosophy of business. The economic doctrine which prevailed during the first 125 years of this country's life was that the man best served his community who did the most business and made the most money. . . . This being the doctrine it is not surprising that we have been known abroad as a nation of dollar chasers. . . . Today, there is a new point of view. . . . Business can succeed only in the long run by acquiring and holding the good will of the public. To do this, it is necessary to render honest, intelligent service at a fair price."[10]

THE "NEW CAPITALISM"

By the late twenties, the idea of service and its allied concepts had come to be known as the "New Capitalism." The converts to this doctrine developed a philosophy in which the role of business was that of the creator of prosperity who paid high wages in a climate of "fair competition."

Vague though the New Capitalism was, it was much more understandable than the parent concept of service, for precisely what "service" meant remained a riddle throughout the decade. To Henry Ford, it meant "low cost production of high grade goods, made by well paid labor, and distributed at a profit." To E. A. Filene, it meant much the same: "mass production at more efficient and lower and lower costs, lower and lower prices, with higher and higher wages." To Gifford, it was a job well done. To Gerard Swope, who thought that "industry is not primarily for profit but rather for service," service meant "responsibility to the public, the worker, the shareholder, and to the duty of perpetuating itself." Swope was anticipating what later became a commonly expressed opinion—the idea that the first objective of business leadership was not profit maximization, but the survival of the organization. This view was perhaps best expressed by Gifford, "The day of pioneering is over. New conditions have called a new type of men to lead the new kind of business organization. . . . Instead of 'captains of industry,' the present requirement would seem to be 'statesmen of industry. . . .' These men must take a long view ahead. They cannot decide questions merely on a basis of immediate advantage, because their company is going to be in business long after they are dead."[11]

Swope's associate at General Electric, the articulate lawyer Owen D. Young, gave the concept its most complete and most famous interpretation. According to Young, "service" meant "trusteeship" or "stewardship." In a widely publicized article in the March 1929 *Review of Reviews,* Young wrote: "Very soon we saw rising a notion that managers were no longer attorneys for stockholders; they were becoming trustees of an institution." As chairman of General Electric, Young thought he had obligations to stockholders, workers, customers, and the general public "to get capital at the lowest rate, to have workers think that the institution was a good place to work and that wages were as good or better than anywhere else . . . products so good and prices so reasonable that buyers would prefer it to other products."

A doctrine as nebulous as "service" was fair game for the cynical. As soon as they discovered it, anti-business critics labeled the theme a shameless hypocrisy, and some business commentators denounced it as lunacy. So far as I know, no business leader openly derided the objective of "service," but some business spokesmen, those who regretted the passing of the rugged individualist, openly scoffed at the whole idea. At the peak of the "service" wave, William Feather proved that a columnist for *Nation's Business* could be out of step with the prevailing tone of business opinion:

> The 100 per cent American believes in the doctrine of selfishness, although he is often ashamed to admit it, a fact which leads him into bleary sentiment when he undertakes to define service. . . . The John D. Rockefeller who gives away millions is not a hero, but the Rockefeller who made a billion dollars out of oil is a hero. The Carnegie who made steel and millions of dollars was a hero, but the Carnegie who gave medals to heroes and built libraries was just a sweet old lady.[12]

This derision had been anticipated and the devotees of service had their answers ready. Said banker Charles Cason, "Andre Siegfried in his book . . . ridicules this idea of 'service' that is so much attributed to businessmen in this country. To him, it does not seem bona fide; to me it does. The best upper class men in business are really genuine in their belief in it and are consistent in its practice."

In explaining their own motives as differentiated from those of the firm, business giants from the nineteenth century on made it clear that for them there were motives in addition to money and profits. Moreover, it didn't matter much whether these giants were owners or professional managers with or without a large financial stake in the firms they managed. When Alfred P. Sloan said, "Making money ceased to interest me long ago. It's the job that counts," he was echoing the sentiments of a great number of business giants. Rockefeller had said in the early 1900s: "Some say that because a man is successful and accumulates wealth, all he is after is to get wealth. . . . How blind! . . . That's the thing—accomplishment, playing the game." The British tycoon Sir William Lever repeated the general opinion in 1911: "My happiness is my business. I can see finality for myself, an end, an absolute end, but none for my business. I don't work at business only for the sake of money. I am not a lover of money as such and never have been. I work at business because business is life." And Henry Ford in 1924 told whoever was listening, "I do not care in the least for money as money. I am in business not to make money as money, but to do many things which I believe are of public benefit."[13]

Businessmen who had achieved unusual success were motivated by a drive for power and the satisfaction of empire building as well as by pecuniary considerations. Above all, however, was the sense of adventure and accomplishment in playing a game where victory meant the satisfaction of a job well done. All this has been said by different business leaders again and again during the last fifty years. It was very well expressed in an unpublished letter which Frank Vanderlip wrote in 1921 to Charles Mitchell congratulating him on becoming president of the National City Bank of New York:

> Your success will be measured very largely by your grasp of the opportunity to make the Bank in truth the leading financial organization in the United States, and I shall measure that success . . . by your accomplishment in that direction rather than by merely what you will do in adding to the Bank's profits. . . . This is not "highfalutin" talk; it is a fundamental truth.[14]

In the middle 1920s, Walter Gifford observed that "more and more he encountered men who regard business not as a means to acquire personal wealth, but as a fascinating profession and an opportunity for accomplishment." And again in 1930, Charles Schwab, a hold-over from the "neanderthal" days of business, wrote: "No first rate American businessman is ever satisfied with what he accomplishes. It isn't the money—it's doing big things and doing them better year after year. Every businessman worthy of his name is sentimental about his business. It is his own child, his own creation."[15]

THE RESURGENCE OF THE PROFIT MOTIVE DURING THE DEPRESSION

Things changed abruptly in the 1930s. The idealism that had been such a popular conversation piece in the prosperity of the 1920s was one of the many victims of the depression. Businessmen were just as convinced as they had been in the 1920s that the robber barons like Havemeyer had been crass, badly motivated, and altogether in error. But because of the depression, comments about the improving moral tone of business were muted. In most businessmen's minds, a high moral tone was bought at the expense of profits, and in an era when profits were almost non-existent, the demand for higher tones seemed gratuitous. In August 1931, Batton, Barton, Durstine & Osborne described, in the language of a jolly Rotarian, what had happened to "high moral tone":

It is a grim fact that most of us . . . have been jammed against stark reality in a way that has made it easy to consider the expediency of compromising a bit on the more idealistic phases of square dealing. Nothing really dishonest, of course, but a sort of liberal attitude toward any device which might ease the strain.[16]

As the depression worsened, the opinions offered by business leaders about their philosophy, their motives, and their objectives took a different emphasis from that of the boom years. Aggravated by what they considered the public's ingratitude, bewildered by economic events, and engrossed in efforts to keep their firms in the black, businessmen had second thoughts about the tawdriness of profits. Profits were now too scarce to be treated cavalierly, and some returned to the unapologetic acceptance of the profit motive as the primary goal of business policy. "Nothing," said Eugene Grace of Bethlehem Steel, "has ever been invented in war time or peace time that would make men work as hard as the lure of money and profits."[17]

To be sure, the sentiments expressed in the boom years still echoed, but they were not heard as frequently. The service concept still had an appeal. It was still understood that there were other motives besides the acquisition of wealth. Edgar Queeny undoubtedly voiced a popular opinion when he wrote: "Acquisition of wealth is not the sole motivating force of a businessman; he is pursuing happiness in a game in which he hopes to prove a winner. I have seen multimillionaires spend an afternoon at poker and take great delight in winning either five or fifty dollars; yet if anyone offered these men many times the amount of their possible winnings to sit at the same table all afternoon and do nothing, they would be insulted. On the other hand, if there were no stakes and no chips to be cashed in as symbols of success, the table would draw no players."[18]

Commentators on business, spokesmen for business, and far-out idealists still spoke of improvements in business ethics as if to say that the twenties had been as bad as the 1890s. *Fortune* magazine told its readers in 1940, "The New Deal has wrought better than it knows, or would like to believe. For the business community today is nothing like it was in 1929, or 1933, or even 1937. An entirely new spirit is in the air." Much earlier at the trough of the depression, E. A. Filene, whose idealism often led him to hyperbole, enthusiastically announced that a vast awakening of businessmen had been taking place since 1921. "Never before," he said, "did great business leaders engage in agitation to keep wages up. Never before has big business worried over the plight of the farmer; and never before has it been stated in so many business gatherings that business, for business reasons, must find a way to abolish unemployment." In his inimitable fashion, Filene soon changed his mind. He came to believe that he had grossly exaggerated the "awakening" and that businessmen were not acting as he thought they should act. With this realization he lost his enthusiasm and resigned in disappointment from the United States Chamber of Commerce.[19]

The service concept had lost much of its appeal, but a new phrase was beginning to enter the businessman's vocabulary: the concept of social responsibility. "I believe," said John D. Rockefeller, Jr., in 1930, "that the purpose of industry is quite as much to advance social well-being as material prosperity." Alfred P. Sloan, then listed as one of the most reactionary of Americans, wrote:

> Industrial management must expand its horizon of responsibility. It must recognize that it can no longer confine its activities to the mere production of goods and services. It must consider the impact of its operations on the economy as a whole in relation to the social and economic welfare of the entire community.

And Lewis Brown, the articulate chairman of Johns Manville, echoed Owen D. Young's famous quote of a few years before:

> In the evolution of a complex industrial society the social responsibility of management has broadened correspondingly. Management no longer represents, as it once did, merely the *single interest* of ownership. Increasingly it functions on the basis of a *trusteeship.* . . . Today the executive head of every business is accountable not only to his stockholders, but to the members of his working organization, to his customers, and to the public.[20]

BUSINESS MOTIVES IN THE POST-WORLD WAR II ERA

In the heady atmosphere that prevailed in the decades after World War II, business leaders, after some slight hesitation, got back into the groove of commenting about the "revolutionary" changes in the conduct, philosophy, and motives of the business world. Much of this comment had to do with the "professionalization of management" and the doctrine of "social responsibility."

Again as in the twenties, business leaders revived the sport of criticizing predecessors for unhandsome, if not vicious, conduct. They hit the glory trail, repudiated their ancestors, and swore to sin no more. A. W. Robertson of Westinghouse expressed a typical view in typical fashion when he wrote: "I'm not suggesting that big business has always been above reproach in its dealings with competitors and the public. It took a depression and a decade in the dog-house to teach some big businessmen that leadership entails obligations to society. The huge fortunes amassed by certain captains of industry in generations past point strongly to the conclusion that the public once paid many times a fair value for what it got. Monopoly is the ugly word for this kind of operation." Some other business leaders were

more blunt. Robert W. Johnson of Johnson and Johnson heaped
much of the world's troubles on the backs of the tycoons of the past
as he rejoiced that "rugged individualism has all but vanished; rugged
individualists managed to make themselves offensive as well as ridiculous. How much harm they did we never shall know. They probably
did not inspire the New Deal's opposition to business, but we may
fairly assume that their bombast and venom helped to crystallize it.
It seems certain, too, that their holier-than-thou, let-us-run-things
spirit inflamed the most hostile and least balanced labor leaders."[21]

The repudiation of the past swept through the business community,
affecting business journalists even more than business leaders. Russell
W. Davenport, editor of *Fortune,* and author of *U.S.A.: The Permanent Revolution,* saw the past as an era of unreconstructed evil.
"Fifty years ago," he wrote, "American capitalism seemed to be what
Marx predicted it would be and what all the muckrakers said it was
—the inhuman offspring of greed and irresponsibility, committed by
its master, Wall Street, to a long life of monopoly."

The new revolution had become such an article of faith that few
business leaders had the courage to express skepticism. Crawford
Greenewalt of DuPont was one of these few. "Some of our modern
critics," he said, "while rebuking the memory of Jim Fiske and Jay
Gould, are sufficiently tolerant to applaud the 'new type' of executive.
I am afraid I find this notion equally wearisome as the legend of the
toolless plumber. It is presented as though, by some process of sex-
less eugenics, the bull terriers and bloodhounds of the business past
had been cross-bred to produce a race of kindly and socially conscious poodles."[22]

THE FURTHER DEPRECIATION OF SELF-INTEREST

Along with the sweeping condemnation of past performance came
a further erosion of the philosophical foundations of self-interest.
Having demolished the hypothesis that human behavior was predi-
cated upon self-interest, the critics did an even more thorough job on
the other prong of the thesis. Far from accepting the Smithian concept that society's interests were best served when everyone followed
his own self-interest, they implied that just the opposite was true, and
helped by the hair shirt which everyone had donned during the depression, they ultimately succeeded in giving self-interest so bad a

name that even the businessmen finally lost their stomach for it. The reaction of Robert Johnson in 1946 illustrated how far businessmen had changed their attitude toward a doctrine which they had once respected: "Herbert Spencer welded Smith's economics to Darwin's theory of natural selection. The result was a system of savage brutality. . . . It made capital of naive doctrines, and to men already battling for wealth it gave authority for competition as ruthless and impersonal as that waged by weeds and wild beasts. It also justified exploitation, made severity a prerequisite of progress, and dignified greed as part of the struggle for existence."[23]

Yet though they avoided the phrase and treated the theory with increasing disrespect, businessmen frequently showed some awareness that behavior was not altogether divorced from self-interest. Examples of inconsistent action during prosperity and depression make a long and tedious list,* for like most other people businessmen found those things good which they thought were good for them. That is, they tended to think that society's interests and the interests of business were one and the same. Their reactions were very similar to those of an economist who once observed, "Sound economics is the economics I agree with, and the economics I agree with is sound economics."

As business returned to a status of respectability in the boom years of the nineteen fifties and sixties, self-interest lost much of its disrepute. What is surprising is that it took so long for this to happen. There is, if one thinks about it, nothing inherently wrong with following self-interest. But society is not likely to cheer such behavior, nor is it likely to praise those who advocate it. Businessmen, therefore, traveled the road back cautiously and gradually. At first, they prefaced self-interest with the adjective "enlightened." Whereas

---

* A few illustrations must suffice. In the 1920s, C. L. Bardo of the New York Shipbuilding Co., one of the most outspoken critics of government help, headed a lobby which successfully accomplished a subsidy for shipbuilding. In regretful tones, Tom Girdler of Republic Steel told a Senate committee that suggestions for improving safety in steel production were never met by questions of how many injuries or fatalities they would prevent, but how much they would cost and how much they would increase output. Robert Lund explained that he did not employ undercover labor agents because "it did not pay," not because of "any moral conviction." Clarence Wooley of American Radiator rarely had anything very good to say about Roosevelt, but after the passage of the National Housing Act, he "took off his hat to President Roosevelt." The American Bankers Association, which was always concerned with making the banking system safer, was in a constant furor because country and city bankers, correspondent banks and independents, argued hotly about branch banking. *Etc. etc.*[24]

naked self-interest seemed egocentric and selfish, enlightened self-interest could be unselfish and altruistic. Gradually, they went still further and removed the word "enlightened" as a qualifying adjective. Once more, they talked about self-interest without appearing to put themselves outside the area of common decency. Indeed, self-interest became something that was actively sought rather than coyly rejected. In a *New York Times* survey of business opinion in July 1966, the phrase occurred over and over again in such sentiments as *"self-interest,* if nothing more, dictates the acceptance of responsibilities . . . ; in business' *own self-interest,* I would hope . . . ; we cannot in *our own interest* sit back and rest on our past accomplishments . . . ; businessmen have learned to assume social obligations if for no other reason than their *own self-interest."*

SOCIAL RESPONSIBILITY

The opinions that business leaders expressed in the years after World War II about business motives and objectives combined the main themes of the prosperous twenties and the depressed thirties—the doctrine of "service" from the former and the respectability of profits from the latter. They were, therefore, a mixture of what had gone before rather than something entirely new. The concept of "social responsibility," which seemed so new, had appeared as early as the late 1930s. It was, moreover, really nothing but a substitute for the word "service," which many people thought had been overused in the 1920s. "There is nothing new in the idea that businessmen have responsibilities," said Eugene Holman of Standard Oil. The newness was the business leader's preoccupation with convincing the community at large that he was responsible. As the *Times* announced in July 1966, "The social responsibility theme seems suddenly to have gathered a steam-roller momentum. . . . A new generation of corporate managers . . . envisions a wider role for business than has been traditional."

What exactly was meant by social responsibility was just as much a puzzle in the 1950s and 1960s as "service" had been in the 1920s. Few businessmen, even among those who seemed to be at home with the notion, bothered to define it. It was assumed, apparently, that everyone knew what this elusive thing was. The fact of the matter, however, was that almost every business leader had his own subjective definition of the term. But all agreed that the whole concept of social responsibility rested on the premise that business decisions have consequences outside of the firm; as one leader explained, business "cannot exist without reacting constructively to the goals of society." To say this in a different way, the decisions that business makes should have consequences that accord with generally accepted social values. But what did this mean? George S. Moore, president of the First National City Bank of New York, explained: "It is not an attitude that a business organization adopts in a fit of benevolence like a decision to hold a company picnic." He thought it meant "enriching society today so that the interacting interests of both business and society will endure tomorrow."[25]

Other businessmen emphasized economic stability, high employment, technological progress, improved living standards, community development, a more active role in politics, the war against poverty, and an effort to improve relations with the government and with academic circles. Harry Bullis, chairman of General Mills and prolific writer in the years immediately after World War II, came as close as anyone to being specific about social responsibility. "Basically," he said, "the social responsibilities of a businessman are no different from those of an individual except in degree."[26]

It was not long before those outside the business milieu became involved in the game of social responsibility. But most of the outsiders had a quite different concept of social responsibility.* They were apt to imply that the Democratic party and the labor unions had a monopoly on social responsibility, and they often intimated that

---

* Professor Howard Bowen in his *Social Responsibilities of the Businessman*, New York, 1953, listed a number of business policies that carried "distinct overtones of social interest." Among these were:

1. Holding prices below market levels in time of inflation.
2. Effective codes of ethics.
3. Overcoming misrepresentation and adulteration.
4. Efforts to improve working conditions—hour reductions, vacations, fringe benefits.
5. Recognition of unions and acceptance of the right of workers to organize and bargain collectively.
6. Reduction of discrimination.
7. Active support of community activities.
8. Conservation.
9. Consideration of social factors in locating plants.
10. Smoothing out seasonal unemployment.
11. Avoiding speculative accumulation of inventory.
12. Smoothing out investment spending.

anti-New Deal sentiments, hostility toward labor unions, and opposition to a greater economic role for government evidenced a lack of social responsibility. On the other hand, a willingness to accept government intervention and an admission that labor unions were here to stay (whatever that might mean) were *sine qua nons* of social responsibility. Most business leaders, being self-confessed Republicans and regarding the average labor union leader as a lineal descendant of Morgan the Pirate, found it difficult to sympathize with this concept, much less agree with it. They, therefore, continued to thrive in a good-natured atmosphere in which social responsibility was defined as one chose to define it.

No matter how difficult to define, preoccupation with the subject of social responsibility continued right through the 1960s, and if anything it became stronger the vaguer the meaning became. In the process, business leaders, assuming that they had discovered something brand-new, once again succumbed to the temptation of looking back at their predecessors with something less than respect. Thus, Clarence Francis of General Foods in 1953 after confessing that "failures and transgressions have been numerous," went on to say that much progress had been made and "every single one of the many advances was accomplished over the dead body of some Scrooge who considered himself a hard-headed, two-fisted, down-to-earth businessman."[27]

In language reminiscent of the 1920s, David Rockefeller in 1962 talked about change being measured by many yardsticks. "In social terms," he said, "the old concept that the owner of a business had a right to use his property as he pleased to maximize profits, has evolved into the belief that ownership carries certain binding social obligations." The president of the Chase Bank continued: "Today's manager serves as a trustee not only for the owners but for the workers and indeed for our entire society." But this sentiment was not new. J. Pierpont Morgan, whom Rockefeller perhaps had in mind as "an old conceptor," also believed that ownership carried obligations, was in fact a trusteeship. Indeed, in the face of such institutions as the Rockefeller Foundation, the University of Chicago, the Massachusetts General Hospital, the Carnegie libraries, the Mott Foundation, Sloan-Kettering and many, many more, the banal remarks about a newly discovered social responsibility were more brashly condescending than accurate.

In the chorus of social responsibility, few business leaders sang off key, but here and there a skeptic delivered a discord. In the middle fifties, for example, Leland I. Doan of Dow Chemical remarked, "It is difficult to go into any sort of industrial gathering without encountering some discussion of management's 'social responsibility,' or 'corporate citizenship,' or operation of business in the public interest. Now I would be the last to quarrel with this. . . . It disturbs me a little bit, however, in that it is always possible to become myopic. . . . Business, if it is to be successful, must operate *within the framework* of public interest. But I hope we never kid ourselves that we are operating for the public interest *per se.*"[28]

THE NEW VIEW OF PROFITS

The substantial differences in business opinions about motives lay first of all in the attitude toward self-interest, that has already been mentioned, and secondly in the attitude toward profit. In the 1920s and 1930s, "service" and profits were considered incompatible. This view gradually changed in the late 1940s and early 1950s.

In the years immediately after the war, as in the 1920s, some of the older leaders again seemed reluctant to talk about profits. They seemed much more interested in emphasizing continuity, survivorship, and the concept of trusteeship. Frank W. Abrams of Standard Oil of New Jersey thought that managers wanted to leave their companies in a sounder and more assured position than they had found them. In order to do so, Abrams thought "management should conduct the affairs of the enterprise in such a way as to maintain an equitable and workable balance among the stockholders, employees, customers and the public at large." Similarly, Clarence Francis, like Young and Gifford before him, thought that most managers operated as trustees, and their task was to keep a balance between employees, investors, consumers, and government while seeing that each got its fair share of industry's rewards.[29]

In the late forties, the younger men in business were soft-pedaling the trusteeship theme and were no longer shunting profits aside as a respectable motive. Rather, profit was being freely accepted as a necessary part of business and not at odds with service. Thus, Harry A. Bullis said that the first responsibility was to earn a "reasonable return," for "profits were the reward that came to those who best served the public interest." At the same time, however, the concept "social responsibility" was coming into ever greater prominence. By the 1960s, the majority of big business executives had found a way of combining profits and social responsibility as equal partners in the hierarchy of objectives. To be sure, there were a few like Thomas J. Watson, Jr., of IBM who thought there was a wide range of choice between genuine self-interest and a concern for social responsibilities. But most business leaders agreed with Gilbert W. Fitzhugh of Metropolitan Life when he said: "I don't think you can really distinguish between what is done for public relations, for the profitability of your company, or what is done in the public interest. They are all the same."[30]

In the middle 1960s, the profit theme was being played as a counterpoint to the main theme of social responsibility. The usual approach was to combine profit and responsibility in a harmonious marriage sometimes with profits first, sometimes with responsibility first.

A minority were so carried away that they dropped profits to a decidedly subordinate position in the list of factors that motivated the firm. "Today," wrote an authority on management, "when one young executive describes another as a good businessman, more often than not, he does not mean a man with a good nose for profits, but rather a man who keeps his records in order, his staff contented, his contacts active, and his pipelines filled." Some leading spokesmen achieved a monumental success in ambiguity. Robert Wood Johnson wrote: "A hundred years ago, a successful business was one that made a profit. . . . Today, we consider a business successful if it meets the requirements of . . . *Service Capitalism*. . . . In saying this, I do not mean that a successful business must give up the idea of earning profits. . . . I do believe, however, that business must meet the needs and desires of human beings."[31] It is hard to visualize how profit could be made without meeting the "needs and desires of human beings."

George R. Vila of United States Rubber in 1964 spoke of what he called a misconception:

Profits seem to be a nasty word in many parts of the world. . . . And this is largely the fault of businessmen themselves. I suspect that misconception arises because the businessman is fond of saying, "We are in business to make a profit. . . ." I believe—and from searching discussions I have had with other corporation executives over a long period of time, I am convinced they too believe—that the businessman really means "We are in business to perform a service and the profit we make is an index of how well we perform this service and hence how much we contribute to society."[32]

Frederick R. Kappell of A.T. & T. said the same thing, but more succinctly. "When someone asked me," said Kappell, "which do you put first in your mind, service or profits? I said naturally I put service first, but we can only serve by earning money."[33]

The majority view, however, was that social responsibility was important, but that making a profit, perhaps even a maximum profit, was clearly the first order of business. According to John E. Swearingen of Standard Oil of Indiana, "Social responsibility begins with being successful—earning a profit. . . . It is obvious that profitability must be the fundamental corporate goal, if only because there is no other satisfactory way to measure what a corporation can and does do." In the same vein, J. P. Levis of Owens-Illinois told the California Manufacturers' Association: "The first responsibility that management has to the community is to run a profitable business." In what was almost an aside in a speech on economic planning, Sinclair Oil's O. P. Thomas said, "Most businesses frankly admit the existence of other, secondary goals. . . . Objectives of this sort, while important, cannot be permitted to displace the basic business purpose [maximizing profit] or to become ends in themselves."[34]

Some business leaders were more circumspect as they qualified the profit motive. Daniel J. Haughton of Lockheed offered an example: "Business' chief job is to make a profit. But profit for today or tomorrow is not the main goal. Companies that want to keep going have to take on a lot of obligations and responsibilities that are not concerned with immediate profits—and sometimes these are at the expense of immediate profits." And an unreconstructed "conservative," Ralph Cordiner of GE, put the matter this way: "Since profit is the lifeblood of business, a chief executive will find himself managing an anemic and dispirited organization if he loses sight of his primary responsibility to earn an adequate profit," but he went on to qualify the profit motive as a long-range thing emphasizing the continuation of the business.[35]

Although the business community was returning to the importance of profits, most businessmen, whatever their views on the firm's objectives, still believed that non-pecuniary rewards were vital. No one went so far as Sloan had done when he said that money had ceased to interest him long ago. The following remarks by James Worthy of Sears, Roebuck were more in accord with the newer world:

> One of the important functions of profits is to serve as a standard of evaluating the performance of managers. But within the structure of the enterprise itself, managers progress in terms of their ability to serve all the needs of the corporation as an on-going institution, not only the need for profits. And the manager's rewards are not limited to money. They are likely to take the form of improvements in position and status, as well as the satisfactions which come from a sense of achievement, power, and responsibility.[36]

At the opposite extreme were those non-conformists who thought that money rewards were so far ahead in the scale of incentives that whatever was in second place was not even in the running. Crawford Greenewalt of DuPont was the most articulate proponent of this view. Wrote Greenewalt:

> Of all the motivations to which the human mechanism responds, none has proved so powerful as that of financial gain. . . . Money is the only form of incentive which is wholly negotiable, appealing to the widest possible range of seekers. As people differ so markedly, it is difficult if not impossible to apply any other common denominator of inducement fully acceptable to all.[37]

BUSINESS RESPONSIBILITY AND IRRESPONSIBILITY

Critics of business, who operated on the assumption that anything short of perfection was the same as failure, argued that the talk about social responsibility in the 1950s and 1960s was just as hypocritical as the talk about service had been in the days of Teapot Dome and Richard Whitney. Certainly, those who wanted to snicker about "social responsibility" could find plenty to snicker about when they compared business opinion with business behavior. Scandals continued. Reputable firms entered into so-called "sweetheart contracts" with disreputable labor union leaders, and thus managed to keep their payrolls lower than those of their competitors. The major electric equipment manufacturers were found guilty of price fixing. An empire builder bilked banks, credit companies, and other financial institutions out of many millions in the "great salad oil swindle," and as always in prosperity, there was a plethora of skulduggery on the security exchanges, involving such unlikely names as Re Sr., Re Jr., Belle, Burrell, Guterma, Tellier, etc. Although none of these modern embarrassing falls from grace was quite as earth shaking as the collapse of Ivar Krueger's empire, they were eagerly pounced upon by those who openly scoffed at business talk of social responsibility. They found it hard to believe that business was sincere when they contemplated industry's contribution to water pollution, the automobile industry's foot dragging on air pollution and safety, the tobacco industry's inhumane attitude on cigarettes and lung cancer, the food industry's hostility to packaging legislation, the Stock Exchange's cynical repudiation of "People's Capitalism" by the imposition of a surcharge on small accounts, and the brokerage houses' discouragement of "the little fellow" whose patronage they had once so eagerly sought. At the same time, the critics forgot or they never knew about business' pioneer attempts to ameliorate some of industrialism's worst by-products. Long before the launching of the campaign to make automobiles safe at any speed and with any driver, the Ford Motor Company equipped cars with safety belts only to find them scorned by the public at large. Similarly, many electric power companies tried for years to persuade utility commissions to approve low-sulphur fuels and cleaning devices in smokestacks. They were always refused on the ground that the public was entitled to power at the lowest possible cost.

Following the anti-trust convictions of certain executives, GE's Cordiner was called upon by one stockholder to resign. "I don't care," she said, "whether you are guilty or not; you are an embarrassment." Cordiner, of course, did not resign. The stockholder then called on Henry Ford II and Sidney Weinberg, GE directors who were sitting on the platform, to say something since they had just been quoted as having deplored evidences of unethical business behavior. But they said nothing, and according to *Business Week,* the majority of the stockholders present at the meeting were solidly in favor of management. Thomas J. Watson's remarks seemed peculiarly appropriate: "The question is how far a company can go toward meeting its social responsibility if this effort detracts from or runs counter to what must be its primary mission—being successful and thereby providing jobs, goods or services, and profits."

But Watson thought business had done a good job. He noted that business had supported "regional planning, urban renewal, employment of the handicapped, equal opportunity, financial support of colleges and voluntary price and wage restraints." He concluded, "there is still a long way to go, but we are miles and miles ahead of where we were before World War II."[38]

Other leaders, very much in the minority to be sure, were not so sanguine. Their misgivings took one of two forms: that most of the talk about responsibility was really nothing more than talk; and that businessmen, sincere or insincere, did not have the talents for the job of nailing down responsibility. An example of the first opinion occurred when Theodore Houser of Sears, Roebuck criticized the high salaries paid to executives:

> If we sincerely believe that the publicly-owned American corporation is the most efficient and most desirable means of serving the material and, to some extent, the cultural needs of the people, then those endowed with the ability to lead these great organizations should begin to conceive of their remuneration partly in terms of the satisfaction of making a real contribution to national progress.[39]

An example of the second opinion was given in a lecture at Tufts University by Alexander N. McFarlane of Corn Products Refining:

> It is evident that many actions on the part of the business manager involve him in social change. It is obvious that for him some social role is inescapable. Despite this fact, too many businessmen are neither confident nor comfortable in the part. Nervously, and with hands groping unsteadily for the public pulse, they follow other power structures in our society—government, education, and the church.[40]

Over the half century, the expressed objectives and motives of business had changed significantly and substantially. During the boom years after the first war, profits and self-interest were as unmentionable as sex in the Victorian era. The depression ended this and forced business to face the reality that profits were a necessary though perhaps a not altogether respectable part of American economic life. Then in the luscious years that came after World War II, profits were mixed with generous amounts of responsibility to make an amalgam that sometimes defied analysis.

PART II

How Business Leaders Viewed the Economy

PART II

How Business Leaders
Viewed the Economy

3. BUSINESS OPINION AND THE DEPRESSION OF 1921

"There is an overproduction of fearful opinions, impressions by professional prophets and pessimists and critics. These destructive forces undermine confidence and scare some people into inaction and undue caution which leads to unemployment."

A. R. Erskine, 1922.

A graph of business activity for the forty-odd years after 1920 looks like a relief map of Death Valley. There are breath-taking peaks alternating with extraordinarily depressed troughs. First came a severe postwar depression, then the long period of prosperity and stock market speculation from 1923 to 1929, interrupted by two slight recessions in 1924 and 1926. From its high in 1929, business sank almost steadily until 1933 when a gradual and uninspired recovery set in and lasted for four years. In May 1937 came another alarming collapse that, fortunately, lasted for only about a year. Then, once again, a slow recovery began—a recovery that ultimately ran into the galloping inflation of World War II. With V-J Day there was a short period of reconversion, and then the economy began a long forward march broken only four times (1949, 1953, 1957, and 1960) by slight recessions.

Businessmen reacted to these toboggan-like movements, sometimes optimistically, facing the present and the future confident that they knew the answers; sometimes in surprise at the turn of events. Occasionally, when the economy seemed to be collapsing completely, they were bewildered and at a loss to explain either the causes of or the cures for what was going on. But over the half century, most of the businessman's opinions about the nature of the business cycle and his explanations for prosperity and recession changed fundamentally, so that there were more differences than similarities between what he said in the sixties and what he had said in the twenties.

THE POSTWAR BOOM AND COLLAPSE

At the end of World War I, businessmen, unlike some other groups, were extremely optimistic. There were, to be sure, a few pessimists, but they met a frigid reception. One forecasting service that started early and earnestly to warn its readers of a coming decline was rewarded by a wholesale dropping of subscriptions. Business was having none of that. Instead, businessmen rushed to buy goods in anticipation of ever rising prices and in eager expectation of ever greater prosperity. What they anticipated came true immediately; what they expected took a little more time to realize. The inflation of the war years continued after the Armistice and prices rose to a record high in the spring of 1920. Meanwhile, in November 1919, the Federal Reserve System, hampered by the Treasury, new at its job and groping in unexplored territory, began to tighten money by raising the rediscount rate first to 4¾ per cent, than to 6, and finally in June 1920 to 7 per cent. The federal government also rapidly cut its expenditures. Stock prices began to fall in November 1919 and bank deposits, in December. The general economy began to sag in January 1920 and by the spring, it had slid into deep depression.

Under the pressure of swollen inventories, tighter money, and less spending, prices tumbled, production fell off, profits declined and unemployment increased. As has frequently been the case, the cataclysm came so suddenly that many did not realize it was here until well after it had begun. This was especially true of business leaders. As with every subsequent recession or depression, it took a long while for them to recognize and admit that prosperity was over at least for the moment, if not for a longer period. The initial reaction was always to treat depression as a state of mind. Judge Gary, for example, told the American Iron and Steel Institute in October 1920, when the depression was only half over: "The business skies are practically without clouds. There may be showers from time to time, but there is nothing in the atmosphere to indicate the approach of dangerous storms. It is up to the business men and women to maintain certain and continuous business activity in satisfactory volume with fair and reasonable profits."

When they finally did realize that a depression existed, the majority of business leaders still kept their courage. To be sure, some volatile tycoons lost their nerve. Years later, Donaldson Brown of General Motors recalled one of the strangest of these instances: "On numerous occasions during a trip in November 1920, one of the men pointed out the economic storm warnings which were gathering (*sic*) on the horizon. . . . It is ironic that this man whose conspicuous pessimism was not shared by others on the journey was W. C. Durant." There was ample justification for the use of the word "ironic," for Durant was to become if not the most prominent, at least the most articulate bull in the subsequent prosperity era, and, as Brown pointed out, his pessimism was not shared by the others.

Despite the severity of the depression—the decline was the steepest in U.S. history up to that time—most business leaders did not think there was any real cause for alarm, and they were right in thinking that the downturn would not last long. "There's no reason whatsoever to despair," said James B. Forgan, chairman of the board of the First National Bank of Chicago, "1921 will be a year of steady though possibly very slow improvement." His brother David, vice-president of the bank, reinforced the opinion by saying, "Hard times will last not for two or three years, two or three months is nearer the truth." And Judge Gary went so far as to think that he "was justified in saying that so far as his information extended, there was nothing unfavorable on the business horizon."[1]

EXPLAINING THE DEPRESSION

Business leaders were convinced that they fully understood the causes of and cures for the depression. Most of them explained what had happened in terms of "market rigidities" and on the premise that what goes up must come down. According to what were always referred to as "the rules of economics," if business became too prosperous, the economy was in danger because beyond a certain point prosperity became "unsustainable." This doctrine, theory, law, hypothesis, or hunch cropped up persistently in every prosperity period in the twentieth century, and in some recession periods as well. It was the catchiest tune in the economic repertoire. Bankers were especially fond of it. Industrialists sometimes doubted that high level prosperity had to end in collapse; bankers accepted the proposition without question, and, furthermore, they put the threshold of high level prosperity very much lower than did the industrialists. The chief reason for this lay in the different way that each group viewed the economic environment. Industrialists concentrated on their own firms and their own industries; bankers dealt with many firms and many industries and were, therefore, more interested in the economy as a whole. Bankers were also more interested in and knew more about economic theory. They tended, therefore, to be more articulate about cycles and depressions than were the industrialists whose opinions usually went no further than a general view of the outlook for a particular industry. Taking the overview, bankers looked at economic theory as though they were playing a very enjoyable game, and being trained players, they were much more faithful to the accepted rules of the game than were the industrialists.

One of the most articulate bankers of the 1920s, Otto H. Kahn, gave a typical banker's explanation for the depression, ascribing it among other things to "excessive expansion" as well as to "a war of unprecedented scope, accompanied by a corresponding inflation of currency and production, a peace equally unprecedented in its ill effects. . . . Governmental incapacity, neglect, and blundering . . ." and "exorbitant boosting of the costs of labor." Charles R. Sabin of the Guaranty Trust also thought that the economic chickens of profligacy were coming home to roost. He told the press in early 1921, "Surely 1920 impressed upon all of us the folly of extravagance in personal, business, and governmental affairs. We should have learned the folly of inefficiency, of unsound and unnecessary taxation, of government participation in private business, of trying to substitute legislative enactments for natural economic laws." The cure for all this folly, extravagance and general ineptitude was to allow the rigidities to work themselves out in the course of time. John S. Drum, San Francisco banker and president of the American Bankers Association, told the bankers convention, "the problems are natural manifestations of a world-wide maladjustment that great natural forces are working to remedy."[2]

What had happened, orthodox observers explained, was that everything had "gone too high." Wages were too high, taxes were too high, credit was too high, prices were too high. John Edgerton of the National Association of Manufacturers summed up what many business leaders thought when he said, "During the war, standards of living were set up that can not and should not in many instances be maintained." Then after the war a "buyers strike" occurred. No one knew exactly why people stopped buying; they just did. According to Judge Gary, "Something began creeping into the minds of the consumer. . . . He began thinking about differences between cost of production and selling price. . . . He decided he'd better hold on to his money: that things would have to come down in price." Bernard Baruch, the financier and former head of the War Industries Board, thought the explanation for what was happening was one of simple supply and demand. According to him, the Armistice brought an end to government buying and government controls. "There followed a popular rush to buy and a soaring of prices, but presently the people began to break away from high-price thought. The law of supply and demand was beginning to assert itself."[3]

Why had prices gone up in the first place? Many business leaders explained the phenomenon by what is today called the "cost-push" theory of inflation. That is, they believed that prices were high because wages were high. Gary, who repeatedly referred to unconscionable prices, was especially fond of cost theories of price and value. "The price of commodities," he said, "rose only after organized labor led a movement for increased pay and shorter hours." The *National City Bank Review* thought the matter was well beyond dispute: "It is evident on every hand that the depression which exists is due to an unbalanced state of industry as regards the compensation received by important bodies of people." Another sizable group supported a "demand-pull" theory, which explained that high prices had been caused by expanded credit and a swollen money supply which acted as fuel to feed demand.

PRESCRIBING THE CURE

Whether the explanation for inflation was "cost-push" or "demand-pull," businessmen followed, at least in theory, an orthodox cathartic cure for depressions. They solidly believed that deflation was both inevitable and necessary, and the quicker it occurred, the quicker recovery would come. No dissent was heard from such opinions. "After a war," said William A. Law of the First National Bank of Philadelphia, "deflation finally sets in and continues until buyers generally become confident that prices have approximately reached bottom." Industrialists shared this opinion as A. W. Douglas of the Chamber of Commerce demonstrated when he testified: "There is a feeling that the situation will improve when prices of commodities reach a figure that will tempt the ultimate consumer to begin purchasing for other than his immediate wants."[4]

The business community offered a four-part prescription for accomplishing the deflation that it thought necessary. First wages would have to be cut ruthlessly. At the same time, government activities would have to be pared down and restored to what "the fathers had had in mind." Then taxes would have to be reduced and reformed from the "improvident, disingenious, and mischievous system adopted in 1917." Lastly, the money supply would have to be tightened.

Except for Henry Ford, E. A. Filene and a handful of others, businessmen were in accord with the first three of these medicines, but there was much disagreement with the fourth. Otto Kahn's view faithfully reflected their general feeling: "The American standard of wages and living does not and cannot and should not mean that extravagant and fortuitous standard that resulted from the war." This meant that wages had to come down. If they didn't, there was no hope for full recovery. But very few businessmen believed that labor would reconcile itself to accepting the inevitable. Labor unions were certainly not willing, and they were much stronger and much more influential than they once had been. Recovery, therefore, would take longer than it otherwise might. As M. F. Backus of the National Bank of Commerce in Seattle warned, "There will be much unemployment, since organized labor has announced opposition to any reduction from the present scale of wages." But wages would eventually have to come down, and since the simple ways of the market place that had worked in the past were no longer in effect, more subtle means of dealing with the problem had to be found. And they were found. In 1921 more than three hundred articles appeared in business magazines explaining various intricate maneuvers that had been used to effectuate wage cuts.

Beginning with the railroads, wage reductions spread throughout the economy. The United States Steel Corporation was allegedly reluctant to go along with the prevailing practice, but it too finally reduced the wages of its common laborers from $5.00 to $3.00 for a ten-hour day. Judge Gary, a master at rationalization, became the spokesman for those who argued that reductions were necessary because man-hour output had declined. "I have seen reports," he observed, "made by the clothing trade that wages in that industry went up one hundred per cent and productivity went down fifty-six per cent. I do not know for certain whether or not these figures are correct, but I dare say they are not greatly exaggerated. The same to some extent was true of other trades."[5]

Bringing the government down to size was perhaps even more important than wage deflation in the anti-depression policies that businessmen recommended. Almost everyone found it possible to applaud, at least in the abstract, Charles Schwab's admonition: "The first thing we want to do away with is any sort of governmental control that affects individual initiative. Let us get rid of regulation by people who have no other motive than that of winning votes." This apparently meant the Democratic party with which most businessmen were completely out of sorts. They cheered when Otto Kahn accused the party and the Wilson administration of establishing "an unparalleled record for inefficiency, wastefulness, and general misgovernment." Kahn called on the GOP "to have the courage to maintain steadfastly the tried and true fundamentals of our social and governmental system, and to resist plausible fallacies." The impeccably elegant banker then delivered a judgment that he must have later regretted: "I welcome with grateful relief the approaching transfer of the executive functions into the hands of that calm, right-thinking, sincere, and high-minded man, Warren Harding."[6]

What businessmen most objected to about government was the "unconscionable" tax burden which would have to be lifted and lifted quickly if the country was to get out of the depression. "Every month's delay in not reducing taxes," said E. C. Dougal, New York banker, "means more, much more than a month's prolongation of business depression."[7]

Otto Kahn, the most indefatigable spokesman on the subject, wrote a long letter to Senator Lenroot, the gist of which was that "good times and abundant employment cannot return as long as enterprise is lamed and the natural flow of capital deflected by oppressive and exorbitant taxation." At this time, Congress was being urged to repeal the excess profits tax, and Howard Beebe of Harris, Forbes & Co. and president of the Investment Bankers' Association, appealed to their common sense because "taxation continues to menace business and to retard the return to a normal state of affairs." Beebe demolished the opposition by asserting: "Those men in Congress who use their position for the furtherance of selfish, political ends to the detriment of their country are traitors to the cause of good government and should be so sternly rebuked that they will immediately change their tactics."

The whole subject of taxes was bound up with larger questions about fiscal policy. On this subject, the most important spokesman for business was, of course, Andrew W. Mellon, the Pittsburgh banker and Secretary of the Treasury. His first report succinctly expressed the business point of view on the place of government in the economy, the matter of government spending, and what should be done about taxes. Mellon called for reduced government spending, rejection of any new spending programs, the elimination of the excess profits tax, and a substantial cut in the surtax. He regretted particularly the demand on the part of the veterans of 1918 for a bonus. Mellon warned Congress and the people that the country could have a balanced budget with a reduction of taxes or with a soldiers' bonus, but not with both, and he made no attempt to disguise his own enthusiasm for the former.

Businessmen and business associations wasted no time in forming organizations to resist the bonus. Chambers of Commerce all over the country "agreed with Secretary Mellon," so did the National Association of Credit Men, and an array of individual executives. With the financial support of Judge Gary, Hornblower & Weeks, Cleveland H. Dodge of Phelps-Dodge, Paul M. Warburg, George S. Davison of the Hanover Bank, H. B. Rust of Koppers Coke, and others in the business, financial, and leisure world, the Ex-Servicemen's Anti-Bonus League was set up as a counterforce to the American Legion. The tactics pursued in opposition to the bonus were to treat it with patience and understanding in the "this hurts me more than it does you" manner. George F. Baker, in a rare public statement, unequivocally asserted that he was not in favor of the bonus, and he didn't believe "thinking soldiers" were either. Judge Gary was in favor of the bonus, "but not now." He urged the veterans to "wait a few years" and appealed to their sportsmanship because "after years of heavy taxes, business is just getting into stride."

The nub of the matter was that businessmen wanted an overly balanced budget and some repayment on the debt, but above all tax reduction and tax revision. When it became evident that recovery was in the wind, that government expenditures were stable, and the budget balanced, the business group shifted its tactics. It ceased to agitate for further tax reduction. Instead it began an intensive campaign to "reform" the tax system. Kahn once again struck the keynote. He denounced the existing tax law as "a measure unscientific, inequitable, cumbersome, vexatious and intolerably complex. It bears the imprint of class and sectional discrimination. It penalizes thrift and industry, but leaves the wastrel and shirker untouched. It discourages, disturbs, and impedes business and places the American businessman at a disadvantage against his European competitor. It tends to curtail production, restrain consumption, and diminish the demand for labor. It facilitates government extravagance. It impairs the incentive to effort. It halts enterprise. It makes for higher costs. It hampers the flow of capital. It has shoved a clumsy hand into the delicately adjusted organization of commerce and industry."

Kahn proposed, as Mellon did, to have a "reasonable reduction" of the surtaxes and to introduce a sales tax "the principle of which is endorsed by the majority of businessmen." Kahn wanted it to be understood that he had always favored the principle of a progressive income tax, "but like every other principle, it must be applied within the rule of reason. We have applied the principle with vindictive unreason."

Other businessmen supported Kahn's cry for justice. "The fairest method of taxation," Gary told an attentive Iron and Steel Institute audience, "is found in the sales tax so called." He "verily believed that with a fair sales tax, business would be better, the country would be more prosperous, and everyone would be happier." James Buchanan Duke, the tobacco tycoon whose career dated back to the days of the "Robber Barons," told Barron, "If the United States should put the taxes where they ought to be—on consumption—and let capital increase, this country would dominate the world." Jules Bache, broker and owner of the largest wire house in the country, offered Congress a comprehensive tax program in which the main innovation was a 1 per cent sales tax. In a *Times* survey of banker opinion, the "vast majority" voted in favor of a sales tax.[8]

Businessmen were fervid enough about a sales tax to form organizations to lobby for it. Among these were the Business Men's National Tax Committee and the Tax League of America. They were joined by the National Association of Manufacturers, the Boston Chamber of Commerce, the New York Board of Trade, the National Retail Dry Goods Association, the National Automobile Chamber of Commerce, and the National Association of Retail Clothiers.

But, again, like most business thinking, this was not a one-way street. Many business leaders and some business organizations that

favored tax reduction were against a sales tax. Their objection was
based on the simple hypothesis that a sales tax was regressive, that
is, it would (in percentage terms) fall most heavily on the poor. The
Tax Committee of the Chamber of Commerce pronounced a sales
tax "not feasible." Instead, it supported a general turnover tax. The
National Association of Retail Grocers also opposed a sales tax.
Among the bankers, Frank Vanderlip criticized a sales tax in his usual
forceful way. M. C. Baker of the Pennsylvania National told the press
that "no sales tax has yet proved practicable." Horatio A. Hunt of
the Rhode Island Hospital Trust ruled out a sales tax because it
would be passed on to the consumer. And E. F. Swinney, president
of the First National Bank of Kansas City, not only rejected a sales
tax, but opposed repeal of the excess profits tax. The proponents of a
sales tax considered the arguments of the opponents carefully, and
concluded that if a sales tax were passed on to the consumer, the same
charge could be made against both an income tax and an excess profits
tax.[9]

THE MONEY SUPPLY AND THE FEDERAL RESERVE

The near unanimity of opinion that appeared on wage and tax
reduction did not prevail when the discussion turned to what should
be done about the money supply and interest rates. Industrialists
thought that wage and tax reduction and a major cut in government
spending were all that the economy needed to "readjust." But bankers
were not of the same mind. They thought "the restoration of the
liquidity of bank credit," or, to put it more simply, a contraction
of the money supply was just as necessary. To them, recovery could
only come about through monetary deflation, bitter as that medicine might be. James B. Forgan, sage of Chicago banking, explained
that in the long run the steep slide of 1920–21 had been a blessing
caused by a deliberate and well-advised tightening of the money
supply. Said Forgan, "The decline in prices, which has brought on the
present sharp depression, was undoubtedly due to the action of the
Federal Reserve Banks in increasing the discount rates; but it must
always be noted that without such action, we should have had continuous inflation which unquestionably would have finally brought
on a catastrophe such as followed 1873 or 1893." Sometimes, in
their desire to pursue deflation, bankers overreached themselves and

talked in contradictions. Thus, one small banker wanted the Federal Reserve System to tighten money by "reducing Federal Reserve note currency as rapidly as possible," but he also thought that "interest rates should go lower," and that according to most bankers was a function of easy, not tight, money.[10]

Industrialists were not able to contemplate liquidation, deflation, and tight money with the same stoicism exhibited by the bankers. They wanted prices to fall, but they had no enthusiasm for tight money, and many looked upon the newly created Federal Reserve as the reincarnation of some sort of Spanish Inquisition. By training, the industrialists thought that the economy had to go through a monetary catharsis to cure its malaise, but they had no feeling for the cure, and in the conflict between what they thought and what they felt, feelings triumphed. By the summer of 1921, when the depression had run its course, the Federal Reserve Board's ears burned as small businessmen, country bankers, and assorted industrialists heaped hostility upon it. As in Jackson's day and as in the post-Civil War period, business opinion was split. The proponents of easy money argued with the champions of orthodox finance.

In typical oratorical language, the Texas Chamber of Commerce petitioned President Harding to limit the Federal Reserve Board to banking and to prohibit the Board from "knowingly using its power and influence for the purpose of inflating or deflating the value of commodities or services, or otherwise interfering with the inherent right of the citizen to labor, to engage in such business, to invest, to spend his savings as he may desire." Shortly thereafter, J. S. Wanamaker, president of the American Cotton Association, asserted that the Fed was under the domination of Wall Street. He called its policies "of price and currency deflation . . . cynical and cruel, financial tyranny and commercial criminality." But the most scathing critic of all, as he would be for the next ten years, was W. C. Durant, the automobile entrepreneur. In a series of attacks that had no trouble making the newspapers, Durant said that bankers' greed and Federal Reserve policy were responsible for the depression. "Much of our present distress," said Durant, "is due to extortionate interest rates and restricted credits. . . . Our great and noble bankers are waxing fat."[11]

The big-city bankers, who had once opposed the system, now sprang to its defense. James A. Stillman, president of the National City, said, "The Federal Reserve Board is the backbone of our banking

system. It is serving the country magnificently." E. C. Dougal labeled
the critics' attacks "ridiculous." The Federal Reserve, nevertheless,
began to ease up on money and in a series of maneuvers in the summer and fall reduced the rediscount rate from 7 to 4½ per cent
and to 4 per cent in 1922. Substantial as these reductions were, they
did not satisfy Durant, who clamored for a 3 per cent rediscount
rate and 1 per cent call money. He did not doubt that "the Federal Reserve Bank has the power to stop profiteering in money, and its failure
to do so is very largely responsible for the general business paralysis
and the surrender of many of our splendid industrial institutions
to the greedy money vultures." To all this, Melvin Traylor of the
First Trust and Savings Bank of Chicago replied that the Fed had
made a mistake in reducing the discount rate. "I feel," he said, "that
the recent action of the Federal Reserve will check the liquidation
which is needed."[12]

Few had Traylor's faith in deflation and the automatic market
mechanism. Few had the courage to follow where the logic of their
economic analysis might take them. Deflation was inevitable, they
thought, but they also knew that it hurt. They, therefore, sought some
loophole, some means of taking the sting out of deflation. This of
course created a series of conflicts between what they thought should
be in theory and what they wanted in practice. Thus, Judge Gary, ever
eager to see the bright side of things, compromised between the moral
good of thrift and the practical need for spending: "Even though
people generally are economical, as they ought to be and hope will
be, still they should and will make enough purchases as to bring a
substantial prosperity." And when Henry Ford said that prices and
wages had dropped because of a scarcity of money, bankers quickly
pounced upon him as an economic illiterate, even though they had
quite clearly called for a contraction of money precisely in order to
bring about a decline in prices and wages. The inconsistency, or
rather the dilemma, was well illustrated by some remarks by Charles
Mitchell: "Let us dispel the illusion that prices and wages have fallen
because of a shortage of money. Let us stamp out the thought that it
is primarily money that creates a demand for things. The old fallacies
and heresies that have vexed society throughout all history are hatched
in every time of disturbance and distress. One of them is the paper
money delusion."[13]

Whether it was intended or unintended, prices did fall and wages
did drop; the former by some 37 per cent between 1920 and 1922,

and the latter by 13 per cent. Prices fell so abruptly that business-men became alarmed and opened a concerted drive to do something about the "buyers' strike" which they thought was responsible for it. Early in 1921, the NAM appealed to the public to end the strike, and in the spring, a group of leading businessmen and bankers, including F. H. Sisson of the Guaranty Trust, Joseph P. Day, the real estate tycoon, and J. S. Bache launched a "Sell Now League" to counteract it.

WHAT BUSINESSMEN LEARNED FROM THE DEPRESSION

Many businessmen thought that recovery would eventually take place "despite labor," but that it would take much longer than neces-sary. Yet, the depression was really short. By 1922, it had become a part of ancient history, and by 1923, an era of prosperity had begun. But in the first days of recovery, the optimism that was shown by business leaders was subdued and wary, rather than enthusiastic and elated. Once again, they feared that the economy might run away with itself. F. L. Lipman, chairman of San Francisco's Wells Fargo Bank, demonstrated the prevailing caution: "The improve-ment in 1922 might turn out to be a reaction upward from precipi-tate deflation carried too far, rather than a step upward on the road to a so-called normal position." The mood of businessmen in general was typified by the ideas of Henry S. Dennison of Dennison Manu-facturing. This thoughtful and articulate businessman had been one of the first to recognize the existence of bad times. Now he presented a complicated forecast of the future. He first ticked off the factors that would encourage rapid expansion: 1) the building boom, 2) shortage of railroad equipment, 3) easy money, a large gold supply, and a relatively low amount of debt, and 4) the relatively large pur-chasing power of labor and of those who had profited in stocks and bonds. He then summarized the factors that would prevent "a too rapid expansion": 1) the small purchasing power of farmers, 2) unsettled international conditions, 3) "businessmen are better in-formed than in 1894 or even in 1903," 4) the *possibility* of strong control by the Federal Reserve Board. And he concluded by saying that he didn't think the current progress of business would continue through 1923, a forecast which he greeted with equanimity, since he preferred "a slow rather than a too rapid expansion."[14]

Despite its relative brevity, the depression had considerably shaken the confidence of business leaders. That it had been a severe experience was evident, for many industrial firms that have since taken their places among the most gigantic of businesses barely managed to keep above water during the 1921 crisis. Ford experienced crucial difficulties. General Motors suffered the only year of financial loss in its entire history and emerged with a new management. Firestone hurried back from Europe to resuscitate his battered rubber business from the effects of a storm which he later claimed he had foreseen. Net income for a sample of large manufacturing companies fell from $610 million in 1919 to $139 million in 1921.

Businessmen claimed to have learned many valuable lessons from the depression. True, many of these lessons were specious. Ford, for example, said that he had learned to avoid bankers. There was, however, at least one really great benefit. Businessmen came out of the depression of 1921 with a new appreciation of the advantages of more efficient techniques in marketing, distribution, production and other allied managerial functions. General Motors was one of the firms that learned the lesson best. Under the new management of Alfred P. Sloan, assisted by the Du Ponts, the whole "strategy and structure" of the organization altered. Controlled decentralization replaced managerial chaos. Independent buying power of plant managers was limited to the requirements of a four-month forecast. Donaldson Brown, vice-president in charge of finance, instituted a plan by which in 1923 each manufacturing division was obtaining ten-day reports from dealers on sales and cars in stock. Production was controlled in line with retail demand as recorded by reports from the field and with reference to the calculable factors in the economic cycle. Businesses, large and small, adopted in varying degrees similar plans of control designed to prevent overexpansion of inventory.[15]

Businessmen did not soon forget the lessons that 1920–22 had taught them about their internal organization and operations, but, as we shall see, the memories of the depression gradually faded and mellowed as speculation and boom superseded depression and deflation in the public as well as the business mind.

4. HOW BUSINESSMEN VIEWED THE BOOM OF THE 1920S

"Everybody ought to be rich."
                                        John J. Raskob, September 1929.

"History, which has a painful way of repeating itself, has taught mankind that speculative overexpansion ends in overcontraction and distress."
                                        Paul Warburg, March 1929.

The seeds of recovery that germinated in 1922 soon blossomed into prosperity. By the late 1920s, the country was enjoying its fruits, and the most succulent of these were, of course, in the stock market. The growth of security capitalism could be measured by the space given to "Stocks and Bonds" in the *New York Times Index*. This topic took less than a column in 1924, one column in 1925, one and a half in 1927, and three in 1929. The *Times* of January 2, 1921, allocated less than a page (220 square inches) to a summary of the transactions in stocks on the New York Stock Exchange for the year 1920. It took more than twice as much (525 square inches) to cover the transactions for 1929. Bond dealings which required more than double the space given to stocks in 1921 took only a trifle more than stocks in 1929.

The great bull market was one of the half dozen most sensational episodes in American financial history. And like every sensational happening, it has been surrounded with a set of legends to make the drama more melodramatic. Many accounts of the events leading up to the great crash give the impression that stocks went up every day until October 1929 when they collapsed and lost in less than a fleeting moment all that they had gained in the preceding nine years.

One also gets the impression that during the upsurge, all business leaders, bankers, and brokers were naïve, if not stupid, or even dishonest in urging the public to ever greater speculation. As the implication has it, all the members of the entire business community were propagandizing a "new era," featuring a never-ending boom and a higher and higher stock market.[1]

There is just enough truth in this caricature to give it the credence it does not deserve. Actually, the market did not go up continually. The stock averages often sagged on the upward journey. Until the last great surge in 1927–29, it was three steps forward and two backward. The *Times* average at its low in 1924 was only slightly above its 1923 low, and the low in 1926 was only 30 per cent higher than the low of 1924. From the low of 1921 to the high of 1927, the composite average gained approximately 125 points. From the high in 1927 to the high in 1929, it also gained 125 points. In other words, it rose as much in the last two years as in the previous six years. Nor was the subsequent decline as precipitate as has been pictured. As late as 1931, after a two-year decline, the well-known averages were still as high as the 1928 low.

The last of the caricature is equally erroneous. All businessmen did not fall victim to the new-era psychosis, if psychosis it was. The majority were accustomed to think of the stock market and general business as two unrelated things. They believed that it was quite possible for the market to go down in the midst of good business conditions, and they thought it was quite possible for stocks to go up while business fell off. Or, to put this another way, they thought the country could experience economic prosperity and financial depression at the same time. This was by no means as unreal as it may at first seem, for in the short run, the stock market and general business often move in opposite directions.

As one would expect, there was a disparity in the way industrialists and bankers viewed the state of the nation. Industrialists tended to ignore the stock market while being optimistic about future business conditions. Their impulse was to agree eagerly with those who had decided that the business cycle was a thing of the past and that depressions were no longer possible. Most bankers, on the other hand, initially regarded the whole new-era business with considerable skepticism. They were among the last to believe that a millenium was about to arrive either in the general economy or in the stock market. In time, some modified their skepticism and some dropped it entirely. Others stubbornly maintained their doubts despite the pressures and temptations of a speculative environment. All adult human beings are congenital bulls or bears, having little control over the optimism or pessimism with which they view the economy, and businessmen, despite rumors to the contrary, are human beings. All through the boom, there were voices of caution that shouted loud enough to be heard even in the din of the speculative babel, but their message went unheeded by a public that had the bit in its teeth and wanted no part of caution.

Almost all the historians of the 1920s point out that *Moody's Investors' Service, Poor's, The Commercial and Financial Chronicle,* Roger Babson, and, especially, Alexander Dana Noyes of the *New York Times* warned that disaster was imminent. No bankers, except occasionally Paul Warburg, are included in this list, but in actual fact there were many bankers among the surprisingly large number of Jeremiahs whom "no one listened to." Not that all pessimists should be given any special praise for their constant warnings. They do deserve credit for having called the turn on the "big one," that is, the crash of October 1929, but over the decade they were wrong more often than they were right. On the other hand, the optimists who struck out in 1929 were right more often than they were wrong in the whole decade.* The saver who finally broke down under the blandishments of the optimists and bought Jersey or A.T. & T. as late as 1927 and sold it at the low of 1929 was still richer than the man who had always listened to the conservative banker and who had, therefore, never entered the market. As for the fortunate fellow who bought Radio or Montgomery Ward and sold it at the high in 1929, the less said about his riches, the better.

THE FOUR PHASES OF PROSPERITY

There were four phases to the so-called "speculative orgy" of the years 1922–29.† The first, from June 1922 to August 1924, was

---

* This must always be true, for the market goes up much more than half the time, but when it falls, it falls much faster than it goes up.

† These phases are not the same as *the* turning points in the business cycle. According to the National Bureau of Economic Research, business reached a peak in May 1923, fell to a low in July 1924, advanced to October 1926, and declined to another low point in November 1927. Thus, during the boom, there were two periods of recession, each of which lasted for over a year.

a period of relative stability on the stock exchange, but it also contained the opening chapter in the great Florida real estate boom. In the second period, August 1924 to February 1926, the market moved up rapidly. The third phase, February 1926 to the fall of 1927, witnessed a short, but decided drop in the stock market and a mild recession. In phase four, the bull market really took off as the averages soared from early 1927 to October 1929. Let us look at what happened in each of the four phases and how business opinion reacted to what was happening.

In June 1922, the *Times* industrial average stood at approximately 100, 33 points above the 1921 low and 40 points below the 1919 high. From then until March 1923, the average climbed with only a slight interruption to 120. The Federal Reserve authorities, fearful that the boom might get out of hand, raised the rediscount rate to 4½ per cent and began to sell securities in the open market "to check the overextension of business." This move to tighter money induced little comment from businessmen, for the Federal Reserve was still new. It was, however, to be the last time that monetary action would be taken almost without notice. Throughout the remaining years of the 1920s there were to be times when general business and the stock market would be in conflict, so that whatever action the Federal Reserve took offended someone.

THE MONEY SUPPLY AND CREDIT

Most bankers and financial people thought that what affected the money supply had something to do with what happened in the economy. They, therefore, expressed themselves freely about Federal Reserve policy and the condition of money and credit. They were on the whole sympathetic to the Fed, for they were tight-money adherents. Their opinion was well expressed by A. W. Loasby of the Equitable Trust: "Easy money has induced various forms of speculation . . . lavish purchase of luxuries. . . . This situation cannot be expected to continue indefinitely and it behooves us to consider the possibility of a change and act with discretion."

As could be expected, industrialists had less to say about money and credit than bankers did. What they did say leaned toward easy money and was generally critical of the monetary authorities. In the spring of 1925, after an increase in the rediscount rate, they began to criticize the Reserve's monetary policy, and their criticisms were sharp enough to cause Secretary of the Treasury Mellon to write an article for *Nation's Business* in defense of the system.

The influential academic economists of the 1920s presented a third point of view. They leaned toward tight money and they treated the monetary authorities with less tolerance than the bankers showed. In December 1925 at the annual meeting of the American Economic Association, Professors Beckhart and Reed and Economists Anderson of the Chase Bank and Chandler of the National Bank of Commerce charged that politics rather than economics dominated the Board's thinking, that European interests had influenced the Board to the detriment of American interests, and that the current stock speculation (which annoyed them inordinately) could have been checked if the rediscount rate had been raised early enough and high enough. Owen D. Young, a governor of the New York Bank, essayed a defense of the Board that was greeted by "a storm of disapproval."[2]

What continued to bother the bankers was the threat of inflation and they saw every expansion of credit and debt as its harbinger. Thus in an otherwise optimistic statement, Samuel McRoberts, chairman of the Chatham Phoenix Bank, pointed out that "we are never free from adverse factors. Some tend to increase in proportion to our prosperity; particularly those resulting from credit too freely extended." When the Federal Reserve raised the rediscount rate in November 1925, Charles E. Mitchell, who would later become to some people the personification of Wall Street speculation, thought it a splendid move and stated that although he saw no signs of "commercial inflation," he believed that "there had been some inflation in the stock market."

It was not only stock-market credit that bothered the conservatives. There was also real estate credit and installment credit. F. L. Lipman of the Wells Fargo Bank took an especially dim view of installment credit. "It will undoubtedly be carried too far," he said.* Some bankers became almost livid when they considered the monstrous evils of buying consumer goods on the hire-purchase system. The president of the Deseret National Bank in Utah wrote a stern lecture to Professor E. R. A. Seligman, who had just written a favorable study of installment credit. Another person of some financial

* At this time, commercial banks did not make consumer loans. The first to do so was the National City Bank in 1928.

attainments advised Seligman to "go back and study another fifteen months in which length of time the event will have proved how wrong you are." The Seligman study continued to provoke comment for the next couple of years. It pleased most industrialists, especially John J. Raskob of General Motors, who was instrumental in financing it. Indeed, it went over so well that William L. De Bost, president of the New York State Chamber of Commerce, found it necessary to rebuke his colleagues with an expression of what had come to be old-fashioned Puritanism: "I can not agree that installment buying is a sound or safe thing, it is fundamentally wrong so far as luxuries are concerned." One of the few bankers who had anything good to say about installment credit, Melvin Traylor, the Chicago banker, thought it "characteristic of us Americans to be continually viewing with alarm. . . . Just now there are many who declare the tremendous volume of installment buying a dangerous menace." If it was dangerous, Traylor said, it was not the bankers' fault. Louis Kaufman went much further by asking the critics "to put up or shut up": "We hear much talk about the evils of installment buying. This is rather much hue and cry without a culprit."[3]

TAXES AND THE RECESSION OF 1924

Either by coincidence or as the result of cause and effect, the economy fell off in mid-1923 shortly after the Federal Reserve took steps to cut the supply of credit. The stock market also fell off, with the *Times Index* dropping to a low of about 100 in October 1923, but by August 1924 it had regained all the ground it had lost. This was a more rapid recovery than general business achieved, for the recession lasted until later in 1924. Meanwhile, in an effort to get the economy out of its lethargy, the monetary authorities reversed the "tight money" policy and reduced the rediscount rate in May 1924 and again in August bringing it down to 3 per cent.

Economic recovery was an invigorating tonic to business confidence which had been badly starved during the depression of 1921. It was not long before there were faint signs that businessmen believed that they were responsible for both the good and the bad days in business weather, an opinion that was to gather strength as the decade wore on. C. H. Crennan of the Continental and Commercial Bank of Chicago told the Academy of Political Science:

> Business men are chiefly responsible for the peaks and valleys in business. . . . Business generates its own stresses like rising costs and tension in the money markets, that turn the rising curve of business expansion into a falling curve of business contraction. Business also develops its own correctives, not always so soon as some people desire, but more economically than under most of the plans offered by politicians.[4]

Most businessmen viewed the future cheerfully. They believed the problems of other groups in the economy were greatly exaggerated. Typically, Fred D. Underwood of the Erie Railroad thought all our troubles were imaginary. This was especially true of the farmer, for according to Underwood, "No more farmers are in trouble than in the past." He diagnosed the plight of the grain farmer with more truth than tact: "They try to make a living by working 90 days; it can't be done." Businessmen also sloughed off the recession of 1924 as a minor fault attributable to temporary disturbances. J. Ogden Armour summed up what many business people thought when he said: "This depression is only the usual flurry due to the coming presidential election."[5]

The revival of confidence, real though it was, did not wipe out all vestiges of caution or obliterate all the problems that businessmen thought were important. Taxes, government, labor, and money continued to annoy the business community. The whole list was admirably summed up in the 1923 report of the Resolutions Committee of the American Bankers Association:

> The menace of unwarranted extensions of government interference . . . is especially pronounced. In defiance of economic laws, groups whose commodities or services are temporarily depressed . . . clamor for government action in their behalf. . . . The multiplicity of government activities, with the amazing growth in the number of public employees, has added enormously to the burden of taxation. . . . Business is confronted with the handicap of excessive labor costs, reflecting wage scales which have been raised out of proportion to general prices or the cost of living. . . .

Taxes were an especially sore subject, and when Secretary of the Treasury Mellon devised a plan for tax reduction, business leaders were enthralled. In a book Mellon wrote in 1924, he explained that the upper-income groups should get the major share of any tax reduction "not to relieve the rich, but because the rates have already passed the point where they can be collected." Taxation, according to Mellon, was not "a means of rewarding one class of taxpayers or punishing another." Disregarding the non-fiscal objectives that had influenced tax legislation ever since the days of Alexander Hamilton, Mellon continued, "If such a point of view ever controls our public policy, the traditions of freedom, justice, and equality of opportunity will have disappeared and . . . we shall have class legislation."

Bankers and industrialists eagerly joined Mellon's campaign. Fred I. Kent, in tones that recalled Otto Kahn's effort of a few years before, summed up the whole point of view in a comprehensive speech based on the widely held premise that "government operation is, of necessity, inefficient and wasteful. Errors of judgment, overemployment, and bad management, instead of standing out in periodical statements . . . are covered by increased taxation." Since government expenditures were unproductive, taxation's function was to support the parasites who worked for government. According to Kent, "Every group of twelve citizens gainfully employed is supporting one citizen in government." But there were other evils, too. Taxes were inequitable; they raised prices, encouraged waste, and drove capital out of productive channels. It was hard to disagree with Kent's recommendation that taxes "be collected from the people in such manner as is fair and just and that will cause the least brake on progress and the method of division should be free from politics, envy, or jealousy." It was equally difficult to measure what was implied in Kent's further recommendation: "Leave a sufficient proportion of income in the hands of men of wealth to furnish them with the impulse to make expenditures for research and investment." Kent ended up with the thought that 12 per cent should probably be the maximum surtax rate under normal conditions, but 25 per cent would "seem a proper rate now."

Other businessmen, less eclectic than Kent, picked one or two items from the general indictment. If their recommendations were adopted, tax reduction would be all things to all men. It would encourage business expansion and at the same time, it would lead to deflation. It would benefit the lower-income groups even more than it would help the rich. According to Mellon, tax reduction for the upper-income groups would encourage saving which would encourage investment, thereby increasing the national income and redounding to everyone's benefit. Tax reduction, far from leading to inflation, would "aid materially in reducing the cost of living." John W. Prentiss of Hornblower & Weeks and president of the Investment Bankers' Association thought that "if ever we are going to deflate, it is time taxes were reduced." Henry Ford thought that "taxes raised the cost of living," a puzzling statement which Lewis E. Pierson explained more fully, "The average man is more concerned with results than causes. . . . He has come to the conclusion that one of the ways to reduce his own living costs is to reduce the cost of government." Because he shared this view, F. H. Sisson favored tax reduction not "for political reasons, but because it would relieve small taxpayers."

Business leaders ignored the possibility that anticipated saving might exceed anticipated investment and thus exert a downward pressure on the economy. But this was not unusual. Almost everyone from the academic economist to the sophisticated man on the street thought that everything that was saved would be invested. Indeed, the fear was that there was not going to be enough saving and that taxes would discourage what little there was. It was of utmost importance, therefore, to "encourage incentives." As far as the businessman was concerned, taxes and government spending being wasteful and parasitic did just the opposite. Asserting that taxes took $7 billion out of a national income of $58 billion, Pierson warned, "If our people ever commit themselves to the theory that the Government can do for Americans that which, for more than a century, they have been doing, and doing well, for themselves, they will strike a death blow at the ambition of every American boy." L. F. Loree of the Delaware & Hudson Railroad asked his stockholders to write their congressmen because "high surtax rates drive capital out of industry." The National Industrial Council, a group of employers' associations, telegraphed the President that their information showed that "industry and commerce are in a materially depressed condition because of the burdens imposed upon them and the uncertainty of the success of the measure you have urged for the relief of these burdens through a reduction of taxes." George F. Baker, who was "strongly in favor of Secretary Mellon's plan," argued that it "would give the people an incentive to make more money and the government would collect more." Finally, Frederic H. Rawson of the Union Trust Company, Chicago, delivered the unanswerable argument in favor of tax reduction: "Taxing business until it has no earned surplus. . . . Taxing private incomes until there is not sufficient residue to finance improvements. Taxing one group while excepting another will encourage a form of communism which means national stagnation."*

The crusade for the Mellon Plan was not without its colorful aspects. The Pennsylvania Bankers Association, in a laudable effort to be objective, invited Magnus Johnson, Non-Partisan League senator from Minnesota, to speak on the Mellon Plan. Johnson began by telling the seven hundred delegates that the plan would never pass because it was a scheme to favor the wealthy. The delegates replied by "hissing the Senator for at least three minutes."[6]

Close behind taxes in the list of aggravations came wages or "the high cost of labor." According to Rawson, "High prices are the result of high wages." As a foretaste of the fervid arguments that would come much later over "guidelines" and "moral suasion," Rawson added: "There is a group of people who believe that prices should be controlled while wages remain untouched. . . . Such a misunderstanding of economic laws!" Soon after the recognition of the recession of 1924, the "Topics in Wall Street" column of the *New York Times* learned that "there has been considerable talk in the important trades" about wage readjustments. This considerable talk came to an abrupt end as business recovered. Sentiment shifted in the opposite direction. Before the end of the year, the so-called "high-wage doctrine," the theory that high wages and prosperity went together, began to achieve wide publicity.[7]

FEDERAL RESERVE POLICY

The policies of the Federal Reserve System were still another source of aggravation. Judged by any standard, interest rates in 1923–24 were high. Prime utility bonds were selling to yield over 6 per cent, and reputable brokerage houses were offering "over 100 issues to yield 5½ to 7½ per cent." Businessmen, finding these high rates irksome, soon directed their resentment at the Federal Reserve, which they held responsible. In early 1924, the *Times* reported a growing demand for lowering the rediscount rate. By April, "The New York Federal Reserve Bank was being subjected to heavy pressure to

* Income tax rates in 1924 were 12½ per cent on corporate income, a maximum normal individual rate of 6 per cent and a maximum surtax rate of 40 per cent!

lower the rate," especially from "a number of economists [who] contended that the country needs cheap money even though it might produce inflation." At about the same time, a small businessman, Emerson P. Jennings of Lehighton, Pennsylvania, cheered on by his peers, filed a claim against the government alleging that the Federal Reserve System was responsible for the deflation of 1920 and for the bankruptcy of his business. "The money trust of Wall Street," argued Jennings, "was in a conspiracy to centralize further holdings of wealth."

Bankers hastened to the defense of the system. In January, Rawson expressed their feelings when he said, "Of money and credit there has been and now is a sufficient supply for all legitimate purposes." At first, there was no expressed dissent from the bankers' support of the central bank. But by April, the unanimity had been broken; bankers were reported divided, many contending that a "cut in the rediscount rate was necessary if the banks were to earn reasonable profits," while others denounced such talk as a "narrow view tinctured with selfishness." When the Fed did lower the rediscount rate, it was roundly criticized by Benjamin M. Anderson, economist for the Chase Bank, and by the *Commercial and Financial Chronicle,* but Charles A. Stone of Stone & Webster, a heavy borrower in the money and capital markets, was elated: "With good prospects of healthy, but not too rapid growth, it looks as if we must have cheap money for a long time." Stone's remark, like so many others throughout the 1920s, played on the theme of a healthy, but not too rapid, growth. As the cliché had it, the hope was for "sustainable" economic growth as contrasted with "unsustainable" economic growth.[8]

It is a little difficult to understand the constant preoccupation with "unsustainable growth." To be sure, the concept has validity. An economy in the first stages of recovering from a deep depression will exhibit an unusually high rate of growth. As more and more resources are put back to work, the rate of growth must slacken, for in a fully employed economy, growth is limited to year-by-year increases in the amount of resources plus year-by-year increases in productivity. But this is not what is usually meant by "unsustainable economic growth," and it is not what the business leaders of a generation ago meant. At all times, even in periods far short of full employment, they were obsessed by fears of the hobgoblins that prosperity might bring. As business recovered from the primary postwar depression, it seemed that its leaders feared boom and rapid growth as much as they feared recession; indeed, it sometimes appeared that they feared it more. Seward Prosser of Bankers Trust wrote to his friend and subordinate Fred I. Kent in May 1923: "Trade has slackened down a little bit and I think it well that it should. The result of it, I think, is in the direction of sounder conditions and I believe guarantees that we will have a longer fling at business activity than would have been the case had we kept continually on the ascent." Later, *Trade Winds,* the publication of the Cleveland Trust, called the recession "a healthy corrective of the threatened overproduction of last Spring."[9]

This kind of conservative, Calvinistic thinking was also occasionally displayed by industrialists. Henry Dennison's analysis of the recovery that began in 1921 has already been referred to. In early 1924, Daniel Willard and Henry Ford joined bankers Louis G. Kaufman, president of the Chatham Phoenix Bank in New York, and Frank Vanderlip in forecasting with satisfaction "good times without a boom." It was true, however, that it was the banking profession that seemed always to be looking at prosperity with one eye fixed on the recession that was over and the other eye fixed on the recession that was about to arrive. By the end of 1923, James S. Alexander of New York's Bank of Commerce agreed that the country was definitely on the upgrade and he believed that we had "won what we won solely because American business had the strength and courage to put away the hopes and methods of the disastrous expansion period and to set to work on the basis of present realities."[10] The bankers feared inflation more than the industrialists did, and their worry did not abate even in the midst of recession. Like most bankers, Kaufman welcomed the 1924 downturn because "at one time there seemed a possibility that expansion and improvement would proceed so rapidly as to lead into a dangerous condition of inflation. But that condition was avoided." This kind of rain welcoming continued throughout the fifty-year period. Indeed, as time went on, it engulfed industrialists as well as bankers.

The vestigial remains of Puritanism caused financiers to worry about other effects of prosperity, such as the public's entrance into the stock market. As trading in securities increased, S. L. Cromwell, president of the New York Stock Exchange, considered it "his duty to prevent men of small means from dealing in stocks," for "they were practically sure losers." Bankers worried even more for fear that debt would ruin the country. Today, it requires an effort of imagination to understand the almost pathological fear of spending, of debt, of "extravagance" that prevailed among bankers, for the bankers' business is debt. But these fears were much more a part of the whole folklore of the early twenties than most people realize. At that time, few people, if any, realized that the national income could only go up if debt went up. To the contrary, it was then believed that debt repayment would in some mysterious fashion enhance prosperity. The September 1923 letter of the Mechanics and Metals Bank, written when business was already on the downgrade, commented: "The American people . . . are not paying for all their current purchases out of current income. . . . The degree that borrowing for unproductive purposes has increased is a matter of much concern." In the spring of 1924, when the recession was just about over, 20 per cent of the responders to a questionnaire sent to ten thousand bankers attributed the recession to politics, and 16 per cent attributed it to "extravagant living" and a "tendency to mortgage the future." To quote a summary of the prevailing opinion: "A period of rapidly increasing wealth is also a period of extreme ambition, extravagant desire, inordinate greed. . . . We are suffering today from the aftermath of such a period. The easy wealth of the war period is over." To be sure, Walter W. Head, the Chicago banker who said this, was a little premature; easy wealth had hardly begun.[11]

PROLOGUE TO THE BULL MARKET

By August 1924, the economy was moving sharply upward, and the market was enjoying one of its "late summer rallies." Except for some minor declines in early and later 1925, the industrial stock average advanced for a year and a half, from about 120 in August 1924 to about 185 in February 1926. Volume also rose. Daily transactions which had averaged 632,000 in 1921 and 863,000 in 1923 soared to 1,663,000 in 1925. The Federal Reserve, in an effort "to lean against the wind," tried to slow down the boom by raising the rediscount rate in February and November 1925 from 3 to 4 per cent. The boom staggered and then went on with a greater rush. In the fall of 1925, there were thirty-one consecutive two-million share days. The *New York Evening Post,* which at that time had the most respected financial section of any daily newspaper, was so impressed by what was going on that it inaugurated a stock-market forecast in its annual financial review of 1925.

The activity on the stock market was not churned up by the professional traders alone. It was evident by 1925 that "the public" had also become deeply involved. Along with the great bulls and bears who pass through the chronicles of the times like villains in an Eric Ambler spy story, odd-lot buyers and sellers were helping to make the price of stocks a conversation piece. Odd-lot transactions, which totaled only 50 million shares in 1921 and 62 million in 1923, passed 100 million in 1925.* But except for the magnitude of the transactions, this was nothing new. It had happened in earlier generations with regularity. De Tocqueville, in the 1830s, had been impressed by the American penchant for gambling. Lord Bryce, in the 1880s, had been amazed by the "universality of stock speculation." And in 1901 when the United States Steel Corporation was founded, the *Times* commented: "The man on the street entered the market, forcing prices up to new levels beyond ransom or worth."

As the stock market became more exciting, some business leaders and economic commentators abandoned the caution that had been so characteristic. On New Year's Day 1925, James Simpson, president of Marshall Field, told the *Times* that he thought business was definitely on the upgrade. He was one of the first to describe the period with a phrase that would go down in history: "There seems to be very good reason," he said, "to believe we are entering a new era." One year later, the *Times* financial editor, Alexander Dana Noyes, forecast "a rise in stock exchange prices such as has probably not been witnessed since 1901." Toward the middle of the year, just before the recession of 1926, the *Times* put its *imprimatur* on the prologue to the great boom by listing "prosperity" as a separate subhead in the *Times Index*.[12]

The euphoria of prosperity led the more optimistic business leaders to believe that "bad times were gone forever." There was little reason for their line of thinking aside from the ordinary human desire to make the wish father to the thought, for the causes of prosperity as they saw them were neither new nor world shaking. Judge Gary believed that prosperity was the result of the automobile, the recovery of the railroads, growing confidence among the people and the spread of property ownership. Victor A. Lersner of the Bowery

---

* Although the number of shares in odd lots went up, their proportion of total transactions went down from 28 per cent in 1921 to 26 per cent in 1923 to 23 per cent in 1925. They were still at 23 per cent in 1927 and by 1929 they had climbed back to 26 per cent.

Savings Bank chalked it up to our resources and "the energy and the intelligence and attitude toward work of the producing population." E. H. Simmons, president of the New York Stock Exchange, believed that "we are justified in believing that never again will the disasters of the past arise in American business . . . because the organized securities markets serve to stabilize not only financial but also industrial and commercial conditions."[13] And Guy E. Tripp, chairman of Westinghouse, thought prosperity was due to electricity.

EXPLAINING PROSPERITY

Many industrialists, especially in small business, believed that the protective tariff was responsible for the growth of the economy—an opinion enthusiastically endorsed by some labor union leaders, a few professional economists, but almost no city bankers. Another popular explanation was the friendly political atmosphere of the time. Businessmen doffed their hats to Calvin Coolidge and the "administration" which "by its economy and its resistance to the dangerous heresies preached by some Congressmen" had done much to guarantee good times. Just before the election of 1924, Judge Gary thought that "it went without saying that business conditions during the next four years depend largely upon the result of the election of November 4." Soon after the election, Thomas N. McCarter, founder of Public Service of New Jersey, moralized: "The great overshadowing fact is that the election results show the country to be safe. Our people are not willing to tear down the government which the fathers erected. The wave of radicalism has been happily checked." J. W. Prentiss was also grateful that "the people have said conclusively that they believe in the Constitution, a reduction of taxes, a suitable tariff, the personal rights of individuals." H. T. Parson, president of Woolworth, regarded the election's outcome in a practical way, "We can now look ahead to four years of good business without any hesitancy." In light of the later expressions of opinion about the impotence of government, this early faith in the power of politics was strange indeed.

Following the dictum that human nature is the same the world over, businessmen often confused their own reactions with the public's. What, therefore, hurt business confidence also hurt public confidence. Some merchants complained that Coolidge's emphasis on economy was having a dangerous psychological effect on public spending; but most of the bankers and industrialists whose opinions were reported in the press thought that "the efficient economic administration" was bolstering public confidence. James Simpson explained that the prosperity which was bringing a new day was founded on the "confidence in the sanity and solidity of our national administration, insuring a splendid tone to business in general." According to Gary, "the apparent change in the attitude of many of the national legislators . . . and the decisions of the Supreme Court . . . have created a feeling of confidence."[14]

Confidence was then, as later, a much overworked word among businessmen. Some seemed to believe that the business cycle was nothing but a state of mind which could be exorcised by a kind of therapy known in the early 1920s as "Coueism" after the French doctor who instructed his followers to keep repeating: "Every day in every way I'm getting better and better." R. F. Grant, president of the United States Chamber of Commerce, admitted the existence of "certain ups and downs in business," but he also insisted that "there is nothing as yet to show that these fluctuations are not to a large degree emotional." And Judge Gary, whose aptitude in public relations was largely the result of a Pollyanna personality, thought that whereas "not very many years ago, most men believed that fluctuations of business were as much beyond their control as the snows of winter and the rains of spring, lack of confidence is now recognized as the basis of the business cycle."

THE HIGH-WAGE DOCTRINE

The most ambitious rationale for the new-era philosophy emphasized distribution, consumption, and high wages. It seemed to the proponents of this view that depressions could be relegated to ancient history if business and the economic system would continue to emphasize ever increasing demand, ever increasing consumption, and ever increasing spending. Mass production would supply the goods, and the new devices that had been invented to exploit mass production—advertising, the installment plan, and intensive selling—would stimulate the demand for goods. It seemed obvious to some that if the key to prosperity lay in these new concepts of distribution, it was imperative to increase the income of the great mass of consumers in the lower-income brackets, and it would be wise to arrange for a more even distribution of wealth, so that the average standard of living could be increased and many more could consume. From these premises sprang the "high-wage" doctrine which, in the years after 1924, brought forth a vast literature explaining the salutary effects of high wages and proving that income was being so widely redistributed that the differences between Judy O'Grady and the colonel's lady were being flattened out.

The "high-wage" doctrine had the good fortune to be enunciated by the most articulate businessmen and very quickly got more publicity than it warranted. It had a hypnotic effect, influencing people to exaggerated expressions of enthusiasm. For example, Lewis Pierson was so carried away that he declared that business had definitely abandoned "the out worn notions of unrestricted competition, of minimum wages and maximum prices, of restricted output and limited consumption to substitute the new gospel of mass production, high wages and maximum consumption." Samuel M. Vauclain, president of the Baldwin Locomotive Works and the man who was later responsible for the "two chickens in every pot" advertisement for Hoover's presidential campaign, announced: "The wage earners constitute the great majority of our population. These people are the spenders of the nation, and upon their ability to spend freely the general business of our country depends. It is the wage of these people that makes good times or bad, dependent upon what they are earning over and above the actual necessities of life."

So it proceeded down the list—Ford, Filene, Vauclain, the Chamber of Commerce, Foster, and Catchings—until it was reported that the trade associations which had opposed the California minimum wage law in 1913 were all for it in 1926. But the truth of the matter was that the philosophy of high wages was not as universally accepted as business spokesmen suggested. As Don D. Lescohier, the Labor economist, concluded, "The thinking of the employer group during the twenties might be summarized by saying that they believed strongly in other employers paying high wages."* [15]

* Once again, it is well to point out that business leaders were not the only ones with ambivalent attitudes. In 1929, Harvard University employed some scrubwomen at 35 cents an hour. When informed that the minimum wage law in Massachusetts required 37 cents, the university fired the women.

SOME SKEPTICISM ABOUT THE NEW ERA

The "new economics" that was exciting the business world did not excite the conservative and cautious businessmen whose opinions had dominated the financial world in the opening years of the decade. They regarded the talk about a new era as an assault on their philosophy, but they thought it about as dangerous as a barrage of cream puffs. In time, some of the more cautious would be converted, but in 1925–26, the majority of financiers, many of the business commentators, and quite a few industrialists were still not convinced that a new era had dawned.

Those who were wary about the future could be divided into three groups. There were a handful who predicted a downturn in the economy. Leonard Ayres, the economist for the Cleveland Trust Company, greeted the year 1925 with a prediction that the rediscount rate would be raised and that would be the end of the bull market. In April, Henry Ford urged price cuts and wage increases to "avoid a slump." A small group who took a middle ground decried the "voices of alarmists who asserted that the United States was reaching the point of diminishing returns because of the end of free land, the decline in population, and maldistribution of wealth"; but they also talked about "economic stability" and the "need for sustaining the high level of production," and said very little about future progress. A third group, by far the largest, did not believe what they saw, suspecting that prosperity was a thing of unsustainability, a booby trap to be approached gingerly lest it blow up in a complete catastrophe. The *Times* annual financial review of January 1925 reported that Wall Street wanted to know how long "the market would last at its present clip." One year later, the *Post* financial review reported that "prominent bankers now ask 'how long can it last?'" The answer was that most bankers believed that it would and should come to a quick end. Early in 1925, Samuel E. Ward of New York's National Bank of Commerce warned the readers of the *Post* that "the principal danger to a long period of really active business is too rapid and intensive expansion."[16]

By 1926, a collection of bankers and financial people were advising caution. In September, just a month before the economy went into reverse, Colonel Ayres predicted a depression. And to Roger

Babson, "a distinct recession and possibly a panic within two or three years would not be surprising." When it came, it would be the result "of overextension of installment business" and it would be temporary, although the market would "drop about 80 points within one to three years." At that time the *Times* average was at 170. If Babson had said between three and six years, he would have been the Nostradamus of the boom years. As it was, he earned a minor place among the clairvoyants of economic history.[17]

THE RECESSION OF 1927

The recession which most conservatives had correctly expected arrived in the fall of 1926 and continued for about a year. As a prelude, the industrial stock average dropped from what was regarded as a "dizzy height" of 186 in February to a low of 138 in March. In these two months, speculators, as stock buyers were called in the late 1920s, watched a whole year's profits evaporate. But then the market began another advance. By the end of 1926, the average was back to about 180 and by the early fall of 1927 when the recession was coming to an end, it had climbed to around 235, half the height it was to reach two years later and four times the low of 1921. Meanwhile, the recession had come and gone and had never amounted to much. In fact, it was so mild that few people knew that it existed until they were so informed some months after prosperity returned.

As had been the case in the earlier years, business opinion was again split between the optimists and the pessimists with most industrialists falling in the first group and most financial leaders in the second. If expressed opinion accurately reflected the consensus, most business leaders were mildly bullish and only a small number were enthusiastically so. The majority believed that business would be good over the long run, but they did not discount the possibility of some "hard times." Or to say this in another way, they had not been converted to the new-era gospel.

Most business leaders still talked frankly about what they expected to happen. The optimists had enormous faith in the people and in themselves; they had wrought so well that business depressions were things of the past like the tandem bicycle and bearded men. The recession had hardly begun when Gary said that he "was becoming more and more convinced that periods of business depression were no longer necessary and that the great bulk of the people would do their utmost to maintain prosperity—by their votes if need be." When the recession was half over, Virgil Jordan of the National Industrial Conference Board explained that businessmen could determine the extent and duration of the ordinary business fluctuation. His colleague, Magnus Alexander, echoed the sentiment stating categorically that "there was no reason why there should be any more panics." But if we did have them, "they would be man-made rather than by natural phenomenon." At the same time Melvin Traylor, demonstrating that even bankers could look at the world with some cheer, conceded that we "could not look forward to an unbroken continuation of expansion at the rate of the last two or three years," but, "we need not fear a recurrence of conditions that will plunge the nation into the depths of the more violent panics . . . of times past."[18]

At the other end of the spectrum that separated the cheerful from the cautious, the *Commercial and Financial Chronicle,* in January 1927 announced with some satisfaction that a business depression was undoubtedly underway. At about the same time, various investment counselors were running ads which asked: "Is the process of deflation under way?" In a front-page article, the *Times* reported that S. W. Straus & Company, one of the foremost real estate bond houses in the country, was of the opinion that a saturation in building had been reached. The *Times* also said that "not all good judges of the market are bullish. Many are frankly bearish." The bears were of course wrong. For by that time (January 1927) the market was already off and running at the fastest pace in its history.

The business recession itself was to continue for another ten or eleven months, but those who were pessimistic about the long-run business outlook were almost as wrong as the bears in the stock market. Thus Victor M. Cutter of United Fruit was a few years ahead of time when he advised his readers that business runs in "Hegelian cycles." According to him, history showed that prosperity never lasted longer than a few years before giving way to depression. He thought we had reached the point "where we were faced with the spectre of overproduction." We were certainly in a recession at the time that Cutter wrote, but it was not a depression, and the "spectre of overproduction" was no more dangerous than most bogeymen.[19]

To offset the drop in economic activity and at the same time to help England and Europe maintain the gold standard, the Federal Reserve System in July 1927 announced a reduction in the rediscount rate from 4 to 3½ per cent. Following a new theory that the money supply should expand to keep pace with a desired rate of economic growth, the monetary directors also began to buy securities in the open market. As was becoming the custom in the twenties, the Fed's action satisfied no one except its most loyal supporters, and even their faith was somewhat shaken. Conservatives, especially among the academicians, upbraided the System for being pussilanimous in fighting speculative inflation; the less cautious excoriated the System for not giving business the encouragement it needed.

The system was attacked even in the homes of its champions—the bankers. To be sure, Paul Warburg, the learned and conservative banker who resisted the blandishments of the new era all the way to 1929 and beyond, "thought the reduction was justified as a duty to- ward our European neighbors who are trying to resume gold pay- ments." And others, like Lewis Pierson, called on one and all to "defend the Fed," but the *Times* reported that most of the people in the street believed that "the arbitrary cheapening of money may en- courage inflation." The most respected academic money and banking men, like H. Parker Willis and Benjamin Anderson, were altogether out of sorts with the Fed, and their influence was apparent at the an- nual meeting of the ABA in October 1926. According to the *Times,* there was hardly a Western or Midwestern banker who did not be- lieve that the Fed had brought on the after-the-war deflation that had left everyone else out on a long limb. But at the convention, Ramsay Walker of the Wallace Bank and Trust of Wallace, Idaho, proved that not all who lived west of the Alleghenies were inflation-minded. "When the Federal Reserve was first thought of," said Walker, "it was intended for two purposes—a bank of issue and rediscount. . . . It should be confined to that. It has been an instrument of inflation ever since it came into being." The *Times* reported that the conven- tion "vigorously applauded," but on the next day the delegates on sober second thought were "very sorry for their uninhibited out- burst."[20]

THE FEDERAL RESERVE AND SPECULATION

The bankers' reaction at the 1926 convention was an omen of things to come. For it was the Federal Reserve System more than any other single cause, that was blamed both at the time and in retrospect for the speculative high jinks that characterized the last years of the 1920s. It was argued that the monetary authorities could have prevented the extremes of the latter part of the bull market had they had the courage, the will, and the determination to use the tight-money tools that they possessed. They were aided and abetted in their mistakes, the argument continued, by the financial and business community which enticed the public into the market with talk about a "new era" and "endless prosperity." This blanket indictment was at best a half truth. To be sure, the subsequent collapse of the stock market proved that the Federal Reserve must have been doing something wrong. But whether it erred on the easy-money or the tight-money side is something else again. Similarly, there is no doubt that the talk about a new era was at best premature, but the whole business community did not make this mistake. Industrialists were much more optimistic than pessimistic, while financiers were always more bear-ish than bullish.* To be sure, the extraordinary market advance of 1927–29 did persuade many business leaders that dreams of never ending prosperity had more substance than they had at first supposed, and some, therefore, became converts to what proved to be naïve optimism. More and more business leaders found themselves echoing that very important person in the French Revolution who said, "There goes the mob; I am their leader; I must follow." Albert H. Wiggin was right when he said some years later in answer to the question of why the Chase Securities Corporation traded in securities: "I think the times . . . There was a great deal of atmosphere. There were a great many people who began to think you did a great injustice to everybody if you did not have equity stocks." And Otto Kahn was equally right when he asked "Who could have stemmed the buyers' tide? I doubt whether anything but a catastrophe could have stopped that violence." It is a mammoth irony that those who belatedly and halfheartedly went along with the new-era philosophy were to be condemned as the pied pipers who led the public into the dreams of quick riches that ultimately turned out to be a nightmare.[21]

Quick riches seemed easily achievable in 1927–29; all one needed was a little capital, a spirit of adventure, and the will to gamble. No other economic indicator in the 1920s did nearly as well as the stock averages. The gross national product increased by some 17 per cent,

---

* After the whole thing was over, Alexander Dana Noyes quoted Walter Gifford as saying that the "important financiers" knew perfectly well in 1928 and 1929 what was going on, but they kept their ideas for private expression.

whereas the stock market tripled between 1920 and 1929. The *Times* industrial average opened the year 1927 at a little over 170 (50 points higher than on January 1, 1920). In January 1928 it was approaching 250; a year later it had passed 330; and at its high in September 1929 it stood at almost 470. The total value of shares on the New York Stock Exchange was $35 billion in February 1926, $50 billion in early 1928, and almost $100 billion in 1929.

The securities business had become a big business indeed. A seat on the exchange which had sold for $300,000 in 1927 cost $600,000 in 1929. Brokers' loans at the end of 1927 were $3.6 billion, 25 per cent more than conservatives had considered alarming in 1926; by October 1929, they were around $8 billion. Prior to March 1928, there had been only eight days in stock exchange history on which over three million shares were traded. There were sixteen such days in March 1928 and four days with over four million shares each. As the *New York Evening Post* described it, "In corners as far separated as Maine and Washington, California and Florida men are hanging over stock tickers just as they are in Wall Street." Playing the stock market had become a great indoor sport like Mah Jong and crossword puzzles, and the public joined the game with enthusiasm. It has been estimated that one million people owned stocks in 1900; two and one half to three million in 1924; five million in 1927; and ten million in 1930. Toward the height of the boom, a panhandler stopped Bernard Baruch with the whispered question: "Want a good tip on the market?"

Conservatives viewed the public participation in the stock market with rising trepidation. They feared the worst, and although it took a long while, their fears were eventually justified. The nature of the fears was well summed up in early 1929 by John E. Rovensky, vice-president of the Bank of America in New York: "All classes from the day laborer to the wealthier businessman are participating (in the market); if any one class is represented to a less degree than others, it appears to be the seasoned investor. . . . It is to be hoped that the excellent business outlook will not be marred by an untoward development in the stock market."

By contrast, there were many industrialists and outside observers who viewed the activity in the market as a very healthy thing. Beginning in 1928, there was a noticeable increase in the number of comments about the market and about the economic outlook, and most of these comments were decidedly more optimistic than had been the case. R. B. Sheffield of the Commander-Larrabee Corporation thought that the increasingly wide ownership of securities was making the laboring man a capitalist. This view was by no means confined to industrialists. In one of the more curious books of the era, Professor Thomas Nixon Carver, Harvard economist, anticipated the concept of "People's Capitalism," which was to become so popular a generation later: "The only economic revolution now under way is going on in the United States. It is a revolution that is to wipe out the distinction between laborers and capitalists by making laborers their own capitalists." Professor Carver went on to say that the proof of the revolution existed in the growth of savings deposits, building and loan associations, premiums paid to life insurance companies, and investment by labor in stocks and bonds.[22]

Clarence Wooley of American Radiator opened the year with the flat statement: "The business cycle in the United States has been adjourned." Walter Chrysler swept a somewhat smaller field by saying, "The day of the wide swing from prosperity is over." William L. De Bost, president of the New York State Chamber of Commerce, explained why: "the Federal Reserve Act . . . the sound financial policy of the Federal Government and the Mellon tax program." Charles Schwab wrapped up the whole package by warning: "This is no country for prophets of gloom."[23]

Schwab's interdict was somewhat gratuitous. There were almost no prophets of gloom. But the cautious still outnumbered those who saw an eternity of prosperity. The people in building construction (T. F. Holden of F. W. Dodge; L. J. Horowitz of Thompson-Starrett; and W. J. Moore of American Bond and Mortgage) were not very optimistic about 1928. Neither were the bankers, who had in Thomas R. Preston, Chattanooga banker and president of the ABA, an excellent spokesman for the recurrent theme that prosperity was the father of disaster. Preston thought that "booms were to be dreaded as much as panics," but the chances of both had been mitigated because "brains and system instead of guesswork and haphazard methods prevail today throughout business." Preston, however, conceded that there were still two problems: agriculture and credit expansion. The latter bothered many other bankers and financial observers, including Charles Mitchell, who thought "it should be watched," and Alexander Dana Noyes, who was not overly enthusiastic about the stock market. A headline in the *Tribune* asked "Will The Bull Market Last Forever?" A headline in the financial section of the little-known *Brooklyn*

Daily Times told its readers "Caution Urged in Stock Market for Coming Year." *Moody's Investors' Service* said stocks had "overdiscounted future progress" and were too high. And there were others. The take-over by the prophets of the new era was, at least in early 1928, greatly exaggerated. But those who listened to the unconverted instead of the converted and stayed out of the market in 1928 later had cause to regret their action. The cautious were still over a year ahead of their time.[24]

THE BULL MARKET AT HIGH TIDE

On March 3, 1928, the *Times* 50-stock average stood at 177.89. Radio Corporation, a darling of the pool manipulators, sold at 94½. B. C. Forbes in the *New York American* said, "The stock market palpably has lost its head." *Moody's Investors' Service* wondered "how long the opportunity to sell at top prices would last." The bankers attending the executive council meeting of the ABA were concerned about "the speculative boom." W. D. Longyear, Los Angeles banker, thought, "The present frenzy of speculation, if continued much longer, will surely bring its own destruction." Sisson of the Guaranty Trust expected a market crash but speculation "contained no direct threat against business in general. The worst that could happen would be for a severe break in stock prices to bring some increase in caution."[25]

Much of the public, some of the industrialists, and a few of the financiers thought differently. They quoted J. Pierpont Morgan's admonition "Don't sell America short," and they recalled that George F. Baker had never sold anything. In late April, "the men who have 'made' this stock market, or at least have been primarily responsible for its great activity" held a dinner at the Biltmore Hotel to wish *bon voyage* to the greatest bull of them all—W. C. Durant. The public would have recognized very few of the guests who included besides Durant, Arthur W. Cutten, Frederick and Lawrence Fisher, Matthew C. Brush ("who probably held more directorships than anyone else"), Duncan Holmes, George Breen, and Joseph Higgins. The *Times* reported that there were no bears present to mar the joviality of the occasion. And it was a jovial occasion, for Radio was approaching 200, and so were General Motors and A.T. & T., while Montgomery Ward was on its way to 150, and the *Times* composite average, in which Durant was probably not at all interested, was also approaching 200.[26]

A week before this Belshazzar's feast, the Federal Reserve Board had begun to raise the discount rate. In May, the New York rate went up to 4½ per cent and the Fed began to sell securities in the open market, hoping to dry up the funds which were feeding the stock market. The financial editor of the *New York American* thought this was the moment of truth: "The public must choose between the Federal Reserve System . . . and the glib customers' men* . . . who assure the gullible that the trees of market prosperity will grow right up to the heavens." He was ultimately wrong, although for one month it seemed that he would be right. The market fell slightly during the rest of the rather quiet month of May. Then on June 11, A. P. Giannini, who had deservedly acquired a reputation as a banking genius, stated that in his opinion Bancitaly was not worth the $200 at which it was selling. At about the same time, the president of Brooklyn Edison and the chairman of Canadian Marconi also said their stocks were too high. Bancitaly immediately fell 53 points, and the whole list underwent a reaction that carried the *Times* average back to 177.75. Those who knew about such things explained that the drop was caused by tight money and the final elimination of Coolidge by Hoover for the presidential nomination.[27]

Bankers regarded the drop in the market with equanimity that bordered on relief. Most of them thought that, in the words of the *Times,* "The great bull market is over." As far as they were concerned this was a good thing, for they agreed with Melvin Traylor in thinking that stock market speculation took credit away from more legitimate uses. They also agreed with Otto Kahn's opinion that the break had brought stocks to a reasonable level. Once again conservative opinion was wrong. The boom had just begun. The *Times* composite average rose 130 points and the industrial average, 200 points in the year and one half after April 1928. This was more than the industrial average had risen in the previous eight years.[28]

Although it reached greater heights here than in any other money market, stock speculation was not a peculiarly American phenomenon. All over the world, against the warning of banking authorities, the public crowded the *Bourse* in the belief that they saw values that experienced financiers were too stubborn to recognize. And there

---

* It must be mentioned in passing that not all customers' men were urging the public to buy.

were many who agreed with them. When conservatives pointed out the danger of an unprecedented growth in stock-market credit, E. H. H. Simmons, president of the New York Stock Exchange, pooh-poohed the whole thing.[29]

SOME PESSIMISM IN THE MIDST OF OPTIMISM

Meanwhile, the Federal Reserve System was suffering the tremors of indecision and criticism. Interest rates were high in 1928, but business, especially in home construction, was dull. Industrialists were positive that one of the main reasons was tight money. But from the financial district came a constant clamor for a more rigid monetary policy, because brokers' loans were over $4 billion and the rate on call loans was 9 per cent. The System itself was as badly split as the business community, with advocates of tighter credit arguing against those who thought that a further turn of the screw would throttle the whole international economy. Then the Democratic party at its national convention joined in. Senator Carter Glass, after pointing out that brokers' loans were four to five times what they had been in the years right after World War I, succeeded in having the convention adopt a plank condemning "the use of the Federal Reserve System to encourage speculation on the stock market." The Federal Reserve was getting it from both sides, and it lacked Solomon's wisdom in arriving at a policy. In July it raised the rediscount rate to 5 per cent and it continued to sell government securities. The stock market took no notice, and the criticism from the conservatives grew so loud that Assistant Secretary of the Treasury Ogden Mills and Owen D. Young felt compelled to come to the defense of the System. Mills explained that the Fed had turned toward easy money in 1927 because "business was in a period of decline" and because "European exchange rates were weak and unless money rates were eased here, there might be a movement of funds to this country" (on the ground that capital tends to go to where interest rates are highest). When it "became apparent that the objectives of the policy were being accomplished, the policy was reversed." Young repeated all that Mills had said and added, "Now I would not have any one think that the Federal Reserve has its eye on the stock market. That is the last thing that enters into consideration. . . . It desires to contribute to stability in purchasing power and to provide proper credits for business at reasonable rates without wide fluctuations."

The news items in the financial pages during the fall of 1928 left no doubt that the business community was worried about "speculation." John J. Raskob, formerly of General Motors, now chairman of the National Democratic Committee and one of the most widely known of the large operators, thought that "security prices have so far outrun demonstrated values that a material readjustment is necessary." *Iron Age,* the voice of the steel industry, also said that earnings did not support prices. The delegates to the annual convention of the ABA were reported to be much concerned, but they could not help but agree with retiring president Preston when he told them—correctly —that credit was tight because of business expansion, not because of speculation. When Colonel Ayres informed them that "stocks were selling on expectation not reality," they were astonished not by what he said, but that he had said it. And they were shocked when Congressman MacFadden of the House Banking and Currency Committee called for special curbs on speculation. Not that they did not want to curb speculation, but they didn't see how. Walter E. Frew of New York's Corn Exchange Bank quickly announced his opposition to any legislation designed to curb brokers' loans, and the *New York Sun* reported that "most of the important bank officers in this city agree that the situation should be left to cure itself." Big-city bankers thought very much as President Buchanan did when the Civil War broke out. They deplored what was going on, but they were sure that nothing could be done about it.

And just as the South had ignored Buchanan, the public paid no attention to the bankers. Signals for a new burst of activity were going up in all directions. At the end of October, W. C. Durant told the press that good stocks were cheap. On November 7, General Motors announced that it would pay a quarterly dividend of $1.25 plus an extra dividend of $2.50 and would split its stock on the basis of 2½ shares to one. On November 18, the *Times* ran a special mouth-watering article on the money that had been made in the market. General Motors passed 215, Radio hit 250, and Montgomery Ward was approaching 400. To be sure, there was a mild break in December, but by year's end the forward march had resumed. What was more important, people who were taking part in this onward march were being urged on by highly respected names in the academic and business world and some of the bears were beginning to see the error of their ways.[30]

This was apparent in the statements about the future that were contained in the mammoth financial reviews published by the press in early 1929. The consensus agreed with Charles Schwab in thinking that the year would be one of magnificent progress for the general economy. Schwab offered ten rules to make prosperity permanent: 1) pay labor highest possible wage, 2) treat labor as a partner, 3) conduct business in the full light of day, 4) remember that the law of supply and demand is inexorable, 5) live and let live, 6) welcome new ideas, 7) never be satisfied with what has been achieved, 8) operate business most economically, 9) look ahead, and 10) smile!

The annual survey by the *Post* found that only six out of fifty-seven dissented from glowing predictions of extraordinary prosperity. Only one anticipated a recession. The remaining five dissented only in believing that enthusiastic enthusiasm should be tempered by a little caution. George M. Reynolds, the Chicago banker, voiced their sentiments when he said he found it "difficult to say whether or not the present prosperity is the beginning of a long upswing." The lone prophet of a downswing, Byron W. Holt of Goodbody & Company made a remarkable forecast: "We will enter 1929 with business about normal. . . . By next spring, business (because of tight money) will decline to below normal. President Hoover's anti-depression remedy may be needed next fall."

In hindsight, Holt's forecast should, of course, have received much more notice than it did. But he was referring to the stock market, and the whole business community was much less optimistic about the stock market than about general business. It was dear money that worried many businessmen, but it worried bankers more than manufacturers and merchants, for it was thought that the money market had a more penetrating effect on stock prices than on general business. Call money was at 12 per cent, and many experts, quoted in the press, thought that such high interest rates would certainly have a dampening effect on stock prices and *perhaps* on general business.

In back of many of the remarks about tight money was the perennial fear that disaster was inevitable. Colonel Ayres was now mildly cautious as he warned that past bull markets had lasted only two years. Alexander Dana Noyes, now a gadfly to the optimists, had no "doubt at all about the underlying strength of the economy," but "the very rash abuse of credit, the resultant abnormal money stringency, the fantastic illusions that are entertained about the economy's future, and the public's appetite for the most restless stock speculation are distinctly disquieting." The financial editor of the *Tribune* was not far behind, although he implied rather than gave the answer to the important question of whether we were really in a new era: "The unusual features of last year were such as to bring about the condition that a new era had been established, that rules of the past were obsolete, that some sort of transmutation had taken place which had created new laws. . . . Almost it seems that there is a grain of truth in such an interpretation and yet there are many who believe that fundamentals are the same as they were years ago . . . that the things that have taken place are merely temporary happenings."

The distrust of the market was even more apparent among bankers and brokers than among financial writers. It was hard to find a financier who agreed with the university professor who proclaimed: "Old standards are not only futile; they are childish." Contrary to what one recent writer has said, many men in the business world questioned the acuity of that judgment. The back pages of the *Tribune* contained a somber warning by E. L. Smith, a manager of an investment company:

> The writer has passed through several periods of stock market activity and optimism in Wall Street and cannot pass without comment the fact that during the time of all such previous periods . . . the cry has been raised (and raised in many cases by people who should have known better) . . . that the prosperity of the American nation has reached such a pitch that all previous experience can be discarded and that speculative transactions can be entered into with a certain hope of definite reward. . . .

R. S. Hecht, articulate New Orleans banker, believed that there was a possibility of further excessive speculation that might bring disaster to the speculator and to business as well. F. L. Lipman of Wells Fargo regretted that "prosperity in industry has become the basis for a huge speculation in securities." Charles Hayden thought "the greatest menace to the stock market is the stock market itself." Charles Sabin of the Guaranty Trust watched the flow of funds into Wall Street and observed that "it would be regrettable if rich opportunities were wasted by a heedless diversion of capital into channels of speculation." Albert H. Wiggin warned the government and business that "neither could afford to rely upon an indefinite continuance of a rising stock market." Percy H. Johnston of the Chemical Bank of New York knew that "many thoughtful people view with apprehension the nation-wide speculation that has been going on."

Although the overwhelming sentiment among financiers was one of caution, some like Mitchell of the National City Bank and Pierson of the American Exchange Irving Trust had been converted to the new era philosophy. They were no longer so sure that what was going on was "unsustainable." Mitchell correctly called attention to the absence of general price inflation. There was, he thought, "A basis for views that lead to rising stock prices," but he conceded "an ever present danger that such expectations may be discounted too freely"; on the other hand, "danger only appears when current savings are inadequate to keep pace with advances in prices and huge borrowings for the carriage of stocks brings a competition for the always limited supply of lendable funds." Pierson was confident that business was "not over-looking the danger expressed in the huge volume of securities," but he was equally positive that "adequate facilities are available for whatever corrective measures may be found necessary."[31]

In contrast to the opinions expressed in the financial world, most merchants and industrialists and many academicians were all-out optimists. To be sure, Graustein of International Paper "saw tight money as unfavorable," and many professors of money and banking, notably Benjamin Anderson and H. Parker Willis, were in the front ranks of those who called for tighter money to prevent the holocaust that would be the inevitable outcome of unsustainable growth. But few could resist the enthusiasm of the day. Charles Schwab confessed, "I no longer see the danger that I formerly saw." Phillip Le Boutillier, president of Best and Co., the department store, subscribed to the then popular feeling that everybody was in the market and that "universal investment has ruined the old ratio between the income return and the cost of money." The year 1929 had hardly begun when Irving Fisher, the brilliant Yale University economics professor, said, "Stock prices are permanently high." Another professor thought that "stock bidders are among the best informed and most intelligent people in America."[32]

Electric as the atmosphere was, the monetary authorities were still being called upon to do something about speculation and especially to do something about brokers' loans which were now well past $5 billion. Some financial experts thought that as things were going, a collapse was just a question of time. Secretary of the Treasury Mellon told a news conference in early March that although many stocks were good investments, some were too high in price to be good buys. "For prudent investors," he said, "now is the time to buy good bonds." In early March, Paul Warburg, in a widely quoted report to the stockholders of the International Acceptance Corporation, deplored what was taking place and called on the Federal Reserve to take decisive, restrictive action. As would be expected of a conservative private banker, he followed the theme of overexpansion and unsustainability:

> Stock exchange operators have for many months governed the flow of money. . . . The Federal Reserve Board, through its failure to check speculative credit, has relinquished the leadership in the money market to the stock exchange operators. The volume of stock trading that is going on is nothing less than a debauch. . . . History, which has a painful way of repeating itself, has taught mankind that speculative overexpansion invariably ends in overcontraction and distress. . . . If orgies of speculation are permitted to spread too far, the ultimate collapse is certain not only to affect the speculators themselves, but also to bring about a general depression involving the whole country.[33]

THE BUSINESS REACTION TO THE FEDERAL RESERVE'S ATTEMPT TO STEM SPECULATION

The financial community recommended an increase in the rediscount rate. No mention was made of using any other monetary or fiscal controls such as open-market operations or a tax increase. The former was still not too familiar and the latter had not been thought of as a deflationary apparatus. The New York District Bank urged a rediscount rate advance, but the Board would not agree. Instead, it tried moral suasion, notifying the district banks on February 2 that "a member bank is not within its reasonable claims for rediscount facilities . . . when it borrows either for the purpose of making . . . or maintaining speculative loans."

The business community reacted immediately with practically no one defending the precise action that had been taken. It did not take long for W. C. Durant to make a melodramatic gesture. Durant thought that those who wished to gamble should be permitted to gamble. "It is well known," he told the press, "that over-extended credit for speculation leads to trouble, but our successful bankers do not have to be reminded of it every few days. . . . Men engaged in constructive undertakings will be overjoyed when the brokers' loans ghost ceases to walk." On April 1, Durant sent a telegram to leading business executives asking whether they thought the price of their stocks was too high. In the telegram he told his colleagues that the attitude of the Board was most harmful to business interests and threatened the prosperity of the country. Two weeks later he announced that 451 of 463 replies opposed the Board's policy. He, therefore, called on the Fed to keep its "hands off business, to reduce the rediscount rate to 3 per cent and to restore the $700 million that had been taken out of the money market by the sale of securities." Arthur Brisbane, the sage of the Hearst press, assisted Durant with the succinct comment: "If buying and selling stocks is wrong, the government should close the Stock Exchange. If not, the Federal Reserve should mind its own business."

Most of the financial community, including those who were most tireless in demanding some action to dampen the stock market, were terrified by the implications of the Fed's move. If it were carried through, it would mean that credit for the securities market, and for all markets for that matter, would be severely curtailed and a disastrous panic might occur. Indeed, the money market did become extremely tight; interest rates soared and the rate on call money jumped to 20 per cent. Michael H. Cahill, president of the Plaza Trust Company and president of the New York State Bankers Association, denounced the Board's action; and the New York District Bank, which continued to call for a hike in the rediscount rate, refused to bring any direct pressure on its member banks to reduce their loans. Instead, Charles Mitchell, one of its directors, announced that his bank, the National City, would offer $25 million in the call-money market at rates ranging from 16 to 20 per cent. The call-money rate immediately broke to 8 per cent. Mitchell explained that he had no intention of encouraging speculation; he had taken action to neutralize partly the withdrawal of $50 million from the market by a large Chicago bank. The National City Bank continued to ask for a 1 per cent increase in the rediscount rate. But no matter what Mitchell's intentions, his action was denounced in Washington with Senator Carter Glass calling for Mitchell's immediate resignation from the Federal Reserve System.

The bankers were quick to come to Mitchell's defense. *The Bankers*

Magazine "found it difficult to understand why the Board had waited until February 2, 1929 to issue a warning against speculation which has been rampant for a year or longer." L. M. Williams of the Richmond, Virginia, banking firm of John L. Williams & Sons called from the heart of the Glass country for the senator's resignation and congratulated Mitchell for allaying a panic. Ex-Governor Stokes of New Jersey, now chairman of the First Mechanics National Bank, told the Board to stop trying to control speculation and to reduce the rediscount rate to 4½ per cent.[34]

A variety of opinion was also evident among the economic consultants, free-lance writers, and professors. H. Parker Willis, who fancied that the Fed had not done anything right since he had left it, charged that the Board did not have the courage to take drastic action and that it was being used to suit the selfish interests of influential bankers. Later, Willis said the Board "was guilty of capricious changes in rates—first too low, then too high." Very few, especially among the younger men, shared Willis' views, whatever they really were. Lionel Edie said, "It is only a question of time until tight money and high interest rates threaten to force a business recession." Foster and Catchings, the brilliant writing partnership of professor and businessman, thought that "the Federal Reserve Board can stop the rise in security prices only by injuring business." The eminent Swedish economist Gustav Cassel could not understand the Federal Reserve attitude. To him, "it seemed scarcely rational to endeavor to check speculation by raising the bank rate or by fixing high rates for loans on the stock exchange." The conservative press was waiting to ambush this innocent foreigner. "For our part," editorialized the *Chronicle,* "we have never been able to understand why so much importance should be attached to the views of Professor Cassel. He seems to be lacking in any comprehensive knowledge of the workings of the Federal Reserve banks and accordingly can hardly be regarded as fully competent to express an opinion with regard to their functioning."[35]

EARLY SIGNS OF A BUSINESS DEPRESSION

The economic events of the spring and summer of 1929 were not confined to the stock market regardless of how sensational that area had become. Business activity had begun to decline from its high. The Federal Reserve Index of Industrial Production dropped off after

June; building construction plunged downward in July; freight car
loadings slipped after May; and factory payrolls, after April. An
occasional economist complained that the money supply was not rising as fast as it should; and one argued that net time and demand
deposits had actually declined since 1928. A few sensed a recession,
but the majority were too busy watching the stock market to consider the general state of business. Those who had by this time become "the old and tired" were still leery of the market. Fred I. Kent,
looking at the world as an objective bystander, wrote: "American
bankers have been increasing their margin requirements and the Federal Reserve has been endeavoring to prevent any developments that
would find the banks indebted to the System in large measure. It is
conceivable that the market can be made to correct itself with the
intelligent exercise of these forces." But it was quite evident that he
didn't think it would. The *Illinois Bankers Association Bulletin* of
July 1929 carried a headline: "Business Showing Slight Decline," on
top of a story reporting that Illinois bankers were antagonistic to "installment selling, mail order and chain stores, and the stock market."
The rate on call money once again advanced to 12 per cent, and a
member of Congress proposed to investigate the effect that the stock
market was having on "normal business credit." In August, the rediscount rate in New York was raised to 6 per cent. The reaction was
lethargic. As the press reported it a month later, "Except in a few
stocks, the break did not amount to more than 1–6 points and all that
and more has been recovered. The boost scared a lot of weak holdings out of the market." Actually, the move had come too late if it
had to come at all. As William T. Foster said at the time, the increase
in the rediscount rate would push the economy downhill. In more detail, the banking house of J. Henry Schroder considered the move unnecessary and dangerous, for there was no inflation in the form that
mattered—high prices.[86]

Despite what some economic indicators were foretelling, fewer
people in the summer of 1929 were expressing the conservative thesis
that unsustainable growth was a danger. Gloomy forecasts seemed at
odds with reality. The new era philosophy seemed much more in
tune. In August 1929, Colonel Ayres finally succumbed and admitted
that "this is truly a new era in which formerly well-established standards of value for securities no longer retain their old significance."
Only eight months after having said the market was too high, John
J. Raskob, in collaboration with Samuel Crowther, informed the

readers of one of America's best-known family magazines that every-body ought to be rich. Raskob thought that "an income from invested capital sufficient to support him and his family in a decent and com-fortable manner . . . ought to be obtainable by anyone." All one needed was to invest $15 a month in common stocks which would produce in twenty years a capital fund of $80,000 which in turn would produce an income of $400 a month. Raskob was not so much saying that stocks would rise continuously, but that if an individual bought stocks on the installment plan, he would in the long run make money. It was said that Bernard Baruch was liquidating his investments, but in an article in the June 1929 *American* magazine, the long-time adviser to Presidents prophesied "a huge volume of business for many years to come with occasional and temporary set-backs." His reasons were: the realization of every banker and manu-facturer that the more money people have the more they can buy, the Liberty Loans that taught the people to save and invest, the War Industries Board that established new co-operative relationships be-tween industry and the government, the better use of statistics, the great increase in human wants and ambitions and, above all, the Federal Reserve System.[37]

The business community and others had immense faith in the Federal Reserve System despite its evident inability to deal with specu-lation. The opinion expressed by Paul Mazur, Lehman Brothers specialist in retailing, was typical of many: "With the assistance of the Federal Reserve System, we may expect freedom from the un-warranted and annoying financial panics of the past." Others were even more rhapsodic. The optimists among the academicians outdid everyone else. One expert on the stock market dashed off a book ex-plaining the new era to the unsophisticated. "Old and tired traders and investors," he said, "expected the bull market to break, according to custom in two years," but "they were confused. Stocks have moved from a lower level to a relatively much higher level which will be permanent for some years to come." A revolution had occurred; the old rules were dead because of "unprecedented fundamental develop-ments in wealth, in the habits of people, in mass production, in efficient distribution, in the world of finance, in the attitude towards investments, and in public confidence." The latter was especially im-portant, for in the old days "the public did not trust the leadership." But new knights, "unhampered by the heavy armor of tradition, have come into the market . . . and finally joined in despair by many professional traders who, after sack-cloth and ashes, had caught the vision of progress, the Coolidge market had gone forward . . . parasang upon parasang. . . ." In November, weeks after the market had crashed, the publishers were still advertising the book.

Another academic observer of the passing scene comforted the faint of heart with some inside information: "The consensus of judgment of the millions whose valuations function on that admirable market, the Stock Exchange, is that stocks are not at present overvalued."[38]

The irony of the situation was that the economy was already in a recession and the stock market was not doing nearly as well as appeared from the daily newspaper headlines. In the first days of autumn, more and more observers either recognized this or at least caught a gleam of the truth. The bulls, after eight years, had finally overstayed their time, and as October succeeded September, it seemed that only Mitchell, a few free-lance writers and a few professors were left holding the bag. But as in the closing days of any brilliant career, there were still to be more moments of buoyant excitement.

THE END OF THE BULL MARKET

In early September, the last of the summer rallies came to an end. At long last, those who had regarded the future with alarm had something concrete with which to support their fears. The *Commercial and Financial Chronicle,* finally right after all these years, displayed a trace of glee when it said the market was falling of its own weight. The *Evening World,* whose sometimes gloomy reactions had always been dismissed as the grumblings of a Democratic scold unhappy in a Republican paradise, reported widespread bearishness among professional traders. The *Post* noticed a "suspicion in some quarters that a recession is under way." It went on to say that it was "difficult to see any basis for a further increase in the rediscount rate." *Poor's* spoke of the "common stock delusion." The English economist T. E. Gregory said, "The miracle of American prosperity is in part unreal and illusory, a mirage produced by a naive and undiscriminating optimism." Roger Babson predicted a great crash. Pointing out that most stocks were below their 1928 highs and that it was "possible to have optimism overrun and submerge discretion," Babson asserted that stocks were due to fall 60 to 80 points and that a "vicious circle will get into full swing and the result will be a serious business depression."

There was no lack of rebuttal from those who looked at the brighter side of things. Irving Fisher said there would be no crash; an editorial in *Barron's* referred to Babson as "the sage of Wellesley" and dismissed him as one who should not be taken seriously because of the "notorious inaccuracy of his past predictions." Hornblower & Weeks warned its customers not to be stampeded.

Those who had not been stampeded felt well satisfied with themselves as the stock averages once again reversed themselves. Somewhere between Labor Day and the beginning of fall, all the averages and some of the most active individual stocks attained their highest prices. On September 19, the *Times* industrial average reached 469.50 and the composite average 311.90. By then, General Motors had climbed to 225; Radio had passed 500; A.T. & T., 310; Steel, 260; and Montgomery Ward, 460. Brokers' loans were still going up, interest rates were high, and call money was at 10 per cent. The *Post*'s financial editor had second thoughts and now conceded that "fears of a recession must be regarded as premature." The Bank of England raised bank rate to 6 per cent because "of the orgy of speculation in New York" which was drawing gold out of London.

It was a time of uncertainty. Business news was disturbing, and no matter what the stock averages were saying, the market was spotty; more than half of the 650 issues traded at the height of the market were selling below the levels of the first of the year. All of this was brushed aside by the optimists. Sailing for Europe in October, Charles Mitchell said: "I leave with no fear whatever as to the prospects for business. Its progress is safe and I look for its continued gain." This was somewhat of a change from the previous spring when Mitchell had been cautiously optimistic and had called for a rise in the discount rate. Later, in an interview in Europe, Mitchell did say that speculation had in some cases gone too far, but the country was really "suffering from brokersloanitis." Still later, on his return from Europe in late October, Mitchell said that he knew nothing fundamentally wrong with the stock market, "If you can show me anything wrong with the situation generally, I would be concerned." Nevertheless, he called for a drop in the discount rate.[39]

It was clear to the press if not to the public that views such as those expressed by Mitchell had lost much of their glow. They were now regarded somewhat in the same way as the opinions of the bears had been regarded in the previous years. When Frederick Ecker of the Metropolitan Life said: "Common stocks are inherently speculative. There will always be an ebb and flow of the business tide. The curve of advancing prices has in the past invariably been offset by cycles of declines of equal degree," his views were accepted with much more interest and respect than had been the case two years before. The market was in a state of stagnation and was about to start on the way down. Any attempts to talk it up were regarded as nothing more than judicious expressions of optimism designed to make people feel better mentally while they were undergoing the cure. Few people thought that these expressions had any substance, and they weren't particularly bothered, because almost everyone had come to believe for some strange reason that the market had nothing whatever to do with the economy. The prevalent feeling was that what was taking place was the inevitable hangover after a long bout of dissolute living, and when it was over everyone would go back to work, forgetting what had happened. So as the market went down throughout October with the *Times* industrial average finally ending the month down 48 per cent from its high of September 19 and losing $32 billion in the process, bankers and brokers, the press and the public thought the debacle had come to an end. John J. Raskob, on October 30, said it was time to buy stocks because "the present decline has carried prices in many instances to levels ridiculously low." Colonel John W. Prentiss, senior partner of Hornblower & Weeks, said that prices would not be so low again in years. The *Commercial and Financial Chronicle* was satisfied that the country would now get back to a normal basis in which prosperity could be enjoyed without speculation. The *Times,* which had always been equally cautious, did not think that the crash presaged a depression. The fledgling *Business Week* did not pay any real attention to the market break until November when it said in a prominent article: "It was inevitable and is healthy. It will affect business, but to a limited extent and for a short time." Advertisements appeared in the press placing responsibility on the pessimists whose continuous forecasts of doom had finally had a psychological effect.[40]

As almost everyone knows, the bottom was not reached then, but a couple of years later, and whether it was necessary or not, business slumped as much as the market did. In the immediate aftermath of the October collapse, the *Times* composite index continued to slip until November 13 when it reached 164½, almost 150 points below the level achieved on September 19. Before the end of the

year, General Motors had dropped to 75; Radio and Montgomery
Ward again saw 100; Steel, 150; and Telephone had dropped below
200. Toward the end of the year, the 5600 top executives whose
opinions on the business situation were collected by *Business Week*
were optimistic about the future. They cited five favorable factors:
1) an early return of stocks to normal levels, 2) co-operative action
by business and industrial powers, 3) return of money to normalcy,
4) improved agriculture, and 5) small inventories. The one unfavorable factor was uncertainty and fear. "Factually," concluded *Business
Week,* "there is little to indicate that there will be a drastic decline
in business." But the new era, it was acknowledged, was dead; and
its eulogy was pronounced early in January. In an article called
"What's Left of the New Era?" the magazine said:[41]

> It was a great car to look at, but they finally had to trade her in for a
> well-used old model. . . . It was an automotive era. It taught us belief
> in prosperity. It enthroned the customer. It established the value of tech-
> nical progress and efficient management. It created a new awareness of
> the power of credit. These things are good and these are the things
> that remain.

5. THE TROUBLED YEARS

> "1929 RICH MAN
> 1930 poor man
> 1931 beggar man
> 1932 thief."
>
> Franklin P. Adams

The economy grew the melon in the years 1923–27; it cut the melon in 1927–29; and by 1930, there was nothing left but the memories—and the seeds of another future boom. But little of this was understood when the wreckage of the stock market crash was being cleared away during "the holidays" in 1929.

As 1930 approached, business leaders, journalists, college professors, and the public in general settled back to relax. Those who had not "lost their heads" had no expectation that the world was about to be visited by the worst business depression in history. To be sure, there had been signs for a few months past that business was falling off. Here and there, a few pessimists were forecasting disaster, but even the gloomiest would have been aghast had anyone told them that the next three and a half years would wipe out all the economic growth that had been achieved in the previous quarter century. By 1933, total production of goods and services had been cut in half. To be sure, prices were also down, but lowered prices were small solace to the one quarter of the labor force who were unemployed. The business community hardly suffered as much but only because it could live off its accumulated capital. Corporations that had earned $10 billion in profits in 1929 suffered a loss of $2 billion in 1932 and again in 1933. The stock market sagged in 1930 and 1931 and then fell to an abysmal bottom in July 1932 when the *Times* average was down almost 90 per cent from its high in 1929.*

* From 312 in September 1929 to 34 in July 1932.

THE FIRST REACTION TO THE DEPRESSION

None of this was anticipated in the winter of 1929–30. To the contrary, it was generally assumed that at worst the economy might experience a recession such as had occurred in 1924 and again in 1927. The typical attitude among business leaders was that the debauch was over. A sober America would forget its recent unseemly conduct and get to the business of enjoying a safe and sane prosperity. Bankers Arthur Lehman, James Speyer, Lewis Pierson, and Benjamin Anderson forecast a "normal" prosperity. In the words of one, "Business during 1930 will be much nearer normal than at the moment anticipated." Industrialists James A. Farrell of U. S. Steel, Gerard Swope, Alvin Macauley of Packard Motors, and A. W. Robertson of Westinghouse thought the "general economic situation thoroughly sound . . . There was no reason why 1930 should not be a good average year with stable prices and stable wages." The entrepreneurs of the non-bank financial intermediaries were also confidently optimistic. According to Thomas E. Parkinson, onetime academic dean and now head of the Equitable Life Assurance Society, and Frederick Ecker of the Metropolitan Life, "so long as our buying power remains sustained, there can be little in the way of a serious depression."[1]

It was apparent that business spokesmen did not believe that the stock market had much to do with business condition. George Roberts, editor of the National City Bank Letter, diagnosed the stock market collapse as an attack of acute indigestion, but he saw nothing wrong with business activity. Colonel Ayres expressed the prevalent opinion when he commented, "There does not seem to be as yet much real evidence that the declining stock prices are likely to forecast serious recession in business. Despite the slowing down in iron and steel production, in automobile output, and in building, the conditions which result in serious business depression are not present."[2]

The economic columnists and apparently the public at large shared the opinions of the business leaders. Standard Statistics, McGraw-Hill, Julius Klein, and David Friday were very optimistic, while *Brookmire's Survey* and *Moody's* were only a trifle less so. Business philosophers had been too successful in convincing the public that they had the business cycle well under control. It was an accepted fact that "all the important millionaires were planning to continue prosperity." Or so at least announced Arthur Brisbane.

Along with this belief that the important millionaires had everything under control went a corollary conviction that everything should be done to preserve confidence. President Hoover tried to convince the country that it was suffering from nothing more than a minor organic disturbance. Like many businessmen, he thought a defeatist state of mind was causing a psychosomatic stomach ache. He sought to bolster confidence by holding conferences and setting up committees. After meeting with a representative group of important businessmen in early November, the President announced the formation of an organization representing manufacturing and commerce which was to "stabilize industry." As they left the meeting, some of the participants co-operated with the President by minimizing the seriousness of the economic crisis. Alfred P. Sloan thought the slump was "healthy" for business. A few months later, he was to say that he was more bullish than ever. A. H. Giannini was positive the crash would have little effect on business. But Henry Ford grasped the opportunity to sound a raucous note without straying too far from the main thesis. Asked about the stock market crash, he said that it had been a symptom of a general decline in business—a point of view contrary to the general consensus that the debacle in Wall Street was an isolated phenomenon bearing no relation to business as a whole.

The business leaders were expressing sentiments that were the opposite of what they really believed. This was not because they were insincere or hypocritical; they were whistling through the woods to scare away the hobgoblin better known as a loss of confidence. The party line had been agreed upon and, like good sports, one and all joined loyally to spread it around. Thus, Secretary of the Treasury Mellon, who, according to reliable authority, believed that the purpose of business depression was to transfer ownership of the means of production from the weak to the strong and that nothing should be done to interfere with the process, now found himself expressing an opposite opinion:

> In this country there has been a concerted and determined effort on the part of both government and business not only to prevent any reduction in wages but to keep the maximum number of men employed, and thereby to increase consumption. It must be remembered

that the all-important factor is purchasing power. . . . The standard
of living must be maintained at all costs.[3]

BUSINESSMEN BEWILDERED

Gradually it became evident that the stock market collapse had not
been an isolated and irrelevant phenomenon. In January 1930, the
National Economic League voted unemployment eighteenth in a list of
national problems. By January 1931, it had moved unemployment up
to number four. In late 1930, apple sellers, inspired by the International Apple Shippers' Association, were appearing on every other
street corner. At the same time, a group of businessmen, led by George
Washington Hill, the advertising enthusiast of American Tobacco,
launched a drive to end the depression by an advertising campaign
designed to encourage buying. Less flamboyant executives, such as
Walter Gifford, did not think the idea could work, and eventually, the
"Buy Now" campaigns did lose their appeal and proved ineffectual.

One of the most disheartening contributing factors to the spreading
pall of gloom was the continued decline in the stock market. The
market had recovered vigorously in the winter and early spring of
1930, giving some substance to the ebullient feeling that ran through
the business community. But then it fell rapidly. The industrial
average, which had risen to 360 by April, sagged to 260 in June,
returned to 300 in September, and ended the year at 200. There were
some periods of weak recovery in 1931, but the average ended the
year at 110; 1932 was even worse, and in July, the average had fallen
to just under 60. At that time Bruce Bliven of the *New Republic* proposed that the government buy all the common stock of 44 of the
largest corporations for $5.5 billion, their market value at that time.[4]

It took almost two years for the unpalatable to be swallowed.
Throughout 1930 and much of 1931, the reaction of business leaders
to what was happening underwent a subtle change, but the consensus
continued to be that the downturn would be short-lived. In June 1930,
Otto H. Kahn was confident that "the prospects of the future are as
great as ever," a view that quickly acquired a respectable following.
Harvey S. Firestone told the press, "The present slump will soon be
succeeded by greater prosperity than America has known for ten
years." Walter Gifford was "as sure as I am standing here, this depression will soon pass," and we would "enter a period of prosperity the

like of which no country has ever seen before." W. S. Farish of Humble Oil announced the end of the depression in six months, for "history will bear me out that no business depression [has] lasted more than two years."

By the fall, this initial reaction was veering toward greater caution. It was still thought that unprecedented prosperity was sure to come back, but the time for its return had been extended. It would now arrive in its own good time—sedately and orderly. A. W. Robertson looked for a "slower, more orderly, and possibly a more permanent return to normal conditions than in 1922." By late 1930, some members of the business community adopted still another tack by announcing that the depression was over. In September, Alfred P. Sloan and George M. Varity of American Rolling Mills simultaneously told the waiting public, "We have reached the bottom of the cycle." In January 1931, Louis K. Liggett, the promoter of a drug chain, told President Hoover "the depression has touched bottom." In April, Frederick H. Ecker wondered whether the American people were not "unduly pessimistic by about six months."

But the downturn continued, and as it did, some business leaders felt their confidence slipping away. The usually inarticulate businessmen were the first to lose patience. In early 1931, N. A. Perry, an Indianapolis banker, told President Hoover that the country had three years of depression ahead of it and that there was too much propaganda regarding the betterment of general business. This realization spread slowly, for like most other people, businessmen wanted to believe that the future would be better rather than worse. James A. Farrell repeated what he had been saying all along, "The worst is over." In August, Hubert T. Parson of Woolworth was "convinced the tide has turned and that the rank and file of business is encouraged, but there is still some pessimism among bankers." But pessimism did not engulf all bankers. Charles E. Mitchell thought that a "multitude of corrective influences are gradually restoring conditions to a return of prosperity." Edward C. Delafield, president of the Bank of America, was sure that "if the business depression has not passed its low point, it has at least reached a level where prices can be considered practically at their low point." Francis Sisson was looking at an even more clouded crystal ball when he reassured an audience of bankers: "The liquidation of the past year has prepared the way for revival. The most reassuring thing is that the banking system is on a firmer base than last year." Paul Warburg was much more cautious,

"Nobody," he said, "may venture to predict when this depression will end but no sane person doubts that eventually it will end."

By the middle of 1931, most businessmen, recognizing that the announcement of the slump's demise had been premature, acknowledged that the country was experiencing the worst economic convulsion in history. There were, of course, exceptions. James A. Speyer, for example, continued to insist "there is no cause for pessimism in this country with its stable currency and its efficient Federal Reserve System." But Alfred Sloan expressed the more typical view when he tempered his previous optimism by conceding that 1931 might be disappointing. Apparently not knowing what else to say, he advised his listeners, "to eliminate the memory of the past from our minds. . . . Nothing is so dead as the past." A more inveterate optimist, Charles M. Schwab, who always had a word for everything, sadly proclaimed, "There are no longer any rich men."[5]

The trend toward less and less ebullience continued into 1932, the worst year of the worst depression. As the year opened, Arthur Lehman told the press, "No boom, no sudden stimulation of values is in sight . . . but one can reasonably hope that the abnormal depression has run its course." Many other business leaders shared this opinion, but it was a time for guarded expressions, as John D. Rockefeller illustrated when he told the Associated Press: "From talks I have had with prominent men and reports reaching me, indications are that business conditions are improving."

Events, it was plain, had come to bewilder the majority of business leaders. In mid-1930, ex-Ambassador James W. Gerard announced that sixty-four men ruled the United States. Reporters immediately dashed to learn from them what could be done. They came away with almost nothing.

Some businessmen did offer an explanation of what was happening and why, but their explanations were so weak that they led Will Rogers to observe: "The whole thing shows there ain't none of them know any more about it than Texas Guinan." Myron C. Taylor of the United States Steel corporation knew that we would learn "something of high importance out of the depression," but he couldn't say what this something would be. In a moment of frustration, Senator La Follette pleaded with Taylor to explain how he would go about getting the country out of the depths. The ensuing dialogue revealed how dazed the business leaders were.

TAYLOR: "Well, Senator, I can only answer you as to the attitude and mind of industrialists generally. . . . They are confident people, hopeful people. They believe in the future. . . . And they are going to use every ounce of their energy to pull this thing out so far as it lies in their power to do it."

SEN. LA FOLLETTE: "I am interested to know how it may be done while the slide keeps on."

TAYLOR: "Well, we are all of us trying to find the remedy."

At the same hearings, Edward D. Duffield of the Prudential Life Insurance Company started confidently to explain the laissez-faire point of view, but he quickly found himself floundering. Asked by La Follette whether it was fair to assume that he was in favor of "letting the depression run its course," Duffield answered that it was "difficult to answer that question yes or no." When La Follette then asked whether Duffield had favored the creation of the Reconstruction Finance Corporation, the insurance executive said, "I did. I do believe that by legislation we should endeavor to prevent unnecessary injury from what in the broader sense must be cured by economic laws."[6]

Other businessmen reluctantly admitted that they did not understand what was taking place. Paul Warburg, certainly one of the most sophisticated, said in 1931: "I have studied finance and economics and international trade all my life, and now, after these recent events, I have come to the conclusion that I know nothing whatever about any of them." The rugged individualist Sewell Avery observed, "To describe the causes of this situation is rather beyond my capacity. I am unfortunate in having no friends that seem able to explain it clearly to me."[7]

"WHAT THIS COUNTRY NEEDS IS A MUSSOLINI"

Forgetting what had happened during the boom, the public soon became impatient with business bewilderment. It seemed convinced that the President and the business class, that he was assumed to represent, were "doing nothing" and "didn't care how much America was suffering." Few charges could have been more baseless. Both Hoover and the business leaders were vitally interested in restoring prosperity; no class had more to lose by the continuance of the depression. To be sure, many businessmen and business spokesmen foolishly and unnecessarily kept infuriating the public by saying that "nothing can be done about it, except very gradually and in a small way as industry is doing." It was not that businessmen were inhumane. It was that they had no understanding of what was taking place. Everything they had said about the causes and consequences of economic ups and downs now seemed like so much pap, and they were left frustrated and generally disillusioned. Their feeling of helplessness was so deep that many of them were more than willing to try the last path of least resistance—turning the whole mess over to a dictator. To be sure, many businessmen had always had some admiration for strong men who could make trains run on time. Early in the twenties, soon after Mussolini came to power, Lewis E. Pierson complimented him because "under his superb leadership, the Fascisti have revived the flame of Italy's aspirations." About the same time, Judge Gary told reporters, "We should be better for a man like Mussolini here too." Somewhat later, Fred I. Kent said, "As far as I can ascertain, Mussolini has been accepted by the Italian people wholeheartedly, and for the next year or two he is probably going to have an opportunity to put into effect many of the very excellent ideas which he has in mind, unless he loses his head because of the adulation which is being heaped upon him."

The depression deepened this empathic admiration. Early in the depression, at a meeting of the Foreign Policy Association, Dr. Elliot of Harvard University, attacked Mussolini, only to find him strongly supported by Thomas W. Lamont and Otto Kahn. Lamont cited Mussolini's accomplishments in eliminating unemployment, balancing the budget, improving the life of the common people, and gaining popular support. Kahn and Mussolini's other business admirers looked at only one side of the coin. Said Kahn: "In the case of every people more essential even than liberty, and therefore taking precedence over it, is order and national self-preservation. . . . Mussolini is a patriotic realist. He is no dictator in the generally understood sense of the word. . . . He set the Italian nation once more on the high road to national achievement. That is a towering feat. . . . I bow in homage to the solitary figure who accomplished it." Andrew W. Mellon saw in the Italian dictator "a strong hand to reestablish the Italian Government upon sound principles and Government by party and not by bargaining. Steps have been taken to abandon Government operation of the railroads, and to cut taxes, and the budget this year will be practically balanced."

As the depression wore on, business leaders lost some of their enthusiasm for Mussolini, but at the same time, their remaining faith in democracy was also considerably shaken. L. F. Loree, the individualistic railroad executive, demonstrated how far this had gone when he recommended to the Senate: the abolition of all direct primaries, a graduated suffrage, a poll tax, denial of suffrage to all persons on the public payroll, and the restriction of local suffrage to taxpayers or those who paid rent of a fixed amount. In an article for *Current History* called "Does America Need a Dictator," the eminent historian, F. A. Ogg stated that "fifty representative men had told Gordon Selfridge [an American-born, English merchant] that they thought with him that democracy could not possibly succeed as a system of government in the United States." Coming back from the 1931 meeting of the Chamber of Commerce, Virgil Jordan of the National Industrial Conference Board reported that businessmen had lost faith. "An economic Mussolini," he said, "could have them parading in red, white, and blue shirts and saluting some new symbol."

W. B. Bell of the American Cyanamid Company in an attack on the labor unions warned that the world was splitting into two groups: those for order and those for chaos. He explained to Congress: "In the case of Italy before Mussolini, the labor unions took control, simply ran wild. . . . As a consequence, you could start a train from Milan without any assurance that you would ever get to Rome. . . . All the conservative elements realized that the choice lay between chaos and anarchy on the one side, and dictatorial power on the other, and the human race is so constituted that broadly speaking when they realize that that is the choice they always let liberty go and take order." By this time, another dictator had appeared—one who would do even more to heighten international tension. But Charles W. Schwab, who "had talked to several German businessmen," thought that Germany was "in fine condition" and that the man called Hitler "was really popular because they credit him with bringing order out of chaos." Kahn, returning on the same boat with Schwab, torn between his love for Germany and what Germany was doing to the Jews, refused to comment.

But businessmen were not the only Americans who longed for the dictator who would bring "order out of chaos." Other Americans from the liberal as well as the Fascist wing yearned for the man on the horse. *The Nation* steadily opposed Mussolini, but the *New Republic* in the 1920s admired the man who had given Italy "increased moral energy" and "a deeply felt common purpose." As the decade sped on Ezra Pound, Stark Young, George Santayana, Irving Babbitt, Kenneth Roberts, Lothrop Stoddard, and Ida Tarbell were responding to "the great intellectual challenge of the age." The depression pushed many of the liberals into the Soviet camp, but so-called conservatives clung to Mussolini. On the floor of Congress, Senator David Reed of Pennsylvania confessed that although he did not often "envy other countries their governments, if this country ever needed a Mussolini, it needs one now." Some of the glossier magazines were openly urging someone to "appoint a dictator." And Bernarr MacFadden, the physical-culture publicist, told his readers "what we need now is martial law; there is no time for civil law. The President should have dictatorial powers."[8]

THE REASONS WHY

Businessmen were far from agreement about what caused the depression or what could be done to bring prosperity back. Their widely divergent social and economic philosophies resulted in a whole congeries of plausible and implausible explanations of the plague that had come upon the country. In the previous severe depression, that of 1921, these differences in philosophy had been subordinated to a secondary role. At that time the nature of depression seemed very clear, and businessmen had no trouble in arriving at a consensus. It was agreed that the war had inflated everything, and all that had to be done to get the economy rolling was to tighten money and deflate prices, wages, and taxes. Such a consensus was impossible in 1930. Prices were not inflated; federal taxes were low; and, if one took expressed opinions seriously, wages were not too high. Given the divergent philosophies, the area of possible agreement was extremely small. Indeed, it was confined to only two aspects of the depression problem. A number of businessmen in all groups put the onus for the depression on the extravagance of the speculative boom, and almost without exception, they believed that no relief was possible unless the federal budget was balanced. Beyond this, each group—bankers, manufacturers, and merchants—framed its own rationale, and within each group, there was a series of variations on the main theme.

With few exceptions, bankers of all types—investment and savings bankers as well as commercial bankers—were disciples of classical business cycle theory. They believed that depressions were the abnormal by-products of the frictions and rigidities that resulted from interfering with the operation of natural market forces. In this impeccably logical analysis, depressions were the inevitable result of the excesses and mistakes of the previous boom.

What were these maladjustments, these mistakes and errors of the prosperity years? They could be grouped under four general headings. First, there were the international dislocations caused by the war and by unnatural interferences with the international flow of goods and capital. This was, as one might suspect, a favorite theme of the international bankers, including Kahn and Speyer. But it was an even greater favorite of the heads of the Chase Bank, Albert H. Wiggin and Winthrop W. Aldrich, who were, with the advice of the bank's outstanding economist Benjamin M. Anderson, the most indefatigable spokesmen for the typical banker point of view. In early 1931, Wiggin explained to the Senate Banking and Currency Committee that the immediate cause of the 1929 collapse was that "the debauch of speculation reached its climax and stopped." But he also gave five underlying reasons for the depression, reasons which prominently featured "excessive tariff and other restrictive policies which limited international trade." In a long lecture to a Senate Committee, Aldrich put even more emphasis on the international causes of the depression. The war, he said, had caused an immense shift in international debtor and creditor positions. Intergovernmental debts, high protective tariffs, and the gold exchange standard had further complicated matters and led to "a strangulation of international trade."[9]

A second cause of the depression in the bankers' list was the "extravagance" and "the speculative mania" which characterized the decade after World War I. Melvin Traylor thought, "August 1, 1914 was the beginning of the depression we are in today. . . . One of the biggest things was a watered state of mind in which we all thought we were richer than we were." Traylor and Kahn both thought, in the latter's words, that "the prolonged speculative mania" had put "an unbearable strain on credit." Fred I. Kent also argued that the war insidiously influenced our time-honored ideals of thrift and industry. According to Kent, "Very often the causes for a depression have very little, if anything, to do with the judgments of those who are operating in the business world. . . . The original cause dated back to the actions of European governments following the Armistice under which men were paid for doing nothing instead of being given work." But according to the Pepys of American business, Clarence Barron, the tycoons of the immediate postwar period were "crazy about Europe's reluctance to go back to work." James Buchanan Duke, the tobacco entrepreneur, gloated to Barron: "I thought when the war was over, impoverished Europe would get to work, send their goods over here, take our money and reduce our prices, but, damn it, they haven't begun to do it yet; they won't work; they are demoralized. There is something about failure in a nation that is demoralizing and destroying to efficiency."[10]

Most of the thinking that blamed the depression on extravagance and speculation was a repetition of the "unsustainable prosperity" doctrine that had been so popular among bankers during the boom years. This "what goes up must come down" analysis was in back of many of the prayers for thrift that were offered during the early 1930s. It is difficult to understand how serious people could call for less spending at a time when total income had been cut in half, but opinions in praise of thrift,* were expressed over and over again in letters to the *Times* and in the comments of business and political leaders. Eugene R. Black of the Federal Reserve Bank of Atlanta and later chairman of the Federal Reserve Board was not exaggerating the prevalent motif when he said:

> I do not agree with those men who are saying that in America there must be no retrogression from the present high grade of living. . . . We have been living in an automobile, a Frigidaire, a radio era, and have been sitting in the atmosphere of a Corona-Corona. We cannot pay our debts and continue in that atmosphere.

"It is folly," echoed John W. Barton, president of the National Bank Division of the American Bankers Association, "to expect to maintain our standard of living against the rest of the world." Joining in the general chorus, the president of the ABA wanted to launch a campaign to "induce our people to be economical and thrifty." And Dwight Morrow prophesied that "recovery is going to be brought

---

* Some commentators did express contrary views. Garet Garrett, the business writer, said: "People may ruin themselves by saving instead of spending. Thrift may become economically disastrous." And Foster, of Foster and Catchings who were always out of order, wrote an article entitled "Must We Reduce Our Standard of Living?"

about by the man who earns a modest living and spends just a little less than he earns."[11]

"Abnormalities in price and wages" was, in the classical view, a third cause of the depression. Wiggin and Aldrich both alluded to "artificial price maintenance" and the "tardiness of prices and wages to adjust themselves." This allegation that the twenties was a period of inflation was not supported by the behavior of the price indices. The cost of living and wholesale prices were relatively stable all through the decade, and price levels at the height of the bull market in 1927–29 were lower than at any time since before the war. But the bankers had a rationale for their view. In other postwar periods, such as after the War of 1812 and after the Civil War, prices fell sharply. They thought the same thing should have occurred after 1918; production was increasing the supply of goods, and consequently prices should have fallen. A stable price level was, therefore, *prima facie* evidence of inflation. This was all explained by Paul Warburg in an address to the directors of the Manhattan Company in early 1931. According to Warburg, "customs and other interferences with supply and demand kept prices high." Installment credit, foreign loans, and easy money gave artificial support to demand and prevented the price decline that should have occurred. Eventually, when new markets failed to develop, demand did collapse, prices dropped, and depression set in.

Still a fourth reason and one that was accused of having powerfully influenced the deplorable trend to extravagance and speculation was the so-called "easy-money policy" followed by the Federal Reserve System in the years before the crash. Almost every big city banker took time out to reproach the Fed because it had not tightened money when the speculative boom was taking off. Wiggin, for example, thought that "a stiffer policy on rates and a somewhat different open-market policy might have reduced the extremes to which the speculation went." Mitchell thought that the Federal Reserve would have turned to tight money much sooner if it had it to do over again. George Davison of the Central Hanover regarded it as "quite probable" that "if rediscount rates had been raised a little faster and with less talk, it might have checked much speculation," and might have stopped "the inordinate rise of all prices (*sic*) including securities." J. P. Morgan said, "The failure of the Federal Reserve Board to take the necessary measures to control the inflation in time encouraged the speculative frenzy which carried the market quotations out of

bounds—so that they were too high in 1929 and too low later."
Marine Midland's Edmund Platt, who had been a member of the
Board, asserted that the "whole easy money policy of the last half of
1927 deserved criticism" for keeping prices artificially high. When
asked how he knew they were "high," he cited as proof the fact that
they had later declined.

Aldrich was the most positive of all the bankers in blaming monetary policy for the catastrophe. He constantly referred to "the unprecedented expansion of bank credit" that took place as a result of
steady inflow of gold from abroad and the "cheap money policies"
of the monetary authorities. Playing on one of Benjamin Anderson's
favorite themes, Aldrich criticized the Federal Reserve Board for
having left the rediscount rate unchanged from July 1928 to August
1929 "notwithstanding the vast speculation then in progress." This
failure, Aldrich added, "had immeasurable consequences and has
come to be regarded as quite the most conspicuous failure of the
Federal Reserve System since its inception."[12] Today, in contrast
to the 1930s, it is generally agreed that Aldrich's remarks were much
exaggerated. Perhaps, the Fed should have tightened the money
market in 1928, but its eventual tightening was much too heavy
handed, and as to "most conspicuous failures," the episode of tight
money in the depression of 1920 was a strong contender for the title.

Aside from the injudicious monetary policy, tariffs, and a failure to
settle international debts, the bankers surprisingly enough did not
find the government guilty of creating the depression. Mitchell and
Davison, like President Hoover, thought that the capital gains tax
did dissuade stockholders from selling their holdings, thus cutting the
supply of securities offered in the market, and contributing to the
unsustainable rise in security prices. But this was the extent of their
criticism.

WHAT TO DO ABOUT IT

The older bankers, who had gone through any number of depressions, had little hope that anything much could be done about the
business cycle or that there was any easy road out of any specific
crisis. Depressions were inevitable, and the automatic workings of
economic law were no more subject to the designs of men than were
any of the other fates. Fred I. Kent thought that "cyclical trends

seem to be due to certain inherent characteristics in men." When someone asked Wiggin whether the capacity for human suffering was unlimited, he replied, "I think so. . . . Human nature is human nature. . . . So long as business goes on, we are bound to have conditions of crisis once in so often." In popular terminology, this was freely translated as: Those who dance also have to pay the fiddler. In Paul Warburg's opinion we were "living in a period when the uneconomic producer, the producer who can only live on the basis of artificially high prices, is being weeded out. A painful readjustment indeed, but an inevitable one that has to run its course." It was the old cathartic cure, and no one knew how long it would take, but nothing should interrupt it until all the poisons were out of the system. In 1932, after over two years of deflation, Frederic H. Rawson, the Chicago banker, said, "In my judgment the situation has not been helped by the various attempts made to escape the inevitable liquidation which should have been allowed to continue its natural course." It was a ruthless sentiment, and those who expressed it were regarded as unnecessarily cruel. Misguided and pigheaded, they may have been, but they were also sincere.[13]

Despite their fatalism and pessimism, the old-line bankers struck a few notes of cheer. Warburg did not hesitate to say that "a few years hence the level at which some of our securities sell today will look as incomprehensibly low as the prices paid seemed unreasonably high long before the crash occurred in October 1929." It hardly seems necessary to emphasize how right he was.

Almost every big-city banker had some positive suggestions for improving things. Most recommended tariff reductions and the settlement of international debts and reparations by reduction or cancellation. Wiggin and Traylor called for wage scales adjusted to price reduction. Actually, wages were already being reduced, but Wiggin was the first to suggest openly that this distasteful medicine was a necessary part of the cure for the economy's sickness. "It is not true," he held, "that high wages make prosperity. Instead prosperity makes high wages." Following orthodox economic theory, he argued that wage reductions would reduce costs; in turn, prices would come down; consumers would be able to buy more; and employment would go up. It was as simple as that, a fact of economic life. The few who regarded it with skepticism and pointed out that wage reductions might reduce demand and lead to further unemployment were in the underworld of economics, not respectable enough to be listened to.[14]

Other bankers added further embellishments to the classical analysis. Aldrich called for "undeviating adherence to sound money and sound public finance," which meant the gold standard, deflation, and a balanced budget. When critics attacked the gold standard as a deflationary device that hammered down incomes and hammered up unemployment, bankers quickly came to its defense. "The gold standard," Fred I. Kent warned, "does its work so smoothly and quietly except when unwise acts of men arise to interfere that the business world and even the financial world is not aware of what it means to them and does not appreciate the extent of the disruption that would accrue if the gold standard were abolished."

To most bankers, however, threats to the gold standard were minor irritants. They never aroused nearly so much aggravation as the failure of governments, especially the federal government, to balance their budgets. But the aggravation did not begin until late 1931, for it took that long before the existence of an unbalanced budget was recognized. Very quickly thereafter, however, businessmen of all sizes and in all walks (and most other people for that matter) worked themselves up to a high state of excitement because governments would not live within their incomes. "There can be no lasting prosperity," said Carl P. Dennet of Boston in a typical opinion, "as long as one-third of the national income is consumed by government."

There was no agreement among budget balancers as to what exactly was meant by a balanced budget. In general, it meant "living within one's income" year by year, but some interpreted this to mean that the government should raise enough income to meet ordinary expenditures and borrow whatever was needed to cover capital expenditures. Budget balancers constantly alluded to the "fact" that an individual who spent more than his income would find himself in most extreme difficulty. They believed that the government was no different from any other household. Indeed, many of them thought that the government was inferior to a householder. They would countenance an individual going into debt to buy a house or a motor car, but would not permit the government to go into debt, except during a war.

Nor was there any agreement as to how the budget was to be balanced. Almost everyone agreed or at least paid lip service to the charge that the government was spending huge sums of money and that these expenditures would have to be reduced. For example, Professor Taussig, the widely respected Harvard economics professor, shocked by a $4 billion federal budget, warned: "A grand orgy of expenditure is a dangerous stimulant likely to be followed by a relapse." Gates McGarrah, the New York banker, wrote George Harrison in May 1932, "Of course, what will be the greatest possible benefit to the United States is the adjournment of Congress five minutes or less after the budget has been securely balanced." Fred I. Kent, at about the same time, was sure that "there is seemingly not the slightest doubt but that the forces delaying the return of prosperity are political and that they are fundamentally due to unwise expenditures of governments, federal, state, and municipal, in most countries of the world."[15]

If spending could not be reduced enough to balance the budget, then taxes would have to be raised. "We are confronted by two paramount necessities," said Francis Sisson, "rigid economy in public expenditures . . . balancing the budget by tax increases if necessary." A sales tax was the kind of tax that was most often suggested. Most congressmen agreed that the budget would have to be balanced, but the Democrats wanted to raise income taxes, and the Administration favored reduced spending and a sales tax. Finally in the spring of 1932 there came forth the largest increase in tax rates in peacetime history. But, alas, the budget was more unbalanced than ever. Yet bankers and business leaders were undaunted. They increased their efforts to talk a balanced budget into reality.

In a long letter in December 1932, Secretary of the Treasury Mills told Owen Young, "Clearly, it is comparatively easy today to bring our budget into balance." Mills's letter expressed very well what many businessmen thought:

> . . . All the evidence . . . indicates that there is no serious purpose on the part of Congress either to make the essential reduction in expenditures, or to provide the necessary revenue to bring the budget into balance. They seem to be living in a little world of their own without genuine realization of the gravity of the fiscal problem and of its relationship to the general economic situation.

To which Jackson Reynolds later added a suitable postcript: "The difficulty is the failure of the Government to live prudently within its income. . . . I appraise what will follow from balancing the budget by the knowledge of what has followed from the failure to balance the budget."[16]

DIFFERENT OPINIONS ABOUT MONEY AND CREDIT

Cheap money policies even in depression were almost as high as unbalanced budgets on the bankers' disapproval list. Soon after the stock market collapse, some of the bolder and more disgruntled inhabitants of the business world proposed to increase the money supply as a means of reinvigorating the economy. *Business Week,* for example, called on the Federal Reserve System in March 1930 to make money cheaper and more plentiful and to do it "now." This was what the Fed did try to do. Whether or not it did so with sufficient enthusiasm and whether it went far enough is open to question. But beginning in late 1929 and continuing through 1930, it bought $560 million of securities in the open market and it reduced the rediscount rate to 2 per cent in New York and to 3 and 3½ per cent in the other districts. It had, however, much to contend with, for most of the articulate bankers took a sour view of these maneuvers.

Following classical theory, bankers thought that manipulating the money supply could accomplish nothing but harm. In their view, changes in the money supply could raise or lower prices, but could have no effect on income or employment. Attempts to bring back prosperity by increasing the money supply could not, therefore, do any good. They could only result in inflation and produce rigidities. In 1933, at the bottom of the depression, when the price level was down one third from the 1926 level, F. H. Sisson still thought "the great menace . . . is inflation. . . . Many persons, weary of hardships and sacrifices, appear to be willing to accept artificial correctives that they would have strenuously opposed several months ago."

At the same time, Winthrop Aldrich said, "I should avoid further artificial efforts to force an expansion of bank credit. It was forced expansion from 1922 to 1928 which was responsible for a great part of our present trouble." He then went on to say that heavy excess reserves in the banks in the "absence of confidence" would not force bank-credit expansion. He argued that all that the excess reserves would do would be to feed inflation and speculation, and as evidence he insisted that government security purchases by the Fed in late 1929 and early 1930, which were designed to feed money into the economy, had been "responsible for the stock market boom in early 1930." Apparently, to Aldrich, the economy was divided into nice neat

pigeonholes, one marked "business" and one marked "speculation."
Most other bankers shared Aldrich's opinion about money and inflation, for they too had been educated in the orthodox tradition.
They worried for fear that cheap money would engender inflation and
threaten the gold standard. They believed in bleeding the patient, for
even though he was now in the advanced stages of pernicious anemia,
he had once weighed twenty stone. Thus Fred I. Kent in 1933, considerably bothered by the inflation talk that was coming louder and
louder from congressmen, farmers, and some manufacturers and
merchants, denied that money had anything to do with depression.
He recalled that "stock market inflation introduced one of the great
depressions . . . and still men cry for inflation in every man-made
economic emergency."

Here again, however, bankers were not the only ones in the community who held what now seem such strange views about money.
In March 1930, a letter to the *Times* asked, "are we sure that business will react favorably to the cut in the rediscount rate to 3½ per
cent? Has it been definitely felt that what business needed was
cheaper money? We can be certain that one result, at least will follow . . . and that will be an increase in speculation." When the rate
was further lowered to 2 per cent, Representative McFadden, chairman of the House Banking and Currency Committee, said it would
stimulate "artificial business" and lead to speculation and inflation.

General Charles G. Dawes, erstwhile banker and now ambassador
to England, wrote the Secretary of State in October 1931, "Cochran
[a Morgan partner] agrees with me that if gold withdrawals continue
on any large scale careful consideration should be given to the idea of
raising the rate by ½ per cent every week." This sort of thinking
was not without influence. In October 1931, in a move which in
retrospect seems one of the most astonishing in monetary history,
the Federal Reserve raised the rediscount rate. The only excuse for
this move toward dearer money, and perhaps tighter money, at a time
when the economy was sagging pitifully was that it was in the orthodox tradition of protecting the gold reserve. The action did not go
uncriticized, and as the depression lumbered on, a number of economists dropped out of the orthodox school and joined in urging "an
aggressive and sustained credit expansion." This was in turn denounced by some of the most respected men in academic circles.
Said one to the Senate, "Abandon at the earliest possible moment the
false philosophy that cheap credit is the source of prosperity. . . .

Let the Federal Reserve resort to its original province of being a bankers' bank and not a money-making device for the Treasury or an 'automatic stabilizer' (*sic*) of the business cycle."

The classicists were no doubt correct in pointing out that Federal Reserve policy had had little apparent effect in the months following the break in the market. But it is probable that they were right for the wrong reasons. First of all, it was not at all certain that the Federal Reserve was following an all-out cheap-money policy; and second, the policy may have failed not for the reasons implied by Aldrich and other financiers, but because the banks were afraid to lend. Certainly, there was much evidence to support this latter hypothesis. Small businessmen were constantly complaining that the economy needed more money, and that banks were overly niggardly in making loans. Some of them bitterly attacked the Federal Reserve for not making money cheaper and more plentiful. One, George W. Armstrong, president of the Texas Steel Company and author of a little-known book called *The Calamity of 1930: To Hell With Wall St.*, told a Senate committee, "It must be obvious that the cause of the depression is the deflation of all values as measured by the dollar. The deflation of 1930 has been brought about by the operations of the Federal Reserve System in precisely the same manner as the system brought on the deflation of 1920, *viz.*, by the contraction and hoarding of money and credit and by advancing the rediscount rate."

Others blamed the bankers rather than the Federal Reserve for the shortage of capital. They wrote to their congressmen and to the President of the United States accusing the bankers of plotting to undermine the American economy. To some extent, this was a symptom of the old antagonism between the industrialists and the financiers. Clearly, that was true in the case of Rudolph Spreckels, the sugar magnate, who had himself been involved in the Kolster Radio pool during the halcyon days of 1929. Spreckels explained that "the depression had been caused by bankers who duped the public in order to protect their foreign loans." But most of those who complained about the banks thought they had more substance to their remarks. W. W. Finney, president of the Empire Kansas Telephone Company, wrote to Senator Capper in 1932 about "the serious situation that has developed as a result of the attitude of most of the large bankers in Kansas." Finney said that one bank in Topeka had called in loans until it had $6 million in deposits and $1 million in loans. He quoted another banker as having said, "There is not a good bank in

New York City that would loan a dollar to anybody at this time under any circumstances. Good banks are all collecting their money regardless of the wreckage it entails." Another letter, written to Capper and turned over to President Hoover, reported that "the banks in Wichita have agreed that they will not under present conditions loan any money for any purpose on any security." All this the banks hotly denied. B. W. Trafford of the First National of Boston said that he "had never heard of anybody not getting money for their commercial needs." Wiggin was quick to agree with him. And Jackson Reynolds of the National City Bank of New York explained that an absence of borrowers was responsible for the lack of bank credit, "You cannot get anybody to borrow now except in institutions for the feeble minded."[17]

A minority of bankers did think that there really was a shortage of money. Harry E. Ward of the Irving Trust Company thought that the Federal Reserve banks should not be confined to rediscounting short-term paper. Although he did not specifically say so, he implied that the central bank should be able to discount anything, so that banks that were in trouble would be able to raise funds even on illiquid assets. It was difficult in 1930 and 1931 to find other bankers who felt the same way. When it was suggested that the rules for rediscounting be eased, the Economic Policy Committee of the ABA* saw serious disadvantages in the proposal, insisting that it would lead to inflation and make reserve credit less liquid. Apparently assuming that the money supply was going down because businessmen did not want to borrow, the committee reported: "It would appear that the banks have no need for enlarged sources of eligible paper since they are using so small a proportion of what they have." And when it was urged that something be done to protect banks from threatened ruin, for example, broadening the power to establish branches or passing laws to establish deposit insurance, most bankers found many ways to express their opposition.

* Consisting of R. S. Hecht, chairman; George Roberts, Leonard Ayres, Nathan Adams (Dallas), Frank W. Blair (Detroit), Walter W. Head, W. D. Longyear (Los Angeles), W. S. McLucas (Kansas City), Melvin Traylor, Paul Warburg, O. H. Wolfe (Philadelphia), among others.

BRANCH BANKING AND DEPOSIT INSURANCE

Branch banking was a subject for spirited debate during the twenties. Most objective experts on banking believed that widening the power to establish branches would reduce the scandalous rate of bank failures. They pointed to the Canadian and British systems where branch banking was the rule rather than the exception and where few could remember the date of the last bank failure. But bankers divided about evenly between the pros and the cons. It, therefore, proved impossible to get more than a token branch-banking bill through Congress. Now as bank failures became ever more common, another effort was made, and again opinion was divided. Country bankers were of course opposed; they were the friends of "the little fellow" and they seemed to imply that independent unit banking and freedom from "monopoly" were worth the price of a few bank failures.

Many big-city bankers either opposed branch banking or equivocated on the question. Cynics charged that correspondent relationships with small banks might have something to do with this, and circumstantial evidence supported their case. The only big bankers who favored branch banking without qualification were Thomas Lamont of J. P. Morgan and Edmund Platt of the Marine Midland. George Davison of the Central Hanover Trust Company opposed any liberalization of the law. B. W. Trafford did "not see any need for branch banking in New England." Albert Wiggin told Congress that "our own preference would be not to see any extension of branch banking." The ABA favored branch banking on a community basis, as did Owen D. Young, director of the Federal Reserve Bank of New York.

Insuring commercial bank deposits showed the same division of opinion, with most bankers opposing the idea. It was easy to understand why bankers in the big cities opposed it. They thought that deposit guarantee would put a premium on bad banking. It was remotely possible that the Chase Bank might close its doors on a day other than a bank holiday, but it was absolutely certain that the Chase Bank would pay premiums to cover the possible losses of a small bank. It was harder to understand why so many small banks opposed the plan. Yet in the congressional hearings, which were stacked in favor of the bill by Representative Steagall, its sponsor, it was apparent that the majority of small bankers opposed deposit insurance, the one thing that at that time might have restored a sense of security for both bankers and depositors.[18]

OVERPRODUCTION, CHEAP MONEY, AND GOVERNMENT SPENDING

Although most bankers followed the orthodox tenets in which they had been trained, there were a few mavericks. Some had idiosyncracies on one specific belief and a few were out-and-out nonconformists. Most bankers followed J. B. Say, the eighteenth-century French economist, in believing that *general* overproduction was impossible. The supply of *some* goods might at times be a glut on the market, but it was impossible for the supply of *all* goods to be excessive. But during the depression there were some who lost their faith and bought the far-fetched idea that the United States was suffering from too much goods and services. W. H. Crocker, the San Francisco banker, explained the depression in one word: "overproduction." Otto Kahn cited "the overstimulation of production" as one of the many reasons for the existing crisis. He recommended the modification of the Clayton Act as a means of dealing with the problem. He also recommended old-age pensions and health insurance, public works, government relief, and at the same time *rigorous economy and modification of the tax structure.* James Speyer, another international banker, also showed the influence of his German background by saying, "Changing conditions make it advisable to change our anti-trust laws enabling our manufacturers, under reasonable restrictions, to combine . . . so as to avoid uneconomic plant expansion and overproduction." Speyer was also far from typical in favoring expenditures for public works and in believing, "a reduction of wages ought to be avoided if possible."[19]

Here and there, a few bankers rebelled against the classical strictures that forbade any tinkering with the money supply. Of these, the most rebellious was Frank A. Vanderlip, the retired head of the National City Bank. Vanderlip occupied the same position in the banking fraternity on the question of money supply that Professor Irving Fisher occupied among monetary economists. Both were regarded as brilliant eccentrics who were quite mad on the subject of money. Fisher believed that prices in general could be raised or lowered by increasing or decreasing the amount of gold in back of the dollar, or to explain this in another way, by raising or lowering the price of gold. The logic was simple and the proposition was plausible. If the amount of gold in the dollar was reduced, more dollars could be created with the same amount of gold, and since money like everything else was subject to the law of supply and demand, a greater supply of dollars would reduce the value of each dollar, so that each dollar would buy less. In other words, prices would go up. Vanderlip agreed wholeheartedly with this reasoning. In November 1932, he brought together a small group of businessmen and formed the Committee for the Nation,* which quickly became a voice for inflation. In the spring of 1933, it recommended that the government raise the price of gold from $20.67 an ounce to $36.17 an ounce; in September 1933, it raised its sights and recommended an increase to $41.34 an ounce. Meanwhile, too, Vanderlip supported a series of bills introduced by Representative Goldsborough instructing the Federal Reserve System to use its powers to raise prices to the level they had been in 1926.

Vanderlip's influence is a matter of debate. He was an intensely dynamic personality, and having been a financial journalist, he could express himself effectively. Within the financial world he did have a few sympathizers: R. C. Leffingwell, a Morgan partner and former Assistant Secretary of the Treasury, and George L. Burr, partner in Lazard Freres and a champion of bimetallism. But Vanderlip had no real allies in Wall Street. As for his political influence, it was insignificant during the Hoover years, for Secretaries Mellon and Mills would see or hear nothing that clashed with the classical analysis. Things were different under the first New Deal. Then, heretical as well as orthodox ideas on money got a thorough hearing. Vanderlip and Fred I. Kent, who had much more orthodox views on money, both tried to keep President Roosevelt informed with written memos and personal interviews. Vanderlips's views ultimately won, but this was probably more because of the efforts of other articulate champions of unorthodox monetary theories than because of Vanderlip's persuasive powers.

On issues other than money, Vanderlip's opinions were those of a

* The committee also included James H. Rand, Jr., of Remington Rand; F. H. Frazier, chairman of the General Baking Co.; Lessing Rosenwald and General Robert Wood of Sears, Roebuck; Vincent Bendix, the airplane tycoon; and Robert Harriss, a broker.

typical big-city banker. He was opposed to government spending and wanted a balanced budget, by the imposition of a sales tax if necessary. As a rebel against the consensus, he was not in the same class as Marriner S. Eccles, the president of the First Security Corporation of Ogden, Utah. Since Eccles later became the head of the Federal Reserve Board and remained in that position for half a generation, his views were undoubtedly more influential than those of any other banker and, therefore, deserve much more space.

Eccles' opinions about the depression were not only different from those of other bankers, but also different from those of the general public and most academic economists and financial commentators. He was one of the early proponents of government spending and government deficits as a way out of the depression. He first achieved prominence when he made a lengthy statement to the Senate Finance Committee in its "Investigation of Economic Problems." What he said at that time came as a traumatic shock to the orthodox. "Along with other businessmen," he recalled, "I believed (in 1928) we had reached a state where depressions and panics were a thing of the past. The American dream had been put on a sound statistical basis." This illusion had been shattered by the great crash, and even though he was more than forty years old, an age at which one's prejudices, biases, and philosophy are supposed to have thoroughly congealed, Eccles' ideas underwent a fundamental transformation. He became convinced that the cause of economic difficulties was not overproduction; it was oversaving. Thrift, he recognized, was a primary social virtue, but because of the passing of the frontier, the lower rate of population growth, and the change from a debtor to a creditor country, "we have now reached the stage where further advance in the national income depends on finding adequate outlets for the nation's savings. . . . Too large a share of income goes into the hands of savers and too small a share into the hands of consumers."*

Unlike some early New Dealers and many businessmen, including Bernard Baruch and Gerard Swope, he did not favor "government planning." On the contrary, he "opposed governmental action which would dictate the terms of our business life beyond what is essential to protect the public interest." What he did favor was "to have the government use its functional powers of taxation, public expenditure, and monetary policy in maintaining a reasonable balance be-

---

* It is clear that Eccles was a precursor of the economic analysis that John Maynard Keynes and Alvin Hansen later would promulgate so effectively.

tween that part of the national income which goes into savings and
that part which goes into consumption."

Specifically, Eccles recommended that the federal government
make a gift of $500 million to the states and that it lend $2.5 billion
or more to cities and states for the construction of public works,
including roads, bridges, public housing, and educational facilities.
By today's standards, these amounts were picayune, but at the time,
they were considered revolutionary. Eccles sought to soften the blow
by explaining that if he had his choice, he would always have a balanced budget, but "experience had demonstrated that the budget cannot be balanced in severe depressions by either increasing taxes or
decreasing expenditures or by doing both. I contend that the volume
of government expenditures should be increased in a depression and
should be so planned, so timed, and so adequately scaled as to result
in diminishing the duration of the depression." He challenged those
who were shouting and pleading for a balanced budget: "Is it consistent to demand at this time a balanced budget by the inauguration
of a sales tax, further reducing the buying power of our people? Is it
necessary to conserve government credit to the point of providing a
starvation existence for millions of our people? Is the present lack of
confidence due to an unbalanced budget?"[20]

Eccles insisted that many businessmen agreed with him and he
cited a couple of them in Utah; but the majority judgment was more
accurately expressed by the president of a Western railroad when he
said, "Poor Eccles! He must have so terrible a time with his banks
that he is losing his mind."

THE CURES AS GIVEN BY NON-BANKING FINANCIERS

Other financiers, life insurance executives, savings bankers, and
speculators shared most of the views of the commercial and investment bankers. It would have been strange if they had not, for they
all ate at the same table. David Houston of the Mutual Life of New
York, onetime Secretary of Agriculture and later Secretary of the
Treasury, told the Senate Finance Committee in 1933 that it "seemed
obvious" that the Great War supplied the background of the depression. Like other financiers, he stressed the ill effects of the "period of
speculation," in which "most things expanded too rapidly." As he
recalled it, "there were few communities in which people of all classes

were not speculating. Even when you tried to stop them it was difficult to do so. Some of us who urged caution in the later part of 1928 and during 1929 were told we were out of date."

Like the bankers, Houston subscribed to the notion that history repeated itself. Depressions were, therefore, like the common cold; not much could be done about them. But he did recommend a balanced budget, and cautioned against precipitate action. He opposed deposit insurance as a "premium on bad banking."

Houston's colleague, Edward Duffield of the Prudential, was more optimistic and equally unoriginal. To him, the "fundamental difficulty was a general lack of confidence" caused by government deficits and fears that "in some way our monetary system will be radically changed." The cure for public unrest was to balance the budget and put an end to the threat of inflation. He did not "doubt that every member of Congress agreed with him" about balancing the budget, but they were not putting their hearts into it, for "it is a factor in the uncertainty that Federal expenditures have for a period of years exceeded receipts."* Duffield also chided the easy-money advocates. "We hear," he said, "a great deal about controlled inflation. But the difficulty is where will you control inflation?"

The questions that Duffield left hanging in the air were brought to earth by Bernard Baruch, who was the star witness before the Senate Finance Committee's investigation of the economic crisis. It is impossible to catalogue Baruch. He was not a businessman, a broker, or a banker. He was, of course, a speculator, but he must have been a "good speculator," for he was admired and respected by many of those who looked down their noses at other speculators. He was a philosopher of the park bench, an adviser of Presidents, and, as Arthur M. Schlesinger said, not so much a man as an institution.

Baruch as always had as much to say about the depression as anyone. He thought that it was caused by the war and postwar inflation, debts and taxes, national self-containment, and overcapacity to produce. He reduced the four horsemen to three: overproduction, unbalanced budgets, and inflation.

In May 1930, certainly as early as anyone else, Baruch told a gullible audience that we were the victims of too much. "For a good many centuries," he said, "the peril of the poor was famine—scarcity

---

* The federal government, on the contrary, had substantial surpluses in every year from 1920 through 1930. It had a small deficit in 1931, a large one in 1932, and was running substantially in the red when Duffield made his statement.

of things. It is a curious paradox that too many things—overproduction—should now be the wolf at the cottage door." What should be done about it? Why, the anti-trust laws should be amended to permit collaboration among business firms against the depression. Consistent in his action, Baruch was a strong proponent of the Agricultural Adjustment Act to control overproduction on the farm and the National Industrial Recovery Act to prevent overproduction in the factory. But at the same time, he saw nothing inconsistent in telling Congress to "reject all plans which oppose or postpone the working of natural processes."

Baruch's second *bête noire* was the unbalanced budget. "Delay in balancing the budget," he lectured Congress, "is trifling with disaster." He recommended that federal spending be reduced to $3 billion (it was running at $4.8 billion), for "from the moment that we balance the budget and return to orthodox policy, money will flow here from all the world and out of every cautious domestic hoard. There is no magic in this conclusion. It is the simple arithmetic of the oldest axioms in the world." Somewhat confusingly, Baruch denied that the balanced budget would mean that there would be no money for relief. "It means that there would be more money. The credit of the government would be increased and bonds could be sold to almost any reasonable extent for the purposes of relief." Baruch also had ideas on money and inflation. "For three years, we have conducted a vast but vain experiment in inflation. . . . Money cannot go back to work in an atmosphere filled with the threat to destroy its value." As for the people who talked about "gradually inflating," one might as well talk about "firing off a gun gradually."[21]

This, then, was the point of view of the financial people. It was very neat, very reasonable, and very plausible. Most bankers and insurance executives felt very satisfied with it, and none of them had the remotest idea that what seemed so brilliant then would in a decade come to be regarded as a tedious piece of antiquarianism.

THE CAUSES AND CURES ACCORDING TO THE INDUSTRIALISTS

Like the bankers, many non-financial businessmen thought that depressions were, as Henry S. Dennison expressed it, "inevitable." L. F. Loree, the picturesque and historically minded head of the Delaware and Hudson Railroad, told the Senate, "These disturbances have occurred intermittently and usually run three to six years." Or as P. W. Litchfield told the same committee, "The inevitable day of reckoning came," and in Schwab's words, the best thing to do was "just grin, keep on working, stop worrying about the future, and go ahead as best we can."[22]

When the inevitable came, businessmen could not resist explaining it. This depression, they believed, was like all depressions, the result of "profound dislocations," including the war, the extravagances of prosperity, and international difficulties. "The major causes of the depression," explained Litchfield, "might properly be lumped together under the embracing title of extravagance. . . . Producing more and more goods, paying more and more wages. . . . Senses of values were lost. The counsel of prudence was hooted." Litchfield brought his analysis to a close with what seemed a premeditated *non sequitur.* "In other words," he said, "we discounted the inexorable law of supply and demand." Twenty-five years later, Litchfield still thought that the depression was the result of extravagant living: "We had gone through an era of prosperity and with people as optimistic about the morrow as Americans are, many forgot the age-old principles of thrift and saving for the rainy day, were living beyond their means, buying things they did not need. As people overbought . . . manufacturers overproduced. Buying fell off. . . . Orders stopped coming in. . . . Manufacturers who had not been prudent had no money to pay wages. . . . Men were thrown out of work, purchasing power declined, the thing built up like a snowball. There was another factor. . . . People bought commodities, securities, and properties on margin. . . . When the market broke, some thirty billion in paper profits went down the drain. . . ."[23]

Thus far, the analysis was very similar to what was being said on Wall, State, La Salle, Market, and Chestnut streets. The point of departure came when businessmen talked, as many of them did, about overproduction and underconsumption, oversaving and maldistribution of income, and tight and easy money.

Unlike the bankers, few industrialists and few merchants were infatuated with classical theory. They were in awe of it, for they had been taught that it was the only true economic theory. But they did not understand it and they did not sympathize with it. The non-financial community found it especially difficult to swallow two of the most important planks in orthodox economics: that competition was "good" and that easy money was "bad." Most, but not all, industrialists were intrigued by easy-money arguments, and many industrialists and most merchants were not at all sure that competition would automatically produce the greatest good for the greatest number. Industrialists argued heatedly for the suspension of the anti-trust laws, so that production would be regulated to "meet demand." Merchants, too, talked about overproduction and underconsumption, and some spoke knowingly about oversaving.

Much of the thinking on overproduction was a holdover from the era of prosperity, when it became fashionable to think that production was a solved problem and that distribution—how to sell the goods that the production mill turned out—was now the great puzzle. Some manufacturers and many merchants came to believe that there was an upper limit to human wants. The limit had been reached by miraculous increases in production. Unless production could be curtailed, a perpetual flood of goods would glut the market.

A report submitted to the United States Chamber of Commerce in 1931 offered the best example of the overproduction approach. It was based on the premise that businessmen, in seeking to maximize their profits, speculate in land, securities, and commodities. This speculation causes an overexpansion of productive capacity and an overextension of credit, leading to overproduction in the sense that more goods are produced than can be sold at prices high enough to produce acceptable rates of profit. Silas Strawn, president of the Chamber and also president of Montgomery Ward, announced that the Chamber's consensus agreed with the report by ascribing the depression to increased production that had outstripped consumption and to "excessive incursions of the state into the domain of private enterprise."[24]

Another sizable group of businessmen, in which automobile executives were prominent, disagreed strongly with this simplified overproduction explanation of the depression. On this score at least, this group of executives was much more attuned to the classical line of thinking than they were to that of their industrial colleagues. They denied emphatically that there was or could be such a thing as overproduction. According to Henry Ford, the most fundamental business principle was "to make an ever increasingly large quantity of goods of the best possible quality, to make them in the best and most economical fashion and force them out on the market."

Still a third group, including many merchants, argued that the difficulty with the economy was not overproduction, but underconsumption. Paul Mazur of Lehman Brothers was one of the most articulate spokesmen for this thesis. In a series of books, Mazur attempted to explain the whole business cycle with its causes and its consequences. In his opinion, low costs and high consumption, encouraged by installment selling, had produced prosperity. In explaining the depression, Mazur agreed with his banking colleagues in their emphasis on the obstacles that stood in the way of a free flow of international trade. But he considered this less important than underconsumption. According to Mazur, underconsumption was a monetary phenomenon. He argued that the supply of money and credit had not kept in step with production; the latter had increased at a geometric rate, while the former had multiplied at an arithmetic rate, thus starving purchasing power and leading eventually to chronic underconsumption. He also believed that most of the talk about overproduction stressed the wrong thing for the wrong reason. It made production the goal of economics whereas consumption should be the goal. Moreover, according to Mazur, "Those who have raised the cry of overproduction have usually delivered their warnings from an overstuffed chair, or in the luxurious surroundings of a Pullman Car."[25]

The underconsumptionists had decided opinions about what caused it. A few, like Mazur, ascribed it to an inadequate money supply. Others argued that the condition resulted from too much saving or from inadequate wages, which produced a maldistribution of income. Foster and Catchings were the most popular exponents of the oversaving idea, but the most indefatigable were E. A. Filene and Henry S. Dennison. Filene tried to convince his readers that the American economy had undergone so revolutionary a change that the concepts that had once been true were now dangerous. In an era when capital goods were scarce, saving was imperative. Even though such saving had resulted in hardship for large numbers of people, it had been beneficial in the long run, for it had made possible the machinery that produced immense amounts of wealth. But now in the machine age, saving was no longer as necessary as it had been. Now there was a plentitude of capital goods, and it was imperative to emphasize spending. And spending was inadequate not because there were too many goods, but because there was too little purchasing power. Filene, therefore, urged a more equitable distribution of income, higher wages, and lower prices.[26]

In the oft-quoted, multi-thousand page Senate "Investigation of

Economic Problems," Henry S. Dennison presented a comprehensive analysis of the great depression. To him the most important aspect of the depression—transcending the long-term declining trend in prices, agricultural stress, and unsatisfactory international relations—was its occurrence "after several years during which, in spite of the rising standard of living of the masses, there was a largely increased proportion of the produced wealth going to the well-to-do, and hence into investment channels, and this just at a time when improved technique of all sorts was making our chief need consuming power rather than renewed investment." Dennison, expressing the industrialist's low opinion of the financier, included as the last in his list of causes of the depression: "a banking management far below the high level of professional standards with which bankers have been credited."

The depression, like politics, attracted strange bedfellows. Liberal businessmen, like Filene and Dennison, were joined by other industrialists, ordinarily considered very reactionary, in thinking that inadequate wages and unequal distribution of income had contributed importantly to the depression. Consider, for example, the case of Ernest T. Weir. Through his activities in the Liberty League and his determined anti-labor unionism, Weir managed, during the 1930s, to build up a reputation as a ruthless reactionary. Yet this was the man who said in 1933, "People have suffered to an extent that I think is not thoroughly recognized."* In explaining the causes of the depression, Weir did not talk the way an arch-reactionary was supposed to talk: "There is no question," he stated, "but that the percentage that went to capital was considerably in excess of a fair division. This had its influence on the breakdown and on the extent of the depression." Sloan, another Liberty Leaguer, told the House, "Unemployment has reached such proportions and has continued over such a long period, affecting the morale and economic position of such a large proportion of the people that most anything is justified that appears to offer a reasonable chance of relief." And John E. Edgerton, in a mood of candor or perhaps of disappointment, admitted, "Unemployment insurance, old-age relief, and the problem of the machine are receiving consideration from manufacturers who would not have thought of them a few short years ago."[28]

---

* Compare this with what Mary Pickford told the "privileged class" in the Welfare Island Workhouse in 1932, "The depression is really a privilege. You boys and girls should consider your time here really a privilege, a sort of exercise for your spiritual muscles."[27]

The solutions proposed by those outside of Wall Street covered as wide a territory as their opinions about the causes of the depression. They ranged from the laconic advice of the utility tycoon S. Z. Mitchell, "more work and less talk" and Harvey Firestone's, "good hard work" to the detailed "plans" of Gerard Swope and the Chamber of Commerce. But in no case did a businessman descend to the fatuous level achieved by Bernarr MacFadden when he said, "find jobs for the jobless. . . . I have maintained again and again that men who cannot find work in the city should go to the country." Nor did they ever achieve the heights attained by former President Coolidge, who explained that "when more and more people are thrown out of work, unemployment results. . . . The final solution of unemployment is work." Some of the free-lance economists also demonstrated that in retrospect they were no more aware of what was going on than were the most banal businessmen.[29]

For the most part, businessmen agreed with the bankers in recommending the settlement of international debts. But, unlike the bankers, they were divided sharply on the question of tariffs with the majority, mostly in steel, defending protection, and the minority, especially in automobiles, recommending tariff reductions. Occasionally, as had always been the case with protectionists who believed in laissez-faire, tariff opinion had its amusing side. Durant, for example, greeted the Hawley-Smoot tariff with the opinion that it would "protect manufacturers and put business on a sound basis when the government stops interfering with it."

A few industrialists, hypnotized by the fear of inflation that was still making the rounds in Wall Street, were resigned to the inevitability of severe deflation. "There is," lamented General Atterbury of the Pennsylvania Railroad, "no panacea for a resumption of prosperity except the slow, painful one of hitting the bottom." But most industrialists and retailers, being much less defeatist, regarded the cathartic approach with something more than distaste. "There is entirely too much talk at present about inflation," Thomas J. Watson told the Jeremiahs. "Persons who mention this subject should be asked to be more specific and to define what they mean." Henry L. Doherty of City Service impatiently asserted, "Economy has become such a fetish in national life that it threatens to defeat its own purpose."

Even though it was true that few non-bankers were resigned to accepting the dour outlook of the classicists, most businessmen remained faithful to the gold standard and to orthodox principles like "sound money." But these principles if followed to their logical conclusion led remorselessly to deflating the money supply, and the price and wage level, and most industrialists and merchants, inconsistent as it was, sympathized with easy money and supported—at least in their expressed opinion—high wages.

Somewhat surprisingly, considering their interest in money, few non-financial executives commented on Federal Reserve monetary policy. Most of those who did seemed to want easy money, but they opposed, at least orally, easy-money policies if practiced by the central bank. In this, they were very much like William Jennings Bryan and the Populist party in 1896; they thought it was right for the government to take steps to increase the amount of money, but wrong for the bankers to do so. Durant was one outstanding exception. He continued to carry on a personal vendetta with the Federal Reserve System to which he "ascribed the hard times" and which he blamed for the coming "more pronounced tendency toward socialism and communism."

On other banking matters, opinion was equally sparse. Some, like Weir, thought the government should protect "the banking situation" but should not insure bank deposits because that would put a "premium on bad banking." Others, including Alexander Legge of International Harvester and Owen D. Young, favored a partial guarantee.

Industrialists also disagreed with the bankers' recommendation that wage reduction was a necessary precondition for economic recovery. All through the depression, Ford continued to champion the high-wage doctrine just as he had done in the previous twenty years. Early in 1930, he said, "wages are too low everywhere. Those who are lowering wages now don't know what they are doing." Ford had plenty of company. General Robert Wood of Sears spoke out against wage cuts. So did James A. Farrell of the Steel Company. "Oh, no," said Farrell in early 1930, "wages in the steel industry are not coming down. If you are going to sell your goods and expect to get it out of the man in the mills, you are mistaken." In October, however, U. S. Steel did reduce wages 10 per cent. E. T. Weir also favored high wages; as late as 1933, he was still insisting that "better wages" would have to be paid, although by then his company had instituted five wage cuts. Sloan tied wages to productivity and denied that big business was leading or even sympathizing with the policy of lowering wages "for the plain reason that unless wages be high—although their cost in production must be low—there will not be enough purchasing power created to move the finished product."[30]

In spite of all this opinion, however, wages were being reduced. In the fall of 1929, nearly four times as many employers reported increases to the Bureau of Labor Statistics as reported reductions. During 1930, the news was quite the opposite; only 125 firms reported increases, while 900 had cut wages. In 1931, over 3500 firms with over 650,000 employees slashed the factory payroll. By October 1932, wage reductions were common and the average size reduction was almost 20 per cent.

Since the campaign to prevent wage reductions was demonstrably a lost cause, many prominent executives, including Taylor, Gifford, and Sloan, listened sympathetically to schemes for sharing what employment there was. K. R. Kingsbury of Standard Oil of California told the Industrial and Banking Committee of the 12th Federal Reserve District that sharing the work even with a pay reduction would have job-expanding results. Assume, explained Kingsbury, that four men are employed at $125 each and that it costs $100 a month to live with $25 "possibly going into the savings bank, more likely into the sock." By sharing the work, five would be hired at $100 each and one of the effects of this will be that $100 will be "added to the buying power and put into circulation."

OVERPRODUCTION, A "PLANNED SOCIETY," AND THE ANTI-TRUST LAWS

Executives talked occasionally about monetary policy and at some length about international debts, tariffs, and wages, but they lavished whatever enthusiasm they could muster on two proposals: first, the various "plans" to combat the problem of overproduction, and later, the need for balancing the budget. As was said earlier, Bernard Baruch was the first to propose a specific method for dealing with overproduction. In May 1930, the former head of the War Industries Board told the Boston Chamber of Commerce: "It may have been sound policy to forbid regulation of production when the world was in fear of famine, but it is public lunacy to decree unlimited operation of a system which periodically disgorges masses of unconsumable products." Baruch then went on to propose the creation of a "tribunal which should have power to suggest and to sanction or license such common-sense cooperation among industrial units as will prevent our economic blessings from becoming unbearable burdens." Louis Kirstein, who, along with Lincoln Filene, ran the Filene department store, wrote Baruch that his speech "made a hell of a fine impression here in Boston." Kirstein continued to feel that the country suffered from too much. In October 1934, he told a group of retailers: "It is your job to create obsolescence. The very idea will be opposed on the theory that it is an economic waste. That idea was probably excellent in days when food was scarce and work was plenty, but it is certainly obsolete in a day when food is plentiful and work scarce."[31]

Baruch's plan was based on a simple premise and a simple theory. The premise was that the country was suffering from overproduction.* The theory was even simpler. If producers could be persuaded or coerced to reduce production, prices could be raised, wages could be paid, and profits could be made. It did not seem to occur to the many who espoused this simple theory that cutting production would also cut employment. What they were proposing to do was to get fat by starving themselves.

In his speech at Boston, Baruch was almost a year ahead of his time. As was always the case, his remarks were given an attentive reception, but there was no rush to join in agitating for his plan. After all, it was not until early 1931 that most business leaders accepted the fact that a depression existed. Then a stream of writing on the problem of overproduction began to gush forth. Most of these writings echoed Baruch's view that the country was suffering from too much rather than too little. In retrospect, it is difficult to understand how such a conclusion could have been reached by sane men when per capita income was down to a little over $600 and falling rapidly. Nevertheless, the world of economics was innundated by proposals for modification of the anti-trust laws, so that business would be in a position "to stabilize itself," as the phrase of the day had it; or as Magnus W. Alexander of the National Industrial Conference Board more bluntly expressed it, "Overproduction and overexpansion require a change in the anti-trust laws to permit combination and control." Anticipating criticism from academic theorists, Alexander warned businessmen "not to permit economic thinking to assume the aspect of a rigid dogma."

---

* Newspapers were fond of printing little fillers demonstrating the "fact" of overproduction. One such item told of competition so cutthroat that one store gave five cents to every customer who accepted a free dress.

It was soon apparent that suggestions for planning could take one of two main roads—one leading to a system of "self-regulation of business" designed to eliminate "unfair competition," to restrict production, and to fix prices; the other leading to regulation of business under a system of planned production that had admittedly received much inspiration from what was going on in the Soviet Union. The former road would make the government an incidental advisory agent with the planners being businessmen; the latter would give enormous power to government with a few supermen acting as planners. The majority of businessmen supported self-regulation. Henry S. Dennison was one of the very few who supported planning under government aegis. When he described his plan at the Symposium of the Institute of Politics, it was immediately denounced by Professor T. E. Gregory of the London School of Economics as "a business man's short cut to economic serfdom."[32]

The various trade associations were the first to jump on the planning bandwagon. Early in 1931, the NAM urged modification of the anti-trust laws,* and in the summer the Chamber of Commerce issued a lengthy report proposing that "business be allowed to enter into contracts for the purpose of equalizing production and consumption." The Chamber did not suggest that the anti-trust laws be repealed, but it did urge the creation of a National Economic Council to "deal with the tendency of productive capacity to outrun the ability to buy." Shortly thereafter, Gerard Swope, a prominent member of the Chamber, addressed the trade association of the electric producers and outlined the most famous of all blueprints for a "planned society." The Swope Plan contemplated the organization of all industrial and commercial companies with fifty or more employees (less than 2 per cent of all firms) into trade associations under the supervision of the federal government. The federal government would act merely as an advisory and regulatory body and as a provider of unemployment insurance where it was "impracticable to stabilize industry and employment." The trade associations would outline trade practices, business ethics, methods of accounting, and would collect and distribute information on the volume of business, the volume of inventory, the standardization of product, and the stabilization of prices. Swope believed that the industries which would take the initiative in "coordinating production and consumption" were long past the point where

* James Emery later stated that the NAM had never favored modification. "We have always opposed exemption from anti-trust laws."

they would "curtail production." What they would do would be to "prevent overproduction." What exactly this meant remained a mystery for some time.

The business world may have been taken by surprise by the Swope Plan, but very few businessmen treated the proposal with indifference. Some thought it the greatest document since Magna Carta. Others thought it provided a staircase for a descent to fascism or communism. Textile and metal processors, more than any other manufacturers, favored restricted production and price fixing. J. W. Cone, a cotton mill operator in North Carolina, said, "Price fixing should be allowed when it is done in the public interest. This would result in increased employment and tend to stabilize legitimate industries." Cornelius Kelly of Anaconda Copper greeted the whole idea with unrestrained enthusiasm. "The time has come," said lawyer Kelly, "when American industry asserts that it must be freed under proper regulations from the artificial restraints of laws that result in a compulsory overproduction of basic commodities, that result in the calamitous drop in prices to levels below the cost of production." C. F. Abbott of the American Institute of Steel Construction was equally enthusiastic. "The Swope Plan," he intoned, "can be called a measure of public safety. . . . We cannot have in this country much longer irresponsible, ill-informed, stubborn, and non-cooperating individualism. . . . Overproduction is comparable to nothing so much as traffic congestion and chaos." Abbott added his own codicil to the Swope Plan. He urged the formation of a cartel which would establish zones and allot orders on a percentage basis. If a firm wished more than its allotted share, it would have to pay a tax.

Other businessmen, such as Edgerton of the NAM, had severe doubts about Swope, and these biased them against his plan. Edgerton thought it was "pretty generally recognized that economic necessities required some modification of the anti-trust laws," but along with some other businessmen, he resented the proposed role of government in the plan. Samuel Vauclain of Baldwin Locomotive dismissed the whole idea with a laconic, "I don't believe in it." President Hoover denounced the plan with a frigid blast, "There is no stabilization of price without price fixing. . . . It is the most gigantic proposal of monopoly ever made in history." Some businessmen, recognizing that the proposals to cut production were the result of quirks in the minds of well-meaning, but naïve people, urged more production, not less. Automobile producers were shocked by what the plans suggested. Machine-tool manufacturer Ralph Flanders thought it "unwise to give us manufacturers power to organize hours and, to use the euphemistic phrase, adjust production to consumption. We had better be adjusting consumption to production."[33]

Whether they liked the Swope Plan or not, more and more and more businessmen urged that something be done to restrict "overproduction" and to fix prices to offset "unfair competition." By 1933, the number of owners and managers who were pleading for planning and clamoring for co-operation could have filled a huge amphitheater with the trade association executives occupying the front rows. The Chamber of Commerce was the leading spokesman for those who desired, if not a complete about-face, at least a strategic retreat from the anti-trust policies that had weathered a very stormy forty years. For over two years, until its efforts finally culminated in the National Industrial Recovery Act, the Chamber recommended that "each trade association, representative of its industry or branch . . . should be permitted to promulgate fair rules for industrial production." The NAM was somewhat more cautious, but one of its long-time leaders, J. A. Emery, was not. "The primary fact," he knew, "is we are confronted with a steadily downward spiral of prices which has led to destructive and demoralizing competition that can be corrected best by enlarging the permissible limits of cooperation within the industries themselves. . . . Let such industries develop their own plan . . . to establish rational standards of competition and employment."[34]

Many individual business executives shared this sentiment. Of the eleven non-financial business leaders who testified to the Senate committee investigating economic problems, seven were in favor of restricting production or of price-fixing of some sort. Three said nothing on the subject, and only one thought such schemes "unwise." Walter C. Teagle of Standard Oil of New Jersey favored "curtailment of production to reasonable demand." General Atterbury, in a long list of things to be done, called on Congress to "materially modify the anti-trust laws" because "competition which for so long had been a fetish in this country is now working industry's own destruction." Litchfield thought that industry and the nation itself were being persecuted by the anti-trust laws, for "were we permitted to establish fair and reasonable prices through group agreements the best interests of the country, social and financial, would be served." Melvin Traylor felt very much the same sense of being mishandled: "I confess I find it extremely hard to believe that constructive, cooperative plans sincerely undertaken by a basic industry for rationally adjusting production to demand and which avoid any attempt artificially to fix or control prices, can be fairly regarded as in restraint of trade or commerce." Another steel man, Ernest Weir, apparently did not believe that industrial prices should be stabilized. At least, his actions were not in that direction, for he was constantly accused of "price cutting," but he did believe in fixing the price of farm products "in harmony with the general domestic price structure."[35]

THE BALANCED BUDGET PANACEA

Although it is probable that the majority of corporation executives favored some sort of curtailment of production and some sort of price-fixing, business did not present a united front on the issue. Some old-line owner-entrepreneurs flirted with the idea of planning, and many career managers pounced upon it as the last hope in a very discouraging world. But other owners and other managers denounced the whole idea as inexcusable folly.

No such schism existed about the desirability of a balanced budget. Almost without exception, every businessman thought that economic recovery was possible only if the federal government learned "to live within its income." As Lew Hahn, the retailer, expressed it, "It is time for all businessmen to get together to demonstrate that government as well as taxpayers must learn to economize." What exactly this meant was as vague among businessmen as it was among financiers and the general public. To some, balancing the budget meant that all expenditures by the government had to be met out of current revenue. Alfred P. Sloan believed that recovery from the depression was up to Congress. It was a simple matter for it to cut expenses, balance the budget, and go home. "The trouble at Washington," he said, "is that large sums have been voted for post offices, pensions and bonuses not justified." General Atterbury agreed, "Budgets should be really balanced. The National Government and its component units should stop making capital expenditures of any kind except those which show a reasonable return on the investment." E. T. Weir and Thomas N. McCarter also opposed expenditures for public works. But others defined a balanced budget more liberally. To them it meant that only "ordinary" expenditures had to be covered by income. Myron Taylor, like most people at that time, thought that the government was just like any other householder. He told the Senate, "The simple rules that we apply in our own lives are those to apply here when our resources begin to shrink. That we live more simply, that we curtail expenditures." But he was very hazy about where the line should be drawn. When Senator La Follette pointed out that U. S. Steel had just paid a dividend despite the fact that it was losing money, Taylor conceded that a balanced budget would allow some borrowing to cover "extraordinary expenses."

But, however defined, businessmen felt a passion for the balanced budget. The member organizations of the Chamber of Commerce voted 1173 to 6 that the federal budget should be balanced. In words that reiterated what the bankers were already saying, Weir enunciated the "well-known fact that even governments cannot carry on indefinitely expenditures in greater volume than income." Daniel Willard, who had a reputation as a liberal businessman, expressed the same sentiment with somewhat less authority. "It has seemed to me," he said, "that there could be no doubt about the desirability of taking early steps to balance the budget. No individual can go on indefinitely living beyond his means." Gerard Swope, considered *very* liberal, also echoed the prevailing sentiment, "It is necessary to bring about a more equal distribution of work. Of equal importance is a balanced budget and a reduction in city, state, and Federal Government expenditures. Just as each individual and private business is constrained to live more simply and economically, so should government. If we are to maintain confidence a definite program should be adopted toward balancing the budget." George H. Houston of Baldwin Locomotive gave the typical business answer to the question of what would happen if government continued to spend more than it took in: government credit would collapse. "The government could not possibly raise sufficient funds through security sales to solve the unemployment problem without disrupting the whole security market." Given the fact that the government was then borrowing at the cheapest rates of interest in history, the answer rated a very low grade.[36]

There was no end to the vague suggestions about how to balance the budget. It was agreed on every side that expenditures would have to be reduced, but just how was not very clear. Some executives, such as Sloan, Weir, and Atterbury, were consistent enough to oppose public works. A few, like General Robert Wood of Sears, Roebuck would have gone even further. They apparently would have put a stop to all federal relief, but if it were given, "it should be on a bare subsistence allowance." But most had no specific suggestions. Daniel Willard, pointing out that governments of all types were spending $15 billion out of a national income of only $40 billion, was positive that costs could be reduced by at least 25 per cent, but he didn't know where. H. I. Harriman recommended cutting the budget by $800 million, one half from the veterans and one half from general government. This was a little more than the $750 million minimum recommended by George W. Rosseter, general chairman of the National Organization to Reduce Public Expenditures.

It was still possible to live in the best of all possible worlds, a world in which expenditures could be cut not only by enough to balance the budget, but by enough to give a tax reduction. This opinion, admittedly that of a minority, was tersely expressed by Eugene Grace of Bethlehem Steel, who thought "taxes must come down, the burden of government costs must be lightened, and the budget must be balanced." A larger group of executives, especially in wholesale and retail trade, would have been satisfied if expenditures could have been lowered by enough to balance the budget without a tax increase. H. M. Karker, president of the Jewel Tea Company, wrote his stockholders urging them to oppose any increase in taxes. C. B. Clark of the National Retail Goods Association was sure no increase in taxes was necessary; "just cut expenses 10 per cent."[37]

But most businessmen were pretty sure that in order to balance the budget, a tax increase would be necessary. Actually, of course, the events of 1932 showed that the budget could not be balanced even with a mammoth increase in tax rates. But this evidence was ignored. What most business leaders proposed was a sales tax, and in some instances, a reduction of income taxes and the imposition of a sales tax. Alexander Legge was not disturbed because the government was "running behind a little in times like this," but lest it last too long, he recommended a sales tax, because the income tax was already too high. Similarly, Daniel Willard favored a sales tax because "the present high tax rates discouraged investment." In the discussion, self-interest was not entirely absent. Atterbury seriously proposed reducing income taxes and eliminating the capital gains tax, which "contributes so largely to speculation," and replacing them with an "ultimate sales tax applied to everyone." Retailers and entertainment entrepreneurs opposed a sales tax, and the automobile industry supported it, if it "were not discriminatory."

HOW THE NON-BUSINESS COMMUNITY VIEWED THE DEPRESSION

Looking back on the years of depression, it is easy to see that businessmen were sadly mistaken in urging the curtailment of production, price fixing, and a balanced budget. They were trying to make society rich by reducing society's income. But they were not the only victims of illusion. Labor union leaders, academic economists, and presidential advisers joined Baruch and Swope in championing grandiose schemes for "planning production." John L. Lewis, Sidney Hillman, Matthew Woll, and William Green argued for "sustained, coordinated planning," and "integrated cooperation within industries." Raymond Moley, Rexford Guy Tugwell, Jerome Frank, and Donald Richberg thought the economy could be lifted by its bootstraps from depression to prosperity through a series of legislated "plans." Some of these advisers later changed their minds, but others continued to carry on the fight. Green, Lewis, and Hillman would eventually lead an all-out struggle for the renewal of the NRA, and Moley thought that "industrial laissez-faire is unthinkable. . . . The interests involved in our economic life are too great to be abandoned to the unpredictable outcome of unregulated competition."

Nor were bankers and businessmen the only ones who supported a balanced budget and the reduced expenditures and higher taxes necessary to achieve it. Three prominent contenders for the 1932 Democratic presidential nomination—Governor Ritchie, former Governor Smith, and Governor Roosevelt—supported a balanced budget. Senator Byrd called for cutting $1 billion out of the federal budget. Governor Smith supported a sales tax. John W. Davis, former presidential candidate, accused President Hoover of following the road to socialism. Governor Roosevelt told the electorate that too often, liberal governments had been wrecked on the shoals of loose fiscal policy. The Democratic platform of 1932 called for an annually balanced budget, and as late as 1935, Senator La Follette said that higher taxes or uncontrolled inflation were the choices.

Matthew Woll, vice president of the AFL, supported a balanced budget and opposed an expanded public works program. Learned professors of economics and money and banking such as Fred R. Fairchild, Norman Silberling, and E. W. Kemmerer, put the balanced budget high on their list of the medicines necessary to restore the country's economic health. In a long letter to Henry Bruere of the Bowery Savings Bank, on leave to the Treasury Department, Professor E. R. A. Seligman of Columbia University, noted authority on public finance, emphasized the need for maintaining government credit by balancing the budget and inspiring confidence.[38]

Some of the most respected journalists in the nation's press were just as sure that a balanced budget was part of the decalogue of economics. In the *Herald Tribune* in January 1932, Walter Lippmann wrote: ". . . the balancing of the Federal budget by reducing expenditures and increasing revenues is the fundamental and indispensable problem before Congress. . . . It should be clearly understood by Congress that the needs of the country at this time can not be met by voting large sums of money."[39]

Why were so very many people so concerned about the balanced budget? Because they believed that without it, the government's credit would be ruined, and, like an individual in similar circumstances, it would go bankrupt. "It must be obvious,"* wrote Lippmann, "that success depends upon maintaining an absolute confidence in the credit of the United States Government. . . . If the feeling can be created that the Government's bonds are secure, that money invested in them is safe, the effect should be like bringing up a new corps of picked, trained, and well-equipped troops behind a shaken army." E. T. Weir put the point much less eloquently and in much fewer words: "A balanced budget would improve government credit." It was just simple economics, and everybody believed in simple economics, except a few odd creatures to whom no one paid any attention anyway.

---

* Strange how much was "obvious" or "perfectly obvious" in a period of frustrating economic puzzlement.

6. THE REACTION TO THE NEW DEAL

"There is always talk, talk about everything and anything from defense of laissez faire in the guise of an Old Tory, to speaking with the beatified and radiant face turned toward the New Deal in the guise of a child of light. The *Filii Aurorae* make me actively sick at my stomach. They are so conceited, so insensitive, so arrogant. But on the whole, the Old Tories are intellectually so moribund. They seem to me as persons more fit associates for gentlemen . . . but are so stupid and emit such dreary, hollow sounds."

Judge Learned Hand, 1934.

Business leaders thought that Calvin Coolidge was one of the greatest Presidents, if not the greatest, in American history. When he did not choose to run in 1928, they were grievously disappointed. But they accepted Hoover. They had no other choice; he was, after all, one of their own, but they were never as fond of him as they were of Coolidge. As the economy ran downhill, they became less fond of him. They even toyed with the idea of dropping him in favor of Roosevelt. Some in fact did, and more of them might have done so had they not feared the folly of "switching horses in mid-stream." Charles M. Schwab told the American Iron and Steel Institute: "Many people want a change because of bad business conditions. I believe the best way to better conditions is to elect Mr. Hoover. This is no time to make a change." James H. Rand of the Remington Rand family warned, "Any man, however wise and able, who comes into office now . . . is going to compel us to stand around and wait while he learns the ropes." Henry Ford also plowed the given line, "I support the best man for the job, Herbert Hoover. Why bring in a new recruit and retard the seasoned veteran?" The Democratic National Committee, in great glee, promptly revealed that Ford had not bothered to register and thus could not vote.[1]

Of the presidents of the one hundred largest corporations, sixty listed their politics, but only eighteen were Democrats, and most of these were from the South. Among the prominent businessmen who supported Roosevelt were Jesse Jones, Texas millionaire; Harvey Couch, Southern utility tycoon; the Reynolds Tobacco family; Rudolph Hecht, New Orleans banker; Bernard Baruch; Jackson Reynolds; Melvin Traylor; Owen D. Young; John D. Ryan; Edward L. Doheny; Nathan Straus; Sam Lewisohn; and Russell Leffingwell.*

Fortune magazine had to look hard in January 1933 to dig out these names. But business no longer spoke the public consensus, for Roosevelt won the 1932 election handily. When he came into office, the country was in a state of shock, and the business and banking community was at the height of despair. The first few electric days of the New Deal gave it new hope. This quickly wore off, however, for the coexistence between government and business was, as always, an uneasy one. Business and government are natural enemies. They have been known to get along, but not usually. Except in times of crisis, most businessmen thought that government was parasitic and served no purpose at all. Fred I. Kent, the retired banker, expressed this point of view succinctly and unapologetically when he wrote in the *New York Sun:* "Government could lapse and if the people were fairly intelligent, and, in general, rightminded, communities could continue—and constructively—provided business did not lapse." According to Kent, the functions of a "proper government" were 1) to allow mankind to live in peace and comfort, 2) to permit the greatest possible individual freedom consistent with safety, 3) to encourage private enterprise under sound government regulation, 4) not to operate business in competition with the people, and 5) to confine government spending to normal amounts. Kent added two subheads under

---

* The largest gifts to the Republican party were from the Mellon family ($53,500); Eldridge R. Johnson of the Victor Talking Machine Company ($50,-000); the Pratt family of Standard Oil ($36,500); the Rockefeller family ($35,-000); Edward Hutton ($35,000); the Guggenheim family ($32,000); Ogden L. Mills ($30,704); Firestone family ($30,000); William Nelson Cromwell, corporation lawyer ($28,000); and Mr. and Mrs. Herbert Straus of R. H. Macy & Co. ($22,000).

The largest gifts to the Democratic party came from John J. Raskob ($125,-000); Bernard Baruch and William H. Woodin ($45,000 each); Vincent Astor ($35,000); William Randolph Hearst and R. W. Morrison of Texas ($25,000 each); M. L. Benedum, Texas oil man ($22,500); and Pierre S. du Pont ($14,-500). The above casts some doubt upon the oft-repeated assertion that consumer-goods businessmen supported Roosevelt and producer-goods businessmen supported the Republicans.

the second edict: "Higher grades of intelligence may not be submerged by lower grades" and "Incentives to the accumulation of private property" should be "furthered." A differing opinion offered by Gerard Swope was unquestionably out of harmony with the general run of business thinking. "Happily when you come to democracy," said Swope, "well-being is much more important than efficiency. The ideal of the American family is to secure the greatest happiness from life, and it is not always the most efficient government that is going to give that."[2]

THE INEVITABILITY OF THE CONFLICT BETWEEN BUSINESS AND THE NEW DEAL

The antagonism that business felt toward government was more a question of power than a question of economic self-interest. Businessmen liked Coolidge because he knew his place. He offered no challenge to their leadership. Brilliant politician that he was, he was willing, indeed glad, in the atmosphere of the time to allow the businessmen to carry the ball. But times had changed, and Roosevelt, moreover, was not Coolidge. Public opinion had revolted against business, and the government was in a better position to exert leadership. As Adolph A. Berle, one of the early brain trusters, put it: "If business is up, the public will put pressure on government to change the rules, but if business is down, the public will put pressure on business to observe the rules. If business would not function, it was up to government to create conditions under which it could work."[3]

Roosevelt intended to be a strong President. Hostility between government and business was, therefore, inevitable. As the economy began to show some signs of slow recovery, Roosevelt lost his fascination for businessmen. For despite all their disclaimers, businessmen were not really ready for any drastic change in economic theory or economic policy. They were still bound to the canons of orthodoxy. So, for that matter, was the President. He too had studied economics under Professor Taussig at Harvard and he never was quite able to forget that fact. But he was in government and not in business, and as he saw his task, it was to experiment again, and again, and again in the hope that the country would eventually find the road back to prosperity. The businessmen, who had at first welcomed Roosevelt's iconoclastic pragmatism, soon came to regard it as at best infra-dig and at worst a sin against eternal truth. They did not understand much of what was being done, and they, therefore, began to regard the New Deal with uneasy and fearful suspicion. A good example of this came from Ernest T. Weir, who was to be one of the most irascible of New Deal opponents. Said Weir in 1949: "Much of its [the New Deal's] original program was good. . . . I do not believe any administration ever had a more unified country in back of it. Then something happened. It became apparent that the Administration . . . intended to transfer leadership of the economy from private hands to government." Time intensified the division between business and government. Within a year, the fire of enthusiasm with which business had greeted the President died to a thin wisp of smoke. Only a couple of embers were kept alive by a few of the loyal and faithful. More than once, the press reported "a new era of good feeling," but these rapprochements never amounted to anything more than news items that died in the borning.

Meanwhile, too, the New Deal itself was changing. Actually, there was not one New Deal, but three New Deals. The first one emphasized recovery; the second put more emphasis on reform; and the third flirted with compensatory fiscal policy. Business leaders found much of the first New Deal to their liking; they were not happy with the second one; and they thoroughly detested the third. By the last part of the decade, resentment between government and business had built up to a feverish pitch. Politicians like Secretary Ickes took a sadistic delight in needling businessmen. Others were overly sensitive and were quick to engage in fruitless arguments over "who was running the Treasury" and "if business was as sovereign as the government." Not to be outdone, businessmen spent much of their time hissing Roosevelt and the New Deal. Some of them proved that they were human by becoming quite irrational about what was going on in Washington. It was said, for example, that every dinner guest at J. P. Morgan's home was requested not to mention the name Roosevelt under any circumstances. It was also said that the mother of George Humphrey of the Hanna coal empire (and later Secretary of the Treasury) always spelled Roosevelt's name with a small r. During the presidential campaign of 1936 hard-headed businessmen were so carried away by their wishes and hopes that they predicted an overwhelming victory for Governor Landon. In the course of a cross-country trip, Harry E. Benedict, Frank Vanderlip's partner and intimate associate, wrote Vanderlip that Roosevelt would not carry

Florida, North Carolina, or Virginia; that New York would probably go Republican; that Landon would easily sweep Pennsylvania, Ohio, and New Jersey; and that "Farley has written off New England." On Election Day, Landon carried Maine and Vermont, and nothing else.[4]

THE EARLY INFATUATION

But be that as it may, businessmen were by and large happy with Roosevelt during his first year. When he took office on a gloomy Saturday afternoon in March 1933, the business world little understood the man or his philosophy, and it never did acquire this understanding. Early in his administration the prevalent business interpretation was that the President was well-born and therefore obviously pro-business. This was clearly stated by the magazine *Steel:* "More than is publicly known he has given assurances to business. Short of shouting from the house tops . . . he has certified to business that he will stand between it and extreme left wing proposals. . . . By birth, training, and environment the President is a patrician. . . . He has quelled a social as well as a financial panic."[5]

It was true, as many Washington correspondents were to testify, that Roosevelt was a bulwark against radicalism. It was also true that he was a patrician. But there was no agreements as to what was meant by radicalism and the business world took too much for granted when it assumed that "patrician" and "friend of business" were synonymous. Indeed, more often than not, they were just the opposite. Roosevelt had never been a businessman in the real sense of the word. He had all the aristocrat's dislike for the ways of business. As Arthur M. Schlesinger, Jr., has pointed out, "the business ethos—its ideas, its assumptions, its goals, its vanities—just seemed to him absurd. He hated the whole thing. It could not, he thought, interpret the experience of most Americans. It did not understand the higher values and ideals of American civilization. . . ." In the first few days of the New Deal, business leaders were not aware that this was what he thought about them and their system. What they were aware of was that he "intended to do something," and this they thought at the time was all to the good. That they changed their minds later is, of course, another story.[6]

One of the things which created an early bond between the President and the business group was that he was in continuous communication with the leading bankers from February 17 on. They wanted him to make a statement that there would be no departure from the gold standard. Many of them also wanted federal credit placed in back of the banking system through large loans from the Reconstruction Finance Corporation, and some wanted a federal guarantee of deposits.[7]

Enthusiasm for the President was further strengthened by the inaugural address and the lightning speed with which the New Deal was set in motion. Never before had the federal government so rapidly passed so much legislation to deal with national problems. Those businessmen who had feared that they "would be standing around while he learns the ropes" must have been amazed at the rapidity of events. With sentiments that they were ruefully to regret, they rained praise on Roosevelt and on the wholesale breaking of precedent that came to be called the "Roosevelt Revolution."

Most of the criticisms of the New Deal that emerged in the famous "first 100 days" came not from the business community, but from liberal and radical sources. The critics included Oswald Garrison Villard, the influential editor of *The Nation;* the editorial pages of the *New Republic;* the Progressive bloc in the Senate; the Communist press; and a number of early Roosevelt supporters, such as Father Coughlin, who quickly lost interest in the experiment. Business, on the other hand, appeared in these early days to have few qualms concerning the direction in which the country seemed to be heading. As in all honeymoons, some most extraordinary opinions were freely expressed. One business leader called Roosevelt "the greatest leader since Jesus Christ," and he hoped "God would forgive him for having voted for Hoover." John J. Raskob, who had led Governor Smith's unsuccessful attempts to achieve the presidency, said, "Few Presidents have accomplished as much in a whole term as you have in a single month." Samuel Vauclain, who had been responsible for the regrettable slogan about two chickens in every pot in the 1928 campaign, once again bubbled over. He now declared himself "thoroughly loyal to Roosevelt," who "has given the country what it needs—unparalleled energy, prompt decision, well-considered action." To be sure, not all business opinion was so unguarded and so uninhibited. Francis H. Sisson, president of the American Bankers Association, regarded the inaugural speech "as a very courageous and inspiring appeal. It is reassuring in its general expression. . . . His suggestion for a high degree of discipline in American private and public life must win universal approval." Said Walter Gifford, president of A.T. & T., "Under his leadership, with the will to win and the willingness of each individual to make any sacrifices for the common good, we can and we will conquer our economic difficulties." At the end of April, James A. Farrell, former chairman of U. S. Steel, told the Foreign Trade Council: "There is an atmosphere of more confidence than at any period during the past three years . . . due to the public utterances of President Roosevelt."[8]

Other bankers and businessmen put more emphasis on the need for change. At one point in the early career of the New Deal, Otto H. Kahn told the Senate: "The New Deal is now being made. It is of the utmost consequence economically and socially. I do not believe any man is wise enough at this moment to express any views or conclusions until these new theories and laws have been tested. I know a good deal must be changed. And I know the time is ripe to have it changed. Overripe in some ways." The President had taken responsibility for changing things and businessmen admired him for it. Said Charles H. Swift of the meat-packing family, "The initiative, energy, and courage of the President in the emergency—his willingness to pioneer in the hope of building a new and better order of things—commands respect and admiration." If change required some compromise with laissez-faire, it had to be recognized that the times also required flexibility and pragmatism. As R. G. Knowland of the Bigelow Sanford Carpet Company put it: "The breakdown in finance, in agriculture and in industry has led to direct measures on the part of Government to rectify the financial and agricultural situations. . . . There can be no question as to the soundness of the intervention when matters of such large importance are in a state of chaos." But few at that time or at any time would have agreed with Owen Young's opinion about why there was a need for more potent government influence:

> We are now learning . . . that we must enlarge our restraints and controls over the economically powerful . . . not only to protect but to develop the economic well-being of the weaker. . . . The question is not how we can secure the largest theoretical liberty of political action for the individual. It is rather how we can get the largest combined political and economic freedom. . . . Business having failed

to discipline itself, I see no escape from some direction and control
by politics.[9]

Even at this early point in the history of the New Deal, the contradictions inherent in the business platform were beginning to
haunt those who had fashioned the planks in that platform. For one
thing, businessmen were not as enthusiastic about the specific legislation that was passed as they were about the philosophy that under-
lay the legislation. They wanted something to be done, but they were
not particularly happy about what was done. Between March and
June, the Administration and Congress attempted to reorganize the
whole American economy through far-reaching enactments in finance,
industry, and agriculture. The business community had mixed feelings
about this ambitious program. This was especially true in the area
of finance. Very early in the New Deal, the Administration took the
country off the gold standard; new security issues became subject to
federal regulation through the Securities Act; and the Banking Act of
1933 separated commercial from investment banking and provided
for a federal guarantee of bank deposits. Industrialists were indifferent to these attempts to alter fundamentally the money and banking
system. What they thought was probably best summed up by James
A. Farrell's enigmatic remark, "The most pressing need is the establishment of sound currencies." As usual, however, there were exceptions. James H. Rand, speaking for the Committee for the Nation,
was ecstatic as he called for a "two-year moratorium on price-fixing
laws" and "a reflation by raising the price of gold."

As would be expected, most of what the financiers said was negative. Almost without exception, they were committed to the gold
standard. Long before we went off gold, Winthrop Aldrich said that
such a possibility was "simply incredible." After the deed was done,
Bernard Baruch thought the worst had happened. "It can't be de-
fended except as mob rule," said Baruch. "Maybe the country doesn't
know it yet, but I think we may find that we've been in a revolution
more drastic than the French Revolution. The crowd has seized
the seat of government and is trying to seize the wealth."

Surprisingly enough, J. P. Morgan, one of the sphinxes of Wall
Street, broke his silence to express his disagreement with the majority.

"The way out of the depression," he told the President, "is to combat and overcome the deflationary forces. . . . Your action in going off gold saved the country from complete collapse." Morgan was probably echoing the opinion of the astute Russell Leffingwell, who believed that money was very important in the economy and that marvelous things could be accomplished by the use of intelligent monetary policy. Leffingwell wrote Roosevelt that going off gold "was vitally necessary, and the most important of all the helpful things you have done." Sometime later, when the President was being beset on all sides for his "reckless" monetary policy, Leffingwell sympathized: "What a task you have between the deflationists who are sadists or radicals and want deflation to bring on revolution; the deflationists who are reactionary like Baruch, Smith, the Chamber of Commerce and my beloved Carter Glass who are still fighting the Bryan-McKinley campaign; and the extreme inflationists . . . who can't know that that too means starvation and revolution."[10]

There was a more equal division of opinion on the issue of deposit guarantee. The big city bankers unconditionally opposed the idea, since they would have to pay most of the costs and would get the least benefit. In almost every state banking association, the majority, over the protests of an articulate minority, adopted resolutions opposing deposit insurance. The leader of the fight against this fundamental reform was Francis Sisson of the Guaranty Trust of New York and president of the American Bankers Association. He regarded the proposal as "unsound, unscientific, unjust, and dangerous." It would put a premium on bad banking and was socialistic and un-American. He promised to have the association fight "to the last ditch" against the idea. A typical instance of Sisson's never-say-die campaign occurred at the Virginia bankers convention after the passage of the Banking Act of 1933 introduced federal deposit insurance. Samuel W. Keys, president of the Virginia Association, said that the Act "marks the greatest revolution in banking since the Federal Reserve Act and possibly the greatest revolution of all time. . . . It is the answer to the public demand for a new deal in banking." Unabashed by this hyperbole, Sisson denounced the Act as stupid and prophesied that it would be repealed "as usually happened with legislation of this kind."

The one thing to which the majority of bankers gave approval was the separation of commercial from investment banking. The small bankers had never been involved in the flotation of securities, and some of the big banks had had such unhappy experiences that they were glad to get out and glad to be forbidden from ever getting in again. Winthrop Aldrich of the Chase Bank flatly advocated the absolute separation of commercial and investment banking. To which W. C. Potter of the Guaranty Trust commented that it was "quite the most disastrous statement ever heard from a member of the financial community." J. P. Morgan once again broke his silence by regretting the bill because it would reduce the supply of capital so necessary for the development of the country.[11]

In agriculture and industry, the federal government attempted to restrain competition through production, price, and wage controls imposed through the National Industrial Recovery Act and the Agricultural Adjustment Act. Just as industrialists showed little interest in commenting on banking legislation, so bankers commented little on these two measures until after they had become accomplished facts. Then a few bankers cautiously expressed misgivings that ran along the general lines of Sisson's opinion that the NRA "threatened to set aside the principle of free competition in business" and William C. Potter's view that "NRA would cost the people a lot of personal liberty, but if it is a success, the loss would be well compensated."

THE AAA AND THE NRA

For the most part, businessmen were not very much interested in agriculture. They had enough to bother them in industry. There were, however, a number of businessmen in the farm implement and fertilizer industries who had a direct stake in the farmer's welfare, and they helped to draft a farm-relief program. Long before the inauguration, Baruch had favored government intervention in the agricultural market place. He and Owen Young were two of the few businessmen who supported the McNary-Haugen bills, which President Coolidge vetoed. With the depression, Baruch began to publicize a plan for the relief of agriculture through acreage reduction and a subsidy to farmers for cutting production. The cost was to be borne by a processing tax. Much of this plan had been worked out by Baruch's wartime associate General Hugh Johnson and his colleague in the Moline Plow Company, George Peek. They had long since become convinced that it was necessary to reduce the supply of farm products by artificial methods rather than through the painful process of waiting for the natural effects of supply and demand. Much the same ideas were pressed by Henry A. Wallace and Professors M. L. Wilson of Montana State College and Rexford Tugwell of Columbia. So well did Wilson put his case that he converted Henry I. Harriman of the United States Chamber of Commerce, who happened also to own a few thousand acres of land in Montana. Through the efforts of these many cooks, the first Agricultural Adjustment Act was passed early in the New Deal.[12]

Baruch and other businessmen were also influential in the creation of the National Industrial Recovery Act. Actually, the NRA was an extremely complicated piece of legislation. It was an omnibus measure with three distinct parts: a program of public works, provisions for raising labor's status and guaranteeing the right to bargain collectively, and the modification of the anti-trust laws in order "to allow production to be based on demand." Neither labor union leaders nor business leaders were enthusiastic about the public works program; but each had a major stake in the other parts of the legislation. The business leaders who favored the type of "planning" represented by the NRA desired, in the words of Paul Litchfield, that "the destructive competition which had marked industry in the past be done away with." Labor leaders wanted the government to give them freedom, indeed, help to organize the workers. The majority of labor leaders were willing to accept what business wanted, but the majority of businessmen were not willing to accept what labor wanted. This inability to arrive at a working agreement soon developed into a vituperative hassle and put a severe strain on the uneasy alliance between government and business.

Businessmen, like the Marxists at the other end of the spectrum, thought that all values were embodied in economics. A blind spot prevented them from recognizing that what made bad economics could sometimes make good sociology. The NRA was economically absurd, but it had some salutary social effects. It was idiotic to assume that the way to make the country rich was to curtail production, fix prices, and hold an umbrella over the submarginal producer. But it was not idiotic to try to eliminate child labor and sweatshop working conditions.

The wide gulf that separated businessmen from labor union leaders and social reformers was apparent as soon as the NRA began to take shape. The prologue to the bill came when Senator Black of

Alabama introduced his thirty-hour-week bill. It was received with
little enthusiasm by the Administration, and business opinion in
general was very much opposed. True, it had the support of Paul M.
Mazur of Lehman Brothers, who was an articulate champion of the
purchasing power theory of business recovery. In a statement prais-
ing Roosevelt's farm and public works programs, the banker called
the Black bill "a most constructive measure, if accompanied with a
minimum wage provision." Other business voices drowned out
Mazur's views. James A. Emery, perennial spokesman for the National Association of Manufacturers, termed the bill a "rigid and
highly centralized regulation, not of commerce but of production."
The Illinois Manufacturers' Association used the same old clichés
in describing the bill as "socialistic, unsound in principle and utterly
impractical."[13]

While the Black bill was being discussed, the leaders of the
Chamber of Commerce pushed ahead with their plans to do something about competition. At the annual meeting, president Henry I.
Harriman, Gerard Swope, and Paul Litchfield told the assembled
delegates that "the economic system was antiquated," and warned
that it was no longer a question of whether competition would be
regulated, but a question of who would do the regulating. What was
being said was heard in the White House and on May 7, the President advised that "well-considered and conservative measures will
be proposed to prevent cutthroat competition, unduly long hours for
labor, and at the same time to encourage each industry to prevent
overproduction." This was followed ten days later with a message
to Congress requesting it "to provide for the machinery necessary
for a great cooperative movement throughout all industry in order
to obtain wide reemployment, to shorten the working week, to pay a
decent wage, and to prevent unfair competition and disastrous overproduction."

As finally adopted, the NRA provided for a general code of practices to apply to industry in general and for special codes to be drawn
up to regulate each industry's wage and price policies. An attempt
by Senator Borah to prohibit price fixing in the codes of fair
competition passed the Senate, but was dropped by the conference
committee. Robert Lund, president of the National Association of
Manufacturers, expressed what many businessmen thought of this
amendment: "Modification of the Borah Amendment makes it clear
that the rigid restrictions of the anti-trust laws are not to apply in

the future. . . . Industry has a right to be encouraged. . . . It will now have an opportunity to police itself against ruthless competition in the form of unregulated price cutting."[14]

The one thing in the final bill to which business leaders specifically objected was Section 7 (a) which guaranteed labor the right to bargain collectively through agents of their own choosing. When the steel code was drawn up, Taylor and Schwab representing the two largest producers refused to accept it because of 7 (a). At a meeting with the President, Schwab said he could not in fairness to the stockholders of Bethlehem Steel go along with the code. Roosevelt asked Schwab whether he had been fair to the stockholders in paying Eugene Grace huge bonuses. "I scared them," said Roosevelt, "the way they have never been frightened before."

The NRA went into effect in a wartime atmosphere, and most of the businessmen to whom the philosophy of planning was anathema remained silent, lest their patriotism be questioned. One of the outstanding exceptions was Ralph E. Flanders. In November 1933, Flanders published an article in which he said, "the limitations on improvement, processes, and equipment; the allocation of sales; the setting of prices was a body of doubtful doctrine founded on the assumptions of too drastic competition and its accompanying overproduction. It was a body of thought concocted by the 'tired business man.'" He thought that shorter hours without a rise in wage rates was relief, not recovery, and increased costs meant increased prices. Judged from the point of view of what was best for the welfare of society as a whole, Flanders' judgment was more than reasonable. If the economy could not produce enough goods in 1929 to achieve a desirable standard of living, it certainly could not do so under the appreciably shorter hours proposed in the NRA.

But less than half of the Who's Who of American business agreed with Flanders. The executives of the textile and steel industries were especially enthusiastic. H. P. Kendall, although aware of the dangers latent in this new philosophy, nevertheless put the responsibility on industry: "Undoubtedly, the Recovery Act means that the Government has taken a long step toward state socialism, which is described as 'cooperation with business.' Will the textile industry carry on in such a way that the Government will not have to exercise further control?" Other textile tycoons took the opportunity to lecture their fellow producers. "It is time," F. C. Dumaine of Amoskeag Mills and Waltham Watch announced, "that an industry incapable of intelligently managing its own affairs should be forced to accept outside control." According to Eugene Grace, "One of the chief benefits has been to relieve industry from the shackles of the anti-trust laws." Charles M. Schwab thought it "was the first time in fifty years experience when the business of the industry could be conducted on a common sense basis." The great steel man went on to say: "Industry must regulate itself. . . . The President offers to the business world the facilities and prestige of our government in eliminating unfair competitive practices with all their ruinous effect on prices, wages, and profits. . . . We need price stability."[15]

Those who were active in the Chamber of Commerce and who had been instrumental in pushing for planning profusely praised the NRA. Henry I. Harriman called the Act "the Magna Carta of industry and labor." E. A. Filene compared the opponents of the NRA to the Tories of 1776. C. L. Bardo, shipbuilder and executive of the NAM, who had just finished criticizing the government for its paternalism, thought the NRA "the most important legislation ever enacted." Alfred I. du Pont saw the beginning of the end of the days of hard times: "I have always been very much in favor of just what has recently been done by way of setting aside the Sherman-Clayton Act and carrying on business as it should be, free from inordinate competition which was always productive of low earnings and of course of low wages. . . . This gives complete control of production which has always been the canker worm of hard times and business depressions."[16]

What these businessmen complained about was "unfair competition" and "ruthless price cutting." What they wanted was stability, which was simply a polite term for price fixing, cartel arrangements, and containment of competition. Of the 557 basic NRA codes, 441 contained price-fixing provisions, and although many of these never went into effect, they went, in theory at least, as far as any of the "stabilizers" desired. In one code or another, the industry was given the power to fix prices and to restrict and allocate output among companies. Prices were to be "fair and reasonable," or "equal to the lowest reasonable cost of production," or equal to the cost of "the lowest representative firm." The cotton textile code limited the number of spindles that could be operated and the amount of new machinery that could be introduced into the "sick" industry. Under the steel code, the directors of the Iron and Steel Institute could judge prices to be unfair on the basis of costs and could require a new and fair base price. No new blast furnaces or open hearths were to be built for the period during which the code was effective. These provisions enraged the consumer representatives in the NRA administration, but the magazine *Steel* cavalierly disposed of them. "To understand what is in back of the movement of protest," it editorialized, "one must delve deeply into the tangled roots of political intrigue, bureaucratic jealousy, clashing industrial interests, and the fanaticism of economic theorists."[17]

It is not meant to imply that all businessmen favored price fixing in the codes of "fair competition." In many industries, there was spirited disagreement, but the opponents of price fixing rarely won the argument. When the National Retail Drygoods Association presented a code for the regulation of department stores, the differences of opinion which had so much to do with the eventual breakdown of the NRA came into the open. The proposed code included a paragraph condemning the sale of merchandise at less than invoice cost plus 10 per cent. Sales at less than that price were designated as unfair competition. Immediately, the fur began to fly. Percy Straus of R. H. Macy, who was positive that those who drafted the code had his company in mind, protested that such a principle was bound to be harmful to the consumer and that price-fixing agreements had always been illegal, but his protests were turned aside by a coalition of small business competitors and a group of department store executives who thought there was something evil about price cutting. In the oil industry, too, most small independent producers demanded that prices be fixed and production be restricted. They had the support of Standard Oil of California and of Harry F. Sinclair. All the other large producers and a few independents opposed price fixing. J. Howard Pew wrote Donald Richberg, "My own conviction is that the same natural forces which alone can be relied upon to set prices, are the same forces on which we must rely to control production. . . . I have uncompromisingly opposed price fixing and every other attempt to hamper free competition." But even within the companies themselves there was strong disagreement. The controversy was so intense that James A. Moffett resigned from the Board of Standard Oil of New Jersey because he favored price control and Walter Teagle did not. Eventually, the oil code was practically dictated by the government, but not before the first draft had been flatly refused by Sinclair because it did not prescribe price control from the well to the consumer.

The automobile industry, which was also on evil days, looked upon the NRA's Blue Eagle symbol as some strange, prehistoric, and long since extinct bird. According to Donaldson Brown of General Motors, "The industry's decision to sign up under NRA was based solely on its readiness to submit to the requirements of Section 7 (a). The committee unanimously rejected the opportunity offered by the law to seek any relief from existing anti-trust statutes." For most executives, there seemed nothing else to do but go along in a resigned fashion. The one maverick was of course Henry Ford who, despite numerous threats of "cracking down" by General Johnson, would have nothing whatsoever to do with the NRA.[18]

In this instance, if in no other, Ford was able to laugh last. The Blue Eagle had hardly spread its wings before most businessmen realized that what they had expected from planning was not materializing. When the NRA became law in June 1933, it was greeted with extravagant enthusiasm. By the fall of the year, feelings had chilled perceptibly, and by 1935, for most business leaders, the Eagle had become a very sick chicken. This gradual erosion in sentiment could be traced in the comments that industrialists and bankers made along the way.

Early in the game, open criticism of the NRA was expressed at great length at the annual convention of the National Founders Association in 1933. In January 1934, Harvey Gibson hinted to the stockholders of the Manufacturers Trust Company that there was some disenchantment: "The net effect of the NRA represents on the whole a net gain. Many who are somewhat hostile to it admit that they prefer it to the old order." By the end of the year, the magic of planning had worn off for some of its most vociferous onetime champions. "A planned economy," said Silas Strawn, "cannot be effective unless the executive is vested with power to enforce it. . . . Do we want dictatorship such as they have in Russia, Italy, and Germany?" In May 1935, Judge Ames, chairman of the Texas Company, said, "Public sentiment had repudiated the NRA." The automobile people, who had never been crazy about the idea, were now a little smug. "The NRA," said William S. Knudsen of General Motors, "brought some complications in the way of attempts by government officials to plan for a business they knew nothing about, and apostles of the so-called social service gospel indulged in considerable finger-pointing." Speaking for those who represented the "conservative" view, David Lawrence, the old Wilsonian, thought the NRA had been "a splendid idea in principle, but that it had been mishandled."[19]

THE REVULSION AGAINST THE NRA

When planning was first broached, many businessmen seemed entirely unaware of its implications. The theory that increased wages would result in increased purchasing power made no allowance for a rise in costs and in prices. Then, too, businessmen entirely miscalculated the labor provisions of the Act. They did not worry about Section 7 (a). It, therefore, came as something of a surprise when a few aggressive labor union leaders interpreted the law to be an open invitation to nation-wide collective bargaining. It came as an even greater shock to find that the Administration was sympathetic to the union interpretation. Businessmen were, for the most part, willing to bargain provided the bargaining agent was a company union, but the trade unions had different ideas. Thomas I. Parkinson, president of the Equitable Life Assurance Society, later recalled, "The effort of the NRA was spoiled by a combination of meticulous detail . . . and governmental encouragement of unreasonable demands on the part of labor." Finally, businessmen objected to the people who were writing and administering the codes under which business was supposed to operate. Louis Kirstein, a stanch defender of the NRA and the New Deal, much later recalled: "The code for retailing, in some of its important aspects [especially its labor sections] was being written by people who had no experience with retailing."[20]

The critics of the NRA had their first opportunity to complain in February 1934. At an unruly meeting held under government auspices, retailers directed a vitriolic attack on the "open price" arrangements permitted under many codes. It was frequently charged that price fixing was rampant, that the codified industries were moving rapidly in the direction of monopoly, and that if price fixing were not eliminated, government regulation of industry could not be avoided. Major Namm, who had been one of the leaders in drafting the retail code, said that the increase in dollar-sales volume had been due to an increase in price, rather than an increase in volume sold. He said that manufacturers were too eager to recoup three-year losses in a matter of a few months, and that the labor provisions of the retail code had increased the costs of business in the retail trades by about

2 per cent. Small businesses were disturbed by this increase in costs which they claimed had not been accompanied by an increase in volume of business. At the annual meeting of the National Chamber of Commerce, much was made of this in reports from over one hundred local chambers. These reports generally supported the trade practices provisions in the codes, but there was extensive criticism of "favoritism toward employees." About 40 per cent of those reporting thought that there had been material benefits from the Act, and 15 per cent thought there had been benefits in some fields.[21]

Toward the end of 1933, business organizations had already become convinced that the NRA as then constituted could not be enforced. The Chamber of Commerce stated flatly that the "NRA was impossible of enforcement and leads to chiseling." It suggested that the Act be made voluntary instead of compulsory, a suggestion that was heartily endorsed by the Act's leading proponent, Gerard Swope. At about the same time, the NAM reported that 98 per cent of the manufacturers of the country (sure an overly huge array) opposed the labor and licensing sections of the Act. The association also reported that 45 per cent of its members favored discarding the Act, 40 per cent favored modification, and 15 per cent, continuation. The Illinois Manufacturers' Association categorically opposed renewal in any form. R. W. Irwin of the National Committee for the Elimination of Price Fixing and Production Control reported that 8000 members of the Southern States Industrial Council divided 43 per cent for abandonment, 34 per cent for modification and 22 per cent for continuation.[22]

It was apparent that the NRA was already critically ill when it was declared unconstitutional in the spring of 1935. Its demise was, for one reason or another, greeted with exultation, satisfaction, and dejection by the business group. Those who, like Flanders, Sloan, Ford, and most bankers, had never had any sympathy for planning, were sure that the nation would take new strides toward recovery now that this yoke on free enterprise had been removed. Those who had supported the Act—the Chamber of Commerce, the NAM (whose support had not been as enthusiastic), the steel executives, the cotton textile producers, and individuals, such as E. A. Filene and Gerard Swope—expressed mixed emotions at the passing of the Blue Eagle. Filene and Swope regretted the whole thing, but the other former advocates hoped that the decision would enable them to throw overboard the labor provisions and government interference while salvaging freedom from anti-trust laws and "the ability to cooperate." The *Times* reported that Wall Street was elated by the decision, but that in some quarters it was feared that "unless Congress enacted a substitute, providing for price and wage fixing in certain industries, deflationary consequences might ensue." Fifteen hundred businessmen, allegedly representing small business, drove to the Capitol in a demonstration for a two-year renewal. William Cheney, a Connecticut silk manufacturer, prophesied that renewal of the legislation would bring prosperity for all business, not for a few powerful monopolists.

Most businessmen were in a state of confusion about the NRA decision. This was most evident in the steel industry. On the one hand, the Court's verdict made some of the industry's leaders as happy as a group of brides at a wedding. *Steel* editorialized:

> The nine justices performed the great service of shocking the nation into a realization of the extent to which the New Deal has violated the tenets of the Constitution. . . . It dashed the dreams of those who hoped for a dictatorship manipulated by brain trusters. It destroyed the system which permitted immature collegians clothed with government authority to tell experienced veterans in industry and finance how to conduct their affairs.[23]

But steel men also feared that some companies might return to wholesale price cutting and that the government might reinvigorate the anti-trust acts. A meeting, immediately called to create a workable code for the self-regulation of the industry, announced that the steel code would continue in spite of what had happened to the NRA. Much was made in this initial statement of price control, and at the first official meeting of the Iron and Steel Institute following the Supreme Court decision, Eugene Grace said that there had been no price cutting, "thank God!" Two hundred leaders of the industry said that they would maintain the basic provisions of the code. All over the nation businessmen reiterated the sentiment of the steel industry. However, in a short while, the NRA became a thing forgotten and pretty generally regarded with condescension as one of the major mistakes of the New Deal.[24]

THE SEPARATION THAT PRECEDED THE DIVORCE

Disappointment with the NRA was only one symptom—a very important one, to be sure—of the general disenchantment with the New Deal that the business group was rushing toward in late 1933 and early 1934. Of course, the breach between the Roosevelt administration and business was not the product of one day. Pressure on the strange alliance had been building up for months as the business community watched with misgiving what the New Deal was doing. What finally triggered the open break was the realization that the economy was finally recovering from the long depression. As profits, employment, and the gross national product rose, the New Deal lost its novelty, and business no longer wanted the experimentation that it had thought was needed at the trough of the depression. This was frankly stated by Henry I. Harriman, the president of the Chamber of Commerce, at the time when the meeting of minds came to an end and open criticism became common.

Once the breach appeared, it rapidly widened in a condition of general deterioration as all the dissatisfaction that had been built up came into the open. The first open acknowledgment that the honeymoon was over came in the late fall of 1933, appropriately enough, at the convention of the National Founders Association—appropriate because the Founders had always been noted for outspoken opinions of an "anti-liberal" nature. S. Wells Utley, president of the association, branded the New Deal as "Socialism" and warned that "if the next Congress did not revise the Presidential powers (given by the NRA), it would be repudiated at the polls." Then, Utley added, "we shall have gone through the greatest revolution in all history, and, in the space of a few months, shall have retread all the steps of progress taken by the English speaking race since that far off day seven centuries ago when Englishmen forced the great charter from King John." The day after the Utley speech, Congressman M. L. Littleton told a receptive audience at the New York State Chamber of Commerce that Washington was experiencing a "program of collectivism, executive dictatorship, and bureaucratic government." On the same day, the national Chamber's directors called on the President to stop experimenting with money and return to the gold standard, a resolution which was cheered by Alfred P. Sloan, Lammot du Pont, and James P. Warburg.[25]

At about the same time, Du Pont, in his annual report to Du Pont stockholders, wrote, "1933 witnessed an adventurous attack by the administration upon the political, social, and economic ills of the country." He then went on to question "the usefulness of a prolonged limitation of the productiveness of our plants . . . the threat of inflation, mounting government expenditures, and credit expansion."

The President replied in kind. As he was to do throughout his administration, he referred to his critics as "certain modern Tories, small in number, but powerful in influence." This nose tweaking was gleefully encouraged by those in the administration—and there were many—who regarded the business world with contempt, suspicion, and hostility. They believed that whom God had put asunder let no man put together. From here on, each time that anyone tried to pour oil on the troubled waters, these critics of business managed to skim it off. What was happening was that the repartee between the business group and the Administration was taking on overtones of a power struggle. For its part, the Administration had no intention of letting business regain the influence that it had had in the days of prosperity; and on the other side, many of those who complained most bitterly about dictatorship continued to flirt with the dangerous and mistaken idea that fascism was "distinctly a business dictatorship with the government running the country in the interests of business." Even as late as 1938, H. W. Prentis, Jr., president of Armstrong Cork and sometime president of the NAM, warned that American businessmen might eventually have to turn to "some form of dictatorship" to bring order out of chaos if attacks on free enterprise continued.[26]

Criticism of the New Deal accelerated so rapidly in late 1933 that the press, the gossip columnists, and astute as well as dilettante observers of the passing scene finally felt that it was worth commenting about. In early March 1934, Kiplinger said that business opposition to the Administration was becoming significant. In mid-March, Julian Mason, one of the carpenters in the Republican Builders, Inc., announced that the era of good feeling was over and that the "fight on the New Deal would begin." In a long editorial in April, the *Times* noted a significant increase in business criticism of the New Deal. At about the same time, Justice Harlan Fiske Stone wrote former President Hoover, "It seems clear that the honeymoon is over and that we may witness the beginning of real political discussion." *Fortune* announced in its April issue that "with the exception of Woodin, Baruch, and a handful of ambassadors . . . there is not now to be found within hailing distance of Mr. Roosevelt a single prominent industrialist named in *Fortune*'s [Jan. 1933] list. . . . They have unanimously accepted their dismissal and left the party to go to hell in its own fashion."[27]

A few businessmen were still loyal to FDR, and most businessmen, though considerably bothered by the passing events in Washington, did not want warfare. They may have had a subconscious desire to picket the White House as unfair to free enterprise, but consciously they had no wish to demonstrate. An excellent example of this "holding back" occurred in a letter that Edgar M. Queeny wrote to Fred I. Kent at the time he published his book, *The Spirit of Enterprise*. Looking back, Queeny wrote: "I restrained purposely in handling the New Dealers because few people know the truth. . . . I addressed myself to that group which is on the fence, and I thought that by treating the New Dealers generously such readers would have greater faith in the points I attempted to make against New Dealers."[28]

As would happen time and time again, cooler heads rushed in to try to keep the rift from widening. In mid-1934, there occurred the first of these many attempts to reconcile business and government. The so-called liberal businessmen and those who desired for one reason or another that the wounds be healed still thought that the President tended toward the right. They noticed that his attitude toward labor was not as distinctly co-operative as it had formerly been. Senator Wagner had introduced his bill calling for a National Labor Relations Board to assist in the settlement of labor disputes and to guarantee free collective bargaining. Despite the fact that one of their colleagues, Gerard Swope, had a hand in writing the bill, businessmen were horrified by it. They were overjoyed when the President did not seem to welcome it with any great enthusiasm.

At the same time, events in the auto industry were also interpreted to mean that the President was becoming more sympathetic to the business view. Auto makers, objecting to industry-wide bargaining and national unions and refusing to recognize the AFL as bargaining agent, drew up a set of principles, including such sentiments as "the government favors no particular union" and "membership in a union would be no guarantee of a job." As part of the plan to achieve harmony, an Automobile Labor Board was set up to mediate in disputes. According to Donaldson Brown, the President accepted these principles, but later repudiated them and the Automobile Labor Board was allowed to pass into oblivion.[29]

Thus the initial attempt at rapprochement failed, and it should have been evident that nothing could put things back together again. The Administration had no intention of turning the wheel back to business, and business had no understanding of the philosophy of the New Deal. Those who had lost whatever faith they had in the Administration began to form organizations to thwart what they were positive was a danger to the system, to business, and to the country. Eventually, there were at least half a dozen prominent organizations trying to overcome the plague of locusts. These included the Crusaders, originally an anti-Prohibition group; the Committee of Americans, primarily the brain child of Frank Vanderlip; and the Liberty League, the creation of Raskob, the Du Ponts, Sloan, and Weir. The latter organization was, of course, the most famous or infamous of them all. When it was formed, Rudolph Spreckels and A. P. Giannini, two of the few who still championed the New Deal, offered to form a counter organization. But Roosevelt made light of the whole thing. And well he might, for from the point of view of power and influence, he was in a most advantageous position in the game of economic issues. He took the public pulse much better than did his business opponents. He knew that the people at large were not primarily concerned with the ultimate effects of programs of reform. They were not very much interested in the "American System." Rightly or wrongly, they blamed business and the business value system for the plight in which they found themselves. Roosevelt was empathetic to their spirit. The recovery program, therefore, marched on apace; 1935 saw the Works Progress Administration, the Social Security Act, the Wagner National Labor Relations Act, the Holding Company Utility bill, the Banking Act of 1935, and new tax measures. Business was opposed to all of these in varying degrees, and grumbling about the New Deal mounted. In 1935, the Liberty League, in its efforts to turn back the clock, spent more than twice as much as the Republican party in advertising its platform which included a dozen recommendations ranging from balancing the budget and eliminating inequities in taxation to overhauling the bureaucracy. The League was in favor of abolishing or drastically revising every major and most minor enactments of the New Deal. Yet, as such things go, the business reaction was not sufficiently vitriolic to satisfy the more impatient critics. Frank Vanderlip, who was becoming perceptibly touchy, complimented William Randolph Hearst on the "fine editorials" he was writing. "I am getting pretty disgusted," ejaculated Vanderlip, "with the way businessmen have acquiesced in some of the more impossible features of the New Deal. Unless some fighting spirit is devolved, we are going to see our old America changed into a different government and a different order of society."[30]

BUSINESS ABANDONS THE NEW DEAL

Haranguing businessmen into a fighting mood seems to have had some effect, for by the time the Chamber of Commerce met in May, relations between the President and business had chilled so deeply that the President neither appeared nor sent a message of greeting. The meeting itself did nothing to restore amicable relations. The sole topic on the agenda seemed to be the New Deal, and more than a few businessmen grasped the opportunity to voice their many grievances against it and against government in general. Those who came to speak for the Administration were unceremoniously squelched. F. E. Powell was ruled out of order when he resolved that the Chamber bore no malice toward the Administration. W. P. Witherow, member of the Industrial Recovery Board, chilled the assembled delegates when he reminded them that "many government interventions have been injected into the business mechanism at the urgent and insistent demand of business itself."

Business feeling toward the New Deal could best be described as impatient. "Businessmen," said Silas Strawn, "are tired of hearing promises to do constructive things which turn out to be only attempts to sovietize America." The Chamber called on the President to suspend work relief, to delay the Social Security Act, and to modify the Securities Act. So acidly did the Chamber condemn each of the major Administration measures that those few who still desired a workable arrangement with the White House, including Henry I. Harriman, Averill Harriman, Thomas J. Watson, Winthrop Aldrich, Gerard Swope, Robert Wood, and Melvin Traylor, left the meeting to visit the President and promise him their continued support.

This attempt to observe the amenities of good taste carried on well into the late spring. In June at the annual meeting of the International Chamber of Commerce, Thomas Watson and E. A. Filene paid warm tribute to Roosevelt with Watson predicting that the United States was "on the verge of one of the best business periods in history."

The progress toward peace and harmony seemed to be proceeding. In a letter to the President, Roy W. Howard, publisher of the Scripps-Howard newspapers and possibly still a New Deal sympathizer, revealed that there was much questioning and uneasiness among business groups, and he inquired whether the President might not give some assurance that would resuscitate confidence among entrepreneurs. The President immediately obliged with a letter in which he announced the famous "breathing spell" for business. "This Administration," he said, "came into power pledged to a very considerable legislative program. . . . This basic program has now reached substantial completion and the breathing spell is here. . . ."[31]

But it was much too late for this kind of nonsense. Most business leaders thought the New Deal was far beyond the point of no return. It took E. T. Weir a little more than a week to formulate the opinion that "to draw any assurance from the President's mention of a breathing spell would not be justified. . . . There is not a sign of a change in the Administration's economic philosophy which has been disturbing to business." C. L. Bardo for the Manufacturers Association was "a little doubtful" about the breathing spell, and the official voice of the NAM, J. A. Emery, characterized the spell as "an interval between a preceding period of strangulation and one of approaching exhaustion."

By 1935, feelings had solidified. Although it was from time to time expressed in different ways, the recurrent themes were drift, suspicion, and hostility. A typical episode occurred in October 1935 when the Chamber of Commerce sent out questionnaires to 1500 constituent member bodies asking for an expression of opinion on the New Deal philosophy. Although friends of the Administration maintained that the questions were so loaded that the vote was misleading, it was, nevertheless, 35 to 1 against what was thought to be the New Deal's philosophy.

Encouraged by the trend and urged on by such stalwarts as Ernest Weir and E. F. Hutton, broker and executive of General Foods, the NAM at its national convention openly announced that it was "out to end the New Deal." The extremely low state of cordiality between government and business was aptly illustrated by certain happenings at the "Better Light, Better Sight" dinner in December 1935. That was just about the time when the plan for breaking up the public utility holding companies was getting into high gear. According to the *Times,* the toastmaster at the dinner, T. N. McCarter, took everyone by surprise when he offered a toast to the President of the United States. After the initial shock, the subtle joke "was greeted with general laughter by the audience of 500 executives of the electric and optical industries."[32]

By this time, almost every trade association dinner concluded with a loudly applauded denunciation of the "Administration," "the New Deal," or occasionally the President himself. The first Liberty League dinner in January 1936 heard speakers denounce the Administration as "unconstitutional, experimental, and opportunist." When the AAA was declared unconstitutional, dining New England business leaders were glad to hear that the decision "presaged the death knell of virtually all New Deal legislation from the Social Security Act to the Wagner Labor Bill." In May, the members of the American Iron and Steel Institute loudly applauded as Taylor, Hook, Weir, Girdler, Irvin, Hugh Morrow (president of Sloss-Sheffield Steel and Iron), and Grace slashed out at the trend of government. In the same merry month, Samuel W. Reyburn of Associated Dry Goods told a meeting of retailers that the New Deal was a "hangover from Hoover's New Economics," and he expressed a hope that "Washington and Albany will soon end extravagance and introduce thrift."[33]

By the time the 1936 presidential campaign rolled around, it was difficult indeed to find any businessmen who were enthusiastically for the Roosevelt crusade. Just the opposite was the case; anti-Roosevelt businessmen believed that they were embarked upon the eighth crusade. J. Howard Pew was not exaggerating the typical point of view when he accompanied a sizable cash contribution to the GOP with the words: "Considering the importance of this campaign, I have felt it a duty and a privilege to make these contributions. . . . The American form of government, the fundamentals of our democratic society, the economic system under which our country has become the greatest in the world, are in jeopardy." "Wall Street," said a pro-business journalist, "is pinning its hopes on the defeat of Mr. Roosevelt. If that hope fails, practical businessmen must need be practical."

ANOTHER ATTEMPT AT RECONCILIATION

Roosevelt really did not need the votes of the businessmen. He was overwhelmingly re-elected without them. Yet, it annoyed the President to be unpopular with any group. He felt terribly persecuted. "Never before in all our history," he said, "have these forces, business and financial monopoly, speculation, reckless banking been so united against one candidate as they stand today. They are unanimous in their hate for me—and I welcome their hatred." The annoyance was so great that the Administration made continuous attempts to deny reality by insisting that only a handful of willful men among the business population opposed what was being done. By October the Democratic National Committee had managed to put together the names of thirty-five businessmen who favored Roosevelt's re-election. Most of these were small businessmen of little national fame and chiefly in the clothing industry. The President's nationally known supporters included Jesse Lasky, the movie entrepreneur; E. A. Filene; John McKinley, former president of Marshall Field; and Samuel S. Fels, the non-conformist Philadelphia manufacturer.

There were a few others who still supported Roosevelt, but they were doing so more silently than they had four years before. Swope, Baruch, and Young continued to be Democrats, but they did not participate in radio broadcasts or in newspaper advertisements. Often, the businessmen who voted the Democratic ticket did so reluctantly. One was Daniel Willard. He had voted for Hoover in 1932 but now wrote his old friend, Albert Shaw, "While I have always been a Republican and still adhere to that name, I find myself in sympathy with many of the objectives which President Roosevelt has at least subscribed to. I am quite out of sympathy, however, with many of the methods which are being followed presumably in an effort to accomplish such objectives. I regret greatly the seeming lack of intelligence and effective leadership in the Republican Party."

Many merchants and some manufacturers and bankers felt strongly that unless they could find some measure of true co-operation with the Administration, all would be lost. Rudolph Hecht, the New Orleans banker, in his presidential remarks to the American Bankers Association stressed the "need of our accepting some of the more moderate evolutionary changes going on at home, lest we, too, may face some of the social upheavals which have taken place and are still taking place throughout Europe." Thus, in the campaign of 1936, the business community divided into three groups. The over-whelming mass supported Governor Landon and the Republican party by original inclination and even more so because of a deep emotional opposition to the New Deal and its architects; a small number supported Roosevelt because they favored the New Deal or some of its subdivisions; and a third group made up of reasonable men who were going to vote reluctantly for Roosevelt because the New Deal was the lesser of a number of evils.[34]

INTRANSIGENCE ON BOTH SIDES

Most businessmen regarded the election as a thorough disaster, and for a long time, they were speechless from the shock. But in 1937, a serious break in the economy rejuvenated their vocal opposition. Business spokesmen got a sadistic psychic income by slyly reiterating Roosevelt's famous phrase, "We planned it that way." Business circles applauded W. A. Draper when at the annual meeting of the Chamber of Commerce he dubbed the steep decline "the Roosevelt recession." They sincerely believed J. D. A. Morrow of the Pittsburgh Coal Company when he explained that "the depression was created in Washington and it will have to be cured in Washington by a frank acknowledgment of some mistakes that have been made." Outside observers like the *London Economist* thought that the commercial community had worked itself up into such a lather of hatred that its fury was "choking the whole industrial and financial machine." Inside observers insisted that business fears were not based on anything real, to which F. E. Frothingham, president of the Investment Bankers' Association, replied with more realism than most people were showing: "It is scarcely a question of whether or not the fears and uncertainties are justified. The fact is they exist." What businessmen were asking for, they insisted, was some concrete action that would restore confidence.[35]

The New Deal's anti-business wing immediately repudiated this call for confidence. Secretary of the Interior Harold Ickes, who would rather be nasty than right, and Assistant Attorney General Robert Jackson, who would eventually distribute justice from the Supreme Court bench and at the Nuremberg trials, became the chief hatchet men in a spate of name calling. Ickes's diary records how little hope there was for the business case. "The President," he jotted down, "was greatly disturbed over the economic situation. . . . At Hyde Park he consulted with some important businessmen," but he felt that "the big money interests were in an unconscious conspiracy to force the hand of the Administration. . . . They would insist upon what would amount to a complete reversal of social and economic policy. Privately, these men admit to the President that they would not want unlimited farm production, that they favor a wages and hours bill, and that they favor some kind of social security. But while they admit these things privately, none of them will say so publicly.* . . . Morgenthau started to tell the President that he ought to reassure business that he is not against business as such. The President almost jumped down his throat." At this point, Ickes, a talented coat holder, wrote on the memorandum pad: "This looks like the same kind of fight Jackson made against the United States Bank. . . . The President read it, looked up at me, and said 'That's right.' "[36]

Ickes delivered a blast at "America's Sixty Families," a title suggested to him by Ferdinand Lundberg's sensational book. Attorney General Jackson weighed in with an address before the Political Science Association on "The Philosophy of Big Business." Few addresses could have displeased business more than these two that accused "big business" of a whole series of deplorable practices, the least of which was "monopoly." Anti-New Deal businessmen eagerly grasped the opportunity to demonstrate why they had lost confidence. Banker Aldrich called "the inflammatory statements by members of the government most unfortunate." The representatives of "small business," who, according to a Gallup poll, were "61 per cent against Roosevelt," demanded that "unwarranted and malicious attacks on business by administration spokesmen be permanently stopped." Banker Percy Johnston and cotton textile spokesman G. A. Sloan admonished the government to let up on business and put an end to name calling.

Businessmen who were still sympathetic to the New Deal wondered, more in sorrow than in anger, why Administration spokesmen felt it necessary to play children's games. General Robert E.

---

* This was far from the truth. Whether they meant it or not, businessmen never tired of stating that they agreed with the objectives of most of the New Deal legislation, but they objected to how it was being done.

Wood, who had often expressed strong sympathy with the New Deal, thought that "the time was never more favorable for capital, industry, government, and labor to cease baiting each other." A. P. Giannini, one of those rarest of creatures, a New Dealer among bankers, bluntly announced that he was "getting fed up with some of the people down in Washington and their antagonistic attitude toward bigness in business." Puzzled by the trend of affairs, a group of friends of the Administration, including Young, Lamont, and John L. Lewis, traveled to the White House and asked for a clarification of policies. This was one of the oft-repeated complaints of the business coterie and whether they got the clarification seems doubtful, for in April, Secretary of Commerce Roper, one of the few in the Administration who sympathized with the business point of view, challenged industry to put men back to work. But business and government were still talking at cross purposes, for Lewis H. Brown replied for the business community by saying that business could not put men back to work until government got out of the economy, amended the Securities Act, stopped attacking profits, stopped using taxes for other than fiscal purposes, and balanced the budget.[37]

Like all wars, the one between government and business made nonsense more often than it made sense. All the criticism which business directed against the Administration was not vituperative. The NAM, in its more flamboyant moments, was not greeted with huzzahs by all big businessmen. Indeed, some were so disturbed by what they considered a miscarriage of public relations that they took steps to take over the direction of the business organizations. Charles R. Hook, it was said, took the presidency of the NAM in 1938 because, among other things, it would "signalize a more liberal point of view in the NAM." Once he was president, Hook presented the following set of principles:

1. Self-improvement of business itself, with full recognition and acceptance of management's social responsibilities.
2. Good employment relations with industry cooperating fully with this objective.
3. More tools to facilitate expansion and increase jobs. Such tools come only through investments, hence industry seeks the removal of barriers to investment.
4. Increased purchasing power for the individual American. This can be arrived at only through increased production of essential goods.

5. Thorough analysis of the whole tax program and the promotion of sound economy in government. We recognize the necessity of types of government expenditures but believe that elimination of waste and extravagance would constitute a marked contribution to recovery.

6. We point to the need of everyone doing everything in his power to foster a wide understanding of the worth and manner of operation of the private enterprise system.

Donaldson Brown's recollections of what happened in the NAM was also most revealing. Brown thought in 1939, and before that as well, that "fundamental changes were occurring under the pressure of public opinion. . . . They appeared to the business community to be departures from the principles of a free and competitive economy. But whether they liked it or not, they were having a major impact." To combat these changes, Brown became chairman of a Coordinating Committee of the NAM and guided the preparation of a Declaration of Principles in 1939. "I had no previous identity with the NAM," wrote Brown, "but had been familiar with prior annual pronouncements. . . . Usually, these were belligerent statements with attacks on governmental activities. . . . It seemed to me that NAM had been resorting to pressure group tactics, presuming to speak for the managers of industry; in other words placing itself in the same kind of light as the very pressure groups which NAM was condemning." The 1939 declaration reaffirmed faith in the free enterprise system and took a strong stand for increased production. Among other things, it said, "The managers of industry must continue unabated their efforts in behalf of increased production and employment. . . . This requires an application of policies basic to the welfare of industry as a whole and to the broader welfare of the nation. Good management will recognize that it serves its own interests best as it strives to serve also the interests of the nation as a whole."

The business community was by this time engaged in an endeavor to "sell private enterprise" back to the American people; in the business world, this also meant an endeavor to upset the New Deal. In a sense this effort never succeeded. Yet, paradoxically, the business point of view seemed to have regained much of its lost ground. A Gallup poll taken in March 1939 found that 52 per cent of the public thought that the Roosevelt administration had not "been friendly enough" to business; a mere 9 per cent thought it had been too friendly, and 40 per cent thought that the hostility toward business had seriously delayed recovery. A *Fortune* survey of Executive Opinion (September 1940) revealed the business community's disenchantment with Roosevelt's policies. In answer to the question "By and large do you favor Roosevelt's policies designed to achieve social reform and recovery?" the voting was as follows:

	Social reform	Recovery
Yes	9.2 per cent	2.0 per cent
Some	65.4 " "	18.9 " "
No	24.4 " "	77.1 " "
No answer	1.0 " "	2.0 " "

In short, three out of four big business executives objected or frowned upon the Roosevelt program. A postscript could be added. In 1940, Young, a lifelong Democrat, wrote to George Harrison: "Everybody protests about the government extending itself further into business, but nobody really does anything about it."[38]

THE NATURE OF THE BUSINESSMAN'S HOSTILITY

The antipathy of business toward government that gradually expanded into apparently irreparable hostility puzzled many reasonable commentators who made the mistake of thinking that human behavior was dictated solely or primarily by *economic* self-interest. William Allen White summed up this puzzlement in his *Emporia Gazette:* "A curious phenomenon of the last two years is this: as the rich get richer, they have hated Roosevelt more bitterly. In 1933, when he was proposing really basic economic changes, hardly a voice was raised in opposition. Now that profits are jumping ahead and industrial activity is almost at the 1929 levels, the rich are hollering their heads off against Roosevelt. The probable explanation: in 1933 the old order had gone so completely to smash that the prosperous classes had nothing to lose but their chains. . . . Now that profits are restored and they have something to lose, they are bitter against all hint of change."

But the matter was much more complicated than White made it out to be. Like many other journalists, the Sage of Emporia implied that the business revolt against Roosevelt was simply a display of peevish temperament. But this was not so. The changes that the

New Deal was instituting in 1935 and 1936—Social Security, the Wagner Act, the Utility Holding Company Act, the undistributed profits tax, etc.—were just as "basic" as the legislation passed in the first hundred days. Then, too, while recovery was taking place, it was much too slow to satisfy any but the most patient; it was little solace to a nation devoted to economic growth that the level of industrial activity in 1935 was on the same plane as that of 1929. This was too much like Alice running as fast as possible to stay in the same place. And even if the recovery had been much more robust, it would have mattered little. The business world was opposed to Roosevelt and the New Deal for reasons that were much deeper than simple economic self-interest. Many spokesmen for the business point of view tried to explain this but never really succeeded. Their explanations always sounded like so much oatmeal and spinach—wholesome and holier than thou and very unpalatable. A typical piece appeared in the *Times* during the presidential campaign of 1936. It began with the usual statement that the financial community was not nearly so far removed from Roosevelt on questions of objectives as it was on methods. It then cited "one one-time supporter of Roosevelt who believed the issue was purely moral" and the head of one of the biggest banks who "could forgive the President everything except that he has stirred up class hatred." A further reading soon revealed that the business community did object to something more than methods.[39]

To be sure, what business leaders found most repulsive about the New Deal was its philosophy and the individuals who were thought to be responsible for that philosophy. But with very few exceptions, they objected to everything about the New Deal. They opposed the AAA, TVA, the Banking Acts of 1933 and 1935, Social Security, the Wagner Act, the Securities and Exchange Act, the Wages and Hours bill, work relief, the undivided profits tax, and, above all, the unbalanced budget. But it would be a mistake to assume that businessmen, both large and small, were the only ones who opposed these measures. When Alfred Sloan was saying that "industry has every reason to be alarmed at the social, economic, and financial implications" of the Social Security bill, a well-known congressman easily outdid him by saying, "Never in the history of the world has any measure been brought in here so insidiously designed to prevent business recovery [and] enslave workers. . . ." Walter Lippmann called the Wagner Act "a legal monstrosity" at the same time that Ernest Weir denounced it as "one of the most vicious pieces of

legislation ever proposed." The Communist party thought it "a
weapon to destroy the power which the workers have gained," while
Sloan called on industry "to fight this proposal to the very last." When
the American Bankers Association was arguing against the Banking
Act of 1935, Professor H. Parker Willis gave the association much
ammunition by denouncing the proposed Eccles bill as "the worst
and most dangerous banking measure that has ever come before
Congress. . . . To allow it to go on the statute books is practically
suicide for independent banking and business." And what of the
businessman's chief *bête noire,* the unbalanced budget? Here again,
he had lots of support. A whole string of Gallup polls showed that
government spending, in the abstract of course, was not popular with
the public at large. As late as November 1936, just before Roosevelt
won his one-sided victory, a poll found that 70 per cent of the people
thought it "necessary to balance the budget." When Roosevelt in
May 1938 proposed to combat the 1937 depression with a $5 bil-
lion spend-lend program, 42 per cent of the Gallup sample answered
"yes" to the question: "Do you think government spending should
be increased to help get business out of the slump?" But in December 1937, February 1938, and June 1938, the same question
elicited only a 37–38 per cent affirmative, and a 62–63 per cent
negative. Among the upper-income groups, only 23 per cent voted
"yes" compared to 57 per cent among the low incomes.[40]

It would be just as much an error to think that there were no exceptions to the business opposition to the many laws passed in the
1933–40 period. Each specific act, including the Wagner Act and the
spending legislation that seemed to be causing the unbalanced budget,
had its friends. Small business approved the Robinson-Patman and
Miller-Tydings acts to limit competition while at the same time calling
for "the strengthening and enforcement of all laws seeking to curb
monopolies." While George Humphrey, Swope, Queeny, Avery, and
Girdler publicly opposed the Securities and Exchange Act, E. A.
Pierce, Paul V. Shields, James V. Forrestal, and Robert A. Lovett
thought it would be better to modify the bill rather than to oppose it
altogether. During the vitriolic exchange that accompanied the discussion of the Banking Act of 1935, Giannini said simply and
bluntly, "I favor the banking bill." One important reason why he did
was that he resented the New York bankers and their most articulate
spokesman, James P. Warburg, because "they wished to continue to
dominate banking as they always had."

Perhaps the Social Security bill was received with more favor than any other measure of the later Roosevelt years. In the House hearings on the measure, Samuel Reyburn and a few other large and small businessmen were enthusiastically for it, and even Emery of the NAM was not his usual self. According to Thomas J. Watson, "Its principles are sound. . . . Such legislation should have been passed years ago." At the other end of the spectrum on New Deal legislation were the Wagner Act and the unbalanced budget. Neither could muster much support, although Gerard Swope had something to do with writing the former and Henry S. Dennison spent many hours defending the latter. On the whole, however, the best that business leaders could do was to reason that an unbalanced budget had to be accepted as an inevitable concomitant of depression. But even this view was unpopular as Jackson E. Reynolds of New York's First National Bank found out when he talked about "The Banker's Responsibility" before the ABA and pleaded: "Is it avoidable that . . . the destitute unfortunate and unemployed must be cared for? . . . May we not be in error in expecting too early a date at which . . . the budget may be balanced; and can any one of us fix a precise date when such balance may be attained without fear that our prophecy will be made ridiculous by subsequent events?"[41]

In the long run, those who were favorably disposed to the actions of the federal government had the satisfaction of seeing a good share of their sentiments accepted. As time passed, much of the New Deal legislation which had earned wholesale condemnation when first proposed came to be regarded more sympathetically and, in a few cases, enthusiastically. Thus polls taken among business executives at the end of the New Deal came forth with the following results:[42]

Legislation	Retain	Modify	Repeal	Don't Know
FDIC	84.7%	3.9%	3.1%	8.3%
1933 Banking Act	64.7%	14.0%	3.8%	17.5%
FHA	56.9%	19.0%	19.6%	4.5%
SEC	44.5%	34.2%	3.6%	17.7%
Utility Holding Company Act	33.7%	35.5%	9.1%	21.7%
Wage and Hour Law	29.8%	47.0%	21.4%	1.8%
Social Security	24.3%	57.9%	17.3%	.5%
WPA	12.1%	41.7%	44.4%	1.8%
Wagner Act	9.8%	41.9%	40.9%	7.4%
Undistributed Profits Tax	8.1%	22.5%	66.2%	3.2%

	Always bad	*Once good*	*Good idea badly handled*	*Continue*
Silver subsidy	90.2	4.5	3.0	2.3
Guffey Coal Act	75.3	2.3	15.9	6.5
Gold devaluation	69.6	14.5	6.4	9.5
Taxation	67.6	2.8	22.0	7.5
Pump priming	61.7	20.2	16.3	1.8
NRA	57.4	12.5	23.2	6.9
AAA	53.6	6.3	33.7	6.4
Wagner Act	48.2	0.6	47.5	3.7
WPA	39.3	10.9	43.2	6.6
Cheap money	32.7	19.4	16.3	31.6
Wages and hours	29.2	1.9	47.7	21.2
Hull treaties	22.4	10.4	14.0	53.2
Anti-trust drive	20.2	7.3	49.4	23.1

Feelings about specific legislation ran pretty high in emotional content, but a much more fundamental cause of the lack of good feeling between government and business stemmed from a mutual suspicion of philosophies and a mutual incompatibility among philosophers. And beneath all the business objections, the suspicions, and the incompatibilities lay very real fears—a fear of change and a fear that the whole position and status of business would be permanently undermined because the process of change would result in the abandonment of the values in which businessmen believed or thought they believed. In the 1930s, business opinion was offering evidence to support the axiom that Epictetus offered in A.D. 60: "It is not things that make men afraid, but their opinions and fancies about them."

Businessmen constantly alluded to the bureaucrats, the impractical theorists, the callow youths of no experience, the intellectuals who were in charge of the New Deal and who had no knowledge or sympathy with business. The Brains Trust was not a thorn in the business side; it was a whole bramble bush. The realization that a group of young, eager, and inexperienced intellectuals was in the process of building a vast empire chilled the conservative mind, outside as well as inside the business system. Very early in the New Deal, Justice Stone remarked: "We are indeed in a theoretical mess, or in a mess of theorists." Editorialized the *Saturday Evening Post,* "If they are competent to plan and run the business of the country, then practical experience and training have lost their meaning." Within the business world itself, spokesmen regularly rang the changes on this most irritating of all the incidental annoyances of the New Deal. For most businessmen, for quite plausible reasons, believed that the "crowd in Washington" was motivated by a desire for power. They also believed that the complex desire for power held far more dangers for the public welfare than did the simple lust for money. "The nation's most immediate danger," explained banker Eugene Meyer, "lies in the inexperience of the young intellectuals who are now directing the policy of the administration." In explaining "what business men think," William Lloyd Garrison, Jr., retired investment banker, told the readers of *The Nation:* "The business and banking community awaits some sincere assurance. . . . It wants to hear . . . an honest purpose to balance the budget. . . . A more helpful and even more significant move would be the inclusion among the President's advisers of more men of high reputation and long experience in the realm of practical affairs." The President did, of course, occasionally ask the advice of eminent businessmen and bankers, including Leffingwell, Kent, Vanderlip, Swope, Baruch, but these consultations usually ended in an altercation in which the President impatiently accused the business community of lacking any positive program and of being pettishly obstructionist.

The New Deal did not understand something that appeared clear to many who were more condescending than empathetic to the business class. During the recession of 1937, John Maynard Keynes tried to explain businessmen and business psychology to the President. He wrote:

Businessmen have a different set of delusions from politicians; and need different handling. They are, however, much milder than politicians, at the same time allured and terrified by the glare of publicity, easily persuaded to be "patriots," perplexed, bemused, indeed terrified, yet only too anxious to take a cheerful view, vain perhaps but very unsure of themselves, pathetically responsive to a kind word. You could do anything you like with them, if you would treat them not as wolves and tigers, but as domestic animals. . . . It is a mistake to think that they are more immoral than politicians. If you work them into the surly, obstinate, terrified mood, of which domestic animals, wrongly handled, are so capable, the nation's burdens will not get carried to market; and in the end public opinion will veer their way.

It was unfair to keep accusing the business community of not having a positive program, for the accusation was not true. Kent offered a widely publicized plan whereby the government would (through the RFC) guarantee selected businesses against loss on normal production and would share the profits. Young suggested that bankers set up an investment organization to provide venture capital. Neither these nor any other positive plans proposed by businessmen aroused any enthusiasm. Somewhat less could be said of the series of "do nots" that business leaders regularly offered the White House as a positive plan for recovery. Ernest Weir, for example, could hardly expect that the President would be wild with delight as he read a plan which began with the statement that the Administration was responsible for the recession of 1937 and continued with the following recipe for recovery: the elimination of "punitive and crippling" provisions in the tax law, amendment of the labor laws "so that they shall be fair," removal of "threats of government competition such as the one overhanging the utilities," and the sending "of the Corcorans and the Cohens and their kind back where they came from." Above all, "to make the program clear and then stick to it." These were the sentiments of the man of action, and as *Nation's Business* put it: "Regardless of how we look at it, the differences between the man of thought and the man of action seem fundamental and irreconcilable." Businessmen thought they supported reliance on economic laws, not empiricism; economy, not extravagance; practicality, not theory.

THE NEW DEAL VIEWED AS A THREAT
TO THE AMERICAN SYSTEM

But in the contest for the President's ear, "the men of thought" had an easy victory, and all that the frustrated businessman could do was reiterate that "it was a hell of a way to run a railroad." In May 1934, Charles W. Nash, the automobile producer, said, "I don't want to criticize the government, but I think it is unfortunate that there is growing up a class of people who are trying to build up hatred between the laboring man and the man who meets the payroll. I think 'Boss' Kettering should be listened to rather than some young men who never earned a dollar in business in their lives. Theory does not always win." The outspoken Tom Girdler told a sympathetic but uninfluential audience of steel men: "The bureaucratic theorists who now presume to supervise American business have never produced the goods demanded by American consumers. They cannot, they never have produced anything. All they do is to tell us to do less than we are doing already."[43]

Business leaders sincerely believed that the government was in evil hands. It was in control of an organized mob that was encouraging class conflict, favoring the great unwashed, and preparing the way for socialism, communism, or some other variety of anti-Americanism. Very early in the New Deal's career, J. A. Emery warned the business class: "It isn't the forward movement of the alley we have to fear, it is the desertion of the avenue. If men of responsibility and intelligence fail to perform their part, popular government will fall into the hands of those whose course of conduct is determined by the number of their supporters." A few years later, A. W. Robertson, chairman of Westinghouse, added a corollary: "One of the first things citizens of the country should concern themselves with is the question of whether or not an individual who receives special benefits from the government should have a voice in the control of the government. In other words, should people on relief have the right to vote." To which people on relief might have rejoined: "Should people on tariffs or subsidies have the right to vote."[44]

In ringing the changes on the evils of bureaucracy and the invidious forces that were breaking down the American system, business leaders and business spokesmen very often resorted to melodramatic hyperbole that left the listener embarrassed and unconvinced. Opinions that saw the end of civilization in every New Deal act were not as uncommon as they should have been. Said one who viewed with alarm, "We have to turn back many centuries to the days of absolute autocrats to find so great a power over the lives of millions of men lodged in the hands of one fallible being." Another thought the New Deal "more strongly resembles the dictatorship of the Fascistic and Communistic states of Europe than it does the American system." Commenting on the Social Security Act, a trade association publication pontificated that "the downfall of Rome started with legislation of this type." Franklin Fort, a Newark, New Jersey, banker and sometime public office seeker, characterized the undistributed profits tax as "a more direct attack on capitalism than any direct attack yet made." Ernest Weir warned his fellow countrymen: "We have taken the first steps along the road which other people have followed in search of a rainbow, only to find at the end no pot of gold, but some form of dictatorship and collectivism." One of the most hysterical spellbinders of the era, O. W. Adams, Utah banker and president of the American Bankers Association, pontificated that a "sound fiscal policy" was the foundation of economic and civil liberties. "Our present government fiscal policies," he said, "are drifting with ever-increasing speed into government planned economy. . . . The inevitable result is ultimate dictatorship."

It was not just the Adamses who feared the trend of government. Calmer voices were equally concerned about the breakdown of the system they admired. Sloan was firmly convinced that "any form of 'Government Regulation of Industry' is bound to result in an ever-increasing interference with the broad exercise of initiative—the very foundation of the American System. . . . If that be so, might not the ultimate logical result be the necessity for the socialization of industry through the breakdown of the profit system?"[45]

AND AS AN OBSTACLE TO RECOVERY

Executives, tycoons, and men of wealth were disturbed by other aspects of Washington policy. They believed that the New Deal delayed recovery. Many years later, business leaders were still convinced, in fact more convinced, that had the New Deal never reached its maturity, the depression would have ended much sooner than it actually did. Paul Litchfield in one of his memoirs wrote, "Government was helping in several ways that it can . . . RFC . . . Public works . . . Direct relief. . . . I do not think that there is any question that America would have worked its way out . . . if the Hoover administration had remained in office. But the new administration had a different idea. . . . It did not talk about the creation of Wealth. What followed was an extraordinary period . . . an Alice-in-Wonderland era, with men proposing to write new laws of economics and to restore prosperity by act of Congress." In writing President Truman after the War, Fred I. Kent averred that the depression had been lengthened by what government had done, and he used the occasion to warn Truman to keep the government out of the economy. George Humphrey, after he had become Secretary of the Treasury and could enjoy the comforts of post mortems, judged that "it was clear that the Government's policies during all the 1930's were wrong and worked badly. . . . The handout principle of deficits of the

1930's actually deterred individual risk-taking and finally became a means of destroying the soundness of the dollar."[46]

Some industrialists thought that the Administration's failure to achieve recovery stemmed from its fascination with "the fallacy based on the thought that we can all have more by making less." If the Administration did so believe, and there was much evidence that it did, it was tragically in error, for that was the road to unemployment and an anemic national income. But some businessmen also believed that "we can have more by producing less." They had never quite given up the NRA notion that an economy can restrict its production and thereby enhance its wealth. In retrospect, it appears that these mature society adherents may have been in the majority. At least, Sloan thought so. He kept alluding to those who "believed that our progress in this world is finished, that we must retrogress." Sloan believed in the opposite point of view that "the amount of available work can be continuously expanded, that progressively higher standards of living will result through broadening the activities of industry. . . . Progress is measured by our ability to reduce the real costs of goods and services. We must maintain the broadest possible spread between income and the cost of the necessities of life." Sloan quoted with obvious disapproval the "rather astounding pronouncement" of Roosevelt that "reduction of cost of manufacture does not mean more purchasing power and more goods consumed. It means just the opposite." Sloan pointed out that "those industries which have been the most successful in reducing costs paid the highest wages." If economic values were the criteria, Sloan was clearly correct, and those with whom he disagreed were incorrect.[47]

Criticism was not couched only in terms of more production or more planning. Bankers, especially, laid all the blame for the slow recovery on the loss of confidence which the New Deal engendered by defying certain inviolate economic abstractions. What they had in mind was a balanced budget, thrift, and a tight money policy. They were not very sure why, but these things were as sacred as patriotism and motherhood.

Business leaders took every opportunity to point out that the Administration consistently ignored the necessity of doing everything to shore up confidence. This emphasis on confidence was not new. The importance of maintaining confidence had been prominently mentioned in the early depression, but in the late thirties it came to overshadow everything else. In 1935, J. E. Edgerton lamented that "at the very hour when wages are highest, hours the shortest and prospects the brightest since 1929, we are witnessing the strange effects of more fear and uncertainty than has perhaps ever been known before." In 1936, Winthrop Aldrich explained that our failure to recover stemmed from a fear that emanated "from the plans and possibilities of the so-called 'New Deal.' It was fear that existed not only in the minds of businessmen and financiers, but was widespread throughout the population that the very nature of our Government was about to be changed." In 1937, Lammot du Pont put into words the uncertainties which vitiated business confidence. "Uncertainty rules the tax situation, the labor situation, the monetary situation, and practically every legal condition under which industry must operate. Are taxes to go higher, lower or stay where they are? We don't know. Is labor to be union or non-union? . . . Are we to have inflation or deflation, more government spending or less? . . . Are new restrictions to be placed on capital, new limits on profits? . . . It is impossible to even guess at the answers." Tom Girdler, fresh from an all-out fight with the CIO, added a further explanation to what was meant by "no confidence." "There are no basic causes making for a prolonged recession," he told the Steel Institute. "The big job is to restore confidence by removing the causes that have undermined it. . . . The national administration actually encourages certain labor leaders in their efforts to foment hatred. . . . We have all manner of inconsistency . . . constant barrage of harassments, inquisitions, and broadside attacks. . . . All the experience of my thirty-five years in business life has led me to believe that employers and employees have mutual interests. I find that I was wrong."[48]

One reason why confidence had oozed was that the New Deal persisted in experimenting. Experimentation had been all right in the beginning, but the beginning was over as early as the winter of 1933–34. The business world was glad to admit that much good had been accomplished, but it was also eager to admonish the Administration not to overdo it. An early example of this occurred in 1934 when the Chamber of Commerce called upon Roosevelt to issue a clear statement that the emergency was over and no more requests for reform legislation would be made. Actually, of course, the Administration's program had hardly begun at that time. But business did not seem to recognize this, for at about the same time, Ernest Weir told the Harvard Graduate School of Business Administration: "We have had more than a year of the present administration. Much good has resulted. Now, however, we have arrived at a most critical time. Business is willing to follow new rules that are reasonable, but it cannot accommodate itself to a routine of almost daily changes." This theme was iterated and reiterated by Weir as well as by other spokesmen for the business point of view. They freely admitted errors of commission and omission, but they wanted these to be rectified slowly, painfully, and thoughtfully. As business viewed it, the way the New Deal proposed to rectify them was quixotic, sloppy, and overhasty, and it would, therefore, accomplish nothing but an undermining of confidence and a delay on the road to recovery.[49]

THE BALANCED BUDGET ONCE AGAIN

Few businessmen had any doubt that confidence would return if the President would forsake his heretical advisers and come back to tried and true principles. T. Jefferson Coolidge spelled these principles out in a private letter to George Harrison: "The principles under consideration are those which enable man to operate for his and others' best interest under the influence of the laws of demand and supply and free from the ever deterring and clumsy hand of arbitrary centralized government. They may be temporarily interfered with under stress of war and upheaval, but once forsaken the need to return promptly is imperative. These principles are the gold standard, the balancing of budgets, absence of government or subsidized competition, freedom of private contract, and maintenance of law and order." To these, others added encomia on thrift and a denunciation of spending. Simon N. Whitney, then with the Chase Bank, characterized as "extraordinary and fallacious the theory that the way out of the depression is by putting money into the hands of those who will not lay it aside but rather will spend it." A. H. Giannini* anticipated anti-Keynesianism by warning against "the new school of progressive economists, some of them connected with government, who would abolish private thrift, substitute lavish spending for saving, and lead us to communism." Major Benjamin Namm spoke for the

* The sons of business leaders were often in the forefront of the rebellion against the New Deal. A. H. Giannini, Charles Sabin, Jr., Frank Vanderlip, Jr., and the younger members of the Du Pont family all played important roles in forming organizations to combat the New Deal. It has even been said that the Liberty League originated because Robert Carpenter found it difficult to find servants.

vast mass of business opinion when he attacked the idea that "we could spend our way to prosperity." But yet there were other entrepreneurs in retailing who did not consider the idea quite so far-fetched. General Robert Wood was somewhat sympathetic to government spending. But the mavericks in the business world were Lincoln Filene, Morris Leeds, Ralph Flanders, and Henry S. Dennison. In their book *Toward Full Employment,* they proposed government deficit financing whenever unemployment passed a specific number. But Dennison did not believe that government spending was a panacea. "Spending could be used for a tonic or amelioration, but not for cure."[50]

Most businessmen, and the public in general, were opposed to unbalanced budgets because it was simply not the thing to do. After all, Roosevelt himself had said in the message accompanying the Economy Act of March 1933, "Too often in recent history, liberal governments have been wrecked on the rocks of loose fiscal policy."

Like Roosevelt, T. Jefferson Coolidge did not think it necessary to explain why an unbalanced budget was wrong. It was self-evident. "Despite the fact that business conditions are reasonably good," he said in 1936, "the budget is badly unbalanced. It is an appalling situation." It was well known that deficit financing was a result of reckless and unnecessary spending and should be stopped by cutting down expenditures. "Unless this psychology of spending is soon changed," warned Percy Johnston, "the piling up of increasingly unsound taxes may easily lead to irretrievable harm to our whole economic structure." Philip Benson, president of the Dime Savings Bank, was one among many who believed that the whole thing was very simple. "Government finances were essentially the same as private," and government expenditures were not unavoidable. "Let us look at the facts," Benson urged. "Is the soldiers' bonus necessary? How about relief? Well, relief can go just so far and no further. It must not bankrupt the nation. Relief must get down to actual necessities. . . . Creating anything with public monies just now that would tend to destroy existing industries and other forms of wealth is wrong, unjust, uneconomic, and un-American. The pump has been primed so often that the paint is coming off it and it is getting rusty at the top."[51]

Businessmen applauded Roosevelt's promises to balance the budget and his early efforts to do so as evidenced by the Economy bill of 1933, which proposed to cut government salaries and certain other payments such as those to veterans, and his resistance to the cash payment of the so-called "soldiers' bonus." When Roosevelt vetoed the soldiers' bonus, Owen Young, who favored its payment and also favored the veto, explained, "To expand an already overloaded budget deficit by $2.2 billion might impair the government's credit. . . . All history shows that the printing press in the manufacture of money is the opium of economics." How much of a debt could the government stand before its credit would evaporate and disappear? No one really knew. In a speech at Atlanta in November 1935, President Roosevelt defended his spending policy and told his audience that bankers had told him in 1933 that the government could stand a $55- to $70-billion debt.* The *Times* found "Wall Street bankers generally inclined to skepticism. They wondered where such an impression was gathered." It certainly was not gathered from Winthrop Aldrich, who did not know of any banker "who has expressed the opinion that the debt could safely rise to $55 billion, to say nothing of $70 billion." He went on to say very much in the manner of offering the President a short lesson in public finance: "There is no magic in Federal Government credit. It rests on the same principles that any other credit rests on. Its credit rests on its taxing power, and its taxing power rests on the productive power of the taxpayers." A couple of years later, when the debt was much higher, Walter E. Frew, chairman of the Corn Exchange Bank of New York, thought that the country could stand a debt of about $35 billion. At that time businessmen who were offering estimates thought that the government should be spending no more than $3.9 billion.† At the time, the government was actually spending more than $8.5 billion.[52]

Quite apparently, business and the Administration were far apart in their estimates of what it took to run the government. The sums suggested by the President appeared staggering to industrialists and more so to the bankers. Panic stricken, the vice-president and about-to-be president of the American Bankers Association, Orville Adams, called for a sit-down strike. As he put it, "Since the Federal Govern-

* At that time (November 1935), the federal government was spending about $7.5 billion a year, about $2.3 billion on relief and $0.8 billion on public works. The deficit was running about $3.5 billion a year and the net debt had passed $28 billion. When the New Deal came to an end in June 1940, the interest-bearing debt was $42.4 billion, and expenditures were running at a rate of approximately $9.0 billion a year, with a deficit of about $3.6 billion.

† $1.0 billion in defense, $1.3 billion for interest on the debt, $0.7 billion for domestic and foreign service, $0.6 billion on pensions, and $0.3 billion for rivers and harbors and other things.

ment cannot spend without using the bankable funds of the nation, it
is up to us to declare an embargo. We must declare that we will not
finance further spending by the government until an honest, sincere
effort is made to restore a balanced budget. The bankers of America
should resume negotiations with the Federal Government only under
a rigid economy, a balanced budget, and a sane tax program."

Holders of bank stocks all over the country were understandably
much disturbed by the awful fate which orthodox bankers were
prophesying. They feared that the United States Government was
about to go bankrupt with its assets sold at a sheriff's auction sale.
Many stockholders objected strenuously to further purchases of government bonds. This made little sense at a time when, either because
of reluctance on the part of bankers or reluctance on the part of business borrowers, commercial loans were almost non-existent and government bonds seemed to offer the only outlet for bank funds. A few
members of the banking profession, chiefly among the young and
among those bankers who specialized in so-called "retail banking,"
that is banking geared more to the general public than to big business,
openly expressed their disagreement with the orthodox view. They
were especially cold to the plea that bankers should go on a capital
strike. When the stockholders of the Corn Exchange Bank expressed
misgivings about the size of the government bond portfolio, Chairman Frew very logically asked: "Which is best—to have the banks
own large amounts of governments or to have printing press money?"
Harvey Gibson, head of the Manufacturers Trust Company, answered
stockholder objections to government-bond purchases by patiently
insisting that governments were the soundest investments a bank
could make. But Marriner S. Eccles was by far the most outspoken
critic of the orthodox view. With typical impatience, he dismissed
"those who talk about boycotting government bonds" and likened
them to "a drowning man to whom a life line is thrown out but who
objects that it is an interference with his individual right and liberty
to drown."[53]

WE HAVE NOTHING TO FEAR BUT INFLATION

What worried most business leaders from Orville Adams to Owen
D. Young was the same old pathological fear of inflation. They knew
that what the government couldn't borrow from individuals and busi-

nesses would have to be financed by borrowing from the banks or by printing paper money. Either method would increase the money supply, and this, *ipso facto,* would mean inflation. In retrospect, it appears rather strange that anyone would be seriously worried about inflation when the price index was 25 per cent below the 1926 level, when the per capita money supply was far below that of 1929, and when Treasury bills were selling at a yield of less than one half of one per cent. This was very much like refusing to give a starving man a piece of bread for fear that it would cause him to become overweight. But worry there was, as innumerable expressed opinions showed. In a speech provocatively entitled "How to Share the Wealth," W. B. Bell, president of American Cyanamid Company, declared, "We are creating vast additional national debt by issuing bonds which banks are forced to buy. Result—inflation." In the middle of the recession of 1937, Fred I. Kent explained the whole thing in simple terms to a group of sympathetic bankers. According to Kent's typically orthodox view, "If expenditures of government are not stopped but are continued until there is no market for government bonds and government must print money . . . we will certainly run into progressive inflation." But Kent had for some time thought that "only time will tell whether our country can escape having similar difficulties [to those of Germany, Austria, and Hungary] because of inflation."

The bankers of the old school had no doubt about the shape of things to come. The whole business came tied in a neatly wrapped package consisting of government spending, unbalanced budgets, inflation, and a general lack of confidence. Winthrop Aldrich thought that "there can be little doubt that the net effect of continued government spending . . . on the volume of business and the volume of employment is definitely adverse. This comes from fear of inflation and fear of government competition."

What Aldrich thought was also the view of orthodox economic theorists. In February 1934, of 845 economists who replied to a questionnaire on money, 51.4 per cent agreed that the "present trend in the United States was toward a dangerous expansion of money." Two thirds thought that "inflation *could be controlled* under existing conditions," but only 41.9 per cent "believed that inflation *was likely to be controlled*." Later in the year, when prices had crawled a little closer to where they had been in 1929, Professor Kemmerer said, "The greatest single danger threatening the American people today is the danger of serious inflation."[54]

Those who were steeped in the traditions of orthodoxy were pursuing a phantom. They knew that the difficulty clearly lay in the failure of credit to expand, but they either blamed this on government or they explained it by saying that there was no demand for loans. The first approach was summed up by Floyd L. Carlisle of Consolidated Edison when he said that "the greatest deterrent to recovery was the log jam in the capital markets which was caused in no small measure by the restrictive legislation of recent years." The other view—that businessmen were not borrowing—had many spokesmen. "It isn't the bankers who are holding back credit," wrote Owen D. Young in May 1935. "They are anxious to make it work, for in no other way can they earn their living. It is business which has not yet been willing to use the credit, for responsible people will not borrow until they can make the money work profitably." A necessary corollary to this conclusion was that monetary policy could not work to alleviate the depression.

Many industrialists, more merchants, and a few bankers dissented from this conclusion. Among bankers, the outstanding dissenter was, as has been mentioned earlier, Frank Vanderlip, who was "inclined to favor completely the President's monetary policy." But in any case, the public at large put a very low value on the bankers' views even on money. According to a survey taken in 1936, the public, when asked with whose views on money they agreed, voted for Roosevelt, Father Coughlin, Senator Glass, and Governor Landon in that order.

According to orthodox opinion, any attempt to use monetary policy as a way out of the depression would not only fail to accomplish any good but might result in disaster. Said Owen D. Young, "The easy money heroes of 1929 have gone; let us beware of the easy recovery heroes of 1935." Fred I. Kent was less cryptic when he explained: "As money was not the cause of the present depression, the inflationary expansion of credit did not lead the way out. Its advocates believed that it would do so and it was the political force built upon this belief that determined this ineffectual monetary policy. There is no doubt whatever but that the monetary uncertainty that exists at present is largely responsible for the holding back of recovery." The bankers and those who believed with them looked upon excess bank reserves as a disease whereas it was really a symptom of an entirely different sickness. Instead of working to expand credit, business leaders took refuge in a nest of clichés and fetishes like the gold standard, etc., and warned against every effort to feed the economy through easy money policies and resisted every effort to reform the banking system. Even though a survey of bankers showed that more than two thirds of the profession thought that "legislation enacted since the crisis had increased the security of bank depositors and stock-holders," the leading bankers persisted in their opposition to deposit insurance. William C. Potter continued to refer to it as "unsound and menacing"; Percy Johnston thought it "the most serious problem confronting the banks"; and Leroy W. Baldwin of the Empire Trust and O. H. Wolfe of Philadelphia called upon their stockholders to resist it.

Uneasiness about the early monetary policies of the New Deal was one of the opening paragraphs in the breakdown of business-government relations. To be sure, the House of Morgan, under the leadership of Russell Leffingwell, supported the President's rapid retreat from the gold standard, but Winthrop Aldrich unquestionably expressed the majority view more accurately when he announced, "I am a believer in sound money; I regretted most profoundly the action taken by the Government in reducing the gold content of the dollar." Aldrich also had plenty of support among the non-financial business-men. In the fall of 1933, Sewell Avery of Montgomery Ward, Alexander Legge of International Harvester, Albert Lasker, the advertising man, and other Chicago businessmen set up a local committee on monetary policy and recommended "the end of experimentation" and "a return to the gold standard." By that time, too, the U. S. Chamber of Commerce was calling for an early return to the gold standard "with complete avoidance of monetary experimentation, greenbackism, and fiat money and with complete recession from theoretical or arbitrary ideas of price index fixation of the value of gold."

When government spokesmen urged bankers to loosen up, the bankers refused to be seduced. The American Bankers Association, in 1933, "viewed with apprehension the propaganda now being featured in the public press which brings pressure upon banks to adopt ultra-liberal lending policies." When RFC Director Jesse Jones, himself a banker and businessman, called upon bankers to make more real estate, consumer, and term loans, the response was far from enthusiastic. Replying for the bankers, Edward E. Brown, president of the First National of Chicago, blamed the government and the regulatory authorities for slow credit expansion.

What all this demonstrated was a lack of faith in monetary policy.

Bankers simply did not believe that anything could be done. In 1935 Winthrop Aldrich told the Senate Committee on Banking and Currency: "Beyond an initial and rather gentle influence, open-market operations, carried on under such conditions as have prevailed, have not succeeded in increasing proportionately the volume of bank credit."

When Marriner Eccles was urging the Banking Act of 1935 on a reluctant Congress, the bankers presented an almost solid phalanx of opposition. The big ones and the little ones, the city bankers and the country bankers objected less to the bill's effects on the money market and the banking structure than to the increased power it would give to the government. F. F. Beattie, president of the First National Bank of Greenville, South Carolina, was of that "school of thought which believed that the business of banking is already unduly controlled and regulated by Government." W. S. Elliot of the Georgia Bankers' Association stated his organization's opposition to "compulsory membership in the Federal Reserve System." Edward E. Brown was "particularly afraid of a board which would be apt to force Government obligations on Federal Reserve banks which the investing public was unwilling to take."

As excess reserves piled up in the commercial banks, bankers of all philosophies—from Winthrop Aldrich to Marriner Eccles—became highly perturbed. By the end of 1935, excess reserves were approaching $3.0 billion, more than half of total reserves. This could conceivably create $30 billion of new loans and deposits, a figure that made staid bankers blanch.*

Almost as though he were pointing to an actual pile of excess reserves, Winthrop Aldrich said, "There it is . . . explosive material awaiting the match. It invites a far wilder speculative abuse of credit than culminated in 1929." As a way "to obviate the probability of an undue and dangerous credit inflation," Aldrich recommended that the Federal Reserve Board sell bonds in the open market and raise the reserve requirements of member banks. But excess reserves continued to pile up, and the banking fraternity became steadily more apprehensive. The panic was contagious and in August 1936, the Federal Reserve System raised reserve requirements by 50 per cent. This gave some comfort to the more orthodox bankers, but they did not think the tightening had gone far enough. In 1937, real per capita

* At the time, member bank loans were $12.2 billion; they had been $26.2 billion in 1929.

income was still less than it had been in 1929, and, according to the best available estimates, some 14 per cent of the labor force was still unemployed. Yet Aldrich greeted the new year with the statement: "Both experience and theory make it clear that, unless additional monetary controls are invoked in time, our recovery can all too easily degenerate into a dangerous boom culminating in disaster." We had, in other words, all too soon reached that familiar ground—an unsustainable boom. Other bankers called on all forces to resist temptation. Said James H. Perkins of the National City: "It is the duty of the banks to do all in their power to avoid the pitfalls which increased prosperity creates." Percy H. Johnston went so far as to anticipate the recession that was about to occur: "In many lines production now exceeds consumption. . . . It is easy to forget, but we should recall 1919, 1920, 1921 when a similar pyramiding of orders caused overproduction. . . . We are in an inflation that is evident and will eventually have to pay the bill which may be confiscation of wealth."

By June, because of the tightening of monetary policy, excess reserves were down to less than $1 billion. The financial world, instead of regarding this as dangerous, was very complacent. As L. E. Pierson explained, "We have reached a point in recovery where selectivity in further credit expansion is becoming increasingly important. . . . The Federal Reserve and the Treasury have already made considerable progress in tightening up some slack in bank reserves. . . . These steps should be followed by other available and appropriate measures to hold further unnecessary credit expansion in check." At that time, member bank loans were on the order of $14 billion, some $12 billion less than in 1929.[55]

Despite the oft-repeated warnings and cries of alarm, the inflation that had been so commonly feared did not appear until the outbreak of war in 1939. Then by some strange process of metamorphosis, the very things that business had blamed for the breakdown of confidence were transformed into the things that created confidence. In the war years, government spending multiplied over tenfold; the budget deficit soared from the $3.6 billion which had seemed so cataclysmic in 1940 to almost $50 billion in 1945. The national debt doubled in two years and reached $279 billion in 1946. The long-awaited inflation at last became a reality as wholesale prices climbed 12 per cent in one year. All that businessmen feared had at last come true, and the business leaders relaxed and enjoyed it.

7. THE READJUSTMENT TO PROSPERITY, 1945–54

"The foolish and the dead alone never change their opinions."
James Russell Lowell.

The outbreak of World War II brought an armistice in the war between government and business. Both sides stopped snarling at each other and turned their attention to the common enemy. The Roosevelt administration formally buried the New Deal, and business did its part in the war effort by meeting production goals that had seemed fantastically visionary when first proposed.

But almost as soon as the war ended, the armistice between the Administration and the business community also came to a jarring halt. Business leaders blamed the government for this. Benjamin Fairless of United States Steel expressed their feeling when he told a House committee in 1950: "It was only a few years ago that the Government gloried in . . . its industrial giants. . . . It called upon U. S. Steel to outproduce, single-handed, all the Axis nations. . . . But when the war was over, all this was conveniently forgotten in Washington."[1]

Government, too, had something to say about the breakdown of the uneasy amicability of the war years. Impatiently, government leaders dismissed the complaints of the business leaders on the ground that like the overprivileged before the French Revolution they had learned nothing and forgotten nothing.

This accusation, like most, was not the whole truth. To be sure, the New Deal's effect on business opinion was negligible, except that it had imprinted on business minds the news that modern government was an immensely influential force. As E. T. Weir realistically and regretfully noted in 1938, "The government had become just as important a factor to business as the cost of raw materials, management policies, sales efforts, or any of the other things with which business-men seem to be more directly concerned."[2]

Unlike the 1920s when government could be and was regarded as a force whose importance could be minimized, business leaders at the end of the Second War went all the way in the opposite direction and became obsessed with the importance of government. Of course, there were other issues besides government about which business-men expressed concern in the immediate postwar years—the same sort of things that had exercised them in the 1920s. Labor always gave them something to think about. Naturally, they were also inter-ested in the economic outlook. Intermittently, too, business leaders were concerned about price inflation which they usually attributed to wage inflation or to "swollen" government spending, "confiscatory" taxes, and "the burden" of public debt.

Just as in the twenties, only more so, many members of the busi-ness group worried about the decline of the "American Way" and the possibility or probability of the ultimate triumph of some form of socialism or communism. And again, as in the twenties, a few, very few, expressed their concern about monetary policy and its effects on the general economy. But no matter which issue was raised, business-men found it almost impossible to discuss it without giving govern-ment a leading role. In the months immediately after the war, when many business leaders were discussing the problems that faced the economy, Charles E. Wilson of General Motors listed six such prob-lems. Of these, he named the "Labor Problem and the Fiscal Prob-lem as basic" with the others "largely resulting from these two."

THE ANTAGONISM TOWARD THE TRUMAN ADMINISTRATION

Management had no difficulty in ticking off why it did not like the Truman administration. Part of the antagonism stemmed from the old natural hostility of business toward government in general. A conviction that the Administration was more than friendly to labor aggravated this latent hostility. According to Robert R. Wason, presi-dent of the NAM in 1946, "The administration's subservience to the CIO is now clear." And as the Truman years drew to a close, Charles M. White of Republic Steel expressed the general business feeling, "This partnership between government and labor has been a disgrace to our country." Wason, White, *et al.* had no trouble in piling up evidence to support their view.

The Truman administration was indeed partial to labor if only because it got along so much better with labor than with business. Its behavior definitely showed this. In the immediate postwar years when the country was immersed in labor-management disputes, the Administration offered a bill to restrict the right to strike. At the same time Representative Case of South Dakota introduced an anti-strike bill. Business considered the Administration's effort halfhearted. It, therefore, endorsed the Republican-sponsored and Republican-supported bill, which Congress passed and Truman vetoed in June 1946. A year later, he also rejected the bill that eventually passed over his veto to become the Taft-Hartley Act.[3]

Subsequent events compounded the business conviction that Washington was becoming ever more biased in favor of the labor unions. In July 1949 the Steel Workers Union announced that it would strike for a fourth-round wage increase. Industry replied in a way that led many to believe that it was saying, "This is most unfortunate, but strike and be damned." Naturally, the Administration was not sympathetic. The President interceded by appointing a Steel Fact Finding Board to find the facts and make recommendations. Management objected to giving the Board the power to make recommendations, but their objections came to nothing, and they reluctantly accepted "action they felt impelled to follow in order to avoid a strike" and in order to avoid alienating public opinion. For its part, the Administration found the business attitude incomprehensible. Never suffering from the pangs of self-doubt, it believed that all parts of the community had the patriotic duty of accepting what the government decided. It charged, in the words of Franklin D. Roosevelt, Jr., that Fairless, who spoke for the steel industry, violated "moral law because he forgets his responsibility to the economy." Government spokesmen, in other words, took the questionable position that they were the final authorities on what constituted moral and social responsibility.

At the first meeting of the Fact Finding Board, Clarence B. Randall of Inland Steel expressed his colleagues' view that the whole procedure was governmental dictation in favor of labor. "Wages shall be fixed," Randall told the Board. "Fixing of profits comes next. No thoughtful person will be deceived that your findings will be recommendations only. . . . This is labor monopoly given its blessings by the same government that cries monopoly at management."[4]

A similar series of events enlivened the conversations between steel and the union in 1952. Once again, negotiations threatened to end in a strike. But this time, the President seized the steel industry. Then the Supreme Court, to the delight of the business community, ruled the President out of order, and there ensued an eight-week strike that ended with a substantial pay raise. Toward the end of the year, the Wage Stabilization Board denied a pay raise to the coal miners, but the President overruled the Board, and the raise was granted.

All of this led businessmen to conclude that the Truman administration was anti-business, anti-profit, and anti-production minded. "The administration," said Wason, "is so concentrated against profit that it can see nothing else." Businessmen's feelings were so intense that they had to exercise their will power to the sticking point to speak calmly about their difficulties with the government. Occasionally, however, especially when talking to friendly groups such as commerce associations, they spoke with an air of uninhibited relaxation, aiming their jibes at two favorite targets: the "Washington theorists" and the "Washington bureaucrats." Benjamin Fairless, after three years in which he "had been through so many Congressional inquisitions that no self-respecting skeleton would hide in [his] closet," pulled out all the stops in a talk that was greeted with extravagant enthusiasm by his colleagues. "In my opinion," said Fairless, "our system is in deadlier peril than it has ever been in my lifetime. . . . I honestly don't know how it can be protected against its self-styled 'friends' in Washington who would literally hack it to death on the pretext of saving its immortal soul." Fairless concentrated his fire on the cavalier conduct of the Administration, the regulatory bodies, and the courts. The courts, he mused, subscribed to the philosophy inscribed on one of Hunter College's buildings: "We are of different opinions at different hours; but we always may be said to be, at heart, on the side of truth." For an academy, Fairless found this very commendable, but for a court, he thought it "a helluva way to run a railroad." Fairless summed up the frustration of the business community: "The greatest single drawback to the effective operation of our modern economic system is the amazing but undeniable fact that the minute any man successfully establishes himself in any business, he automatically becomes a potential jailbird."[5]

What Fairless was touching upon was an extraordinarily popular topic among industrialists and bankers in the first half of the 1950s: a gnawing and constantly increasing fear that the American Way was being destroyed. So real was this fear that the *Commercial and Financial Chronicle* eventually listed "The American Way" in its index. In one six-month period—October 1952 to March 1953—there were thirty-two articles on the subject by such representative businessmen as Charles E. Wilson of GE, Fairless, Sloan, Harold Bache, L. L. Colbert, Henry Ford, Arthur Homer, and Charles E. Merrill. In an article called "Are We Going Totalitarian?" W. Alton Jones of Cities Service wrote: "Two ideas are at grips. One camp contends a small group should plan for the rest of us. . . . The other believes we should center our efforts on the making of men and women who are themselves competent and disposed to do the right thing."[6]

As business saw the situation, it was the federal government together with a breakdown in morals and a rejection of old values that was threatening the continued existence of the American Way and its replacement by some form of collectivism. General Motors' Wilson wrote about the rising tide of government in terms of the parable about the camel which pleaded with its master to allow it to put its nose inside the tent on a bitterly cold night. The master agreed and shortly the whole of the camel was inside the tent and the whole of the Arab was outside. Wilson's namesake in General Electric, who served the Truman administration, deplored the drift to nationalization and socialism as he recalled that he had been overruled in Washington by one man who had never been elected to office but "had more power than the President." Robert Wason said that "the problem of our domestic economy is the recovery of our freedom." To L. R. Boulware, vice-president of General Electric, "The principal problem before us is to decide on whether we can keep what we have and get more of what we want by voluntary individual action . . . or by sending each successive problem to Washington." In 1947, H. W. Prentis, Jr., of Armstrong Cork and the NAM responded to his own question, "Can we preserve our freedom?" with the answer that we could by exercising initiative and self-reliance and by refusing to be wards of the state. But five years after the question was raised, Sun Oil's Joseph N. Pew, Jr., despondently said, "It is obvious that the government has no intention of lessening the weight of its dead hand in business affairs."[7]

Business was convinced that the tendency to run to the government for help was a part of the malaise of the time—the hunt for security.

Early in the postwar period, one extremist, a small businessman from Philadelphia, named "social security as the root of all political evil." L. M. Giannini, president of the Bank of America, had a more complex explanation, one that came closer to voicing the consensus of conservative thought: "The substitution of paternalistic cradle-to-the-grave philosophy for the self-reliance which built this nation is probably America's greatest weakness. . . . The delusion that an unearned luxurious living is anyone's right has become ominously popular." Shortly thereafter, Fairless tried a different variation on the same theme: "We should take thought, serious thought, that in our overall approach to planning security, we do not adopt methods which will wither the spirit while catering to the needs of the flesh." And again James E. Shelton, who viewed many things with alarm, told his fellow bankers, "It is startling to see how far the American people have been led down the road to ultimate economic and political enslavement." By this time, businessmen had become fond of pointing to the awful experience of the British people, who "for some fifteen years have been drinking deep draughts of the poison of communism from the cup of socialism."[8]

All this sounded rather strange and unreal in the late 1940s when the economy was bustling, when employment was full, and when output per man-hour was increasing faster than at any other time in the history of the statistics. The country's economic performance hardly gave proof that "no one wanted to work," or, in the words of Clarence Francis of General Foods, that "there was a frightful tendency among all groups to take rather than make." But one could dispose of the facts to his own satisfaction. Some realized that the price of prosperity came very high. They sensed that large gains in material things came at the cost of some deterioration of the spirit. Others simply denied the existence of the prosperity that seemed so apparent. To these few, the shadows of shibboleths and fetishes made a mockery of the substance of reality. "Beguiled by the diversions and feverish activity of an inflation-induced false prosperity," said William C. Mulendore, Pacific Coast utility executive, "we are acquiescing in the slow strangulation of the principal factors of our strength, namely limited government, sound money, a free market, and other basic elements of our free enterprise economy." Along the same lines, Walter S. McLucas, chairman of the National Bank of Detroit, told its stockholders: "People generally are aware that something has gone wrong. . . . Many have decided that thrift, saving, and honest

effort are no longer worth while; that some power is operating to
defeat the wholesome purpose of those whose instincts are to practice these age-old virtues. . . . Yet these conditions have been accompanied by the outward appearance of prosperity." Apparently,
many had given up the struggle, believing as A. V. Bodine, president
of the Bodine Corporation of Bridgeport, Connecticut, did, "thoughtful Americans have been deeply concerned over the trend toward
socialism. The truth is that we already have socialism."[9]

To cast out the Truman administration and eradicate the New and
Fair deals occupied a high rung on the 1946–52 ladder of business
objectives. When the Republican party in 1946 gained control of
Congress for the first time in almost twenty years, business leaders
were elated. "America," said Charles E. Wilson of GM, "has chosen
the fork in the road that leads to freedom and personal liberty. The
majority of our citizens have had enough, enough of bureaucratic
government planning; enough of the false theory of prosperity
through scarcity; enough of unbalanced budgets and governmental
extravagances; enough of organized unemployment."

Elation was beaten into the dust by the galling disappointment of
the Truman victory in 1948, and the crusade had to begin all over
again. A footwear manufacturer in Columbus, Ohio, circulated membership cards in the "Freedom Party 4-H Club" organized "To Help
Hurry Harry Home!" Others who had little understanding of American politics and who had often come defeated and frustrated from
the political arena lost their interest in the whole game, and cast a pox
on both parties. Ernest Weir, for example, was quite sure that the
"political leadership of both sides is not measuring up to its responsibilities." The events of 1952 added to the disenchantment. Most
businessmen, it seemed, favored Senator Robert Taft, and General
Eisenhower's nomination was something of a letdown. In the middle
of the campaign, Don G. Mitchell of Sylvania Products and H. E.
Humphreys, Jr., of U. S. Rubber—one by flat accusation and the other
by implication—charged that both candidates were failing to give due
recognition to the problems of business and industry: whether "we
were to have more government in business, or more business in government," more equitable taxes, a pause in deficit spending, a halt in
unnecessary government intervention, an understanding of the business system, an end to the instability of the dollar, and labor-
management relations free of political overtones.[10]

ECONOMIC FORECASTS, 1946–48

The new conflict between businessmen and government officials first flared up because of disagreements over the outlook for the postwar economy. As the war came to an end, many government and academic economists and many laymen, disregarding what history had to offer, anticipated a severe and long drawn-out depression in the immediate postwar period. Public opinion polls concluded that almost half of all Americans expected higher prices, about one out of three expected lower prices, and almost two out of three foresaw lots of unemployment and lower wages. At the same time, many prominent economists, trained in the "mature economy" environment of the 1930s, predicted severe unemployment unless the government injected large doses of spending.*

Most businessmen did not agree. Just as in the early 1920s, they did not think that there was any threat of a serious depression. The most sophisticated statement of the majority business view came from Russell Leffingwell, who, in 1945, outlined the course of the economy in the next few years. He looked forward to two to five years of full employment. During this period, inflation would be the major domestic problem, for "nobody has invented a way of stopping inflation without making money dear as in 1920 and 1929, or relatively scarce as in 1937 and so bringing on deflation, depression, and unemployment." Leffingwell recommended gradual and selective withdrawal of controls, maintaining taxes at a "pretty high" level, and a not too rapid debt reduction. But Leffingwell warned that after two to five years of boom prosperity, it might be difficult to maintain full employment so that a tax reduction and easy money might then be called for.[11]†

---

* "A number of economic models relating to the national budget recently developed on the basis of prewar income and expenditure patterns have demonstrated that severe depression in the years immediately following the transition period is highly probable in the absence of a national policy to assure full employment." Jacob L. Mosak, "National Budgets and National Policy," *American Economic Review*, March 1946.

† "The Federal Reserve authorities overdid it [cheap money] in 1927 and this was the chief cause of the disastrous inflation in stocks and real estate which occurred in 1927–29. Our government permitted the consequent deflation to run too long and too deep." Government then pursued an inflationary policy, but it did not take. It will not take "unless the money issued circulates with velocity."

As things turned out, the business leaders were not only more accurate than the academic economists, but more accurate than they had been twenty-five years before. In the twenty years after World War II, total production of goods and services grew at a compound rate of 3.4 per cent annually. There were two hundred months of recovery and prosperity, forty months of mild recession, and no depression at all, easily the most impressive performance in a long history of economic growth.

In the period under discussion here, that is, the years from the end of World War II to 1954, total production in dollars of the same purchasing power grew from about $300 billion to something over $400 billion, or at a rate of about 3.4 per cent annually. It was not, however, all uphill. There were two very mild recessions, one from November 1948 to October 1949 and the second from July 1953 to August 1954. Recovery and prosperity ruled in the other eighty months.

The whole eight and two-thirds years could be divided into four subdivisions. The years from 1946 to late 1948 witnessed the usual reaction to the preceding war economy. This was a time of severe and long-drawn out labor disputes and of sharp inflation with the wholesale price index rising more than 30 per cent. Yet, it was not a time of widespread speculation. Trading on the New York Stock Exchange averaged a little over one million shares a day. In the entire three years there were only five three-million-share days. The *Times* composite average ranged from 105 to 150. Indeed, the market was so lethargic that many public-spirited citizens in and outside of Congress were constrained to express concern. When stock averages lost about 11 per cent in 1946, the brokerage firm Harris, Upham & Co. took an ad in the *Times* to explain that the primary causes of the decline were "man-made regulations, experiments in price control, and wage increases in excess of labor's ability or willingness to increase production." But although the pundits and the soothsayers were alarmed, business leaders in general did not seem to be much bothered by what happened to the price of stocks. At least this is indicated by the way they responded to the questions about the stock market posed by the Flanders Committee investigation of profits in 1948. Typical was the statement by Clarence Francis of General Foods that he knew nothing about the company's stock and that he was "interested only in a sound merchandising procedure," leaving the stock to fend for itself.

For most business leaders, the mood during the first couple of years after V-J Day was one of cautious confidence and optimism. If they did not expect a serious depression, they did not entirely rule out the possibility of a downturn in a few years. This was more a matter of intuition, of feeling, than of fact. "There is no law, divine or economic," enunciated Gale F. Johnson, president of the Mercantile Commerce Bank of St. Louis, "that says we must have a depression after even a $350 billion war." With some surprise, Alfred P. Sloan answered a question about the business outlook, "I haven't any feeling at all that we are going to have a serious recession in this country. I don't see how that can be possible."[12]

In early 1947, the National Industrial Conference Board found only a minority of businessmen expecting a recession. The prevalent mood was well expressed by General Robert E. Wood of Sears, Roebuck. After admitting that he had been pessimistic when we first entered the war, the General went on to recall how incorrect many of the immediate postwar forecasts were. "In the summer of 1946," he said, "we were warned by private sources that a serious recession was impending. . . . I have never believed that any depression was in store for us in 1947, and I doubt whether it will come in 1948." The warnings to which General Wood referred were not just a phase of summer complaint in 1946. Many professional forecasters, but by no means all of them, had started on the bearish road in 1945 and they continued well into 1946. Business leaders naturally delighted in gloating over those who had gone wrong. As early as the spring of 1946, Lewis H. Brown reminded his colleagues how wrong "the bureaucrats in Washington were in forecasting depression." In September 1947, Charles E. Wilson of General Electric still saw no recession and criticized "some Washington economists for wrongfully predicting a depression."[13]

Washington economists were, of course, not the only ones who began with bearish notions and pigheadedly held to them. In the spring of 1946, Major Angas was advertising, "Already 55 per cent of the stocks on the Stock Exchange are below their October lows. Why do people talk of recession, when historically, depression is more likely?" And another advisory service was announcing that 90 per cent of traders were bearish. Some financiers and industrialists who rode special hobbyhorses also warned the public to seek an economic bomb shelter. Arthur J. Morris, founder of the famous Morris Plan, was sure that unless the public went on a buying strike a recession would occur. Robert Cutler of the Old Colony Trust of Boston took an extremely pessimistic view of the long-run future as he recalled Mellon's 1929 statement about bonds vs. stocks. Then, Philip Cortney of Coty International, who had a fixation about classical economic theory, warned that we were in for heavy weather. To all of which, Earl Bunting, president of the NAM, replied that he was dismayed by three fears that were gnawing at American confidence: fear of war, fear of depression, and fear of runaway inflation.[14]

WANING OPTIMISM

In October about 80 per cent of New York credit men expected a "business slump" in the second quarter of 1948. This did not mean a depression, and for the short term, most executives were still optimistic. The *Chronicle*'s annual collection of businessmen's statements about the outlook was sunny. In its annual review of January 1948, the *Times* saw some resemblance to the "new era" outlook of 1929, but it was quick to say that the "real business leaders are well aware that the boom-bust cycle still operates." Millard D. Brown, a highly opinionated textile manufacturer, thought we would have a depression in another seven or eight years, but not at the moment. Morris Sayre of Corn Products Refining thought there would be "reasonably good business for at least another year or two." In May 1948, Sloan told General Motors stockholders that "good business" would obtain for another two years. Still later, Benjamin Fairless gave a fuller explanation of how the majority viewed the outlook. "I think," he told the Flanders Committee, "two things are going to happen. I would think the present demand is not going to continue, and by that I do not want to be quoted as forecasting a depression. There is quite a difference between a depression and receding to some reasonable extent from the present high demands of production."

During this initial period of postwar prosperity, a number of businessmen eagerly explained what had to be done to avoid a slump and to achieve prosperity. Bernard Baruch had the most comprehensive list. In testimony before the House Banking and Currency Committee in 1946, he recommended: more production, an end to the expansion of the money supply, no tax reduction while the budget was unbalanced, a one-year extension of modified price controls, no favoritism to any particular group, reduced government costs, and the elimination of strikes for one year. As usual, Baruch had a little something for every ideology. In this case, he threw a sop to those who believed in a compensatory fiscal policy by adopting their cardinal rule: In time of deflation we should spend; in time of inflation, we should save.[15]

Most businessmen would have voted for most of the ingredients in the Baruch recipe, but they cheered loudly when Robert Wason named "Three roadblocks to prosperity: lack of equality between labor and management before the law, production-preventing controls of OPA, and an inflationary fiscal policy based on continued deficit spending."

Here and there, a few businessmen were not so sure that the economy could keep rolling without a plan or without a push. J. J. Nance, vice-president of Zenith Radio, warned his colleagues: "We must create and sustain a desire for goods to steadily increase consumption. . . . If industry fails to provide millions of jobs required to maintain a high degree of prosperity, the socialist minded boys will say . . . 'See, you have failed again, just as you did in 1932. You cannot and will not take up the slack. Government must come to the rescue.' "[16]

THE REACTION TO THE 1948 AND 1953 RECESSIONS

Everybody knew that the economy would turn down sometime. It was merely a question of time, and in 1946–47, the most popular concept of time was two years. It, therefore, came as no particular shock when business activity did fall off in mid-1948. H. E. Smith, chairman of United States Rubber, accurately reflected general opinion by saying, "A serious recession is unlikely, but there will undoubtedly be some adjustments." Most of his colleagues regarded the recession as a pause for breath that did not warrant any special discussion or any elaborate treatment. In fact, many businessmen, as in the 1920s, seemed to welcome the slump as a seventh-inning stretch that was badly needed to prevent economic activity from becoming unsustainable. Don G. Mitchell of Sylvania thought it would make business "fundamentally sounder." At the American Bankers convention, where opinion was divided about equally between those who thought 1949 business would be off less than 10 per cent and those who thought it would be off more than 10 per cent, a comfortable majority thought the decline "healthy" because it would make prices "more realistic" and labor "more productive." Here was a subtle difference from the prevailing opinion in the 1920s, when prosperity was regarded with alarm because of a belief that depression inevitably followed boom and followed it in the same magnitude.[17]

Yet businessmen had not completely forgotten what they had learned as students of classical theory. They were still impressed by nature's niggardliness and they still believed that a little growth was about all that one could expect in the cruel world of economics. When President Truman, in one of his rasher moments, called on the steel industry to increase its productive capacity, he was met with the hostility that usually greeted his remarks. Ernest T. Weir led off. "It is obvious," he remarked, "that the huge immediate demand for steel is abnormal and temporary. It would be foolish and damaging to build permanent capacity in proportion to this passing situation." Other steel leaders agreed, but the matter did not end there. More than a year later, Charles E. Wilson of General Motors chided steel executives "to get the dust out of their eyes and go ahead with the rest of industry." Still the steel industry had the last word as Charles White, in the middle of the Korean Police Action, complained that steel's profits were too low and warned that to seek a 130-million-ton steel production could bring a repetition of the slump of the 1930s. With which Weir and Roger Blough of U. S. Steel enthusiastically agreed.

By this time, business activity had long since climbed out of its doldrums. When the Korean action broke out in June 1950, recovery was already eight months old. The Korean episode did not, therefore, bring recovery. What it did bring was full employment, a resurgence of price inflation, and a more active and more buoyant stock market. By the spring of 1951, when the second round of inflation ended, the wholesale price level was almost half again as high as it had been in 1946. Daily volume on the New York Stock Exchange which had averaged barely a million shares in the late 1940s climbed to well over a million and a half in the early 1950s. The stock averages, which at their peaks in 1949 were lower than they had been in 1946, doubled between 1949 and 1954.

Yet, in the midst of all this, most business leaders, most economists, and most of those who kept both eyes on the economic indicators continued to be cautiously optimistic. The accepted consensus for 1950 among economists was for "a golden year," while businessmen once again were reported to be "optimistic but cautious" and resigned to the fact that business had returned to normal and the "sellers' market" was over. The forecasts that were made on these premises came reasonably close to the bull's eye with the consensus predicting total production at $267 billion compared to the actual $284 billion.

A few business leaders and economists persisted in their anticipation of complete collapse. Of these, Sewell Avery of Montgomery Ward was the most notable. "We have had a collapse after every other war," he said, "and I think it is inevitable that the same thing will take place again. The thing that hit us in 1929 cannot be assumed not to happen again. I have been waiting for years for the ax to fall." But his rival in the competition between the bulls and the bears, General Robert E. Wood, thought altogether differently and much more correctly. While he admitted he was "not in the confidence of the Administration," he was "firmly convinced that they will use money management to stave off incipient recessions" and he "could see no reason why they should not be successful over a number of years." Opinion had certainly changed from what it had been before the war when the mood of businessmen was one of worry and unease.[18]

As the Korean fighting wore on, optimism became much more cautious, especially among the economists and the stock market forecasters. In October 1950, many market analysts were predicting a 25 to 50 per cent drop in the stock averages, but some others thought that the peak of the market was still in the future. As 1950 and 1951 drifted into 1952, there was a further noticeable increase in bearish sentiment. Yet toward the end of 1952, a survey of over 1300 executives found "wide optimism for the first quarter of 1953." This was playing it close, for the economy did begin to falter in early 1953, and by the summer when the "police action" ended, after a year and a half of peace rumors, we were in a recession.

Among professional economists, the only questions were how long would it last, how severe would it be, and how strong would the recovery be? Some economists, mostly the same ones who had predicted a postwar depression, again foresaw a severe drop, but others, like Sumner Slichter and Arthur F. Burns, thought the whole thing would be over by June or July 1954.

For their part, the majority of businessmen were even more sanguine. Despite the evident downturn in economic activity, they rejected the possibility that we were in a recession. In January 1954 when the business slump was already six months old, Paul G. Hoffman "saw no justification for a recession." J. Luther Cleveland and William L. Kleitz of the Guaranty Trust in New York went further. In their annual report to stockholders, they pronounced the economic climate the "most wholesome in two decades." The business community thought that any letdown in business was psychosomatic. They talked incessantly about resisting "depression psychology." For example, Crawford Greenewalt told DuPont stockholders, "Whether there will be a recession will depend largely on the national psychology and on decisions that are influenced less by rational economic reasoning than by simple confidence and optimism."

Businessmen indulged in much hairsplitting about the difference between a readjustment and a recession. In an inspired phrase in February 1954, Secretary of the Treasury Humphrey summed up the prevalent business opinion by saying the economy was in a "rolling readjustment." As to the idea that we were in danger of a depression, the very thought struck business leaders as ludicrous. That is, except for Sewell Avery, who announced with evident delight that we were in a "distressing situation." A much more typical judgment was offered by Greenewalt, who thought the future limitless. "It is interesting to note," he correctly pointed out, "that when anyone in the past attempted to predict the long-term future, his forecast turned out to be hopelessly shortsighted and pessimistic." By coincidence, Greenewalt's warning was followed by an outbreak of long-range predictions, all of which were wide of the mark. Thus, Samuel Bronfman of distilling fame thought he was quite daring when he "saw a $600 billion national income in twenty-five years," or by 1979. (National income passed $600 billion in 1967, or twelve years before Bronfman's target date.)[19]

ONCE AGAIN THE FEAR OF INFLATION

Because they viewed the economic future optimistically and because the postwar years were ones of above-average economic growth, bankers and businessmen were more concerned with inflation than with recession. They spent much time talking about what it was, why it was evil, what caused it, and what could cure it. And, as in the

1920s, they exaggerated the extent of the problem. Of course, other groups were also fascinated by inflation. "We have been plagued by inflation" was a common expression among politicians, economists and, in different terminology, among housewives, professionals, and the clerical and kindred. Polls showed that the public was more interested in reducing the cost of living than in anything else that the government could do. Economists who in one moment warned of imminent depression found it easy to shift in the next moment to lectures about what should be done about inflation. As prices continued to mount in late 1948 and early 1949, despite the recession, President Truman urged that taxes be increased, and Senator Douglas and the CED argued for a cut in government spending to avoid a deficit.

Preoccupation with inflation was a discontinuous thing that followed the movement of the wholesale price level. Thus it reached a high pitch right after the war, subsided in 1949 as recession stopped the rise in the price index, and came back with increased strength in the first year of Korea. The index of the *Commercial and Financial Chronicle* offered a fever chart of the inflation psychosis. There were only six entries on inflation in the first three quarters of 1947. Then the issue warmed up and by spring 1948 it became torrid with 101 entries in one quarter. In February 1949, Lewis Brown announced that "inflationary forces are about spent unless we start a new cycle of deficit finance." He was evidently correct, for in the first quarter entries dropped to forty-three and they averaged only three in each of the last three quarters of 1949 and the first two quarters of 1950. Interest was, of course, rearoused with the Korean incident and entries on inflation rose to eighty-five in April–June 1951. Then as prices stabilized, the subject again subsided, and by early 1953, entries were running at about twenty-seven a quarter with most of the articles explaining what inflation was and why it was over.

Like other members of society, businessmen thought of inflation as a rise in prices, but they ordinarily defined it with a monetary slant. Joseph M. Dodge, president of the Detroit Bank and later Director of the Budget, resorted to the useful cliché that inflation was "too much money chasing too few goods." Morris Sayre said it was a case of "money increasing faster than production." George Johnson, president of the Dime Savings Bank of Brooklyn, defined it as "a sharp increase in the volume of money and credit relative to the amount of goods and services available."[20]

Almost everyone agreed that inflation was evil, and most people professed to believe that it was 100 per cent evil. Indeed, when Sumner Slichter, the much respected Harvard economist, argued that a little inflation was on balance a salutary thing, bankers and businessmen reacted as though they had just seen Aunt Agatha under the influence of marijuana.

Hostility toward inflation followed three general lines. First, it was immoral, unfair, and anti-American. Inflation, it was charged, led to excessive and misallocated spending. According to George Johnson, it "enabled people to buy things they did not need . . . and caused buyers to bid up prices beyond the true value of the article." Similarly, James E. Shelton, Los Angeles banker and president of the ABA, thought that government-induced inflation "encouraged citizens to go on a reckless spending spree which developed a frenzied business activity which was mistakenly called prosperity." Or attacking it another way, inflation discouraged saving and "saving" was good, while "spending" was bad. Thus W. S. Bucklin of Boston's National Shawmut Bank observed in 1947 that "the problem of inflation is becoming much more serious, saving is declining." Again, inflation was out of keeping with the American way, as indeed it was, but for none of the reasons that the bankers and businessmen raised. United States Steel's Irving S. Olds saw the campaign issue of 1952 as "inflation or freedom," for inflation was "incompatible with free enterprise." J. Stewart Baker of the Bank of Manhattan warned that "the relation between inflation and socialism is closer than one may think." And, of course, many businessmen pointed out that inflation was unfair because it put a disproportionate burden on fixed-income groups.

Secondly, inflation was economically evil. "If something is not done to slow this [inflation] down and to bring it to a stop," Secretary Humphrey told Congress, "this country is in for just the sort of catastrophe that we have seen going on in all the countries, well practically all the countries in Europe and the rest of the world." Inflation killed incentives, discouraged saving, slowed down investment spending, led to maladjustments and eventually to economic chaos. Joseph M. Dodge summed up this whole argument in one sentence: "The effect of inflation is very much the same as that of depression."

The third criticism of inflation emanated from pure self-interest. Life insurance executives made no secret that they opposed it because it hurt their business. Other executives, in Eugene Holman's

words to the Flanders Committee, "as a matter of self-interest wanted
to see an end to inflation," because it raised replacement costs.

In all the discussions about the evils of inflation, business leaders
paid no attention to the other side of the argument: the hypothesis
that inflation was an effect, a part of the price paid for full employment and high level economic growth. Those who took a more tolerant attitude pointed out that in a country such as the United States,
which was oriented toward economic values, inflation was a sometime thing. It occurred in steps not as a steady upward movement.
They argued that full employment and a high level of investment
spending inexorably put an upward pressure on the price level which
caused inflation to break out intermittently, but after a sharp but
short-lived upward movement, price levels settled at a new plateau
as the flood of goods from robust economic activity came on the market. Consequently, inflation in the United States ate itself up which
led to the conclusion that the kind of galloping inflation experienced
in some other nations was impossible here. All of this was either ignored by or unknown to those bankers and businessmen who expressed their opinions on the subject of inflation.

LABOR AS A CAUSE OF INFLATION

Business leaders were just as positive about the causes of inflation
as they were about its evils. Bankers and businessmen both agreed
that government deficits and easy money as well as high wages were
responsible for high prices. In the jargon of the professional economist, they explained inflation in terms of "demand-pull" as well as
"cost-push." The two groups differed, however, on who was responsible for easy money and easy credit. Non-bankers distributed the
onus for the swelling volume of credit and the expansion of the money
supply equally between the bankers and the United States Treasury.
But bankers were quick to exculpate themselves, and in so doing
they demonstrated a superlative aptitude for rationalization.

Long before the war ended, in fact soon after it had begun, some
business leaders were already putting the burden of price inflation on
labor, labor unions, and skyrocketing wages. When the war ended,
this view managed to monopolize the platform. In November 1945,
A. W. Robertson of Westinghouse expressed "deep concern over
the possibility of runaway inflation" and somewhat reluctantly

chalked it up to "wage increases." The business community undoubtedly shared this opinion.

For its part, labor, expressing itself through powerful unions, demanded substantial increases in wages. Management was anything but eager to grant them, but labor was very determined and the first couple of years after the war were colored by severe strikes and a first and second as well as a third "round of wage increases." Business tycoons saw in this nothing but disaster. As they visualized it, every round of wage increases would be followed by price increases, and finally inflation would somehow or other bankrupt the nation. In a moment of exasperation, Eugene Grace told Bethlehem Steel stockholders: "This thing is becoming serious. It is a cycle that should have stopped before, long before this. If you stop the wage cycle, you will start a trend that will eventually lead to lower prices."

Two things kept rankling businessmen. There was a general belief that labor productivity was way down. Yet, many of those who were most dogmatic about this conceded that their own plants had shown a respectable improvement in output per man hour. Thus, Millard D. Brown, after bewailing labor's reluctance to work, said in 1947 that productivity in his woolen mill was 5 per cent higher than it had been in 1941. Considering the disruptions and chaos that had come as a result of the war, this was quite an achievement.

The second aspect of the labor-price calculus that bothered the executives was, in the words of Lewis H. Brown, the "new theory expounded by the CIO that wages could be raised drastically without affecting prices." Unlike the 1920s when labor unions had not been powerful and wage discussions had paid little homage to economic theory, businessmen in the generation after 1929 made much of the "monopoly power of labor" and in their discussions of wages, they especially emphasized the importance of productivity. They were convinced that powerful labor unions could and would raise wages far beyond increases in productivity and would thereby make inflation unavoidable. "Inflation," said John E. Rovensky, former banker and now chairman of the American Car & Foundry Co., "used to be triggered by heavy buying by merchants, manufacturers, and speculators, but now it's the monopoly power of unions." Philip Reed of General Electric expressed what the overwhelming majority of businessmen believed: "Just as long as powerful labor unions, with or without assistance from Government, succeed in forcing employers to grant wage increases not justified by gains in productivity, the increases will always be followed by a rise in prices."[21]

THE GOVERNMENT AS A SOURCE OF INFLATION

As has already been mentioned, business leaders in the years between World War I and Korea allocated responsibility for inflation about equally between labor and government. Whereas labor was responsible for "cost-push" price rises, government was mostly to blame for "demand-pull." In some businessmen's minds, the relationship between government and inflation was very simple. Government spending equalled inflation, and the higher the spending, the greater the inflation.* To other businessmen, the important thing was whether the Treasury spent more money than it took in; if it did, inflation was sure to take place regardless of how the deficit was financed. To a third group, the connection between government finance and the price level was more complicated. Inflation did not occur merely because the government increased its debt, but because the increase in debt was accompanied by increases in the money supply. The links in the chain were somewhat as follows. The Treasure engaged in deficit spending and met the increases in debt by borrowing from the commercial banking system. This caused the money supply to rise at a faster rate than the supply of goods; ergo, inflation.

To still other businessmen, chiefly bankers and other financiers, the government was guilty of causing inflation through its control over the Federal Reserve System and its obsession with low interest rates. In the years up to March 1951, the Treasury exerted a great deal of influence over the central bank, and the monetary authorities were committed to maintaining low interest-rates, a policy that required easy money. As Philip Le Boutillier, department store executive and a champion of the gold standard, said, somewhat inaccurately, "The Federal Reserve whose original functions were to control the business cycle and flatten out the ups and downs of business has become chiefly a political instrument."

But no matter which bill of particulars was emphasized, government, in the eyes of the business and banking community, was the

---

* Ironically, this hypothesis, which had almost no following among professional economists in the period here discussed, gradually gained ground until today it is popular as part of "the balanced-budget multiplier."

chief culprit in the inflation debacle. John W. Hanes, North Carolina
banker and onetime Treasury official, thought that inflation was "the
product of the past mistakes of the New Deal." James E. Shelton
called inflation "a matter of deliberate government policy over a
period of almost twenty years." Le Boutillier ascribed inflation to
"the foolishness of F.D.R. in adopting Lord Keynes's theory of deficit
spending." Robert G. Dunlop of Sun Oil told the Flanders Committee, "It should be clear that the surest way to bring on more inflation
is to resume deficit financing practices by the Federal Government
through increasing the money supply." A number of statements offered between 1948 and 1952 by Irving S. Olds, chairman of United
States Steel, added up to the opinion that inflation resulted from
"expanded money supply" for which government deficit spending
was the "real cause." According to Charles E. Wilson of General
Motors, one of the two basic reasons for high prices was "wage
inflation"; the other was "the fact that we did not finance the war
in terms of money as we went."[22]

THE RESPONSIBILITY OF THE BANKS

Since an expanded money supply was considered to be one of the
root causes of inflation, many non-bank executives thought that banks
were at least partly responsible. The leading exponent of this point
of view was Thomas I. Parkinson, former university dean and now
president of the Equitable Life Assurance Society. In many speeches
and in many interviews, Parkinson distributed the blame for expanded
money and inflation equally between government and the banks. In
this, he had the ardent support of his industry. In a typical opinion,
a group of insurance executives were quoted in 1948 as saying, "Nor-
mally, one would expect some concrete suggestions from the bankers
to restore . . . the soundness of our currency . . . but our bankers
have had so large a participation in what has been going on and are
themselves contributing so much to the maintenance and increase of
the large money supply that little is to be expected, and actually little
has come from that source."[23]

Bankers immediately took umbrage. From 1948 until well into the
Korean episode, bank executives seldom missed an opportunity to
explain that expanding bank credit was an effect not a cause while
expanding government debt was a cause, not an effect. J. P. Morgan

said, through George Whitney, "Control of the supply of money is in the hands of our fiscal and monetary authorities, not the commercial banks." Joseph M. Dodge, president of the Detroit Bank, put the same thing in different words, "The banks cannot be held responsible for the inflation situation. . . . Bank loans are a symptom not a cause." S. Sloan Colt of the Bankers Trust explained that "the big expansion in the money supply started through gold imports and deficit financing before the war and continued during the war. . . . The present volume of business loans is a result of inflation rather than a primary cause. . . . Any attempt to interfere with bank loans could create the risk of serious deflation." Colt, nevertheless, called for self-restraint by bankers, and in this he was joined by the ABA, which, after reiterating that bankers were not responsible for either the expansion of money or prices, announced a voluntary program against inflation.[24]

The theme of the primacy of government and the innocence of banks in the inflationary surge continued to be repeated with slight variations until 1952. After the outbreak of hostilities in Korea, bankers, including J. Luther Cleveland and William L. Kleitz of the Guaranty Trust and F. N. Belgrano, Jr., of the Bank of America reiterated the opinion that government spending, not credit expansion was the culprit. Surprisingly enough, bankers did not think that credit expansion was taking place at an unusual rate. "I submit," John P. Rowe, a Cincinnati banker, told his colleagues, "that the increase in bank deposits and money in circulation is not disproportionate to the volume of business, the cost of living, and taxes . . . money goes up as a consequence of higher prices—the two causes are payrolls and taxes." George Johnson of the Dime Savings Bank, argued that it was not credit expansion, but certain kinds of credit expansion that produced inflation. In his division between good and bad credit, mortgage financing was, of course, good.[25]

The whole discussion of inflation was certainly not distinguished for loyalty to accuracy. The discussants acted on the incorrect premise that prices were moving up steadily and at a faster pace than at any other time in peacetime history. To be sure, prices did move up sharply from 1945 to 1947, but the rise slowed perceptibly thereafter, and prices were lower in 1950 than in 1948.

It was also assumed that the federal budget was badly unbalanced and that the money supply was expanding at an unreasonable rate. The truth was that federal cash receipts in the fiscal years from June

30, 1946, to June 30, 1950, were greater by $14.5 billion than expenditures.* The money supply rose slightly until December 1947, then declined steadily until shortly before Korea. Meanwhile, bank loans rose steadily while bank holdings of government bonds fell.

The attempt on the part of the bankers to deny involvement in the inflationary pressure was an understandable but feeble gesture. Credit and debt were the fuel that fed the price furnace, and if inflation was bad, then bankers had both hands in the guilt, for they were the chief manufacturers of both credit and debt. What had happened was that the private demand for credit and capital funds had suddenly awakened after half a generation in the doldrums. And, understandably enough, all the financial intermediaries—insurance companies and savings banks as well as commercial banks—were unloading their low-yield governments as fast as possible in order to take advantage of more attractive private loans and investments. In the process, the economy roared along, and businessmen and bankers enjoyed the ride, but resented paying the mileage charge. They liked the growth of income, but they did not like the rise in prices that was the other side of the coin.

THE SUGGESTED CURE FOR INFLATION

Businessmen were not at a loss for solutions to the problem of inflation, and each time the issue came back into the spotlight, they attacked it with a barrage of cures. Each time, too, the therapeutic mix was somewhat different from what had previously been proposed, but always each participant in the economy—government, the Federal Reserve System, management, and labor—was supposed to do its part.

Management was called upon to do everything it could to raise production and reduce costs, to plow back earnings, and to increase investment spending on plant and equipment. Labor, in turn, was called upon to raise its output and to restrict its wage demands to conform to increases in productivity. In a ten-point program to thwart inflation, Charles E. Wilson of GM exhorted management and labor

* The cash deficit in the fiscal year ending June 30, 1946, was $17.9 billion. The Treasury accumulated a $16.7 billion cash surplus in the years 1947–49, then ran a cash deficit of $2.2 billion in 1950. There was also $8.0 billion in cash surplus in 1951 and 1952.

to increase production, to keep costs and prices down, to work longer hours, and to reduce inventories and avoid waste. In another ten-point program, Earl Bunting, president of the O'Sullivan's Heel Company and also president of the NAM, called on management "to redouble efforts to increase production and cut costs" and on labor to "forego demands for wage boosts without a corresponding increase in productivity" and "to eliminate restrictions on production except where required for safety." When prices threatened to break upward, many business leaders joined with eminent politicians and eminent economists in calling for a moratorium on wage and price increases. Here and there, more audacious executives came up with complicated schemes to put wages and prices into a strait jacket. Earl B. Schwulst of the Bowery Savings Bank proposed that labor increase its output by 20 per cent while wages and profits remained stationary.[26]

Still bolder executives attempted to take matters in their own hands by making well-advertised price cuts at times when demand at the old price levels was clearly outrunning supply. In January 1947, for example, Ford announced: "Although more than one million of our customers are waiting for delivery of their cars at present prices, we are immediately reducing the price of every Ford car, some models as much as $50. This is our down payment toward a continued high level of production and employment. We believe that the shock treatment of prompt action is needed to halt the insane spiral of mounting costs and rising prices." In August, Ford, acknowledging that its effort had failed, raised prices beyond what they had been in the spring. General Motors and Chrysler followed immediately.

The whole procedure was repeated in the steel industry in 1948. In April of that year, it became "crystal clear" that inflation could not be held back. Proof came when New York City abandoned its hallowed five-cent subway fare. In the same month by coincidence, the steel union asked for an increase in wages. United States Steel refused to grant the "wage demand." Instead, it announced price cuts of "almost $25 million in lieu of a wage increase." Other businessmen were enthusiastic. Ernest Weir "hoped it was an example which other branches of industry would find it possible to follow." Gwillym Price of Westinghouse said, "The action agrees with our own thinking." Government economists were reported to be privately applauding. But by July, the whole thing had fizzled out. Wage negotiations were reopened with the union asking for a raise of 12½–13 cents an

hour, and the steel companies admitting that the price reduction had
not worked. Some steel executives blamed higher prices on the Supreme Court, which, in June 1948, had ruled illegal the basing point
system of fixing steel prices. One of the industry elders, Eugene G.
Grace, called it "regrettable that the law required the abandonment
of a long-established pricing policy around which much of the industry of the country had been built." E. J. Kulas of Midland Steel
simply called it "a tragedy."[27]

Businessmen had no doubt that management was doing its part;
there was no hope, as far as they were concerned, for labor; which
meant that it was up to government and the monetary authorities,
especially the government, to stop the "inflationary spiral."

All through the immediate postwar years, a small group of businessmen, economists, and financiers argued that the best way of beat-
ing inflation was for the government to return to the gold standard.*
J. H. Frost of the Frost National Bank of San Antonio called for a
return to gold because the "departure from sound money threatened
economic disaster." After a new outburst of inflation during the first
year of Korea, Floyd Cramer, president of the Washington Heights
Savings and Loan, called for a return to gold. So did James E. Shelton, president of the Security-First National of Los Angeles. George
A. Sloan of the International Chamber of Commerce also argued for
restoration on the ground that "academic debates notwithstanding,
practical life seems to have proven that there is no substitute for
gold."[28]

But the days of the gold standard were definitely over. The agitation
for its return reached a peak in 1954, and thereafter it had fewer
and fewer champions, and these were among the small businessmen,
the small bankers, and the professionals. Most of the big-city bankers
had never been very enthusiastic about returning to gold, and the
House of Morgan was altogether against it. In February 1948, a committee of bankers and businessmen, including John M. Schiff of Kuhn
Loeb, John F. Bierwirth of the New York Trust, Alexander C. Nagle
of the First National, and Joseph P. Ripley of Harriman Ripley, recommended that a return to the gold standard be deferred. Meanwhile, Russell Leffingwell of Morgan carried on a running debate

_____
* The most articulate organization in the movement back to gold was the
Economists' National Committee on Monetary Policy led by Professor Walter
E. Spahr of New York University.

with Professor Spahr about the advisability of restoring the gold standard.

DISAGREEMENT ABOUT MONETARY POLICY

Most of the articulate bankers were more concerned with the emancipation of the Federal Reserve System from Treasury control. Bankers like S. Sloan Colt of the Bankers Trust and J. Stewart Baker of the Manhattan Company, insurance executives like T. I. Parkinson, industrialists, including Lewis H. Brown and Earl Bunting, and businessmen's associations such as the NAM, called for the Treasury and the Federal Reserve to end the pegging of interest rates, the abandonment of the low-interest-rate philosophy, and the return to the kind of money market in which interest rates were freely determined by the interplay of the demand for and the supply of money and credit.

Although they pleaded for an end to pegging and argued for restoring the independence of the Federal Reserve, most bankers favored taking it very easy. As late as December 1948, the chairman of the Government Securities Committee of the Investment Bankers' Association said that most banking opinion continued to favor the peg, but he "confessed to a significant change in views. . . . We have lost our unanimity. . . . A minority now believes that the pegging has been too stubborn." As usual, the Morgan partners were more daring in their opinions. Russell Leffingwell, for example, laid most of the blame for inflation on the war and the cheap money policy that was then being followed through the mechanism of having the Federal Reserve control interest rates. As he saw it, an end to inflation required the withdrawal of the peg. But, unlike other bankers, he quickly asserted that this did not mean that he recommended tight money, for he "dreaded deflation more than inflation." George Whitney supported his partner's opinion by explaining, "The authorities must exercise controls with caution and wisdom. . . . Too drastic a course such as was followed in 1920, 1929, and 1937 might bring severe results. . . . Inflation is bad, but deflation is worse."[29]

Bankers also danced an extremely thin rope when they were asked what they thought about extending the Fed's control over the money market. When the Board, feeling itself hobbled by its agreement with the Treasury to maintain low interest rates and desiring nevertheless to do something about inflation, asked in 1946 for an extension of its powers, most bankers were visibly cool to the request. Indeed, they always seemed cool to any request made by Marriner Eccles, which was probably one of the reasons why Eccles eventually said, "Private banking leadership has failed to meet the changing needs of the economy. . . . It has fought every progressive step."

Industrialists, as was usually the case, were even more reluctant to embark on a tight money voyage. In the midst of the recession of 1949, Henry J. Kaiser in an allusion to the Fed's previous tight money policy, called on the American people to thank "our American democracy that there are Congressmen with the guts and gumption of [Representative] Wright Patman to check the Federal Reserve Board from plunging the nation into a wholly needless, man-made depression." And Cyrus S. Eaton warned the nation that "an official policy of tight money and high interest rates . . . is not helpful to the general economy."[30]

No matter from which point businessmen began their journey through the labyrinths of inflation, all roads led eventually to the government, for, according to the modal business leader, government held final responsibility for curing as well as causing inflation. Winthrop Aldrich put this in a few words when he entitled a 1951 speech, "Sound Government Action Can Check Inflation."

PRICE CONTROLS, TARIFFS, AND OTHER INTERFERENCES WITH THE MARKET

Businessmen were well aware that one thing that the government could do was to maintain or reinstitute direct controls over prices and wages. In the years from 1946 to 1952, opinion on the issue changed significantly and fundamentally. During the war, business had chafed under the OPA, and with V-J Day, it was hoped that direct controls would be quickly abandoned, but at first only the most daring urged an immediate end to OPA. In March 1946, a poll taken by *Modern Industry* showed 53.6 per cent of 2315 businessmen favoring an extension of price control beyond June 30. Shortly thereafter, a distinguished group of economists, ranging in their economic predilections from Paul Sweezy on the left to Henry Simonds on the right, addressed a letter to the *New York Times* supporting extension of price controls for another year and urging no further tax reductions, continuation of deficit reduction, and the maintenance of credit controls and non-inflationary wage policies. At about the same time, the *Times* also carried an ad signed by Jack I. Straus of R. H. Macy recommending the retention of OPA.

But already qualifications were being introduced. To D. C. Prince, vice-president of General Electric, it appeared "highly desirable that price controls be extended," for "there can be no doubt that without such price controls the boom and bust of 1919 and 1920 would be repeated." *But,* "on the other hand, OPA officials must recognize . . . that without enough increase in prices to cover costs business cannot proceed." Other businessmen, including Ralph Flanders, Henry Kaiser, and Paul G. Hoffman, suggested an extension for another year. But Lewis H. Brown wanted OPA controls limited to only a few items; the Board of Directors of the Chamber of Commerce called for an end of all controls except on rents by October 30; and J. Howard Pew of the Sun Oil Company charged that controls "penalized the law-abiding." He denied that OPA prevented inflation and added that "the only effective ways are to balance the budget and to stimulate production."[31]

As the spring wore on, the question of what to do with OPA became the most hotly debated issue in the postwar economy. In June, Congress extended OPA's life, but President Truman vetoed the bill. At the same time, the NAM announced that 97 per cent of its members felt that price controls were hampering production. It took full-page ads in the daily press to argue that if OPA were discontinued permanently, "production would mount rapidly and prices would quickly adjust themselves . . . and America would enter the period of prosperity that everyone has been hoping for." But this was much too heady a draught for most people and most businessmen to quaff. Congress in July passed a revised OPA bill and Truman signed it. Then in October, OPA began to decontrol the economy, and the AFL asked for an end of all controls except those on rents. OPA finally came to an end in June 1947.

Yet so long as inflation kept threatening, the issue of government price control kept coming back into the news. In the spring of 1947, twenty-three manufacturers and merchants including Wilson of GE, and Allyn of National Cash Register, signed a statement calling on businessmen to reduce prices because "Today's abnormal conditions severely limit the reliance that can be put on the semi-automatic regulation of prices by the market and correspondingly increase the responsibility of businessmen." Businessmen could not rest easy so long as the President intermittently alluded to controls as a way of containing inflation. In 1948, Leffingwell and Whitney warned the Administration that "wage and price controls and allocations . . . will not solve the problem, but many of them will only aggravate it." The sentiment was repeated by Harold Boeschenstein of Owens-Illinois, who thought price pressures rose because "the ratio of wages-to-prices-to-production was out of balance."[32]

With Korea came renewed agitation for the reinstatement of sweeping direct controls. But business leaders, unlike during the war and immediate postwar years, were now strongly opposed to price and wage controls. There were, of course, exceptions. Charles E. Wilson of GE, who had been involved in administering controls, was in favor, and Eugene G. Grace was quick to say that if he had a choice between "a controlled economy and inflation," he would "certainly vote for controls." The opposite point of view was much closer to what most businessmen believed. Morris Sayre insisted that controls fed inflation. "Much of the pressure for controls," he charged, "comes from small power-loving bureaucrats who would like to be big bureaucrats."

Most businessmen wanted to fight Korea with fiscal and monetary tools rather than with price controls. In their lists of things to do, the most popular item was "reduce non-defense spending." Harry A. Bullis of General Foods, F. Raymond Peterson, president of the ABA, A. L. M. Wiggins, banker and railroad executive, Russell Leffingwell, Lewis H. Brown, the Life Insurance Association, and many, many others advised the Treasury to hew as close to "pay-as-you-go" as possible by reducing "non-essential spending," to maintain a free market as far as possible, to follow a tight-money policy, and, as a last resort that few would admit as necessary, to increase taxes. By the spring of 1952, businessmen had become completely disenchanted. Fred Lazarus, Jr., called for a vigorous policy of selective decontrol permitting an orderly return to a free market "if we are not to strait jacket the economy." Irving S. Olds wrote the finishing touch to the businessman's condemnation of price controls by telling his colleagues, "for about 4000 years, the Economic Witch Doctors have invariably come up with the same prescription. They report solemnly that the nation is suffering from high prices and that prices must therefore be frozen."[33]

Businessmen disagreed more basically about tariff reduction as a way of abating inflation. Bankers, like Colt, Aldrich, and Leffingwell, and automobile executives, like Charles E. Wilson, stumped for free trade or trade on a "two-way basis," but textile manufacturers, steel executives, and some electrical machinery makers were sure that a reduction in tariffs would mean more ill than good fortune for their economy and the economy as a whole.

GOVERNMENT FISCAL POLICY

There was much greater agreement about what the government should do about its fiscal affairs. Businessmen, with a few important exceptions, regarded with uneasy suspicion the increasing respectability of compensatory fiscal policy, that is, the doctrine that the federal government's expenditure and revenue policies should be guided by the ups and downs in the business cycle. Russell C. Leffingwell, who believed in the policy, explained what it meant: "The Government should manage monetary and fiscal policies, including the public debt and taxes, in such a way as to maintain a climate favorable to free enterprise and high employment and to avoid either inflation or deflation." Practically no one at this early stage would go along with the Morgan banker. Paul G. Hoffman "accepted the possibility of deficit financing," but he was careful to state that he was not an enthusiastic supporter. Meyer Kestnbaum, the clothing manufacturer who was associated with Hoffman in founding the CED, told a *Fortune* reporter, "I am opposed to the doctrinaire view that everything was fine when the national budget was $15 billion. Nevertheless, I put great importance on performing the functions of government with efficiency and economy." Lewis H. Brown was in closer harmony with general business thinking when he said: "We have in our country now a hybrid Keynesian-welfare state. . . . It has the objective of smoothing out or stabilizing the business cycle by far-reaching government intervention. Those who believe in this policy are not too concerned over any consequences that might result, such as permanent inflation, debauchment of money, fruitless and costly public works projects."[34]

In these early postwar days, the belief that the government could actually do something vital about the state of the economy was groping for acceptance. The term "full employment" was still a dirty word, for with it were associated the threat of inflation and the fear of socialism. When the Murray full-employment bill was introduced in 1945, the business reaction was less than enthusiastic. With few exceptions, such as Beardsley Ruml, F. R. von Windegger of the Plaza Bank of St. Louis, and Clarence Avildson of the Republic Drill and Die Co., businessmen thought it would result in a planned economy, lower standards of living, more government spending, and eventually the destruction of economic and political freedom. Fred I. Kent, who was in the front rank in opposition to the bill, was complimented for his views by Leroy Lincoln of the Metropolitan Life and congratulated by O. A. Taylor of S. H. Kress who wrote, "Government can do little directly to encourage large employment. It can do a great deal to prevent it." Taylor added that without exception all the businessmen with whom he discussed the bill opposed it as leading to dictatorship and encouraging bureaucracy.

Ten years later, business thought was still extremely hostile. In 1954, the *Commercial and Financial Chronicle* printed a speech by a Mississippi University economist arguing that attempts to assure full employment would result in inflation and collectivism. The speech brought forth a fulsome collection of letters from bankers, utility executives, manufacturers, railroad leaders, and especially small businessmen. Wrote one, "Of course we want full employment and perpetual motion; but it isn't likely that we will have either." Others insisted that full employment was synonymous with galloping inflation, the elimination of the middle class, and state socialism. Big businessmen were much more restrained. One of them, John L. Collyer of B. F. Goodrich thought, "We must recognize that full employment generally has been accepted as one of the desirable goals of national policy."

All through the years after the war, businessmen of all sizes and political allegiance continuously called on the administration and to a lesser extent on Congress to reduce government spending and thereby balance the budget both in order to dampen inflationary pressures and because it was the right thing to do. "Until the budget is balanced," concluded Robert Wason, "we cannot sweep back the rising tide of inflation." It was also a canon of orthodoxy that the sins of overspending would eventually lead to bankruptcy. "In 17 of the past 20 years," announced George Humphrey in 1954, "this government has engaged in deficit financing. . . . This course for a government, as for a family, can only lead to eventual disaster."

Yet when questioned, it often turned out that businessmen did not really believe what they seemed to be saying about the balanced budget. Consider the following colloquy between Senator Flanders and banker S. Sloan Colt:

SEN. FLANDERS: In the unhappy event that we get into a depression, would you feel that the best way of handling that depression was to balance the budget through hell and high water?

MR. COLT: I would not feel that. I would feel that you would probably have to go in debt.

SEN. FLANDERS: That is, the national debt is something that at times you might have to add to; at other times you should be diminishing, with probably, on the whole, over good times and bad times, a slow decrease. Would that be your idea?

MR. COLT: Exactly.

SEN. FLANDERS: That idea is all right with me. That is all I wanted to say.

Sometimes, the government was admonished to "eliminate over-spending and over-lending" or to "eliminate unnecessary and non-essential spending." Occasionally, a business leader would actually point a finger at some specific item that he would ruthlessly slash in order to balance the budget. Colt called upon the government to balance the budget by "cutting welfare spending." Earl Bunting explained in 1947 that the budget could be reduced from $37 to $31 billion by paring defense expenditures, agricultural subsidies, and outlays for veterans and social welfare. Fred I. Kent cut another $1 billion from the NAM figure and estimated that "$30 billion wisely spent would undoubtedly enable the government to meet every proper obligation."[35]

Businessmen recoiled in shocked astonishment because Congress found it difficult to reduce expenditures by 10 per cent from the President's $37 billion budget (which, incidentally, was over $3 billion more than was actually spent in 1947). James Mooney, president of Willys Overland, in an impassioned plea for economy in spending and a reduction in taxes, expressed this frustration with a misleading historical analogy: "The budget items of the various departments and services of the Federal Government seem so astronomical when set down by the side of the same items in the budget of 1930 or even 1939 that the conclusion must quickly be drawn that never before did the government perform its responsible tasks or the present expenditures are excessive luxuries and entirely unnecessary."[36]

Mooney was no expert in financial history, for what was happening to government spending was the same thing that had happened after every previous major war. Because of inflation, increased charges on a greatly expanded debt, and higher costs of veterans' pensions and benefits, government expenditures after each major war settled at a level of four and one-half to five times the previous peacetime average. Thus, after the Civil War, expenditures averaged around $300 million compared to the previous average of around $70 million; and as a result of World War I, expenditures jumped from $700 million to $3½ billion. After World War II, the budget settled at about $40 billion compared to about $8½ billion during the last years of the New Deal.

One reason why most people in and out of business wanted to reduce spending and balance the budget was a ubiquitous belief that the national debt should be reduced. To be sure, Beardsley Ruml, the treasurer of R. H. Macy, did warn against "reckless and mischievous proposals for debt cuts" because "the income and standards of living of the poor are not what they have to be to absorb our great productivity." But Ruml was a minority of one, and he wasn't really a businessman anyway; he was a Ph.D. out of Chicago University and a onetime academic dean. Earl Bunting was much closer to the popular line in calling for a systematic plan for paying $2½ billion a year on the debt, as was Charles E. Wilson of GE in recommending a 10 per cent cut in the $270 billion debt.[37]

Debt repayment could, however, be a source of great embarrassment, for it followed overzealously, it would severely restrict the possibilities of tax reduction, and tax reduction was for most businessmen the *raison d'etre* of fiscal policy. What executives said they wanted was a reasonable mix of debt and tax reduction, so that economic growth could continue at an admirable, but not excessive, rate. Here again, opinion differed from the orthodoxy of the previous generation. Many executives had come to realize that debt reduction like all good things could be overdone. As S. Sloan Colt told a Senate committee, "Let us remember that in the reduction of debt, much as I am for it—I don't want to give the impression that I am not—you are, in essence, deflating, and I don't think you ought to deflate too fast. I think you have got to compensate the deflationary picture by perhaps a reduction of taxes to lift up consumer buying. So I favor a division."

THE DILEMMA OF TAX REDUCTION VS. BALANCED BUDGETS

There were other ways of having the cake (tax reduction) while eating it (debt repayment) too. In answer to the inevitable question about which should come first, debt or tax reduction, GM's Wilson replied, "Frankly I am about like the average taxpayer. I have the feeling that until we reduce the taxes, the Government bureaus and the Government are not going to reduce expenditures. . . . If I thought that tax money was going for debt reduction, I would take it a little better." An even more popular rationale was to relate taxes to national income by incentives. Fred I. Kent thought there was "no question but that government debt should be reduced and as rapidly as possible. On the other hand, if present taxation is maintained, there is also no doubt but that government will receive a constantly decreasing income."

The argument was the same as that advanced by Secretary Mellon twenty years before. Tax reduction would spur saving and incentives which would spur investment, which would spur production, which would spur income, and everybody would be much better off. Any sort of tax reduction would do. Herman Steinkraus of Bridgeport Brass and the Chamber of Commerce called for "prompt removal of wartime excises" on the ground that this would increase net government receipts. But the income tax, just as in Mellon's time, was the favorite target.[38]

In the years immediately after the war, the three presidents of the NAM—Wason in 1946, Bunting in 1947, and Sayre in 1948—were the most articulate in pushing the Mellon "trickle down theory" of accelerating economic growth by judicious tax reduction. Wason opened the assault with the conclusion, "The tax structure must quit suppressing enterprise." Bunting and Sayre explained that "an immediate reduction in our highly progressive income tax" was necessary "so that people can again save and invest." Other executives with widely divergent philosophies joined in extolling the salutary effects of tax reduction. Lammot du Pont emphasized how taxes discouraged incentive. Neil H. McElroy of Proctor and Gamble and later a member of President Eisenhower's cabinet added another item to the long list of things that were obvious to businessmen. "There is no doubt," he told a Harvard conference, "that income taxes today are actually oppressive to the fullest application of management initiative. . . . It is management's job to make this point clear to those who write our tax laws." This was a theme that management never tired of playing. When the Knutson tax bill was being debated in the 1947–48 period, Don G. Mitchell of Sylvania Products and chairman of the NAM's tax committee said, "Obviously, if the bill should be revised so as to diminish the amount of tax reduction . . . the legislation would do less toward meeting the fundamental needs of the economy." James Mooney was only slightly less positive, for he thought it "readily plausible that a 20 per cent reduction in taxes would sufficiently stimulate business and raise income until total revenue would exceed that received by present rates." In the midst of the Korean war, president Hood of U. S. Steel, once again insisted that "tax policy must be altered to restore incentives for risk taking."

Objective experts in the field of taxes and fiscal policy were not so positive about the deleterious effects of taxes on incentives. They were in more agreement about the effect of tax reduction as an aperitif for the economy, and in the immediate postwar years, they were not so sure that the economy needed a stimulant that might carry it to inflation rather than real growth. Earl O. Shreve, president of the Chamber of Commerce, disposed of this argument in June 1947 by simply stating, "The fear of aggravating inflation no longer has validity as ground for opposition to tax reduction." Not that inflation was still not a threat, but high taxes, instead of being deflationary were really inflationary, for they "were a brake on production, killed initiative, and denied incentives."[39]

Congress apparently agreed with Shreve and not with the majority of economists. Urged on by every business group from the NAM to the CED, Congress, in 1947, passed a tax bill which reduced rates by 10½ to 30 per cent and revenue by an estimated $4 billion. President Truman imbedded himself further in business' ill graces by vetoing the bill. Then in 1948, both Congress and the President repeated their actions, but this time Congress had the last word by passing the bill over the veto. In retrospect, the congressional view seems to have the best of the argument. Federal revenues did decline by almost $4 billion between 1948 and 1949, casting some doubt on the business claim that tax reduction far from reducing net revenue, would actually increase it. But it must be remembered that 1948–49 was a recession period, and revenues would have fallen even without a tax reduction. Given the recession, tax reduction was at the time a wise anti-deflationary move, even though that was not exactly the original intention.

Long after the war, in the days of the Eisenhower administration, the great dilemma—the calculus between debt and taxes—was still annoying the policy makers, the business community, and the public at large. The Administration, which had such high hopes of achieving a balanced budget, had far less success than the Truman administration in accomplishing those hopes. This, in spite of the fact that George Humphrey was Secretary of the Treasury. Typically, Humphrey showed how deeply the businessman felt the *sturm und drang* between striving for a balanced budget and desiring a decrease in tax rates. Like his colleagues, the secretary started out very much on the side of the angels who believed in balanced budgets and debt reduction. At first, the issue was plain. In 1953, Humphrey put the question bluntly: "Are you going to balance the budget first, or are you going to cut taxes regardless of the deficit involved?" Then in time came second thoughts. By 1955, with the budget somewhat out of balance on the deficit side, Humphrey had succumbed to what he had once thought to be the siren song of profligacy. "We have not abandoned the goal of balancing the budget," he wrote, "and neither have we stopped cutting taxes. . . . We will keep trying to cut Government spending. At the same time, our expanding economy can provide greater tax income even at lower rates because it is on a broader base." Unbeknownst to him, Humphrey was an advance agent of the "new economics" that was to stride into the limelight in the Kennedy-Johnson days.[40]

Businessmen knew what they wanted. They believed that since all taxes were passed on to the consumer, they spurred inflation and could bankrupt the nation. In general, businessmen favored a reduction of corporate tax rates, the elimination of the capital gains tax along with double taxation of dividends, individual rates of 12–15 per cent minimum and 50 per cent maximum, and the encouragement of investment spending through high depreciation allowances. If tax increases were necessary, as some business people were willing to concede during the Korean war, the favorite suggestion was for a sales tax of about 5 per cent on everything except food, housing, and utilities.[41]

EISENHOWER—THE FIRST FRIENDLY ADMINISTRATION IN TWENTY-FOUR YEARS

The difference of opinion over taxes was only one of the things that businessmen held against President Truman. When Eisenhower was elected, business reacted very happily as it looked forward to a new day. Alfred P. Sloan, in a speech called "The Road to Serfdom Blocked," hailed the election as signifying "a socialistic economy receding in the distance." A survey by *Mill and Factory* showed 69 per cent of the sampled businessmen believing that taxes would be materially reduced by cutting expenditures; 57 per cent believed that strikes would be curbed; well over two thirds expected significant reductions in spending for government bureaus, foreign aid, and subsidies. N. B. Jackson and Harold Helm in their annual report to Chemical Bank stockholders showed an unrestrained quality of mercy in observing that "while the public has gained from social and economic reforms over the past twenty years, we have seen the encroachment of socialism." Morton Bodfish, chairman of the Executive Committee of the United States Saving and Loan League, predicted the easing of inflation with somewhat higher interest rates and concluded, "It will be hard indeed to imagine the Government in the role of a friendly ally instead of a critical, if not malicious overseer." But Clarence Francis warned that while the country "faced the greatest opportunity in history," it still faced dangers from "inflation and deflation, huge Federal budgets and deficits, and creeping socialism."[42]

Business was wallowing in tepid self-gratification. The world was again its oyster, and the end of the Truman administration was like the beginning of Milton's *Paradise Regained*. It seems superfluous to point out that in economic life the Eisenhower administration accomplished little of what was hoped for it. It did reduce taxes, but it could not maintain a balanced budget, and it did not end inflation. But business did not really care about this. What it did care about was, in the words of Henry C. Alexander, "one of President Eisenhower's important achievements—the great change in public temper. He and his administration have given business a chance to show what it can do, and have let the people compare that performance with the dire predictions of business baiters." What Alexander was saying was that business *felt* better. Or as Leland I. Doan, president of Dow Chemical, told a Middle-West gathering: "Five years ago, I was deeply concerned about a sort of insidious galloping socialism that seemed to be rapidly approaching the point of no return. . . . We have at last an administration which is not anti-business. . . . We have taken a long step away from government intervention and control."[43]

8. BUSINESS OPINION IN THE AGE OF AFFLUENCE: 1954–67

"The richer the community, the wider will tend to be the gap between its actual and its potential production, and therefore the more obvious and outrageous the defects of the economic system."

John Maynard Keynes.

Somewhere around 1954, give or take a year and a few months, a few important but subtle changes began to take place in business opinion. What was happening was gradual and easily exaggerated, but nonetheless real. The imperceptibility of the change was unintentionally illustrated in a speech by W. C. Mullendore, chairman of Southern California Edison, in May 1955. Mullendore introduced his talk by saying that it represented the third in a series. The first, in 1931, was entitled "Apostles of Hate." The second, in 1944, seriously posed the question: "Why Worry About Free Enterprise?" This one in 1955 explored "The Dynamics of Prosperity."[1]

TOWARD A CONSENSUS

One of the planes in the many-faceted transformation of business attitudes was a narrowing of opinion. On almost every subject, there was much more of a consensus than there had been in the 1920s and even in the 1940s. To be sure, on one issue at least, that of government fiscal policy, opinion varied very widely. But on other important economic questions, the mixture of opinion was impressively homogeneous. There was little deviation from the party line on wages, labor unions, profits, taxes, inflation, and business recession. There were, on any issue, far fewer "way out" opinions among the articulate. Certainly, there were none to match Filene, Dennison, Fels, and Leeds of an earlier generation. But this did not mean that businessmen were necessarily slaves to conformity. Despite the artistry with which sociologists painted a portrait of the man in the gray flannel suit, there were probably just as many, and possibly more, individualistic executives and tycoons than there had been in the previous generation. A score of names quickly crosses one's mind: Arthur Roth in banking; Norton Simon among financiers; Sherman Fairchild in technology; Joseph C. Wilson and Sol M. Linowitz, the copy kings; Yelen and Willensky in discount retailing; Lawrence Harvey in metals. Many of these new individualists were unknown to the public at large. A few were articulate but not on the great economic issues of the day. If they had dissident opinions, they were known to only a handful of people.

Some of the old tycoons, the rugged individualists who were supposed to have clawed their way to the top in a previous epoch, were still around, but they had shifted their interests. Alfred P. Sloan had retired; Ernest Weir had for some years been commenting more on foreign than domestic issues; Cyrus Eaton made occasional cryptic comments on domestic issues but he seemed now more interested in Canada and in cementing better relations with Russia.

On the whole, businessmen talked much less than had been their habit. There were fewer speeches and there were fewer articles. There was, moreover, much more emphasis on technical matters and on specialized subheads of business operation and business management than there had been.

CHANGING OPINION

Some changes also occurred in what businessmen seemed to believe. Opinion shifted significantly on at least two matters. First of all, there was no longer so strong an urge to look upon every period of recovery as the prelude to inevitable economic disaster. Even among bankers, it was no longer *de rigueur* to warn at every opportunity against the evils of speculation and of eating too high on the hog. But the shift in opinion that really monopolized attention and led many commentators to the feeling that a revolution had occurred in business thinking centered around the nature and importance of fiscal policy. By the late 1950s, it was clear that the sanctity of the balanced budget had lost a great deal of ground. It was apparent that many business leaders regarded federal deficits as a useful tool in combating tendencies toward recession. To be sure, evidence of this had already been discernible in the immediate postwar years. Among the bankers and businessmen of that period were non-conformists like Russell Leffingwell and Paul Hoffman, who accepted the notion that it was part of the government's business to regulate its spending and tax policies with a view toward balancing the economy. There were also some who when pressed would admit, reluctantly to be sure, that in periods of economic depression, it was advisable for the government to spend more than it took in. What was different about the post-1954 era was that a great many more businessmen freely accepted the so-called "New Economics"* with its compensatory fiscal policy and among businessmen in general there was less reluctance to espouse the notion that the government should run a deficit in times of depression.

There were a number of reasons for the changes. Some of these were in the internal structure of business and some were in the external economic and political environment. For one thing, businessmen were getting accustomed to prosperity. They had survived the nightmare of depression; they had less fear of its return; and they were beginning to suspect that prosperity, or something close to it, might last forever.

Another stimulus came from the slow but steady alteration in the personnel that made up the business community. The higher echelons of the business world were being continuously infiltrated by younger men who had been educated by a new generation of economists, professors whose allegiance was to the "New Economics" rather than to the classical and neo-classical school that had reigned in the years before the depression. By 1956, twenty years had passed since the economics of John Maynard Keynes had penetrated the colleges. It was an odds-on choice, therefore, that a budding executive, a *wunderkind* of forty-odd in 1957, would have been exposed to the New Economics in his student days. As Keynes him-

* The "New Economics" referred to here is the Keynesian scheme of things that swept the boards in the years after World War II. This is not to be confused with the "New Economics" that came into vogue in the middle 1960s, and certainly not to be confused with the "New Economics" that was abortively announced in 1921.

self observed, anyone who is concerned with economic matters is usually the slave of some defunct economist.

Even more important than the academic background of promising entrepreneurs, business firms were hiring more professional specialists and relying more heavily on them in writing speeches, in making forecasts, and in expressing views on the big issues that were enlivening the economic world of the late 1950s. In the 1920s, and even later, some business leaders enjoyed participating in the game of forecasting the course of the economy. But in the 1950s this was no longer true. The task of crystal-ball gazing was now altogether in the hands of the professionals, and the professionals were for the most part in the business world, but not part of it.

Still another reason for changing business opinion was the Korean episode. No peace followed the armistice at Panmunjon. Businessmen as well as other groups became aware that the cold war had become chronic, and that under the circumstances any call for a return to limited government could leave nothing but a hollow echo.

One final reason for the newer way of business thinking was that the administration of Dwight D. Eisenhower had had much more influence than was readily apparent. Some of the things that had been abhorred in the New Deal and in the Fair Deal, notably deficit spending, an unbalanced budget, and more government regulation, were accepted by most of the business community when they came wrapped in a different package, tied with different intellectual string. To be sure, there were some expressions of disillusion.* H. E. Humphreys, Jr., of United States Rubber told an audience of manufacturers, "For a time there seemed to be considerable improvement. . . . But lately there have been many signs that the problem of big government with its excessive spending, huge national debt, inflation, runaway welfare plans, threatened controls, and progress-stifling, back-breaking tax load is still with us. I am beginning to get the feeling that our new Administration has discovered in the back of a closet in the White House the old hat worn by previous Administrations and has found that it fits." But Humphreys was definitely in the minority of business leaders. The majority, having watched Ike's

* In May 1957, when the President was in the midst of a small storm over his $72 billion budget, a Midwestern banker said, "Ike's turned out to be no better than Truman and the New Deal crowd." According to a New England industrialist, "Eisenhower's all right, but he's surrounded by a bunch of socialist egg-heads."

administration and having found it to their liking, resigned themselves to the fact that big government was here to stay.[2]

BUSINESS AND THE KENNEDY ADMINISTRATION

By the late years of the Eisenhower administration, the anti-
government tympany had passed its crescendo, but it never died out
altogether. Soon after President Kennedy's election, it could again be
heard, for the business world had favored Nixon,* and it looked forward with trepidation to the return of the Democrats. Henry C.
Alexander, chairman of the Morgan Guaranty, expressed the feelings
of most business leaders shortly after the election: "Back in 1933, we
were in the first stages of a political era . . . which was to carry . . .
the stamp of being generally hostile to business. . . . That twenty-
year era was followed by eight years in which the atmosphere was
different. There was a turn away from the direction of constantly
more government intervention. . . . Now again the nation prepares
for a change in national administration. . . . I hope no generation of
businessmen will automatically and instinctively lapse into a persecution complex about government."[3]

But Alexander's hopes were somewhat abortive, for as Paul Gorman of Western Electric said, "opposition to Federal programs is a
predisposition—almost a conditioned reflex." According to some businessmen the last constructive thing that government had done was
done when Queen Isabella subsidized Columbus. Part of this opposition stemmed from a failure to understand that business life
and political life were not the same. According to Senator Charles
Percy, formerly of Bell and Howell, "It's a terrible plunge into an
icy bath to jump from business, which is essentially an autocracy,
into government, which is a democracy." When thwarted by government, business leaders, like other groups in society, chalked it up
to something vague called "politics," and blamed it all on the uninformed voter. In such moments, businessmen agreed with Logan T.

---

* Of thirty-one prominent businessmen who contributed $1000 or more to the
1960 campaign, only three contributed to the Democratic party. In 1964, eighteen contributed $500 or more to the Democrats and twenty-four, to the Re-
publicans. In 1966, the tide was still running strongly toward the GOP. A group
of prominent Pittsburgh businessmen were reported "enthusiastic" about Ronald
Reagan and reported that he would receive "their financial support," presumably
as a candidate for governor in California.

Johnston's comment, "Government is not in a popularity contest. Its function is not to win votes by trying to keep everybody happy . . . or to prove that America is best because our people are given the most and best things." This sentiment, which was by no means unusual among businessmen, was not so much different from a statement uttered by a proponent of the "New Economics" when his prescription for fiscal policy was not followed: "Governments," he complained, "usually operate to maximize votes, not social welfare."[4]

But misunderstanding was only a small part of the story. In addition, businessmen were convinced by long experience and much thought that the government's influence on the economy was at best negative and at worst pernicious. "Perhaps the greatest marvel of our economic system," diagnosed John E. Swearingen of Standard Oil of Indiana, "is not simply that it has been so productive as to become a revolutionary force of world impact, but that it has done so in the face of persistent governmental attempts to tinker with it in ways which threatened to throw it off the track at every turn." H. E. Humphreys was somewhat less damning but equally emphatic. "Since I believe in freedom," he explained, "I believe in the right of the American people to have as much government as the majority want. But I also believe they have a right to know what they are letting themselves in for. There is one important truth the people just don't seem to understand: the government produces nothing. Whatever it spends for people, it must take from people in taxes."[5]

The friends of the Kennedy administration found the business attitude incomprehensible. To them, it seemed an irrational contradiction of self-interest to oppose so vehemently an administration under which business conditions were extremely good; profits, high; prices, stable; and the outlook for tax reduction, favorable. What mystified them even more was the devotion of business leaders to the Eisenhower administration, which had failed to accomplish its specific economic goals. The President found the business reaction wryly amusing. He was, according to Theodore Sorensen, understandably impressed when a group of New England businessmen, who had pestered him about cutting federal spending, asked him to vote more funds for airport construction. Journalists who favored the New Frontier found the puzzle unsolvable. "Any calm analysis," one wrote, "should convince one that John F. Kennedy was not anti-business. On the contrary, he went further than most Republican Presidents . . . in making significant overtures to business."

Seymour Harris, a devoted friend and economic adviser, wrote to the *Times*, "President Kennedy did much more for business than President Eisenhower ever dared. . . . Businessmen should have revered him, not only for what he did for them directly—and especially on special tax measures—but for his contribution to a highly prosperous economy. . . . They never had it better." But this "rational" analysis with its exclusive reliance on *economic* interest missed the whole point. Professor Harris at least had an inkling of why businessmen were not reverent when he wrote, "I suspect that his [Kennedy's] affection and high regard for academicians and eggheads generally, men who introduce new elements of uncertainty for harassed businessmen, may have contributed to his unsatisfactory position with the managerial class." Having written this, it is astonishing that he was astonished because the business community did not embrace the Kennedy administration.[6]

The controversy from beginning to end demonstrated a lack of understanding of business sensitivity. Businessmen simply did not feel at home with the Kennedy administration. Their money incomes undoubtedly went up, but they earned no psychic income. In the Eisenhower administration, they were part of the "in group." In the Johnson administration, they were at least not in the "out group." In the Kennedy years, by contrast they felt like poor relations who had been invited to the wedding to watch the intellectuals, the artists, and the politicians dance. It was not the Kennedy policies, but who administered them that irked businessmen. It was not the ends that drove men to bitter words; it was the means for achieving the ends.

ATTEMPTS AT AN UNDERSTANDING

Many business leaders sought to make peace and chided their colleagues for being myopic. It was freely pointed out that reaction to government policy was often a question of whose ox was being gored. Business was far less loath to accept gratuities and subsidies from government than to see them go to some other group. During the 1950s and 1960s, pleas for tariff protection again became common; in transportation, the automobile industry lobbied for more highways, and six out of seven railroad executives who "disliked subsidies" thought the time for them had come. "A lot of the people who protest about the growth of government," said Daniel J. Haughton of Lockheed, "seem to have forgotten that in most cases they have brought it on themselves." Clarence A. Randall, chairman of Inland Steel, condemned the "businessmen who don't measure up to the responsible side of free enterprise." He included in his indictment the one "who fails to live up to vigorous competition and the one who seeks government subsidy" in the form, for example, of encouragement to "buy American," a subsidy for ships, or a high tariff.[7]

Some business leaders had become convinced that regardless of whose fault it was, business would be well-advised to adjust itself. John S. Coleman, president of Burroughs, urged businessmen to stop resisting change and play "a creative role in controlling and directing it." Coleman thought that the things business stood for were negative, whereas the politicians catered to what their customer-voters wanted. "It is obvious," said M. J. Rathbone of Jersey Standard, "we now have a mixed public-private economy. And that is a fact with which we must work. Unless we believe we can turn the clock back, that must be the starting point of any realistic discussion." Devereux C. Josephs of New York Life had no intention of turning the clock back. "Government," he prophesied, "will become an increasingly important factor in our lives because it will have to perform many functions of adjustment and alleviation which are not clearly the responsibility of any of us. Fine as the old adage is that the best government is the least government, it must be interpreted as the least government consonant with the problems confronting the governed."[8]

In calling for an end to the belligerency between government and business even before it had begun, Mark Cresap, president of Westinghouse, admonished government people to realize that "most businessmen are neither soulless, dripping with greed, nor unconcerned with human welfare." But businessmen for their part had to understand that "most leaders of government are not petty tyrants, bungling bureaucrats, or power-hungry demagogues." Sidney J. Weinberg, senior partner in Goldman, Sachs, holder of numerous directorships, and long-time participant in government service, thought that "most business leaders clearly agreed with him" that "not every criticism of business is an attack on the free enterprise system. . . . Not every change in the laws affecting business is a step toward socialism." Frederick R. Kappel of A.T. & T. believed at the end of 1961 that "President Kennedy has taken pains to emphasize that he and his administration are not anti-business. The force and sincerity of this position seem perfectly clear to me." Unlike many businessmen, Kappel later had opportunities to amend and clarify his views. In 1967, he told a *Times* reporter, "A big change took place in 1960. . . . Business had spent a rather restful time till then. Since then Government has made a big move to involve itself more in business than ever in the past." Shortly thereafter, he cleared up this seeming inconsistency by explaining that a "restful time was not necessarily good for business." "For the past several years," he added, "there has been a rather lively dialogue going on between business and government and on the whole it has been a constructive one for both sides. On business' part, there is a greater awareness . . . of private enterprise's responsibilities to help meet national economic and social goals. And I believe that we have a greater appreciation among government people of the importance of profitable business in achieving these goals. However, there still seem to be some people "who hold the simplistic notion that lower profits is the way to lower prices and that they know more about the way a business should be run than business does. In the main, however, I think the trend is the other way."[9]

On rare occasions, a business leader was much harsher in judging his colleagues' peccadilloes. Ben W. Heineman, chairman of the Chicago and North Western Railway, used a Chamber of Commerce meeting to condemn both the "indiscriminate attacks on all government programs" and the urge to "bulldoze the whole Government establishment into the Potomac River." Heineman expressed a belief that business attitudes toward government had changed, but "the public voice of business is hardly distinguishable from the one that resonated 25 or 50 or 100 years ago." It "still views the demands of the people for social services as the irresponsible clamor of the mob for bread and circuses and government acquiescence in these demands as steps toward inevitable socialism and slavery."[10]

THE FAILURE OF RECONCILIATION

All the pleas and cajolings of those who sought a rapprochement between business and government achieved little success. There were too many in the public at large and on the periphery of business who were eager to hold the coats while big business and government sparred and fought with each other. Opinion polls showed that small business was way off to the so-called "right." In a typical survey, only 19 per cent of big businessmen but 40 per cent of small business did not believe that the government should guarantee a job to any one looking for it. On the question of federal aid to education, 23 per cent of small business were opposed, contrasted to 7 per cent of big business. On the other hand, small business voted overwhelmingly in favor of fair-trade pricing and government loans to small business.

Small business had usurped the role of the carping scold which had once been the hallmark of the spokesmen of the NAM and C of C. Enunciated one pristine "conservative" who could not quite make up his mind about what was the worst evil, "The country is being absolutely destroyed by the eggheads in Washington. . . . The national debt is destroying this country. . . . This country is being destroyed by labor unions."

Many of these way-out opinions paid no attention to historical accuracy. According to the president of a small loan company, the country had been enjoying *"laissez-faire* at the turn of the century." But "in the 1930s under NRA, we adopted the idea that we could spend our way to prosperity." Now this was "no longer a free enterprise economy but a controlled economy." This oversimplified opinion came forth in protest against the federal government's attempts at consumer legislation, especially the "truth-in-lending" bill, although the speaker was quick to claim, "Don't get me wrong; I'm in favor of the consumer."

Among the worst *agents provocateurs* in the conflict between government and business were free-lance writers and the newspaper columnists and trade association officials who enjoyed a reputation as spokesmen for business. In the late 1950s, J. M. Hornor, one of the most prolific of the free-lancers, contributed often to the *Commercial and Financial Chronicle* and did the conservative cause much more harm than good. In a series of articles entitled "Put on Your Specs," "Cancer on the State," and "Thoughts on Statism," Hornor espoused the gold standard and the real bills doctrine, and was positive that "the Federal Income Tax was an instrument of tyranny that should be abolished" along with the Federal Reserve System. Meanwhile, the editors of trade journals hardly missed an opportunity to encourage a sense of self-pity and a feeling of government persecution among businessmen. There were many examples of this indoor sport of throwing logs on the fire of hostility. A typical one appeared in a trade association newsletter which greeted President Johnson's 1967 message on consumer legislation with the meaningless insinuation, "It would appear that the proposals in this year's consumer message were selected as much to serve political and bureaucratic interests as the public interest."

But even if they had not been continuously provoked, business leaders would have found enough reasons to object to government. Despite whatever vociferous protests they might make, most business leaders believed that government, like children, should be seen and not heard. In a romantic reading of American history, L. B. Worthington said, "The wisest course that the American Government could have chosen at that time [1776] was the one they elected to follow. It was a system of perfect liberty—the proposition that industry, if left to itself, will naturally find its way to the most useful and profitable employment." Government's role should be that of a provider of a suitable climate for business; in the words of B. F. Biaggini of the Southern Pacific Railroad, "This challenge of creating jobs is fundamentally our responsibility as businessmen and the important role of government is to see that a favorable climate is provided." Eugene Holman conceded that "modern life makes the intervention of government in individual daily lives unavoidable," but "such intervention should be kept to a minimum. . . . It should aim primarily at the establishment of a climate which will give maximum free play to competitive forces." These were time-honored views, but views were changing as displayed by the broad interpretation of government's role given by a big-city banker. He thought that "in dealing with the imperfections and limitations of the economic system, government has three vital roles: first, to strengthen the operation of free markets; second, to encourage steady growth and minimize swings in the level of activity; and third, to supplement the market system in the areas where it alone cannot as well provide essential needs."[11]

DISTRUST OF BUREAUCRATS AND THEORISTS

Business leaders, as always, had a specific bill of particulars against government—against its actors, its activities, its apathies, its arrogance, and its aspirations. They had not given up their belief that government was trying to do too much. Theodore V. Houser of Sears, Roebuck, who philosophized more than most businessmen, thought that government was always overtaxing itself. "Government," he said, "has large, complicated, and important functions. To perform these functions well strains the government's capacity for wisdom, objectivity, and flexibility. Government is not helped . . . by accepting the additional burden of trying to do what the private economy already does well."[12]

To many businessmen, if not most, the straining to do too much was clearly the result of empire building by government bureaucrats and advisers. James F. Oates, Jr., of the Equitable Life Assurance Society, who did "not regard the noticeable trend toward a bigger and bigger Government as an unmixed blessing," struck a responsive chord when he explained, "History teaches us repeatedly that Government and Government leaders have an appetite for increased power and authority—the satisfaction of which involves the diminution of personal freedom." This reiteration of Lord Acton's thesis had been and continued to be a well-known theme among business leaders. "Are we," asked Herbert V. Prochnow, Chicago banker, "expanding the functions of government faster than necessary as we seek more rapid economic growth? Are we moving into more centralized government with the gradual loss of many individual freedoms?" To the business world in general, the answer seemed to be an indubitable "yes," and it was chiefly the fault of the administrative agencies, the advisers, and officials who had never been elected to office. But on occasion the fear of loss of freedom seemed to be a façade. What businessmen really objected to was the same thing they had always objected to—the anti-business attitude of the theorist. What provoked the businessman was the theorist's impracticality, his flexibility, his cavalier dismissal of rule and law. "Too often," said Albert L. Nickerson, chairman of Socony Mobil, "we sense a halfhearted, apologetic, and even occasionally an antipathetic response to our legitimate requests for cooperation from U.S. officials both here and abroad."[13]

G. S. Kennedy, chairman of the executive committee of General Mills, agreed that there was a widespread view among businessmen that the government was less friendly than it could be. He thought the basis for this was the legislation which the Administration was asking for together with the anti-business statements of people below the cabinet level. Joseph L. Block of Inland Steel, who was considered very sympathetic to the Administration, conceded that although he himself did not feel any hostility to government, other businessmen generally did so feel, because the government did not show fiscal responsibility and because government leaned too heavily on the advice of professors and others who were more theoretical than practical. W. C. Stolk of the American Can Company didn't feel business was hostile to Washington, although, to be sure, there "are many people in Washington with no business experience who are inclined to do a lot of loose talking. A professor who has never met a payroll . . . can create the wrong impression." Bankers were of much the same mind. One Middle West investment banker thought the Administration uninformed about business if not actually unfriendly, and a New York banker saw "real danger in the steady grasping for more power by Federal administrative agencies."[14]

Executives and tycoons, bankers and industrialists insisted that they would not find the government agencies nearly as repugnant if only they understood the rules. They agreed with the statement of Stuart Saunders of the Pennsylvania Railroad, "Business is better served by imperfect rules than by none at all." Business leaders thought they knew why government bodies turned a deaf ear on calls for rules and statements of objectives. "It would appear," enunciated J. Edward Warren of Cities Service, "that the numerous administrative agencies in government are solely concerned with scoring points against industry. They seem not to know nor care about the effect of their actions on society as a whole. . . . Implicit in regulation should be the questions: Will these policies foster economic growth and create jobs? Or are they blind adherence to outworn regulatory concepts?"[15]

THE STEEL IMBROGLIO

The theorists and professors whose value in the government and the economy businessmen were continually questioning, were the *dei ex machina* whose machinations spelled trouble in capital letters to the business community and for free enterprise in general. Business leaders were convinced that well over a majority of theorists had no reverence for the market system. In fact, if they had their way, the economy would become controlled, from wages to profits, from production to consumption by some governmental body. No opinion was more often reiterated in business circles than that "government is working its way toward crippling controls."

The whole subject was brought into sharp relief by the famous or infamous steel incident in the spring of 1962. The incident was not a simple melodrama starring Roger Blough and President Kennedy as protagonists. On the contrary, it was a highly complicated economic and political piece of business. It led to some of the wildest hyperbole that came forth from a hyperbolic generation.

The steel controversy did not begin in 1962, nor did it end then. It began in the late 1950s, and its aftermath stretched at least to the late 1960s. One of the things that bothered businessmen all through the late 1950s and increasingly in the early 1960s was the so-called "cost-price squeeze." As early as the spring of 1956, steel executives were clamoring for higher prices and more rapid depreciation allowances to provide the extra earnings that they insisted were needed to finance expansion. Following a strike in the summer of 1956, prices were increased an average of $8.50 a ton. But most steel men thought, in the words of A. C. Adams of Jones and Laughlin, "The price increase . . . is grossly inadequate in . . . covering our total anticipated costs." To meet the inadequacy, prices were again raised an average of $6 a ton in 1957, and a further increase followed in 1958 just before the 1959 strike, the longest in the industry's history.[16]

Still, steel people did not think they were getting enough. "Take a look at the trend of profits since 1955," Roger Blough told a news conference in October 1961. "Then compare it with any other index you want. You'll find the portion of the sales dollar going to industry is alarmingly low." Two implications inevitably followed from all this: The industry was not getting enough to keep its equipment in a competitive position with that of other countries, and price increases were necessary. There was also running between the lines a feeling that the government was pro-labor and was giving the unions preferential treatment while at the same time "being unmindful of the importance of profits."

In March 1962, just before the renegotiation of a new contract with the United Steel workers, Leslie B. Worthington, president of U. S. Steel, in one of his rare public statements, claimed that the industry needed more profit for investment to meet the challenge of international competition. At that time, the economy was faltering and demand was dropping sharply. Although it was not directly germane to the economic issues involved in the case, Steel stock was selling at about $80 a share. Since 1946, it had split 3 for 1 in 1949 and 2 for 1 in 1955. This meant that 100 shares in 1946, when the stock was selling at about $100 had grown to 600 shares in 1962. In other words, $10,000 invested in Steel in 1946 had grown to $48,000 in 1962, not including dividends paid in the interim.

Mindful of the fact that six strikes had already taken place in the sixteen years since the war, the Kennedy administration exerted pressure to prevent another one, and it was very pleased when a new contract was signed on March 31, three months before the expiration of the old one. It was expected that everyone else would be happy too, but the steel executives were saying nothing.

On April 9, Edmund F. Martin told Bethlehem stockholders that even though labor costs had risen, it was not a propitious moment to increase prices because "We shouldn't do anything to increase our prices if we are to survive. We have more competition both domestically and from foreign firms." Big Steel did not appear to be of the same opinion, for on April 10, Blough issued a press release announcing an across-the-board 3.5 per cent increase. Eight other companies went along, which led government officials to the conclusion that the whole thing was an example of administered prices, that is, of manifest collusion.

President Kennedy was stunned when Blough told him what had been done. Believing himself to be the victim of deliberate guile, he is reported to have said that his father had always told him that all businessmen were sons-of-bitches. All the wheels of government were turned toward rolling prices back, and either because of this pressure, or because the marketplace would not tolerate a price rise while demand was falling and supply was increasing, three smaller, but nevertheless important producers—Inland, Armco, and Kaiser—did not join in the increase. The movement collapsed, and on April 13, Bethlehem followed by U. S. Steel rescinded the action of three days earlier.*

There was nothing brilliant about what Blough and Steel's Board of Directors had done. Indeed, it was reported on the highest authority that most business leaders thought the action very stupid. Certainly, it was bad public relations. As Clarence Randall of Inland Steel said, the public had developed a "plague on both your houses"

---

* The incident was blown up out of all proportion. One writer said Blough's action had shaken the government more than the Bay of Pigs incident had. "The reverberations . . . struck at the foundations of the economy."

attitude toward both management and labor in the steel industry which might lead to public regulation of the industry as a public utility.

Yet of such strange stuff is history made. When the President opened fire, it no longer mattered what businessmen thought about Blough's wisdom or public relations. They looked upon him as David combating the governmental Goliath. A flood of bitterness against the President and the men who surrounded him gushed forth. Businessmen could not tolerate the government's display of power. They were in no mood to forget the remark about the ancestry of businessmen, especially since it purported to come from a businessman. For its part, the Administration had no empathy for business. It regarded anything it did for business as a gift of charity. Its views were well expressed by the President himself when, at Yale, he lectured business on the myths it believed in and castigated those who "ignore the realities of economic life in a neurotic search for unending reassurance." Whether true or not, and much of it was true, the tirade accomplished nothing. There could be no rapport between business and the President; they didn't like each other and they didn't speak the same language.

Relations between business and the government deteriorated almost to the nadir of the days of Roosevelt and Truman. But, as before, some efforts were made to return to a state of non-belligerence. The President made some serious overtures, and business made some half-hearted ones. Soon after the steel episode, Gerald L. Phillippe, president of General Electric, asserted that the nation could not afford a "cops and robbers antagonism between government and business." He then went on to say that although he did not underestimate the influence of government policy on the economy, profit-making business was the true source of growth. There was little doubt that this was the overwhelming consensus. In June, an opinion poll reported that 75 per cent of the country's executives thought government policies would not be very helpful in stimulating growth; a year earlier, only 55 per cent were of such mind.[17]

THE FEAR OF CONTROLS

Downgrading such matters as tariffs, quotas and subsidies, business really thought that the only thing it wanted from government

was to be let alone. "Business and industry," said Robert Dunlop of
Sun Oil, "function today under an increasing pressure of uncertainty
arising from non-economic forces—to put it bluntly, from political
forces. . . . U. S. Steel found that out while the whole country
watched." What continued to worry management was the threat of a
controlled economy. J. Ward Keener of B. F. Goodrich protested
strongly at a government-industry conference against "a planned and
controlled economy." Harold H. Helm of the Chemical Bank told
his stockholders: "Business confidence was shaken by the [steel]
incident. Business felt it was facing a new challenge from government. Fears were expressed that this action might mark the beginning
of government price fixing which could well vitiate the economic effect of supply and demand."[18]

As the economy recovered rapidly from its slight doldrums in
1962, inflationary threats again appeared, and Washington tried once
again to prevent by indirection price increases in basic materials.
The Eisenhower administration had flirted with the idea of setting
guidelines for wages and prices. The Kennedy administration pushed
the idea further, and in the early Johnson years, the guidelines were
made specific. All of which gave some bankers and businessmen a
bad time, especially since it appeared that "a façade of friendliness"
might be developing between business and government, and from
the point of view of the unreconstructed, nothing could be more regrettable. George Champion of the Chase Bank was especially bitter:
"This is no time to be timid of tone or fearful of economic reprisal.
. . . There are guidelines for wages and prices, guidelines for labor-
management behavior, guidelines for antitrust enforcement, even
guidelines for how much you put in the collection plate on Sunday,
and we bankers have been given a special set of guidelines for the
balance of payments and for lending rates. In fact, there seem to be
guidelines for almost everything except the size of the Federal Government. . . . In my judgment, the new trend toward government
by guideline is one of the most insidious and dangerous on the national scene today."[19]

At about the same time, Edward A. O'Neil of Monsanto Chemical
was saying much the same thing. It was not that he was opposed to
government, "for 78 of Monsanto's employees in St. Louis held some
type of government office." But despite whatever had been accomplished by this moonlighting, it appeared to O'Neil that the free
enterprise system had lost much of its freedom of operation. With

the exaggeration that sometimes featured such talks, O'Neil explained, "We are not exactly free to do what we want about prices, markets, competition, wages, and benefits, or earnings for that matter. I certainly am not saying we should try to turn the clock back. . . . But I do say that we must check this trend before the right to earn a profit is legislated out of existence." Friends of business found much of this sentiment hard to swallow, for it had always been a cornerstone of business economics that no one was "free to do what he wanted about prices," etc. That, as United States Steel always insisted, was the function of the free-market system.[20]

In October 1965, the Johnson administration and the guidelines ran afoul of a crisis not unlike that of April 1962. One essential difference was that unemployment was below 4½ per cent and demand was high. So it made much more sense when aluminum producers raised their prices. The Johnson administration, believing that a political mistake had been made in 1962, resorted to indirection in combating this economically more justifiable price increase. It was rumored that the President had been "sputtering mad," but this was immediately denied. Then the White House asked for a meeting to discuss the disposal of some surplus aluminum from the government's stockpile. Later it was announced that the government would sell 200,000 tons, then 300,000 tons, but this, it was said, had nothing to do with the price rise. By coincidence, however, the industry canceled the increase less than two weeks after it had been announced. In November, much the same sequence of events happened in the copper industry. At the end of the year it was steel's turn once again, but this time the issue was compromised with the industry keeping part of the rise and rescinding the rest.

Once again, business was growing restive under the latent fears about controls. David Rockefeller, president of the Chase Bank, thought "The strong reaction to the price increase in aluminum is a profoundly disturbing case of artificial and arbitrary control of wages and prices." A Chicago businessman told the press that when aluminum raised prices, half of the businessmen he talked to thought the industry was wrong, but then came copper and steel and they thought the President was wrong. But probably the reaction was best stated by Paul Wren, president of Boston's Old Colony Trust Company, "Business support has been cracked but not shattered by the President's recent successful attempts to control prices by threats and persuasion."[21]

THE BALANCE-OF-PAYMENTS PROBLEM

What they thought of government and its place in the economy, important as it was, was by no means the only problem in which businessmen were interested. In the new and much more complicated era of the late fifties and sixties, businessmen found many more issues to be concerned about than ever before. Probably because of the proliferation of professional economists in academic, business, and political life, economic issues became something of a fad. It sometimes seemed as though at the end of every year a group of the initiated met somewhere—ideally in a pipe-smoke-filled room—and selected the economic issue for the following year. The game started out rather slowly in 1955, when the automobile union raised the question of the guaranteed annual wage. The *Commercial and Financial Chronicle* ran an article on the subject and invited comments, but responses, especially from big businessmen, were disappointedly meager. Harrison L. Amber of the Berkshire Life Insurance Company favored the idea, and F. W. Specht of Armour and Company thought it impractical. Robert E. Wilson of Standard Oil of Indiana, in a talk to the NAM, feared that a guaranteed wage would cause unemployment. He suggested as alternatives industrial research, better management, and continuous economic growth. A few other business leaders said much the same thing, and the issue faded away.

By 1956, economic issues had picked up steam. In that year, the question of whether controls should be reinstated over consumer credit, which had reached the "staggering total" of $42.5 billion,* vied with tight money for first place. By 1957, the game had taken on the peculiar fascination of a routine. Philip Reed of General Electric selected union power and "the subject of corporate size," but prosperity and inflation were much more popular. In 1958, the business recession enlivened interest. In 1959, public attention swayed back and forth among three rather unharmonious issues. How to encourage economic growth was a prominent question all through the year. But this naturally led to the question of how to encourage growth without encouraging inflation which in turn made a conversation piece out of tight money and its advantages and disadvantages. By

---

* But approximately $100 billion in 1967.

1960, these issues had lost much of their glamour as the balance-of-payments problem, lurking in the wings since 1958, took over most of the stage with the "cost-price squeeze on profits" occupying a close second in most businessmen's minds.

An adverse balance of payments had existed all through the 1950s, but it did not become a *cause celebre* until 1958 when the Treasury gold stock fell below $20 billion. This new dollar glut created a great sense of surprise, for the world had been in a serious dollar shortage for over a generation, and a favorable balance of payments for the United States was considered one of the few certainties in a terribly fickle world. Indeed, when the unrecognized balance of payments was already a number of years old, a well-known university economist wrote an article for a financial magazine with the title "Europe's Impending Dollar Shortage."

In 1959, John J. McCloy of the Chase Bank announced, "we are rapidly approaching, if we have not already reached, a balance of payments problem of our own." What was so frightful about this course of events, according to McCloy and an army of bankers was that "without a sound dollar, not only our trade but the whole world's trade and I dare say the whole world's welfare is in real jeopardy." Equitable Life's James F. Oates drew an even more gloomy picture. If something wasn't done, we would run out of gold; foreign bankers would begin a run on gold; we would be forced to devalue; the consequences would be unthinkable; there would probably be a reversion to the jungle warfare and economic chaos of the 1930s.

What could be done to alleviate this new international difficulty arising from the supply of dollars outrunning the demand? Most businessmen regarded the issue with impatience and put the blame for it on government irrationality and recalcitrance. The solution, wrote Cyrus Eaton to the *Times,* was simple: eliminate foreign economic and military aid and reduce taxes and the whole problem would evaporate. Said Walter Harnischfeger, "We are paying for our own funeral with foreign aid."

Some other businessmen and almost all bankers urged the government and its agencies to adopt additional solutions. They were not unmindful of the desirability of tax reduction, and some reluctantly favored cutting foreign aid, but they put more stress on monetary policy and the manipulation of interest rates. Harking back to the rules that had prevailed in pre-World War I central banking, they called for higher interest rates which, they were certain, would attract investment funds away from European money and capital markets and slow down the flight of funds out of the United States. Lawrence Litchfield, Jr., of the Aluminum Company told a German audience that an important way of solving the balance of payments was to counteract capital outflow by "1. letting interest rates assume levels comparable with other industrialized nations, 2. by improving the U.S. business investment climate through tax reduction, more adequate depreciation, and other measures, 3. by keeping government expenditures in line with tax revenues."

Bankers fully believed that money and credit would have to be tightened in order to raise interest rates. As George Champion put it, "a root cause of the balance-of-payments problem lies in the policies of easy money and credit which have been pursued in the midst of general prosperity." Critics pointed out that tight money and high interest rates might discourage investment, dampen business activity and kill the goose that everybody was allegedly trying to save. But financial circles deigned no reply, leading some of the unsympathetic opposition to infer that the balance of payments would have to be protected even at the price of a business recession.

The Administration meanwhile turned once again to guidelines and moral suasion. In February 1965, it asked businessmen to cut down voluntarily their overseas investments. Businessmen were not happy; they complained that the government would be better off to set its own house in order by reducing foreign aid. Fred J. Borch of General Electric spoke for them in expressing alarm at "resurgent nationalism, mushrooming restrictions, and restraints on international trade and investment." Bankers, on the other hand, expressed general approval, although, as David Rockefeller, Thomas S. Gates, and George Moore said, they would have been happier if the President had been more positive on monetary policy and monetary controls.[22]

THE COURSE OF THE ECONOMY, 1954–67

But balance of payments, the idiosyncracies of government, and the squeeze on profits, exciting as they were, were not the subjects that absorbed most attention. The matters with which businessmen continued fundamentally to be concerned were the bread-and-butter issues that had concerned them ever since 1946 and even before.

These were the rise and fall of economic activity and the rise and fall of prices—boom and recession, inflation and deflation.

From 1955 to 1967, total production in dollars of the same purchasing power grew at a rate of about 3.6 per cent compounded annually. This was about the same as the rate from 1946 to 1954, and meant that the gross national product in 1958 dollars rose from about $315 billion in 1946, to over $400 billion in 1954, and over $660 billion in 1967. This doubling of total production every twenty-one years or so did not take place without occasional interruptions. There were short, almost unnoticeable recessions of ten months beginning in July 1957 and again in May 1960. But from February 1961, the economy moved ahead in the longest uninterrupted advance in peace time history.*

Wholesale prices moved upward in stages rather than as part of a steady progression. From 92.7 per cent of the 1957–59 average in 1953, prices moved slowly to 93.2 in 1955 and then more rapidly to 100.4 in 1958, around which they settled until 1965 when they again advanced rapidly to 102.5 in 1965 and 106.1 in 1967.† All the evidence added weight to the hypothesis that sustained growth and low unemployment would, after some time lag, push prices up, whereas economic recession and unemployment of 4½ to 6 per cent of the labor force would result in stable prices or even in some price decline.

The securities markets, in which, surprisingly, businessmen seemed to take little interest, performed somewhat differently from the economy in general, but very similarly to their behavior in the 1920s. The *Times* composite average rose over 80 per cent, or by 125 points between 1946 and 1954. In the next eight years, it went up another 125 points or by 50 per cent; and between the high in 1962 and the high in 1966, still another 205 points or again by 50 per cent. The average rose more in five years in the 1960s than it had in the previous fifteen years.‡

* Three times during the 1954–67 period (1956, 1962, and 1967) the economy faltered without going into what, according to the National Bureau of Economic Research indicators, would be called a "recession."

† The so-called cost of living index, which included services as well as goods, moved differently, advancing slowly year by year with only one exception (1955) from 93.2 in 1953 to 116.3 in 1967.

‡ The industrial average did even better. The familiar Dow Jones soared 782 points from 1946 to 1966—191 points between 1946 and 1954; 322 between 1954 and 1962; and 269 between 1962 and 1966. In the eight years between 1958 and 1966, it rose as much as in the previous twelve.

Again, this advance was not without its nasty breaks and its traumatic shocks. On three occasions, a crisis in the White House caused a one-day collapse in the averages. On September 26, 1955, President Eisenhower had a heart attack and the averages fell some 20 points. Again in June 1956, the averages plummeted when the President had a minor operation. The third time was on Friday, November 23, 1963, when the assassination of President Kennedy wiped out over $11 billion of market values as the averages dropped more than 20 points. In each case, however, the market recovered more sharply than it had dropped.

Longer slumps in share prices were associated with recessions and slowdowns in the overall economy. Presaging the downturn of 1957–58, the market began to drop perceptibly in the late summer of 1956 and continued down until the fall of 1957 for a loss of some 20 per cent. Then in January 1960, shortly before the beginning of the fourth postwar recession, the market sold off until October with the averages declining somewhat over 15 per cent. There were, in addition, two other short but very precipitate drops that foreshadowed a marked slowing down in general business. In the spring of 1962, stock averages dropped over 25 per cent and many young men in the Street expected that they were about to experience the excitement of another 1929. All divisions of business—large and small, banking, brokerage, and industry—blamed the collapse on the President and anticipated that a severe depression would follow the "Kennedy Market." Their logic was marred by a couple of facts. The stock slump had begun in January, long before the steel incident, and although business did slide off, it came back fast. By the fall it was behaving famously and by April 1963, the stock market had broken into new high ground.

In the spring of 1965, some nervousness again bothered financial circles. In early June, Governor Martin spoke on the similarities between the 1920s and the 1960s. He made a very good case, for in two months, the market melted off over 10 per cent of what many experts thought was speculative fat. This time, however, the rest of the economy paid no attention to the "Martin Market," and stock prices quickly recovered to set new records. Then in February 1966, as brokers and customers watched the Dow Jones rush toward 1000, the market, under the pressure of tight money and to the surprise of almost everyone, collapsed. In 240 days it went down 25 per cent.

Again business slowed down, and this time the recovery seemed much more sluggish.

Judged by the same standards that were used in the 1920s, there were many indications that this too was a market of speculation. In the 1920s, it was said that every adult was in the stock market; in the 1960s, the *Times* carried an ad for a *Teenager's Guide to the Stock Market*. But brokers' loans were far less than they had been in the 1920s, although the same kind of frenzied activity characterized both eras. Up to 1954, with the exception of the flurry that greeted the outbreak of Korea, the market was dull. But thereafter it rose to an astonishing pace, from a little over 500 million shares in 1954 to over 2 billion in 1967. By then, an 8-million-share day began to be considered light trading. Up to the end of 1968, there had been eighteen normal trading days on which activity exceeded 15 million shares; seventeen occurred in 1968.* Yet, because of the immense multiplication of shares, the turnover rate fell far short of that of the "Great Bull Market." In 1929, the whole market changed hands at least once. But this was nothing compared to the early 1900s when the turnover rate was over 200 per cent a year. It was, however, far higher than the 12–15 per cent rate that prevailed in 1947–53, or the 16 per cent rate of 1965 when ten times as many shares were listed on the New York stock exchanges as there had been in 1929.

HOW BUSINESS VIEWED THE COURSE OF THE ECONOMY

The market's pronounced speculative aspects did not seem to disturb many people. In March 1955, Professor Galbraith told the Fulbright Committee investigating the stock market that speculative signs were beginning to appear. Occasionally, too, Stock Exchange President Funston issued perfunctory warnings about speculation by the uninitiated. But the prevalent view was that it was not the same stock market because now there were millions of investors, not just a few speculators. Speculation, moreover, was regarded altogether differently, especially in the business and banking world. "Speculation," remarked New York University's highly respected Professor Marcus Nadler, "goes hand in hand with economic progress." Even in the banking fraternity that had never lost an opportunity to warn against

* This does not include eleven Thursdays that followed tradeless Wednesdays and saw abnormally high activity.

speculation's evils, there was now nothing but silence on the subject.

On the whole, bankers and businessmen were much more optimistic than they had been in the previous boom era. For the short run, they were especially bullish. In the 1920s, almost every year gathered a great harvest of cautious forecasts and warnings to "look out" lest the boom be a booby trap. In the decade after 1954, almost every year was greeted with forecasts of records that were about to be achieved. In January 1955, Harlow Curtice spoke for the business consensus with a very optimistic forecast. As 1956 approached, banker S. Sloan Colt expected a slight downturn, but Harry A. Bullis saw the country "on the threshold of the greatest period of prosperity we have ever known." And the Dun and Bradstreet annual poll of over 1300 large- and medium-size manufacturers found a "clearcut majority" expecting a better year.[23]

In early 1957, five out of six executives told Dun and Bradstreet that they expected better business. In May just before the economy went into a mild recession, "leading figures" mistakingly predicted "continuous improvement for the rest of the year." According to T. V. Houser, there had been "a significant change from some pessimism to more widespread optimism." Ralph Cordiner, in seeing stability for the next year and then a resumption of the decline, was much closer to what actually happened.[24]

At the opening of 1958 when we were more than halfway through the recession, Dun and Bradstreet reported that 109 company presidents looked upon the economy somewhat as follows: 42 per cent were mildly pessimistic, 25 per cent were just as confident as they had been in 1957, 19 per cent were more so, and the others would not venture a guess. By April, the *Times* reported that after seven months of following a gradual downward slope, the optimists were still optimistic and the pessimists were still pessimistic.[25]

The mood for 1959 was on the gray side as business expected a "continuous improvement, but no boom." As 1960 approached, however, the clouds rapidly dissipated. In November 1959, Dun and Bradstreet found 58 per cent expecting somewhat better things, 38 per cent for no change, and 4 per cent seeing a downturn. But before long, forecasts became overwhelmingly cheerful as visions of the "soaring sixties" took hold. One hundred top executives surveyed by the *Herald Tribune* were confident that 1960 would be a record smasher. The consensus estimated total production at $526 billion (the actual GNP in 1960 was $504 billion).

Disappointed by the recession of 1960, forecasters were subdued for 1961, but they awoke and hit the mark almost exactly in 1962. Then came the steel crisis and the Kennedy Market, and predictions turned as grim as at any time except during an actual recession. The Business Council reported that "a great majority of the technical consultants expects economic activity to peak out by year end and turn down in first quarter of 1963. . . . It seemed to many that government interference in the pricing process, coupled with government acquiescence in continuous wage increases, had adverse implications for profit prospects, business confidence, and business investment." But this was in October. By December, forecasts had become somewhat more mixed. Homer Livingston of the First National of Chicago anticipated some "edging up." Joseph L. Block regarded the outlook as "cloudy." Austin F. Cushman, chairman of Sears, looked for business to be "moderately higher." James M. Symes of the Pennsylvania Railroad expected a "gradual decline," and John E. Swearingen of Indiana Standard Oil thought a minor recession was still a possibility.[26]

With such a set of forecasts, the robust recovery of the economy came as a surprise to the many in and out of business who had expected at best a desultory performance and at worst a recession. But if nothing else, forecasters must be resilient, and they were equal to the occasion. In 1964 and the following years, the outlook became increasingly roseate both in reality and as the prognosticators saw it.

Short-term forecasts of the stock market did not do nearly as well as those for the economy as a whole. Indeed, they did not do nearly as well as the market forecasts of the 1920s. In 1959, the *Times* reported that five out of six of the Wall Street analysts who were interviewed were bearish. The most pessimistic thought that the market might be in for a 20 to 30 per cent drop. They were two years too soon. But when the market was about to go into a tailspin in 1962, most forecasters were bullish. To be sure, at the beginning of 1962, some analysts recommended that "equity positions be reduced 25–30 per cent"; others recommended that "traders stay relatively liquid"; and some believed "that the present degree of thoughtless speculation is such that the possibility of an old-fashioned bear market cannot be ruled out." But the prevalent tone was still very bullish. One Chicago house thought it "more likely that the Dow will go to 800 than a 10–15 per cent reaction." To another, "a continuation of a favorable business climate and firm stock prices seem indicated through 1962." A highly respected analyst advised that "common stocks still seem to represent the best haven for surplus investment funds." An equally respected expert saw "little or no likelihood that the great disillusionment of the first half of 1960 will be repeated." Still another thought it "rather improbable that top quality stocks will ever become cheap or even reasonable by conventional standards." As the Dow began dropping from 400 to its ultimate 285, the *Chronicle* reported that Wall Street opinion was still on the optimistic side. Three reputable houses promised that the "next move will be a test of the highs rather than the lows."

After the break subsided, opinion shifted the other way. It was commonly assumed "that the stock market break will adversely affect business. The road back will be rough." A market letter brought the dour news that this was "a serious bear market headed lower for the next year or two." And the ultimate obituary, "The break marks the end of an era."

Again in 1966, few analysts saw the break coming and they did not seem to believe it when it happened. One saw "enough factors to justify caution"; another advised building reserves on values; and still another did not think stocks were cheap. But even after stocks had begun to break badly, one widely quoted authority called it "a purely technical affair." There were a great many who "continued to have confidence" and advised a "policy of placing orders to buy at prices under the market." As late as August, the *Times* carried a headline: "Oversold Market Is Cry of Brokers Puzzled by Slump." Ironically, however, it was a pessimist rather than an optimist who deserved the prize for a far-out forecast. Early in the slump, he concluded that by "utilizing the strategy of ascertaining what the Industrial Average itself is predicting, a market student would be warranted in making the prediction that the Dow will probably decline by 88 per cent to a price of close to 63."[27]

The economic forecasts of the businessmen, their advisers, and those to whom they paid attention, optimistic though most of them were, fell short of the actual results. Even among those who had always enjoyed (or suffered from) the reputation of being arch optimists, there were many who were willing to settle for less than what actually fell from the cornucopia. But this would be what one would expect. Most people have to gulp twice when told that in another two generations family income in today's purchasing power will average

$35,000 a year. Yet that is no more than has taken place in the last two generations.

The cumulative effect of habitual underestimates made long-run forecasts, even by those who had considerable expertise, considerably off the mark. In 1955, the Twentieth Century Fund predicted a $414 billion product in 1960. At the same time the standard estimate for 1965 among academic economists was $465 billion. In 1956, the standard forecast was $570 billion in 1965 and $670 billion in 1975. In 1957, an academic economist with a noted reputation for forecasting set the target at $565 billion in 1965. In 1958, Leo Cherne, in an article called "Are We in the Foothills of the Fabulous 1960's?" thought a $600 billion GNP by 1970 was not impossible. All of these estimates were in dollars of 1955–58 purchasing power. In reality, the GNP (in 1958 dollars) reached $488 billion in 1960, $610 in 1965, and $660 in 1967. In short, the optimistic goals set in the middle fifties were achieved in a little more than half the time allotted.[28]

With all their shortcomings in the arts of clairvoyance, the 1950–60 business leaders did better than their predecessors. They knew a whole lot more. They had more expert opinion on which to rely. They were more precise and had more numbers at their command. And their reasons for recession and recovery were more sophisticated. Admittedly, echoes of the past could still be heard. Bernard Baruch, for example, when asked for his solution to the recession of 1958, presented a set of cures that had been orthodox *circa* 1930: cuts in spending, no tax relief, debt repayment, and price reductions. Others still thought that recessions grew out of the excesses of the boom, so that, in the words of Carrol M. Shanks, "The safest thing to do with a boom, if we are to avoid a depression, is to control it, not let it mount until it tops out." But there were also new-fangled notions about fiscal and monetary policy, taxation and spending. And above all, it was no longer such an absolute certainty that depressions and recessions were inevitable—the plagues that were visited on a sinful and unrepentant people. Henry C. Alexander expressed his contempt for "the feeling that the sins of the boom must be expiated and the only way to do it is by sweating out the slump by suffering a little. It's the old Spartan determination to show that we can take it, coupled perhaps with a belief that we'll be better off for the experience." And Donald C. Cook of American Electric Power, who had had some experience in government, helped to lay another myth to rest: "The past five years of uninterrupted growth have demonstrated that there is no inevitable regularity to recession, that the pattern of expansion and recession does not, like the tides, follow any natural law. Instead, it is now apparent that, as the product of human activity, it is subject to intervention and considerable modification."[29]

INFLATION AGAIN

Since most of the years following the post-Korean recession of 1953–54 were years of high-level business activity, inflation continued to be the most pressing economic issue, lurking importantly in the background even when not first on the list. Concern and fear over inflation subsided in the recession of 1953–54, but as the economy recovered, the smoldering embers began to flare and by 1957 they had again burst into flame. The *Commercial and Financial Chronicle* did not list "inflation" in its index in early 1956, but by the fourth quarter, there were thirty-nine entries and in late 1957, when inflation had again run its race and the economy was again in recession, there were over fifty listings. When preoccupation with inflation was at its height, the *Chronicle* ran a number of articles with such titles as "Inflation: the Termite of Civilization." A banker wrote under the title "There Has Been No Mandate to Encourage the Tragedy of Inflation." A conservative economist warned that we were "approaching a point where the foundations of our economic and social structure are threatened." An insurance executive called for controls over consumer and mortgage credit. An industrialist, at the end of 1957, beseeched the nation not "to relax its fight against inflation," and a prominent banker thought the downturn in business and in stocks "did not mean the end of inflation."

Again, however, the issue simmered down only to burst forth once more as prosperity began to reappear. As 1959 opened, bankers Harold Helm, Henry C. Alexander, and H. P. Davison, and industrialists Roger Blough, Ernest Breech, E. J. Hanley, and others took pains to point out that "they were worried about inflation." The *Chronicle* in the January–March index had forty-five entries on the topic. The sixties demonstrated the same pattern; in January 1962 the *Times* reported that financiers were still "wary of inflation" and before the end of 1964, some early birds were saying that the economy was again "approaching an unhealthy situation."

Businessmen were not the only ones who were concerned. In

1957, President Eisenhower told a press conference that controls would be put on the economy if prices did not stop going up. "Business and labor must discharge their responsibilities," he said. "Unless this happens, the United States then has to move in more firmly with so-called controls and when we begin to control prices, and allocations, and wages, and all the rest, then it is not the America we know." In January 1959, Senate majority leader Lyndon B. Johnson delivered a speech called "Inflation: A Key United States Problem," and as President both he and his predecessor sought to control prices by moral suasion and the use of executive power.[30]

On the subject of inflation, as on so many others, business opinion showed some subtle differences from the opinions of the past. Some businessmen (admittedly a minority, but nevertheless more than in the past) thought that inflation was inevitable in a fully employed economy, and they did not understand the reasons for the alarm that was being expressed on all sides. Frank E. Jerome, a Seattle banker, told a congressional committee, "It is not possible to avoid inflation and deflation completely." James T. Leftwich of Woolworth's said to the same committee, "It is questionable whether we can avoid periodic intervals of inflation and deflation." In the same hearings E. H. Leavey of I.T. & T. said there was no cure for inflation in a democratic society. He put price stability a poor third to "growth" and "stability of production" in the list of desired economic goals. He agreed with the conclusion of Harlow H. Curtice of General Motors that "a period in which prices are stable is not usually a period of growth." Frazer B. Wilde, president of the Connecticut General Life Insurance Company and a leader in the CED, thought the problem was unquestionably the result of heady economic growth. "Our country," he said, "is struggling on three fronts: the struggle against the world-wide advance of Communism, the problem of maintaining high employment and a steady advance in our real standard of living, and the struggle to resist a steady deterioration in the buying power of money. These problems are all interrelated. The American people are trying to get more out of the economy than it is capable of producing. This is natural and good, but also dangerous."[31]

Another handful of business leaders thought that inflation was inevitable but also evil. Donald B. Woodward, chairman of the Finance Committee of Vick Chemical, was one of those who bemoaned fate. "We shall experience," he said, "a rising price level for the rest of our lives; the rise may be irregular, but it will be unmistakable." These determinists drew the scorn of the majority of bankers and businessmen, who thought that inflation was neither predestined nor salutary. There were some among this group who believed that inflation was so evil that it would be well worth the price of a depression to control it.[32]

R. C. Gerhan of Republic Steel compared inflation with being "attacked by an armed robber." Over and over again, Bernard Baruch, the patriarch of Wall Street, pronounced, "Inflation is the most important economic fact of our time—the greatest single peril to our economic health." H. Bruce Palmer, insurance executive, agreed that it was "the single greatest peril to our nation's economic progress. Don't take my word for it," he said. "Examine the facts for yourself —reach your own conclusion—and then believe." A pathological fear of inflation had taken the place of a pathological fear of government. In a letter to a fellow conservative, the broker E. F. Hutton wrote, "What I fear—more than the cold or hot war—is inflation. It's galloping." O. W. Adams, who was not known for his moderation, lamented the extent of economic illiteracy which prevented people from understanding what evil lurked in the economy. "If only they knew," lamented Adams, "the citizenship of this country would be willing and anxious to go through a period of painful deflation and consequent recession in order to restore economic sanity. . . . People who bewail unemployment are at the same time undermining the currency." William A. McDonnell of the First National Bank of St. Louis was milder but along the same lines. After stating that our number-one problem was how to achieve prosperity without inflation, he suggested, "Maybe it is time to level off for a while—not quit growing, but simply quit increasing the rate of growth."[33]

Some business leaders sincerely believed that inflation would mean the end of the American way of life. Said Harold Quinton of Southern California Edison, "The economic destruction which results from inflation creates the excuse for the welfare state." A spokesman for business warned that "if the present complacency and apathy of the American public is not soon altered, the present creeping inflation will result, within the next twenty-five years, in the loss of our present form of free government and our lapse into state socialism."[34]

Carrol M. Shanks of the Prudential propounded the question: "Is Inflation a Good Thing?" and then answered it by calling the question preposterous. He insisted that we could have both stability and growth. His fellow insurers eagerly agreed, and went further by arguing that growth was impossible under inflation. What "shocked" Frederic Ecker was that there were "so many businessmen who did not seem to be concerned and who subscribed to the view that further inflation was inevitable." He denied that full employment required creeping inflation, insisting on the contrary that "growth could best be achieved with price stability." He urged Congress "to write explicitly into the Employment Act of 1946 that the administering Government agencies have a responsibility not only to attempt to maintain high employment but also to avoid inflation." This suggestion was not new with Ecker. It had already been made by Ray D. Murphy of the Equitable in 1956 and picked up rapidly thereafter.

Insurance executives in general seemed more concerned about inflation than anything else. Both Ecker and Edmund Fitzgerald of the Northwestern Mutual in listing the goals of economics put price stability first and growth third. Bankers agreed with the line of reasoning outlined by the insurance executives. J. B. Forgan of the First National of Chicago regretted that many people thought constant price rises part of the future destiny of mankind. After pointing to the well-known experiences of France and Germany, he concluded that we "could not tolerate creeping inflation." George Champion also concluded that "creeping inflation was something we could not afford . . . for the positive harm it would do to the domestic economy and the profound impact on our world position." J. M. Symes of the Pennsylvania Railroad and Eugene Holman of Standard Oil added the opinion of businessmen in other industries. According to Holman, "There are insurmountable obstacles to maintaining full employment with a dollar which is always decreasing in purchasing power."[35]

"Today," said J. Cameron Thomson of the Northwest Bancorporation of Minneapolis and a very active member of the CED, "we worry at least as much about inflation as we do about recession." He and many others thought this "healthy and constructive." Why seemed self-evident, because, according to some, "history shows that creeping inflation usually ends in galloping inflation, leading to ultimate collapse." Or because, according to L. du Pont Copeland, it was "the most cruel tax of all." Or because, according to Thomson, inflation falls on fixed incomes, makes business planning and investment hazardous, ends in liquidation, economic paralysis, and even in political and social upheaval. And, if this was not enough, it also made workers relate their demands to the cost of living rather than productivity, weakened normal incentives, and encouraged the manufacture of shoddy products. There was nothing really new about this comprehensive indictment, but it was still the bill of particulars in which most of the business group believed.[36]

In explaining inflation, business leaders relied on the same explanations that had been fashionable in the previous decade but there had been a decided shift in emphasis. A greater number had come around to the opinion that full employment and an accelerated growth rate could not help but create strong inflationary pressures that had to break out in rising prices every so often. Then, too, there was less emphasis on government fiscal policy and much more concern with cost-push analysis and with monetary policy.

The leading spokesmen for the cost-push explanation of inflation were the executives of the United States Steel Corporation. To begin with, they were more sensitive about inflation, for according to many economists, "as steel went so went the price level." Then, in addition, there was a widespread belief among academic economists, government personnel, and the public at large that steel prices were "administered prices," that is, that they were set under conditions of partial monopoly with little regard to supply and demand. Benjamin Fairless, Irving Olds, Clifford Hood, R. C. Tyson and Roger Blough spent much of their time explaining that this was not true. To them, the complicated subject of the causes of inflation was an open and shut affair. There were elements of fiscal responsibility, but it was wages and fringe benefits—the cost of labor—that pushed prices up. The whole matter was very simple: labor unions, wielding "monopolistic power in industry-wide collective bargaining," compelled management to accept "annual increases in employment costs." These increases "far exceeded increases in man-hour output." They starved profits, prevented investment in more efficient plant and equipment and "automatically compelled inflation." It seemed clear to Clifford Hood, and he assumed it was just as clear to many others, that as a matter of ordinary arithmetic the way to close the inflationary gap was either to step up the overall rate of productivity increase, or to lower the overall rate of cost increase, or both. "I know," said Roger Blough, "that many believe that the greater the power of labor . . . the more likely it is that there will be overreaching by labor of any productivity improvement. . . . To avoid giving a disproportionate share of the total product of an industry to labor, one of two things must happen: The first is necessary price increases, which have the effect of converting the money gains of labor into lesser gains in real wages. . . . If this is done, capital investment is less likely to be stifled and investment, which is the only real source of improving the lot of everyone, will not dry up." Blough was even willing to accept guidelines if they would mean that wages would be kept within the bounds of productivity increases.[37]

Few businessmen disagreed with the belief that the price of labor was the trigger in the inflationary spiral. Said Clarence Randall, "The largest single contributor to inflation is unquestionably the all but irresistible pressure on industry to pay wages not supported by equivalent increases in total product." According to R. J. Cordiner, "The greatest of the inflationary pressures is the wage-price spiral. . . . The driving force behind this spiral is the monopoly power of the unions, which has been created in large measure by Federal policy and legislation." To Ernest Breech, there was "one economic problem of exceptional urgency . . . the problem of wage inflation—the kind of inflation that threatens us . . . with increasing business failure and unemployment and a direct assault on the very foundations of our whole economic system."[38]

To those who argued that fiscal policy and monetary policy were more fundamental and more important than labor costs in creating inflation, the cost-push adherents again had a simple answer. "Inflation," said Philip Reed of General Electric, "has become the greatest whodunit of our time. . . . Ten years ago, economists spoke confidently about what caused it and what had to be done to halt it. They described it as too much money chasing too few goods and most appeared to agree that it would pass as soon as the money supply was stabilized, the budget balanced, and the country had plenty of goods. During the past year all these things have been done and yet the value of money has continued to decline." Why? The answer according to Reed and Mark Cresap of Westinghouse and many, many others was that inflation would continue just as long as wages increased faster than output per man-hour.[39]

THE COMPLICATED WORLD OF MONETARY POLICY

Cost-push descriptions of the inflationary process were probably closer to the feelings of businessmen than any other set of rationalizations. But they were felt to be self-evident and therefore required little exegesis. Monetary policy and the decisions of the banking authorities were something else again. Here, it was freely admitted, the environment was much more murky. Here, too, there was a decided absence of the kind of consensus that made labor costs a prime factor in raising prices. Indeed, on the subject of monetary policy, business was split along the same lines that had existed in the 1920s and late 1940s. Bankers tended to favor tight money at most seasons of the business cycle while industrialists and retailers chafed under restraints.

In the period 1954 to 1967, the objective of monetary policy, in the words of its leading spokesmen and practitioners, was to "lean against the wind." Critics soon pointed out that in following this objective the Federal Reserve Board seemed to think that the winds blew much more strongly in the direction of inflation than deflation. Early in 1954, even before inflation had got off the ground, chairman Martin warned Congress, "Surely it would be the height of folly to ride the witch's broomstick of inflation to the inevitable crash." By the next year, he and many of his colleagues joined with many in the financial community in deploring the tendency to accept the "notion" that creeping inflation was an unavoidable and not too tragic condition of modern life. Holding that there was "no validity whatever to the idea that any inflation . . . can be confined to moderate proportions," the System gradually tightened the screws on money and credit and continued to tighten them all the way to November 1957. In the process, it switched from emphasizing growth to "sustainable growth" and from "preventing corrections" to "moderating" them. During the almost three years of restraint, the rediscount rate was raised from 1½ to 3½ per cent, and the money supply was kept under tight rein, growing only from $132 billion to $136 billion. In the ensuing recession, policy switched again to ease, although those who were unsympathetic to the Fed charged that this conversion was reluctant, belated, and niggardly. Nevertheless, during a period of ten months, the rediscount rate was lowered to 1¾ per cent; the System bought back the bonds it had previously sold; and the money supply grew to about $142 billion. Then in mid- or late 1958, restraint again became the order of the day. By September 1959, the rediscount rate had been pushed up to 4 per cent, and the growth in the money supply had been brought to a halt. It was freely charged that this policy was responsible for the recession of 1960, and the monetary policy makers were subjected to severe criticism. This criticism, together with the change in political administration, appears to have had some influence, for the Fed throughout the boom years after 1961 followed what most people thought was a policy of "active ease" reaching a great climax in 1964 and 1965 when the money supply rose by almost 7 per cent. As complaints about imminent inflation became louder and more penetrating, the Fed in late 1965 again reverted to a more stringent policy. Indeed, it tightened the screw to such an extent that some of the more timorous became panic-stricken from fear of monetary asphyxiation. But before this horrible denouement occurred, the Fed again made a sudden radical shift to considerably easier money.

The business community reacted to the manipulations of monetary policy much as it had always reacted. Again, however, there were slight variations from the pattern of the past. More industrialists and non-financial executives favored tight money than seemed to have been the case in prior periods, and, on the other hand, there seemed to be some fissures in the solid wall of tight money erected by the banking fraternity.

Among the non-financial group favoring a more stringent policy, W. C. Mullendore, the "conservative" Pacific Coast utility executive, was certain that inflation was the result of "an increase in the supply of the media of exchange." He thought rising wages were symptoms, not causes, although he was quick to express his antagonism to "labor-union monopoly." C. R. Smith of American Airlines, when asked how he rated the Fed, said that "on the whole, monetary policy has been excellent; although with the advantage of hindsight it is possible to criticize minor details." At the same hearing, K. S. Adams of Phillips Petroleum thought "Federal Reserve policies have been about as good as can be expected," and R. G. Cordiner believed "the credit policy has been administered with as much success as can reasonably be expected." In 1959, Carl R. Megowan of Owens-Illinois Glass paid oblique homage to monetary policy and to tight money by regretting that "both parties still act as if they were committed to the policy that easy money or low interest rates are desirable in both good times and bad." In December 1965, when the Board raised the rediscount rate to 4½ per cent, the *Wall Street Journal* announced that business was "strongly behind the Fed," and in support of this it cited Howard Newman, president of Philadelphia and Reading, and an assortment of middle-size businessmen. At the same time, a Chicago retailer told the press that he was "turning against" President Johnson because he "had attacked Bill Martin" by disagreeing with the discount rate rise.[40]

Life insurance executives were not as pro-tight money as they had been, although they were still far from being easy-money minded. R. D. Murphy of the Equitable, who was not adverse to rising interest rates and less easy credit, thought that most businessmen were wrong in thinking that monetary policy caused tight money. Following classical economic theory, Murphy explained that the whole thing was the result of supply and demand and that tight money would rectify itself, because high interest rates would reduce the demand for funds and at the same time increase the supply by encouraging saving. Frederic W. Ecker of the Metropolitan also followed the classical lines as he threw bouquets at the Fed because "its overall objectives and operations have been splendid and have met with considerable success." Equally complimentary was the opinion of Edmund Fitzgerald of the Northwestern Mutual that monetary policy had been "generally constructive. It is only with the wisdom of hindsight that we can say that on balance a more prompt and vigorous policy of credit restraint . . . might have had a moderating effect on the excessive credit expansion that brought on the 1955 boom."[41]

Most bankers thought the Federal Reserve was doing a good or a splendid job. George Gund, the extremely successful but virtually unknown Cleveland banker, gave the Board good marks since the accord. Frank E. Jerome of Seattle believed that since 1951 (the date of the accord between the Treasury and the Board) the "Fed had made intelligent use of normal tools of monetary policy . . . an excellent job." Still later, J. Luther Cleveland and William L. Kleitz of the Chemical Bank praised the Fed for refusing to be pushed into easy money during the recession of 1957. And in 1965, it was said that bankers "universally applauded the switch to tight money." At that time, Wallace B. Dunckel of the Bankers Trust said, "The move is timely, useful, and indeed necessary."[42]

As was to be expected, the mass of banking opinion regarded flirtation with easy money as rash and foolhardy, if not wanton and reckless. Proponents of this once-orthodox philosophy thought in terms of "unsustainable growth," in "overheating," and a generally non-optimistic outlook of the country's potential. They were constantly intrigued by the question: "Are We Growing Too Fast?" In a speech with this title delivered in 1956, David Rockefeller of the Chase Bank pointed out that each of our past periods of growth had ended in a period of overexpansion that was followed by a depression. What we want, he judged, was "the maximum rate of growth that the nation can sustain without generating an unhealthy and, therefore, unstable expansion." It appeared to him that we had reached a point "where we stand on the verge of trying to grow too fast." Under the circumstances, there was "much to be said for the Federal Reserve's policy of credit restraint." But later when the economy had been in a recession for six months, Rockefeller still did not believe that inflation was over and he did not favor a "drastic cut in the rediscount rate." Still later, he thought that higher interest rates were needed to overcome the balance-of-payments deficit, and he dismissed as "greatly exaggerated" any fears that tightening of credit would slow or halt the expansion in business activity.

Yet to the obtuse, it seemed that a slowing down of expansion was exactly what tight money was supposed to accomplish. By September 1957, a writer in the *Commercial and Financial Chronicle* was saying, "The bank community's interest is now concentrated on how long the money tightness will last, how strongly it will accelerate the now taken-for-granted recession and on the responsibility publicly ascribed to the bankers for the monetarily induced depression which may be ahead." But to the mystification of those who were somewhat slow to react, the bankers found it easy to run the tightrope between saying that we needed tighter credit because we were expanding too fast and denying at the same time that tighter credit would slow down expansion. The easiest way out of this dilemma was to ignore it. When disgruntlement with the Fed's restrictive policy was at its height, Ben H. Wooten, president of the First National of Dallas, said it would be difficult to prove that tight money had had a bad effect, for the "economy was essentially dynamic and sound." Again in 1959, just about the same time when the Treasury was offering notes at 5 per cent (the so-called "magic fives"), the highest interest rate obligation issued in over a quarter century, Henry C. Alexander of the Morgan Guaranty added some oil to the troubled waters of monetary debate by saying, "Fears have been expressed that our prosperity may be threatened by high interest rates, or a shortage of credit. There is even talk here and there of a coming money panic. Panic talk is without foundation. . . . Just as too little money can hamper growth . . . too cheap money will find its outlet in inflation." But as per usual, it was easy to argue the case from either side. Opponents of the Fed's policy argued that tight money was unnecessary simply because the economy *was* dynamic and sound. Brokers who watched stock prices deteriorate thought that "one might argue that the Fed has actually increased rather than restrained the demand for money." They rested their case on the proposition that an increase in the cost of something brings about an increase in demand whenever the demanders believe that cost is likely to increase further.[43]

Those who followed a rigidly classical approach to the theory of interest rates and monetary inflation pooh-poohed all this questioning of their point of view. To them tight money was simply a calculus between the supply of saving and the demand for capital funds; the Federal Reserve, in short, had very little if anything to do with it. Yet, the once-orthodox and always essentially bearish view of money, credit, prosperity, and inflation, while still in style in the financial community, was much less prominent there than it had been in the 1920s. Those who were skeptical about monetary policy in general and the Federal Reserve in particular emphasized four things: timing, the cost-push analysis, the limited scope of monetary tools, and general disillusionment with the economic effects of monetary policy. Some bankers relying on their recollections of what had brought on the depression of the 1930s, faulted the Fed for tightening too little and too late in 1956 (if not in 1955). Again in 1965, there were some who, in memory of the 1927–29 picnic, called for a rigid policy. There were far fewer bankers, although there were some, who argued that tight money throttled the economy. When such opinions were uttered, they were given cautiously and with much tact. Thus Emmet G. Solomon of the Crocker-Citizens Bank in 1965: "It would be an understatement to say that the rate of credit and debt expansion has not presented certain threats. . . . But this is not to say that a policy of less aggressive ease would have been free of risks. With the economy operating at considerably less than full employment, certainly one cannot dismiss lightly the argument that a more niggardly credit policy might have made it difficult for us to attain a satisfactory level of income and output."[44]

Most bankers and financial people who were skeptical about monetary policy were so because of their preoccupation with wages and fringe benefits. George Gund put it very simply in the standard line: "Wages are going up faster than productivity." Lewis Douglas, chairman of the board of the Mutual Life of New York, referring to this period as "perhaps appropriately called 'The Great Inflation,' " hinted that monetary policy would not work well as long as wages rose and government budgets remained unbalanced. "The question," he suggested, "is not whether the policy of the Federal Reserve Board to restrict credit is right or wrong but whether the restraint of credit, with the consequent rise in interest rates, can in practice arrest an inflationary movement . . . until it has been applied so vigorously that the spectacle and fear of significant unemployment begin to appear." Another banker, admittedly in the very small minority, believed in what economists call the Gurley-Shaw thesis, that is, that the area that could be controlled by monetary policy was too limited to permit effective control. "It is evident," said S. Clark Beise of the Bank of America, "that the inability of existing instruments of monetary policy to reach non-bank financial institutions directly, coupled with the understandable reluctance to require an actual contraction of bank loans and investments, places rather narrow limits on the effectiveness of an anti-inflation policy."[45]

THE INDUSTRIALIST'S VIEW OF TIGHT MONEY

The hard core of opposition to tight money still emanated from the industrialists, retailers, and non-financial men in general. Moreover, these critics, unlike their counterparts in the academic world, did not vent their hostility so much on the personnel of the Federal Reserve System as on the theory and principle of credit restriction. They were, in other words, not so anxious to get Governor Martin's neck as they were to avoid tight money and its implications. Quite early in the Federal Reserve's 1955–57 tight-money policy, Harlow H. Curtice of General Motors began to express industry's disagreement. After announcing a reduction in his estimate of car sales, Curtice said in May 1956, "I still believe the Board's policies unwarranted and should be reversed. . . . I have seen no evidence that would indicate the necessity to fight pressures of inflation. I think they are non-existent." Taking time out from his efforts to reshuffle the railroad system, Robert R. Young denounced tight money. He explained that as a businessman he dissented from George Humphrey, who had recently "boasted of the stability of the Republican dollar, implying that the rise in the cost of living under the Democrats was due to arbitrarily cheap and plentiful money." Not so, said Young; "Easy money encourages capital investment and automation which make operations less costly, thus slowing the rise in the cost of living"; the "real culprits are the wage spiral and the export of capital." George Romney of American Motors shared the opinion that if nothing were done about the wage-price spiral, monetary and fiscal policy would do more harm than good if used to deflate the economy. Theodore Houser of Sears also agreed with Young. He argued that wage increases encouraged employers to invest in equipment to raise productivity; but tight money impeded the employer's search for capital funds, thereby pushing the economy toward inflation. "I have never seen," said Houser, "a tight money policy restraining monopoly unions from the exercise of their power."[46]

Some other businessmen were opposed to restrictive monetary policy simply because they thought it impeded economic growth. J. W. Keener of Goodrich Tire reflected cautiously that it "was possible that monetary policy in recent years has been too restrictive." Henry J. Kaiser went much further. "I believe," he said, "the beast of deflation can be worse than the beast of inflation. . . . It is vital that policies of credit and other government regulations not be carried to the point of artificially creating deflation and depression." But the executives of American Electric Power, Donald Cook and Philip Sporn, were the most specific critics. "Certainly in the last few years," said Sporn, "the Federal Reserve Board in its efforts to be conservative has, in fact, been overcautious in its monetary policies and its attitude toward economic growth." In 1965, Cook expressed his disapproval of Governor Martin's warnings about the similarities between 1965 and 1929. "There is," he said, "a potential threat to the present favorable outlook. . . . It is that the monetary authorities might permit themselves to be misled into prematurely imposing monetary restrictions and higher interest rates either because of international monetary pressures or as a result of misleading and faulty analogies between the present and 1929."[47]

FISCAL POLICY

In contrast to previous periods of chronic inflation, only a few business leaders put federal fiscal policy at the top of the list of causes of inflation. A great many alluded to it, but more as an afterthought or postscript appended to some other explanation such as cost-push or tight money. Typically, George Champion of the Chase Bank, after asserting that "nothing has been more conducive to inflation than the present tendency of wages to outrun gains in productivity," suggested as remedies balancing the budget and tightening credit. Other financial leaders thought that balancing the budget was an absolute necessity in periods of prosperity. The Economic Policy Committee of the ABA under the chairmanship of Jesse W. Tapp called at the end of 1958 for a balanced budget in 1960. "This is not," the committee reported, "another budgetary crisis nor is it a matter of making a fetish of a balanced budget. Our fiscal situation has become a serious inflation threat." Still others who had been won over to a compensatory fiscal policy—Carrol Shanks, Frank Jerome, and Frazer Wilde, for example—naturally thought that inflation could be modified by balancing the budget in periods of high employment. And E. H. Leavey of I.T. & T. went so far as to say, "Fiscal policy probably does more in controlling inflation than monetary and credit policy." But this was a far cry from the less typical opinion of T. F. Patton of Republic Steel: "Competent economists agree that government spending with deficit financing is the prime cause of inflation," or even of David Kennedy of the Continental Illinois National Bank, who thought the cause of inflation was "government spending."[48]

Business leaders were concerned with the relationship between fiscal policy and inflation as they always had been, but they no longer concentrated only on that phase of fiscal policy. They now believed that fiscal policy had much wider ramifications than had previously been recognized. They had come to comprehend the intimate relationship between government spending, taxation, and deficits on the one hand and employment, interest, and prices on the other. One simple illustration of this was the different reaction to government spending in the recessions of 1953 and 1957. Businessmen made it clear in the earlier downturn that one thing they did not want was for the government to embark on an all-out or even a deliberately strong expansionist policy. By 1957, a significant change had taken place. More than half of the score of businessmen who testified in the "Investigation of the Financial Condition of the United States" allotted an important role to fiscal policy, some holding that a decline in government spending had been a primary cause of the downturn and others suggesting an acceleration or increase in the rate of government spending as a means of alleviating the downturn. The details of this change in opinion—which has always been offered as the most important example of a major metamorphosis in business attitudes—can perhaps best be described by tracing what happened to the businessman's view of fiscal policy in general and to his view of government spending, taxation, and government debt in particular.

A poll of small businessmen taken in August 1964 found that almost 90 per cent thought the federal budget should be kept in balance except during war; only 5 per cent voted "no" on the question. Over 90 voted in favor of having a definite percentage of the national income applied annually to the retirement of the national debt. Almost 80 per cent thought that welfare programs should be postponed until there was ascertainable revenue to pay for them. If a similar poll had been taken at the same time among big businessmen, its results would have been altogether different.[49]

As early as 1954, J. Cameron Thomson, speaking for the CED, said: "Thirty years ago if anyone, especially a banker, had announced a talk on balance in fiscal policy it would have been assumed that he was going to talk about balancing the budget. It still means, in part, balancing the budget but in a new sense of balancing under conditions of high employment, not under all conditions." At about the same time, Thomas J. Watson was "trying to make a New Dealer" out of President Eisenhower. "As for the size of the Federal debt," he told the President, "it isn't the amount of money owed that is important; it is the ability of the borrower to repay that counts."[50]

In 1958, Carrol M. Shanks of the Prudential, reviewing the recession of that year, strongly advocated compensatory fiscal policy and deplored the reduction in federal spending that had occurred in the three postwar recessions. By the middle 1960s, there were some articulate businessmen who spoke the new economics with little or no tongue tripping. In a lecture at New York University in 1964, Rudolph A. Peterson of the Bank of America demolished four myths about debt: that debt is too high, that debt has grown many times more rapidly than our ability to pay it off, that the recent high growth of federal debt is a major problem, and that federal debt must be reduced, or at the very least, cannot be allowed to expand further. "Let us look at the mythology of debt in the United States," said Peterson. "These fears are expounded at banquet tables. . . . The speaker warns of the dire results of reckless spending and heedless prodigality. He hints at the awful day of reckoning when we shall have to repay. He righteously denounces the burden we are leaving our children. He castigates the Federal Government as the prime source of this hideous evil of debt. And, finally, he urges us to mend our ways, get out of debt, and be saved. . . . The banquet speech is wrong, not because there are no seeds of truth in the general concern about debt, but because so much of the sermon is devoted to aspects which are not true." Donald C. Cook also attacked what he called the mythology that in the past inhibited the development of sound policies. "The experience of the last five years," he said, "has at long last produced widespread acceptance of modern fiscal and monetary policies. . . . In particular, it has been shown that Federal fiscal policies can be formulated to promote the objectives of sustained economic growth and full employment. . . . At the same time, it has been demonstrated that blind pursuit of an annual balanced budget can prove to be self-defeating."

Cook was somewhat anticipatory, for his views were still not freely accepted by the majority of business and banking groups. The dominant opinion had reached the stage expressed by Henry T. Bodman of the National Bank of Detroit: "A well-known European banker recently said: 'If you want your dollar respected abroad, you must treat it with respect at home.' This means to me that our government must balance its budget over the business cycle. Persistent deficits in good times and bad alike historically have been the source of serious inflationary problems." And there were still many who had not come to accept even this.[51]

FISCAL POLICY AND ECONOMIC GROWTH

In the middle fifties, opinions on the nature and place of fiscal policy were brought into sharp relief when the problem of economic growth began to be a topic for more than passing discussion. By 1959, the issue had surpassed all others, and in the presidential campaign of 1960, it became a kind of celebrated cause; but most businessmen met it conservatively and cautiously. Late in 1955, Henry C. Alexander anticipated his banking colleagues by saying, "We must not succumb to the temptation to force growth along." He warned against "such doses as increased government spending or tax cuts without a balanced budget." In 1959, James F. Oates, Jr., president of the Equitable Life Assurance Society, warned that "to push the growth rate considerably above 3 per cent (the historical average) would require large scale expenditures and deficits by government resulting in either inflation or controls neither of which is acceptable." How much opinion changed in the next half dozen years was illustrated when Oates, in 1965, said, "I give considerable credit for the economy's good performance to courageous, new, and imaginative fiscal measures." Other bankers reacted to "growth" in very much the same way. George Moore, in 1963, disagreed emphatically with those who thought that restrictive monetary and fiscal policies would have an adverse effect on growth. Dale Sharp of Morgan Guaranty expressed himself similarly, "The stimuli usually recommended are easy money and easy spending, which, like prayer, seem easier, which is to say more palatable to the voters, than creating a climate encouraging to growth." What he and Moore meant by an "encouraging climate" was one in which taxes would be reduced substantially and efforts would, nevertheless, be made to balance the budget. These sentiments seemed to reflect those of the business community in general, for a General Electric survey of opinion in 1963 found that almost 70 per cent thought that government policies inhibited growth; about 60 per cent thought that the government should set a target rate, and that rate should be 5 per cent or more. Over 80 per cent thought that if the government cut spending and taxes by $10 billion, it would speed investment and growth, and about 10 per cent believed that such action would result in a recession.[52]

Very clearly, the concepts embodied in the new economics of fiscal policy had acquired some converts, but they were still in the minority in 1965. At the same time, there were many who stuck steadfastly to the philosophy that had been overwhelmingly dominant in the 1920s. Ralph Cordiner of General Electric took an essentially Smithian approach to government. To him, "the fundamental objective of fiscal policy should be to provide the Government with the money it needs to perform the services which individuals and business organizations cannot perform themselves, with a minimum of interference to the economy." Cordiner was convinced that this had not been done. "The level of Government," he said, "has been for years swollen by un-needed services, unwise expedients, and overgrown bureaucracy." Needless to say, he favored a balanced budget. Frederic W. Ecker, who was "not convinced that deficit financing is the way to bring the country out of a recession," favored a provision for a systematic re-duction of the national debt, for "we must pay that debt ultimately or pass it along to our children." Some business leaders gathered in great gulps of psychic income by viewing with alarm. Said Roger Blough, "There are a few in government who have the old-fashioned idea that the government should try cutting expenditures. . . . The interest on the national debt is already eating us out of house and home." O. W. Adams, the Utah banker, regarded the deficit in the federal budget as "America's number one national menace. What has happened here could not happen anywhere else." In a combina-tion of speeches, George Champion warned the country that "un-balanced budgets are like trousers without suspenders; you can't keep them up forever." But he recognized the gradual change that was taking place as he said, "If you raise a question in Washington about balancing the budget, you run the risk of being hauled off to the Smithsonian for preservation as a quaint curiosity alongside the whooping crane and the dodo bird."[53]

TAXES IN INFLATION AND DEFLATION

Naturally enough, taxes represented the facet of fiscal policy that absorbed the most attention among businessmen. In their general views on the nature and impact of taxes, businessmen at mid-century thought very much as their ancestors had. They believed that the whole tax system needed reorganization and reform, that it destroyed incentives and impeded investment, and that there was far too much burden on high incomes, profits, and capital gains. On all sides— among bankers, industrialists, and tradesmen these sentiments could be heard. "Taxation," said Clifford F. Hood of U. S. Steel, "has be-come a political and social instrument and is draining off the finan-cial resources of this nation" by killing the "fourth dimension of economics—confidence, incentive, initiative." Hood's co-worker, Roger Blough, accused tax rates of having "already reduced the American body politic to a state bordering on pernicious anemia." Oil executive K. S. Adams of Phillips Petroleum criticized the tax system for "bearing down unfairly on incentives to save and invest, to work hard, and to exercise initiative and enterprise." Banker Harold Helm cited "two things as fundamentally wrong: aggregate taxes on production are too high and the impact of taxes stultifies the incentive for work and constructive investment." Lamar M. Fearing of International Paper stressed the interrelationship among taxes, profits, and a balanced budget by saying: "Industry cannot produce the profits that are necessary to balance the budget if it is constantly being hit over the head by big government through taxes that discourage the will to grow." According to Logan T. Johnson of Armco Steel, "Tax rates have reached a ridiculous extreme. They destroy the ability to save for productive investment and kill the willingness to gamble with a new idea."[54] E. H. Leavey, who had certainly been impressed by the new economics, nevertheless thought: "Individual income taxes are . . . confiscatory. . . . Incentives to expand exist only . . . in the satisfaction of accomplishment."

To lighten their burdens, business executives proposed a set of "reforms" that bore little resemblance to the "reforms" favored by other tax experts. For the most part, the latter shied away from sales taxes, and were interested in increasing the capital gains tax and in eliminating what they called "special privileges." The executives, on the other hand, detested the income tax, desired a more liberal treatment of capital gains, and as a substitute favored a sales tax. Captain Edward V. Rickenbacker of Eastern Airlines, somewhere to the right of Louis XIV, had no doubt that "the tax law will go. Everybody hates it. Nobody understands it. The Communists want it. It cannot be enforced, and should be replaced with a lottery." After the 1964 tax reduction, James F. Gates, chairman of Equitable Life, proposed a further reduction in corporate taxes and the adoption of an added value tax. But most businessmen who expressed a desire for an income-tax substitute or a means of raising additional revenue expressed a preference for a sales tax. T. F. Patton, during the slowdown of 1962, called for an immediate cut in income taxes and the adoption of a sales tax. Frederic W. Ecker thought "It would seem desirable, if possible, to utilize some other form of taxation rather than to rely on the income-tax approach."[55]

What did change quite decidedly were the businessman's views on which part of fiscal policy should take precedence—tax reduction or a balanced budget. All through the post-Korean era, tax reduction was constantly being suggested as a means of giving the economy an injection of vitamins. Three times in the decade after 1954 substantial tax reductions were passed. The Revenue Act of 1954 reduced individual income tax rates; the one in 1962 provided for a tax credit against business spending for equipment; and the 1964 act cut corporate and individual rates. In addition, at various times during the period, excise taxes were reduced and accelerated depreciation was encouraged by more liberal tax treatment.

The tax reduction of 1954 was greeted with jubilation, for, influenced by the infectious enthusiasm of Secretary of the Treasury Humphrey, businessmen thought that the budget would be balanced despite the drop in rates. As a matter of fact, however, the cash budget did not again come into balance until the fiscal year ending June 1956.

The clamor for tax reduction broke out again with the recession of 1957. In March 1958, the CED called for a 20 per cent cut, and Harlow Curtice of General Motors urged Congress to make a substantial cut in income-tax rates and in the excise tax on automobiles. Shortly thereafter, Henry C. Alexander called for a $5 billion tax cut and L. L. Colbert of Chrysler proposed the removal of the automobile excise tax and the liberalization of depreciation allowances. But, despite their assiduous pursuit of the objective of tax reduction, most business leaders were not able to disabuse themselves of the knowledge that tax reduction meant an unbalanced budget and inflation. They were, therefore, unable to accept without qualification the new economics whether it came in the form of a resurrection of the Mellon trickle-down theory or a set of variations on a theme originally composed by the Reverend Thomas Malthus and Lord John Maynard Keynes. Thus in the middle of the recession, Bernard Baruch said he could think of "no greater folly than a cut in taxes." In fact, he proposed an increase. And at the same time that Alexander was proposing what would have been a small across-the-board cut of $5 billion, thirteen out of fourteen business leaders who responded to a Senate Finance Committee questionnaire opposed a tax reduction. D. B. Jenks, the railroad executive, summed up their opinions with the remark: "A reduction of taxes could only mean an increase in the public debt."[56]

Desultory discussions of taxes in the prosperous years after 1958 brought forth few suggestions from business leaders. In late 1961, Champion called for a 10 per cent cut, but he added an amendment that made his suggestion impracticable, namely, a $30 billion debt retirement in the 1960s. The Kennedy administration brought the subject to the front of discussion when it proposed a tax credit as an incentive to stimulate capital spending. Strangely enough, businessmen acted coolly to the proposal. *Business Week* reported that "the great majority were turning a cold shoulder" because they regarded it as a "gimmick" and as inequitable. What they wanted was something to close the cost-price squeeze—a larger tax credit and much faster depreciation. As *Steel* put it, "We got an aspirin when we needed a wonder drug."[57]

When the stock market sagged and business slowed down in 1962, talk about tax reduction revived. This time, the discussion continued through 1963 and part of 1964, and in the process of discussion, many more business leaders resigned themselves to accepting tax reduction even though the budget remained unbalanced. In June 1962, the Chamber of Commerce called for sweeping tax reduction* even at the risk of a deficit. J. Doyle DeWitt of the Travelers Insurance Company delivered a typical example of the new look, but still the way-out look: "I do not believe businessmen should insist on a balanced budget before they will buy any tax legislation. Despite the natural abhorrence of deficit spending, there should be an awareness that a too sudden *drop* in government spending would tend to magnify the present sluggishness of the economy." Although they no longer regarded remarks such as these as those of a pariah, most businessmen found them to be much too rich and much too indigestible. DeWitt himself added a postscript: "I think most of us are simply looking for a recognition that the annual *rate* of increased spending must be controlled and gradually reduced if any kind of program of incentives is to be meaningful."[58]

After the Kennedy administration began to push a tax bill laboriously through Congress, three thousand businessmen, under the leadership of Henry Ford, Stuart Saunders, and others, offered their assistance by forming a Business Committee for Tax Reduction. But they were still reluctant to buy a tax reduction at the price of an unbalanced budget. Arjay Miller, president of the Ford Motor Co., expressed what many others† were thinking: "The biggest obstacle to a prompt tax cut is the rising level of government spending. With-

---

* A reduction of maximum individual rates from 91 per cent to 65; corporate rates from 52 to 47 per cent.

† David M. Kennedy of the Continental-Illinois Bank, James F. Oates, Jr., of the Equitable, Henry Ford, Stuart Saunders, among others.

out better control of spending, a tax cut could lead us directly into a permanent policy of inflationary deficits." Other businessmen and the general public seemed to agree. A poll of medium- and large-scale enterprise in 1963 showed 85 per cent for a tax cut with a similar cut in spending and only 11 per cent for a tax cut and *no* cut in spending. Among the general public, polls showed over 60 per cent favoring a tax cut, but only 41 per cent thought it should come ahead of a balanced budget while 36 per cent thought a balanced budget should come first. Too, there were some who thought the economy was doing so well that they did not want a tax cut at all. Said D. M. Thompson, president of the Mortgage Bankers Association, "We do not have to act in haste. There is no reason for panic." Quite evidently, the condition of the economy had become the most important criterion for tax policy. In 1966, this considerable and important change was clearly shown when the CED called for a tax increase and a reduction in spending sufficient to produce a $3 billion surplus to neutralize inflationary pressures. Philip Sporn was the only dissenter, and he dissented because "signs of slowing down are sufficiently strong to make the desirability of a tax increase doubtful at best." But Sporn was more a scientist than a businessman, and it was his custom to disagree with the majority business opinion more times than he agreed with it.[59]

PART III

Concerning Theory and Institutions

9. ON COMPETITION, PRICES, AND OTHER MATTERS OF ECONOMIC THEORY

"If economic theorists really knew what they were talking about, they'd have all the money in the world."

Anonymous Businessman, 1962.

"There is no theorist as dangerous as the man who has no theory."

Alfred Marshall.

The slow change in the businessman's thinking about fiscal issues that has just been recounted illustrates the vast gap that has existed between the opinions of the professional economist and the business group.

It wasn't always so. Before the great depression the theoretical lenses through which businessmen viewed the economic world were often prescribed by academic economists. It was a world of complex confusion and plausible inconsistencies. It was a world that believed in laissez-faire mixed with generous doses of economic nationalism. In those days, businessmen stood firmly on a platform designed by the architects of classical and neo-classical economic analysis, Smith, Ricardo, and Marshall, and constructed by the American proponents of high tariff protectionism, the Careys, Raymond, and List. It was a world in which costs were important. It was a world in which the forces of supply and demand operating in an impersonal market were constantly driving the economy toward equilibrium. It was above all a world of economic law, the law of supply and demand and the most inviolate law of all: There is no such thing as a free lunch.

It was a world, moreover, in which businessmen could find themselves at home. Their relationship with the professional economists was as close as any relationship between two different groups with differing objectives could be. Of course, there were differences; there always were and there always are, but the differences in the 1920s were not of any great consequence. Some businessmen made no pretense of knowing anything about theory, and few businessmen appeared at their best when being questioned about the intricacies of economics, for abstract theory was not their dish of tea. To hardheaded businessmen, "practical economics" was the worthwhile economics; theory was something to be used as rationalization by business spokesmen. "Businessmen," said C. H. Crennan, "have to see and foresee and forecast future conditions in making commitments. Economists have too often been reluctant to take similar risks. Perhaps they have too often been engrossed in the futile search for the cause of value."[1]

ECONOMIC LAW AND SELF-INTEREST

Like other groups with irons in the fire of what was "practical," businessmen often succeeded in analyzing economic controversy in a manner that was most convenient to them. They insisted that economic laws were inviolable and they would continue to insist on this long after the rigidity of those laws had proved to be exaggerated. In the 1920s, Andrew Mellon warned that "labor and capital must act in harmony with and not in antagonism to those great economic laws which work so inexorably whether we like them or not." Half a generation later, the NAM proclaimed, "there are fundamentals inherent in our economic and social system which do not change." And after another fifteen years, James E. Shelton of the Security-First National of Los Angeles again warned, "We know by experience that neither men nor nations can violate the simple but very fundamental facts of business and economic life without paying a staggering price in terms of human misery."[2]

The laws and facts that could not be broken were well known to most businessmen. "You cannot borrow and spend your way to sound prosperity," and "the Government cannot produce wealth," were as familiar as the fact that any "attempt to do" away with such a fundamental economic law as that of supply and demand and to substitute involved economic controls devised to prevent people and nations from paying the price of their folly and extravagance never has worked and never will. "Anyone with even the barest knowledge of American history knows this country grew into the world's most powerful and prosperous nation through the relatively unfettered performance in the market place . . . the give-and-take of supply and demand."[3]

But rock-ribbed as these laws seemed, businessmen succeeded in evading them. Early in the post-World War I era, Harding's Comptroller of the Currency Daniel Crissinger pronounced, "The law of supply and demand is as dead as a New England salted mackerel. Manufacturers, jobbers, wholesalers, retailers, laborers are all in some sort of combination to frustrate this fundamental law of economics. Each is out to get his first." It appeared that the business group selected those opinions of the professional economist with which they sympathized and dismissed with ingeniously rationalized arguments the opinions they did not like. In the words of a member of a later generation of business leaders, W. B. Murphy, president of Campbell Soup Company, "There is a constant conflict between expediency and economics in every economic unit. Each of us has to fight the tendency to underrate the facts of life if they are at odds with a pet theory, plan, or what not. Economic facts are too easily pushed aside when facing them is difficult."[4]

After the depression, business leaders moved slightly from the center of the classical platform while academic economists, disillusioned rather than frustrated, moved in all directions. Economic theorists no longer talked the dialect or used the symbols that were familiar to the businessman. Their orientation was entirely different from what it had been in the ante-depression period. The older generation of economists had been much concerned with the economics of the single firm, or microeconomics as it is called in the classroom. The new generation, shocked by the cataclysmic proportions of the business slump, turned for understanding to the total economy or, to repeat the language of the classroom, to macroeconomics. This by itself was enough to alienate the businessman and make him a stranger in a house he never made, for he was interested primarily in the economics of his own firm, and was concerned with the economy as a whole only so far as it influenced his firm.

BUSINESS REACTION TO THE POSTDEPRESSION
REVOLUTION IN ECONOMIC THEORY

There were, of course, other reasons for the widening gap between the two groups. Depressions shake up theory and sweep aside the dust of complacency that accumulates in prosperity. During the depression, something very much like a revolution took place in the physiognomy of economics. Reflecting the new interest in macroeconomics, economists again became concerned with the task of measuring total production and total income, an occupation that had lain dormant for the better part of three hundred years. Largely from the labors of Professor Simon S. Kuznets came the concept of gross national product as well as a refurbishing and reinvigoration of the older national income. Although these aggregate abstractions were on the periphery of businessmen's interests, they had no fault to find with them, for attempts to measure output in specific terms fitted their ideas of what was neat and what was practical. The same, however, could not be said for the other innovations in fundamental principles: the theory of monopolistic competition and the whole collection of premises, hypotheses, concepts and conclusions known as the Keynesian system.

At the risk of much oversimplification, the bundle of ideas known as monopolistic competition theory, developed more or less independently by Professor Edward H. Chamberlin and Mrs. Joan Robinson, denied the adequacy of the classical theory of how prices are made. Classical theorists asserted that all prices (except in rare cases of monopoly) were determined by the interaction of supply and demand operating in a purely competitive market. They defined pure competition as a market structure in which two or more sellers were each trying to maximize their incomes without regard to the behavior of the others. The proponents of monopolistic competition theory defined pure competition quite differently. To them, it was a market structure in which there were many sellers and buyers all of whom dealt in a homogeneous product and none of whom could by his own action affect the market. A monopoly, on the other hand, was one seller dealing in a product for which there was no substitute. They argued that neither pure competition nor monopoly could exist. Instead, every market possessed elements of both monopoly and competition and was, therefore, a hybrid form to which they gave the generic title "monopolistic" or "imperfect competition," the subdivisions of which included oligopoly, duoply, and product differentiation. Prices in such a market were not set by the automatic operation of supply and demand in a non-personal market. On the contrary, they were "administered," that is, they were to a greater or lesser extent set by the seller at a point which would maximize his profits.

Businessmen were congenitally incapable of understanding or sympathizing with this theoretical framework; the very word "oligopoly," which became part of the bread-and-butter vocabulary of the professional economist struck them with horror. But if they found monopolistic competition theory incomprehensible, businessmen found the Keynesian system altogether antagonistic. The New Economics, as developed by John Maynard Keynes and his followers denied many of the classical precepts that were part of the businessman's long-cherished beliefs. Classical theory, with its emphasis on the seesaw of equilibrium, taught that the economy was always driving toward full employment, that the supply of goods created its own demand, that saving and investment would always be balanced by the movement of interest rates, and that money could influence the price level, but not the level of employment or income. In the classical framework, therefore, chronic unemployment, inadequate effective demand, general overproduction, and excess saving were impossible. In the Keynesian system, none of these was impossible. Indeed, they could become the routine characteristics of economic life. In the course of time, an economy, because of declining population growth, the settlement of the last frontier, and the presence of large-scale enterprise, could become mature. Then as income increased, there would no longer be attractive investment outlets for increased saving. Spending would fall, and since spending is the reverse side of income, income would also fall and the economy would be in a constant funk.

There was, however, a way out; consumption could be invigorated and demand could be pushed up by discouraging saving and encouraging investment. This could be accomplished through low interest rates aided by increased government spending or lower taxes, or both. In the businessman's mind, this diagnosis of the economy's ills and the prescription therefore made Keynesianism synonymous with spending, debt, and inflation—three of the many horsemen that the business group looked upon with great repugnance. Keynes was not without his defenders, but for every Henry Dennison who believed that saving need not be automatically invested and that effective demand might thereby be reduced, there were a dozen who took cudgel in hand to refute the thesis. Their attitude was summed up in a series of pat phrases. J. P. Seiberling, of the Seiberling Tire Co. used a typical one when he disposed of the new economics in a talk called "Humbug and Double Talk." Said Seiberling, "Possibly the most astonishing piece of humbug which has been solemnly asserted in our times and widely accepted was the idea sold here by the British Lord Keynes that we needn't be concerned with the size of the national debt because we owe it to ourselves." A similarly typical statement by Winthrop W. Aldrich went like this, "This is the doctrine of spending our way out of the depression, the doctrine of creating prosperity by creating public debt. Mr. J. M. Keynes has been the leading exponent. . . . British friends of mine have expressed to me their amazement that Mr. Keynes' theory, although thoroughly discredited in England, threatens to become the dominant policy in the United States."[5]

It would be unfair and misleading to imply that the business class remained impervious to what was going on in the interior of economics. Some of the ideas in this new economics did rub off on individual businessmen here and there. After all, it required loyalty well beyond the call of duty to remain faithful to a set of principles that had shown as many holes as classical economics seemed to show during the depression.

In the pessimism that prevailed in the 1930s, some businessmen flirted with the idea that the economy had reached maturity. General Robert E. Wood, whose opinions always deviated from the business consensus, quoted approvingly Alvin H. Hansen, the leading exponent of the mature economy thesis. Said Wood, "A decline in population must inevitably result in a lower rather than a higher standing of living. . . . It means that the sun has passed its zenith and the shadows of afternoon have begun to fall."

But most businessmen scoffed at notions of maturity and retained their faith in the doctrine of unlimited wants. Said J. Howard Pew in 1939, "There is no limit that we may discern either to mankind's capacity to consume or to the resources from which demands may be met." As the economy recovered, those who had been tempted stopped flirting with economic maturity and the "secular stagnation" thesis and returned to a more optimistic frame of mind. By 1947, General Wood was saying, "To my mind the greatest of the many fallacies enunciated in the 1930s by the New Deal was that this country was a finished country."[6]

The elements in the new economics that seemed to have permanently affected business opinion were those that were associated with business-cycle theory. In the post-World War II era, there was, perhaps as a direct result of the new economics, much more emphasis on monetary and fiscal factors and much less emphasis on speculation, extravagance, and unsustainable rates of spending than had once been the habit. In the 1958 investigation of the recession, for example, Frederic Ecker, D. B. Jenks of the Missouri Pacific Railroad, and Homer Livingston of Chicago's First National Bank stressed the importance of inflation and unsustainable growth, and Ralph Cordiner emphasized the role of labor unions. But James T. Leftwich of Woolworth, C. R. Smith of American Airlines, Harlow Curtice, S. C. Beise, E. H. Leavey, and Edmund Fitzgerald all cited some aspects of government spending and taxation or of Federal Reserve policy as factors in the cause and cure of the slump.

THOUGHTS ON COMPETITION

Aside from business-cycle analysis, the pieces of economic theory that most interested businessmen were those that were once taught in the academies of learning as value and distribution and are now referred to as microeconomics. These include views on competition and price making, as well as explanations of why who gets what out of the economy in the form of wages and profits.

During the prosperous 1920s as well as the depressed 1930s, admiration for and faith in the essential "goodness" of competition weakened significantly. Throughout the boom years, there was much talk about profitless prosperity, overproduction, unfair competition, and co-operation and collaboration. Although most businesses enjoyed unprecedented prosperity, some industries were extremely sick. The executives of these sick industries together with many small businessmen blamed their "profitless prosperity" on competition and the Sherman Act. They were encouraged to do so by business spokesmen operating through the business journals and trade associations. Thus, for example, the *Bankers Magazine* for January 1928 expressed the opinion that business leaders should be aware of the state of competition inasmuch as rugged competition might lead to a decline in profits and thus to the end of prosperity. Even earlier, in 1924 in fact, Bernard Baruch had proposed "the establishment of a Court of Commerce, before which business men would come with such questions as to whether in time of overproduction and low prices, they could cut down production and fix a price."[7]

Cotton textiles, one of the sickest industries, led the campaign for "self-regulation" of business. At the height of prosperity, W. P. MacCall, president of the National Association of Cotton Manufacturers, expressed what most textile entrepreneurs thought about competition and allied matters: "Our industry needs real leadership such as is apparent in the steel industry which is so well organized that production is regulated to meet the demands of the consumer. . . . Whatever action we should take to bring about changes in the antitrust laws will be worthy of our time and effort. I believe we should have the right to organize and regulate production and establish uniform cost standards under proper Government control. . . . Our chief complaint is that prices are abnormally low. . . . Production exceeds consumption." This typical opinion was shared by many small manufacturers in other industries. J. H. Williams, an ironmonger, told the readers of the *Atlantic Monthly:* "Gradually the Sherman Act had come to be interpreted . . . as prohibiting gentlemen's agreements between any competitors that tended even theoretically to influence a price level, to limit production or to apportion territory according to natural markets, and also quite regardless of whether the effect was beneficial or otherwise."[8]

Few businessmen were foolhardy enough to criticize openly competition, for competition was one of the sacrosancts in the American value system. Criticism usually took the form of throwing stones at "unfair competition." But what exactly was meant by this term remained an unanswered puzzle. It was generally accepted that blatantly acquisitive or predatory practices were "unfair." Among these would be slander of a competitor and commercial bribery. As the United States Chamber of Commerce expressed it, unfair competition embraced "all acts characterized by bad faith, deception, fraud or oppression, including commercial bribery." But most trade associations went much beyond this and defined unfair competition to include sales below cost, use of loss leaders, and attempts to "steal" customers or employees.

Many times, unfair competition simply meant competition. One of the basic points in the International Association of Electro-typers' code was "to never install a new machine unless an old one is taken out, or unless really necessary because of a steady growth of permanent business. Idle machinery will weaken the stiffest backbone and make it impossible to maintain fair prices." The National Selected Morticians aimed "by the efficiency of their members to make it unnecessary that there should be more than 15,000 funeral directors in the nation." Sharing the available business was another major objective. The American Institute of Steel Construction proposed that members whose business exceeded a "reasonable ratio" of the total should pay additional dues on the ground that they were enjoying a greater share of the benefits from research and promotion.[9]

Yet, according to those who knew about these things, activities of this sort were greatly exaggerated. Soon after he took office as Secretary of Commerce, Herbert Hoover came to the defense of the trade associations. He explained that they had been subject to a great deal of criticism "because some very small minority . . . have undertaken practices that were in fact or in suspicion a violation of the restraint of trade act. A short time ago a canvass was made of trade associations to find the number that embraced in their category of effort those particular functions that are subject to a suspicion, and it was found that less than ten per cent of the trade associations have any functions of that character."

The confusion between the critics and the apologists arose because of the different definitions of competition which each group followed. To the theorists co-operation was the antithesis of competition, but to the businessman competition could be co-operative. Julius Klein, Hoover's aide in the Commerce Department, cited as "conspicuous among the newer forces of control, the vastly increased cooperative and collaborative element in modern business." Klein quoted Hoover as saying, "We are almost unnoticed in the midst of a great revolution, or perhaps a better word, a transformation in the whole super-organization of our economic life. We are passing from a period of extremely individualistic action into a period of associated activities." Somewhat similar sentiments were voiced in entirely different language by Judge Gary, who was always in favor of some sort of federal regulation to promote the "stability" which he continuously sought. "Now I am not against competition," said Gary, "I believe in it thoroughly and believe it is a great thing. I believe in the Sherman law. However, I do not think everyone fully comprehends the very great difference between honest, fair and decent competition and ruthless, destructive competition. There can be perfect competition and at the same time perfect cooperation."[10]

The disenchantment with competition reached its zenith in the early years of the depression and culminated in the experiment with the National Industrial Recovery Act in 1933. But the thinking behind the NRA has already been recounted. Suffice it here to say that the benefits that business hoped to receive from the control of competition greatly exceeded the benefits that reality produced. A remark attributed to James B. Duke after the 1911 breakup of the Tobacco Trust would have been appropriate in 1935-36. Duke is supposed to have said, "As hard as I fought for the dissolution of the Trust, I'd fight even harder against any effort to put it back together again. We made more money after we were broken up and had competition."[11]

CHANGING CONCEPTS OF COMPETITION

What was happening was that the definition of competition was beginning to change. As early as 1930, David Sarnoff, the man behind the Radio Corporation of America, was defining competition quite differently from the way it was being defined in the contemporary economics texts. "True competition," he said, "is the rivalry between well matched factors for the maintenance of established markets or for the creation of new markets, for better and more economical public service, for higher standards of industrial achievement." This was similar to the definition of monopolistic competition that was about to emerge from the theories of imperfect competition spun by Chamberlin and Robinson. And as time passed and as the idea of competition regained its respectability, the concept of competition used among businessmen resembled more and more the concept of monopolistic competition described in the later economics textbooks.[12]

Of all businessmen, the steel tycoons were the most preoccupied with "competition." And of all the steel men, those of U. S. Steel were the most preoccupied. By the late 1950s, and early 1960s, Roger Blough was explaining, just as were the monopolistic competition theorists, that there was no such thing as "perfect competition." What existed in Steel's theory was "workable competition," a term associated in the economics classroom with Professor John M. Clark. As Blough explained it, "With respect to pricing and marketing, no longer is there the competition of a peddler with a pack of pots and pans on his back and a different price to every customer, nor the 'perfect competition,' sometimes suggested in textbooks. Today's competition is the competition of pricing policies, of quality, of consumer surveys, of mass advertising and of mass distribution devices, of research, and of production practices and conditions of employment. This kind of competition is the only kind that is workable in a society like ours, which requires large productive groups constantly moving forward to bring improved standards of living. The advantages to the consumer resulting from this naturally evolved competition are far greater than could ever be possible under the theory of 'perfect competition.' "

The corporations' spokesmen could be more specific about what they meant. They told the House Committee on the Judiciary in 1957: "Much has been written and said about both the theory of competition as well as what actually happens in practice. . . . The most significant aspects of competition in steel are these: 1. Steel prices are not static; they fluctuate widely and often. 2. Published prices always have and still do differ to a marked extent between competing producers. 3. Actual prices are highly competitive and frequently vary from published steel prices. 4. Quality, availability, and service, as well as price, are decisive factors. 5. The vigorous competition in steel assures continued improvement in quality and continued development of new steel products. 6. Last, but generally overlooked, steel must compete vigorously with the products of many other industries."[13]

The inferences that economic theorists and businessmen drew from the same set of words were poles apart. Economic theorists viewed the steel industry as an oligopoly and insisted that prices were administered or, in a plainer word, fixed. Business leaders viewed the steel industry as an example of salutary workable competition in which prices were set by the market place. Each accused the other of not understanding what competition meant. Practical men, it was said in the world of business, viewed competition realistically—not as an imaginary state of affairs. Said Roger Blough to Senator Estes Kefauver, "I don't think you understand competition. I think you understand the word, but do not understand the concept."

Kefauver, in charge of the hearings investigating prices, was trying to prove that prices were largely rigged in a game of follow the leader. Concentration, price leadership, and administered prices were the *bêtes noires* of Kefauver and associates, and businessmen regarded their views as unfair, injudicious, and wrong. They knew that the nature of competition had changed. It was now more a contest between marketing departments than a duel over prices. As Charles Mortimer, who had come to the presidency of General Foods via the marketing department, put it: "It used to be that the management of a business had only to worry about the other companies in its industry. Today, it must worry in addition about three competitions: the competition of other industries, the competition of scientific breakthroughs, the competition of swiftly and drastically changing public tastes, habits, and expectations."[14]

But no matter in what guise, management thought that competition was vigorous; it was healthy. Businessmen ridiculed the notion that big business—concentrated economic power—had destroyed or even endangered the competitive game. "Now what are some of these industries where the 'concentration of power' is so great as to menace our national welfare and to arrest the pursuit of happiness?" inquired Benjamin Fairless. "You'd never guess. . . . There are 173 entire industries which are more highly concentrated than steel. . . . There is the pretzel industry . . . and there are the candle-makers too. Then there are straw hats, and streetcars, breakfast foods and chewing tobacco. . . . Then we have women's neckwear and boys' underwear. And, oh yes—window shades and garters." Fairless went on to say that four, or eight, or fifty companies would always do 40 or 80 per cent of the business "as long as free and honest competition exists. If the top teams in any baseball league don't win the highest percentage of the games, how are they going to stay on top?" Robert E. Wilson, chairman of Standard Oil of Indiana, summed up the businessman's answer to the critics of his kind of competition. "Economists generally regard freedom of entry . . . as the acid test of the existence of a true competitive situation. . . . In 1902, we did fully 85 per cent of the total oil business in our territory. Today we do less than 20. Who can believe that there is or has been for decades any lack of competition between oil companies? . . . Yet we constantly have to meet the demagogic charges of monopoly. I wish some of our politicians had to operate a service station and learn what competition really is."[15]

THE ATTITUDE TOWARD ANTI-TRUST

Businessmen's attitudes toward competition were clearly ambivalent. This was well illustrated by three aspects of the problem of competition: government anti-trust policy, the tariff, and price making. Some business leaders thought the anti-trust laws were a throwback to Neanderthal man and as such served no useful purpose. "The anti-trust laws," said M. J. O'Neil of General Tire, "were written before the Industrial Revolution." Others thought that the law should be more strictly enforced against industrial monopoly. George Romney in 1957 proposed that when any one firm exceeded a specific percentage of total industry sales over a specified period, it be required to propose a plan of divestiture that would bring its sales below the specified level. Most businessmen were between these extremes. They insisted that they had a great admiration and respect for the general idea of having the federal government follow an anti-trust policy. But, on the other hand, they were never satisfied with either the administration or the interpretation of the anti-trust laws. According to Charles E. Wilson of General Motors, "Ours is the only country in the world that has recognized the importance of free competition as evidenced by its enactment of antimonopoly and antitrust laws." But he thought that they were not being applied to labor organizations in the same way that they were being applied to industry. Echoing Wilson, businessmen felt that in administering the anti-trust laws, government carried prejudice and flexibility to extremes of inconsistency. "We need anti-trust laws," said Lammot du Pont Copeland, "because businessmen, like any other group, will always include an unscrupulous, dishonest minority who will seek what, in the vernacular, is called a fast buck. . . . It seems to me, however, that anti-trust policy should be directed toward the elimination of unfair competition rather than toward the breaking up of enterprises which have grown because they were successful in meeting human needs." This general opinion was repeated in a variety of ways by industrialists and bankers. R. R. Deupree of Proctor and Gamble called for a new approach to the Federal Government's controls over competition—"an approach based on *three* simple principles. First, *competition is good and necessary*. Second, *certain legal controls of competition are good and necessary*. Third, these controls should be designed to *preserve competition* and *protect consumers* not to protect the *inefficient* producer."* M. J. Rathbone sounded another note of business annoyance in saying that "the anti-trust laws are often directed at bigness rather than monopoly. Underlying this is a series of legal and economic premises that do not conform to economic reality to the detriment of economic growth." In much the same vein and with equal justification, Myron A. Wright, chairman of Humble Oil and president of the Chamber of Commerce, accused the anti-trust policy of working "at cross purposes with economic objectives of maximum growth and development." He insisted that the goal should be "to maintain conditions under which all companies realize that success or failure depends on their ability to compete vigorously and effectively."[16]

TARIFFS

The tariff issue illustrated as well as any the sharp disagreement among businessmen and the ambivalence of business economic theory in general. During the fifty years following World War I, the Federal Government made a sharp turnabout in its tariff policies. During the 1920s, the Fordney-McCumber and Hawley-Smoot tariff acts pushed the nation to new heights of protectionism. But this trend was reversed in the 1930s when the Hull Reciprocity Agreements, extended and further liberalized by successive amendments in the post-World War II era, moved the nation toward freer trade. Business opinion is supposed to have shared in this turnabout, for opinion polls taken in the 1930s and again in the 1950s demonstrated a sharp drop in protectionist sentiment. But like many other things the movement toward free trade was greatly exaggerated. It was probably true that forty years ago, two out of three businessmen voted themselves protectionist compared to less than one out of two today. But this hardly means very much. For one thing, it is impossible to tell how deep the feelings run. Today, it is much more fashionable to be an anti-tariff internationalist than to be a pro-tariff isolationist. So that a slight shift in the winds of business may easily carry a free trader all the way across the indefinite boundary to protection. Thus Philip D. Reed, chairman of the Board of General Electric, constantly

* Deupree's italics.

reiterated strong support for the removal of trade barriers when he was with the International Chamber of Commerce, but in 1953 when General Electric was asking for some help in international trade, Reed said, "We believe that U.S. markets should not be closed to foreign competition. We also believe that foreign competition should not be permitted to enter this market at prices so low that no American producer can meet it." Sometime later when some American manufacturers were waxing enthusiastic over possible modifications of trade restrictions, Lammot du Pont Copeland inserted a note of warning, calling for the "exercise of extreme care and most informed judgment" in all tariff negotiation. There was another reason for questioning the extent of the conversion to free trade; the most vociferous supporters of lower tariffs in the 1920s, the big-city bankers, were comparatively silent on the issue in the later decades.[17]

In every tariff negotiation and debate, from the Fordney-McCumber Act in the 1920s to GATT and the last Kennedy Round in the 1960s, textile manufacturers and, to a lesser extent, steel and chemical producers were articulately in favor of protection. Automobile manufacturers, retail tradesmen, and the bankers in the big cities provided the opposition.

When the United States emerged from World War I as a gigantic international creditor, a few business leaders at the very least were aware that some fundamental changes in international economic relations were in order. According to the impeccable logic of classical theory, a creditor nation had to have an unfavorable balance of trade —that is, if it expected to be paid what it was owed; and most Americans fully expected that. Following the precepts of classical theory, Thomas W. Lamont, partner in J. P. Morgan & Co., declared himself in 1921 sympathetic to "a tendency toward freer trade" which was in any case "bound to come, for imports pay for exports and in the long run a country gains, not loses, by ample imports." Lamont also favored reduction or cancellation of the interallied war debts and internationalism in general. But this was pretty strong stuff for a nation whose businessmen and bankers had always inclined to the protective tariff and a strong belief in self-sufficiency. It was a kind of moral victory for classical economic theory when Otto H. Kahn compromised his old views by saying, "I am in favor of the principle of the protective tariff to the extent that its application is necessary to preserve our industries and the American standard of wages and living. But that principle can no longer be applied with safety and advantage to the country and with fairness to the consumer. New factors have entered into the problem."[18]

These opinions showed that some business leaders had done some strenuous economic thinking, but most businessmen still favored protection. Immediately after the inauguration of Warren Harding, an array of industrial groups rushed into print with enthusiastic support for a return to permanent protection. They rationalized their opinions with talk about protecting American industry, helping the American worker, safeguarding the country's future, and guaranteeing a high standard of living. The Chamber of Commerce urged a protective tariff for any "enterprise important to any part of the country," and high enough to "protect against destructive competition from abroad." Judge Gary, a past master in the art of walking on both sides of the street, explained: "Personally I am not in favor of a high protective tariff, one which permits the possibility of oppression or injustice to any one, nor one that is higher than enough to protect industry, including both producer and workman, against undue and unreasonable foreign competition which has the advantage, if such it may be termed, of cheap labor. Everyone should be satisfied with a protection which maintains the position of this country on a parity with all other countries and with nothing less."[19]

The old game of give-and-take, live-and-let-live logrolling of former tariff legislation was resumed. The West Coast Lumbermen's Association supported a tariff on Canadian lumber which the lumber dealers protested; the glassmakers demanded high protective rates, but the thermometer makers protested; the motion picture industry wanted a tariff on motion pictures, but protested against a tariff on raw film because it would be "economically wrong to give Eastman Kodak control of the industry." And so the Fordney-McCumber Act came into being.

For the next couple of years, the protectionist wave continued to roll. A few examples may demonstrate how influential this wave was. In July 1923, the American Bankers League was formed to provide a medium for small bankers to express their views. Claiming a membership of 9000 banks, its primary purpose was to resist tariff reduction. In 1925, H. T. Parson of F. W. Woolworth told the press that he agreed with President Coolidge's views on tariff, immigration, and war debts. Coolidge believed in the McKinley Tariff, the Quota Act on immigration, and the repayment of international debts because the allies had "borrowed that money; hadn't they?" In a sophisticated article, W. L. Clause, chairman of the Pittsburgh Plate Glass Co., explained that we could not become the world's banker. Admittedly, we had the resources, but it was hardly likely that we were willing to accept goods in payment. To do so, we would have to abandon protection. But, asked Clause, "Can this be done without wrecking American industry, or at any rate without reducing our labor to a basis that would at least put our industries on a competitive basis with the cheap labor of Europe—particularly of Germany?" But business leaders, it is important to point out, were by no means the only supporters of high tariffs in the Coolidge prosperity years. There were still some protectionists among college economics professors as well as among high school and grade school teachers. Labor leaders G. W. Guthrie and Matthew Woll told Coolidge in 1926 that the protective tariff was the reason for prosperity.[20]

The first important change in business opinion on the tariff came in 1926 when the big-city bankers, who had been cautiously questioning the protective policy, issued a manifesto calling for a major tariff revision. Signed by such leading figures in the world of finance capitalism as J. P. Morgan, Albert H. Wiggin, Gates W. McGarrah, Melvin A. Traylor, and J. J. Mitchell of the Illinois Merchants Trust, the manifesto contained the following forceful statement: "It is difficult to view without dismay the extent to which tariff barriers, special licenses and prohibitions since the war have been allowed to interfere with international trade. . . . At no period in recent history has freedom from such restrictions been more needed." The manifesto, which appeared on the front page of the *Times,* must have been too strong a brew for the day and age, because the bankers had immediate second thoughts, which Mitchell expressed in the following qualification: "The manifesto pertains exclusively to Europe. . . . It should be distinctly understood that it in no way refers to American tariffs." This was transparent claptrap and apparently was said in deference to the extent of protectionist opinion among industrialists. That there was a great deal of such opinion was made overwhelmingly clear in the preliminaries to the Hawley-Smoot tariff of 1929–30.[21]

Under the guise of protecting the American worker, stabilizing prosperity, and enabling American industry to compete with foreign cartels, textile tycoons, chemical managers, and steel producers argued for further increases in the tariff rates that were already at a record high. Nathaniel Stevens of the National Association of Wool Manufacturers showed how extreme textile opinion had become.

When Representative Cordell Hull asked how we could sell our surplus abroad if we shut out everything, Stevens conveniently replied,
"We leave that to Congress." S. M. Wilder of the Manufacturing
Chemists Association reasoned that "if it be unlawful for American
manufacturers to confederate with their competitors, then surely it is
not just to open wide the doors to foreigners to reap the fruits in this
market of a system of business which the United States Government
denies its own citizen to practice." John A. Topping of the Republic
Iron and Steel Co. argued that American labor had to be protected
by "sufficient duties on iron and steel to maintain the industry on a
reasonable basis of profits and also to enable it to maintain the present scale of wages." The whole set of opinions was admirably
summed up by W. L. King of Jones and Laughlin, who declared that
the country was prosperous, but not prosperous enough; ergo, what
was needed was a higher tariff.[22]

The automobile industry and the bankers were about the only ones
who took a dim view of the Hawley-Smoot tariff. Alfred P. Sloan
thought that it would be "a bad thing because of America's status as a
creditor nation." Bankers Lamont and Kahn regretted the whole affair, remarking in their usual staid fashion, "The passage of the tariff
bill was most inopportune." The tariff bill was being debated when
the economy collapsed, and some bankers went so far as to blame
the latter on the former. The coincidence was also not without its effects on the opinions of some non-bankers. Thomas N. McCarter of
the Public Service Company of New Jersey confessed that between
1924 and 1932 he had changed his mind and now realized: "We
will have to readjust our tariffs so that other nations can sell to us to
the extent that they buy from us." In its Annual Year Book, Swift
and Company declared that "the doctrine that we should strive for
national self-sufficiency is antagonistic to the doctrine that a high
standard of living is desirable."[23]

But those who were committed to protection remained adamant
even as the depression worsened. Said Myron C. Taylor of U. S.
Steel, "It is inconceivable that in the narrow interest of pushing forward our foreign trade we should reduce those protective barriers
of tariff which have enabled us freely to raise our standards of living." His colleague James A. Farrell thought the tariff axiomatically
correct. As he saw things, "the tariff far from being responsible for
secondary causes of the depression has proved inadequate security
against injurious competition." Eugene Grace demanded higher tar-

iffs to offset the depreciation of currencies that was taking place throughout the world. M. D. Brown, Philadelphia woolen manufacturer, as late as 1940, denied that the tariff had anything to do with the depression. When reminded that over 1000 economists had urged Hoover not to sign the bill, Brown said, "There is a lot of difference in theory and practice in these things."[24]

Part of the explanation for these views on the tariff lay in the typical businessman's theories about price. Basically, he believed that costs determined prices and that the demand for his product was inelastic, that is, he thought that regardless of what happened to prices about the same amount would be sold. This attitude was apparent in the discussions surrounding the Hull Reciprocal Trade Agreements in the early days of the New Deal. Said E. T. Weir at the time when the plan was being discussed, "We have back of us a history of many years of protective tariff under which we have developed a standard of wages and living and wealth and prosperity that speaks for itself. We certainly cannot afford to speculate by trying out new tariff theories, particularly in a time of such serious depression. . . . Radical departures will be a factor in destroying confidence." Lesser industries joined in. The lace industry pleaded against the bill on the ground that it had been an infant industry created by the Payne-Aldrich tariff of 1909, and that it would not be fair for the government to abandon its position of protection. Its spokesman, H. A. Phillips, declared, "The rest of the world does not possess anything we want. I predict that the treaties made under this bill will not aid at all in the restoration of prosperity. These treaties can only act as instruments of despair." The National Association of Wool Manufacturers was back again with Arthur Besse asserting, "We oppose the bill because in addition to its positive defects, it cannot accomplish its purpose, being based on a totally incorrect economic theory."

The opposition moved on apace. The steel pen manufacturers, the machine knife industry, the saw manufacturers, the American Paper and Pulp Association, the glass industry and the toy industry, the wool hat manufacturers, and the Match Institute all expressed their opposition. No one testified for the heavy metals industries, although in an aside, W. A. Irvin, president of United States Steel, said, "Our present anti-dumping laws should be supplanted by one that is effective. Our tariff rates should be high enough to protect American industry and labor against the cheap costs and pauper labor rates of foreign countries." Once again, the National Automobile Chamber of

Commerce was among the few industrial organizations that supported
the bill. Its argument was based on its belief that the automobile
manufacturers of America would be able to sell a million cars a year
in foreign markets.[25]

Despite years of practice, it was still a difficult thing for business
and banking leaders to throw overboard their long-cherished beliefs,
notions, and theories. Even so internationally minded a figure as
Winthrop W. Aldrich, who often criticized the "strangulation of international trade," could not forget what he had learned from his
father, Senator Nelson Aldrich, who also fathered the Payne-Aldrich
tariff. Said Aldrich, in 1936, "I am myself a firm believer in the principle of the protective tariff. . . . I consider that the protective tariff
has been the cornerstone upon which has been erected the prosperity
which this country has enjoyed since the Civil War and until recent
years."[26]

With the end of World War II came a strong resurgence of protectionism very much the same as had followed the War of 1812 and
World War I. There were other similarities, too. After World War I,
the issue of the tariff was bound closely to reparations, interallied
debts, and the efforts to restore and maintain the gold standard. After World War II, the tariff issue was bound closely to American
military and economic aid, gold flows, and desperate efforts to solve
the international balance of payments problem.

Even before we had entered the war, some American producers
were anticipating severe foreign competition as soon as things returned to normal. In a somewhat exaggerated expression of this opinion, M. D. Brown told a Senate committee: "When we again have
peace on earth, and Europe and Asia have exhausted themselves;
when they have added greatly to their already burdensome debts;
when their currencies are greatly depreciated; when their returning
armies are willing or are conscripted to work for a mere pittance to
keep from starvation, the influx of imported farm and industrial products will be a more serious threat than ever before."

It was no coincidence that the speaker was a wool manufacturer.

As soon as the war ended, the textile producers resumed their
role as the most articulate spokesmen for protection. In 1945, William C. Planz, speaking for the cotton textile industry, called for the
imposition of rigid controls on textile production in Japan and Germany. He asked that production be limited to domestic needs and
that excess spindles be destroyed or sent to China. But he also warned

that "cheap Chinese labor should not be exploited to build and expand the textile export industry."

In time, other mainstays of protection rejoined the campaign. Matthew Woll, the labor leader, urged Congress to adopt tariff rates "which really do equalize the differences in labor costs—American and foreign—of competitive imports." But Congress continued to press down rather than increase tariff rates. By the 1960s, producers of petroleum, non-ferrous metals, textiles, chemicals, meats, and many other commodities were objecting loudly or softly to further tariff reductions. R. T. Stevens urged the government to impose a quota on textile imports, for the "predicted collapse of the industry had arrived." At each textile convention, speaker after speaker pointed out that the tariff policy was not only making healthy growth impossible, but was responsible for at least half of the balance of payments deficit. Steel producers were equally vocal in calling for a "temporary tax" on iron and steel imports because, as Leslie R. Worthington, president of United States Steel, explained, employment costs in Japan were less than one third of those in the United States. When the press chided the industry for its stand, Edmund F. Martin, chairman of Bethlehem, put up a stout defense. Wrote Martin: "The American steel industry, faced with a large and growing surplus of steel supply in the world market and world prices which are below full production costs, has reluctantly concluded that it cannot continue to go it alone. We have asked, therefore, that our Government face squarely the same questions faced by the governments of other steel producing nations—does the country need a strong, efficient steel industry and, if it does, does the industry need Government assistance to offset adverse trade conditions? In the real world of today, the answers to both questions must be 'yes' as they have been in other countries." The only remaining articulate supporters of free trade among the nation's big businesses were the automobile and the shipping industries. J. Peter Grace thought "a genuine loosening of tariff barriers would be a desirable goal," and Henry Ford hoped for a "removal of tariff barriers." But even the bankers who were once outspokenly opposed to the tariff now said very little, and sometimes where local industry was pro-protection the local banker lent his support.[27]

PRICE THEORY IN THE 1920s

Despite the fact that their views on the tariff did not always bear them out, businessmen believed that competition should determine and did determine prices. The theory in which they professed to believe operated simply. It assumed that in a competitive market sellers and buyers freely made bids and offers for quantities of goods. Market prices tended to settle somewhere around the point where the seller's supply price met the buyer's demand price. No one supplier could for any considerable period maintain a price higher than that determined by the market, for some keen competitor would immediately grab the market by offering goods at a lower price. On the other hand, competitive bidding among buyers would prevent the sale of goods at a price lower than that determined by the automatic mechanism of the free market. Thus the market acted as a seesaw weighing bids and offers and determining prices without the interference of the fallible human mind. Judge Gary explained the mechanism in a few words: "Prices are made by the sellers and purchasers together; they must agree. Unless there is some artificial control or influence the selling prices depend upon competition, which is always active, and which is taken advantage of by the purchaser to secure the goods he desires at a price which he considers fair to be paid. Sometimes prices are much larger for the same commodity than they are at other times; that is because the demand is greater."

In the prosperous 1920s and in the depressed thirties, businessmen expressed a deep faith in supply and demand. Indeed, the words took on a sacrosanct quality. Gary went so far as to say that "anyone who by word or deed has interrupted or hindered the operation of the natural law of supply and demand" was "blamable" for recession and depression. In the best of all possible worlds, supply and demand acted in tandem to produce a price that resulted in maximum satisfaction for both buyers and sellers. But as with all religions, the practitioners could not conform 100 per cent to the faith. Once again, theory was badly mauled by the stresses and strains of the "practical" world. The *law* of supply and demand was compromised over and over again until it became nothing more than a statement of a general *tendency*.[28]

Despite their oft-repeated assertions, most businessmen in the twenties and thirties did not really think that supply and demand were equally potent forces in price determination. Instead, they followed a cost theory, that is, they put more stress on the role of supply than on the role of demand in explaining why prices were what they were. And among the factors on the supply side, labor costs were considered most important. In somewhat oversimplified terms, what all this really came down to was a belief that wages determined prices.

Once again, the leaders of steel were most articulate. Said Myron C. Taylor, in commenting on the causes and cures of the great depression, "Prices are determined by supply and demand. . . . The medium by which products are exchanged follows in due course. . . . The price of steel has fallen or risen with the price of labor. . . . Labor costs are 156 per cent of 1914. The price of rails is the same." Not very much later, E. T. Weir, who had been accused of price cutting in the early part of the depression, said, "You must charge a price, under any given condition, which covers all of your costs—including the cost of carrying unused capacity—and returns a reasonable profit."

From the standpoint of the economic theorist, Weir had weird ideas about supply and demand. He thought that prices should go up when demand was low and down when demand was high. He tied all price-making decisions to costs. Thus he said, "When we have a high demand and costs are down and earnings are satisfactory, we go beyond the point of a satisfactory return, and the industry should reduce prices." On the other hand, in response to the question, "Doesn't your theory lead to this—that as the demand declines and with it the cost increases, of necessity the price would have to keep going up?" Weir answered, "absolutely," and added a postscript, "I realize that this is what has been condemned as maintenance of a rigid price structure by the long-on-theory, short-on-experience economists in the bureaus down in Washington."[29]

There was a second and more important reason for the business leaders' bifocal view of price making in the years when wholehearted loyalty was being pledged to supply and demand. That was that the sacrifices entailed in classical theory were too much for the average human being to accept. Classical theory, with its Spartan view of the niggardliness of nature, envisaged a profit *and loss* system. Under the irresistible hammering of competition, prices would fluctuate, but they would also in the long run be driven down to a point low enough to eliminate all profits over and above what was absolutely necessary to call forth the effort of the entrepreneur. For almost obvious reasons, this sort of destiny would not sit well with businessmen big or little. Most of them wanted "stable" prices, and the older and more stable the industry, the more it wanted stable prices.

Once again, steel management led the way in opposition to price cutting, and to sales at a price that would asphyxiate profits, and to prices that fluctuated on the way up as well as on the way down. Judge Gary was very proud of his company because "it did not join in the wave of inflation which swept over the country in 1919 and 1920, notwithstanding wage increases, advances in prices of raw materials, heavy advances in freight rates, and tax increases." The price of this self-discipline was high, for "at the close of 1920 in a number of lines, the margin between costs and selling prices is practically nil." There was a widespread belief that stable prices were more popular with everybody than were freely floating prices. As George Whalen, the enterprising promoter of the early 1920s and founder of United Cigar Stores, explained at the time he was launching a cast-iron pipe merger: "We can advance the price, stabilize the industry and everybody will be satisfied. The people who buy pipe want to know that the price is stable. . . . This is more important than how much they pay for it." Along with this went an attempt to show that price cutting was anti-competitive, not pro-competitive. George Eastman of Eastman Kodak carried on a persistent campaign for legislation that would establish the principle of retail price maintenance. Eastman refused to admit that price cutting was a form of competition. He argued that the retailer's margin was so small that if he did cut prices, no substantial saving would result to the consumer. Competition, to him, was "lowering costs and giving the public the benefit of it." Price cutting would only tend toward monopoly, since the field would be left in possession of the strong.[30]

As a result of the incessant agitation for stability, the Capper-Kelly bill for retail price maintenance was introduced in Congress at various times during the period. Business opinion was heavily divided on the subject. The United States Chamber of Commerce polled its members several times and obtained no conclusive result. The membership twice supported the legislation and once opposed it. When the question was worded: "Should there be Federal Legislation permitting a seller of identified merchandise sold under competitive conditions, under a distinguishing trade name, trade mark, or brand, to control the resale price thereof?" the vote was 1079 for and 911 against.[31]

The depression intensified rather than weakened the furor for "stabilized prices." It was said that rising prices meant prosperity as indeed they did. But prices were an effect, not a cause; it was boom that made prices rise; rising prices did not cause the boom. The proponents of stable prices had it the other way around; they thought the way to get out of the woeful state in which business found itself was to raise prices. James A. Farrell told the Iron and Steel Institute, "The main trouble with the steel industry is that certain conditions exist. . . . I refer to price cutting. By what manner of means do people get it into their heads that if production goes down, they must sell cheap? It is rising prices that stimulate buying and consumption and a return to prosperous times." As Farrell lectured, the Capper-Kelly bill was reintroduced. It was opposed by Benjamin H. Namm, Percy Straus, and the National Retail Dry Goods Association. It was supported by W. T. Grant and the New York Board of Trade.[32] The latter set up a committee and proposed to include in its membership such illustrious business leaders as Edsel Ford, A. R. L. Dohme, Chester Colby, Frank Waterman, William Woodin, Walter Teagle, A. W. Robertson, Samuel Insull, Owen D. Young, and Walter Gifford. Edward Plaut of Lehn and Fink was suggested as chairman, and only he and Dohme seem to have consented to sit on the committee. Upon assuming the chair, Plaut said that although he had been a warm advocate of the Capper-Kelly bill, his attitude toward the price cutting—price maintenance controversy was entirely unbiased.[33]

The matter of price maintenance was a ticklish one, for it was certainly not true that all businessmen supported it; some were as opposed to it as others were for it. An alliance of automobile producers and chain store, department store, mail order retailers led the opposition. Said Alfred P. Sloan in the midst of the enthusiasm for NRA, "There has been much discussion with respect to the economic justification of the fixing of industrial prices. Many industries . . . have developed formulas which stripped of all verbiage result in nothing more nor less than the suspension in whole or in part, of the effects of competition. . . . It is a false doctrine to attempt to perpetuate the inefficient."

At a later time, he referred to stabilization as "a direct attack on the American system." He was joined by Paul G. Hoffman of the Studebaker Corporation, whose views rarely resembled Sloan's. Hoffman argued that price fixing was a necessary feature of a planned society, and a planned society necessarily meant the sacrifice of civil liberties. Hoffman paid his compliments to the Federal Trade Commission and the Sherman Act, but he excoriated such price-fixing laws as the Guffey Coal Act, the Miller-Tydings Amendment, state licensing statutes, and the NRA. He also thought that "obviously if you raise the price of a car $100, you cut down the volume of demand."[34]

Yet, though opposed by some able and influential business leaders, the price fixers had more than passing success. According to Professor Frederick C. Mills, prices in the period between two wars showed a tendency toward greater stability "with fewer of those abrupt changes which characterized the nineties of the last century." Most of the academicians of the 1920s regarded this with approval and many businessmen regarded it as a healthy and socially responsible development. Judge Gary, said Ida M. Tarbell, brought the steel industry "from a condition of chronically drunken prices to where its prices are as stable and, on the whole, as reasonable as those in any industry." Gary had indeed wrought well. Steel prices allegedly remained unchanged from 1922 to 1930 when, despite the onset of depression, they were raised $1 a ton. At the bottom of the depression in October 1932, they were reduced from $43 to $40 a ton. To be sure, there were secret price cuts and the offering of extra service and other inducements all through the depression. But it was still possible for Eugene Grace to say in 1934: "What the steel industry has done with the price structure is to put it on a basis similar to retail trade, with announced prices so that the public will know the rock-bottom figure, and will be sure that everyone else is buying at the same price from any one supplier. The system permits the freest sort of legitimate competition. . . . There are penalties . . . against establishment of prices which are unfair taking into consideration cost of production and other factors." And *Fortune* said in 1936, "The steel industry still functions for the most part under a price system which is artificial, wasteful, discriminatory, and non-competitive."[35]

PRICE THEORY IN THE YEARS AFTER WORLD WAR II

Because opinion and behavior, theory and practice were so far apart, the faith in the simple mechanism of supply and demand in a completely competitive market gradually corroded and disintegrated. By the latter part of the period here considered, the years after World War II, price making did not seem nearly so neat, orderly, and simple as it had seemed in the years before the depression. In fact, many business leaders were innocently offering explanations of price making that were very similar to those being given by the administered price school. To put this another way, it was not the theory of administered prices that businessmen objected to; it was the implication that administered prices were arbitrary, sinister, evil, and anti-social.

There were, to be sure, vestigial remains of a cost theory of price, of a notion that demand was extremely inelastic and a concept that reducing prices could lead only to chaos. Thus, C. M. White of Republic Steel, "In every period of decline, we see companies repeating the mistakes that have led to disaster. When sales slow up, the first impulse is to reduce prices. If the product is properly and competitively priced in the first place, price reductions will not result in increasing the volume remotely commensurate with the damage they do to profits, the very life blood of business." But there were, on the other hand, many whose views were 180 degrees away from those of the steel industry. Said Henry Ford in 1947, "The Ford Motor Co. will continue to succeed only if it can produce more and more at lower and lower costs so that more and more people can buy." Then, too, in contrast to the continuous efforts by railroaders to raise rates in good and bad times in the twenties and thirties,* Ben Heineman of the Chicago and North Western said in 1959, "Our markets will be regained through price. . . . For the indefinite future, the railroads must resist every temptation to increase their rates, regardless of inflationary pressures. For a generation the railroads have responded automatically and without regard to competitive factors . . . by seeking higher and higher rates."[36]

How did people think prices were made in the new era? According to Fairless, it was definitely not on a basis of cost plus. It was a question of whether the customer would buy the product at the price the producer had in mind. Ten years before, Fairless had thought, "A price is reasonable if it nets a fair return." Now he thought, "A price is perfect when the producer would rather have the money than the product and the consumer would rather have the product than the

---

* Daniel Willard in 1922 said that rates were declining as rapidly as the public had a right to expect. He opposed pushing them down "artificially." In May 1931, seven of the leading railroad men in the country asked for a rate increase.

money." This was similar to the classical analysis, but not all businessmen and not all steel men echoed it. Roger Blough had an entirely
different idea when he said, "My concept is that a price that matches
another price is a competitive price." Nothing much about supply
and demand here! It sounded much like Senator Kefauver's statement, "Administered prices are those fixed by management and kept
in effect over a period of time, without letting the law of supply and
demand play any particular part in their operation. In other words,
prices in a concentrated industry where one company usually makes a
price, and all of the others follow." But Kefauver interpreted this to
mean that firms in the position of price leaders, especially the United
States Steel Corporation, had absolute power to keep prices high:
"As an example, we have United States Steel making the price and
maintaining it; even if the cost of scrap goes down, they do not reduce
it. Plant production is down to 55 percent and hundreds of thousands
of people are idle over the country and still the price stays up." No
businessman believed this. Nor did any believe that conspiracy or
collusion were important. Witness the following exchange between
Senator Hart and General Robert E. Wood:

MR. HART. You think high prices are not due to anything except the
absolute working of the economic laws and these prices are not a result of any conspiracy or collusion against the public interest.

GENERAL WOOD. With very few exceptions. . . . I think the public
will break the price. I mean where they are unreasonably high.

Businessmen thought that prices were made somewhat in the fashion described by Harlow Curtice of General Motors. "Pricing," Curtice explained, "is like a tripod. It has three legs. In addition to cost,
there are the two other legs of market demand and competition. It is
no more possible to say that one or another of these factors determines price than it is to assert that one leg rather than either of the
other two supports a tripod." Curtice continued by "emphasizing
again that competition is much broader than price." There was the
extremely important factor of style as well as the availability and quality of service.

Once the three-legged tripod had determined price, Curtice went
on, the individual manufacturer had to answer the question of how

he knew whether or not his unit costs were being kept below the unit price. He admitted:

> It is impossible for an automobile manufacturer to forecast his unit costs accurately in relation to the price he has announced. Nor can he keep adjusting his price to costs as they may vary. This would lead to market chaos. Our approach to this cost problem has been the use of the concept of standard volume. Standard volume may be defined as the estimated rate of operations which represents the normal or average and annual utilization of a capacity that must be large enough to meet the cyclical and seasonal peaks which are characteristic of the automobile industry. In General Motors this average annual utilization is estimated at 80 per cent of capacity. . . . How do we make use of the standard volume concept? First, labor and material costs that are directly applicable to each unit produced are calculated on the basis of current wage rates and material prices. Indirect or overhead costs are then determined on a cost per unit basis by distributing them over the determined standard volume. . . . This method of estimating unit costs on the basis of standard volume gives us a benchmark against which to evaluate our cost-price relationship. . . . It is obvious that if our benchmark shows that costs are high in relation to price, efficiency has been reduced—unless, of course, cost increases represent a general rise in what the industry pays for labor and materials. In the first case, steps must be taken to reduce costs. In the latter case competitive forces will cause prices to rise.[37]

A DIGRESSION ON THE CONFUSION ENTAILED IN THE BUSINESSMAN'S PRICE THEORY

It was impossible for businessmen and the proponents of administered price theory to bridge whatever gaps existed in their mutual understanding or misunderstanding. This was made evident in a colloquy between the chief executive of National Steel, former Secretary of the Treasury George Humphrey, and Senator Kefauver; and more colorfully in the confrontation between President Kennedy and Roger Blough on steel prices.

Humphrey's opinions on price determination did not fit any particular theory or school, and neither he nor Kefauver could explain to the other what system was being played. Humphrey began by telling the senator, "Congress cannot legislate with respect to economic conditions and pressures any more than you can legislate with

respect to the law of supply and demand . . . and you cannot legislate on the law of supply and demand in a free country any more
than you can on the law of gravity." Senator Kefauver waded in with
what seemed to him an obvious question: "Do you think that you
would sell more steel if you had your price down?" To which he got
the quite unobvious answer, "I do not think we would, no. I do not
think that a dollar for a family for a whole year is going to have much
effect on whether or not they will buy canned goods." Still unabashed,
Kefauver then asked Humphrey why he "let United States Steel set
the price." To which the former Secretary said, "We cannot fix it
higher if they want to put this price in. There is no way we can sell
our commodity and get business if they will sell theirs and take less,
unless we are willing to sit around and shut down and put these people out of work. . . . We propose to keep competitive."

Somewhat punch drunk, Kefauver came back for more with the
question, "If you reduced your price just a little bit you would get
more business, would you not?" Answer: "That is what you think.
I do not think so." Kefauver then recalled that Humphrey had said,
"If I can not get $6 where the other fellow got $6, rather than shut
down, I will take $5 and take some business and that is the way it
works." He then asked, "In the first quarter of 1957 you were running at 98 per cent of capacity. You are now down to 80 per cent
of capacity. How far down in reduction of capacity do you have to
go before you think your formula here takes application?" Answer:
"To the point where we believe that a change in the price would
make a difference in the demand and would stimulate demand and
increase total demand, and that is not at the present time." Question:
"Can you give us any idea on how far you would let your production
go down before you would put in your—" "No. It depends upon a
great many conditions." Question: "I cannot understand . . . why
a reduction in the price to $5 which you are talking about here would
not give you more business." Answer: "All I can tell you, Senator,
is perhaps if you had some experience in the steel business you would
understand it better. I have tried to explain it as best I can."

THE STEEL EPISODE OF 1962 ONCE AGAIN

The famous steel episode in the spring of 1962 revealed still more
about the ubiquity of administered price theory. Quite early in the

Kennedy-Blough go-round, Blough had written the President explaining his views: the cost-push theory of inflation, the inadequacy of profits measured on the basis of per cent of sales, and business' fears that peacetime control of prices might be instituted when the "causes of inflation in a highly competitive economy" were "clearly associated with the fiscal, monetary, labor, and other policies of government." But the Administration, thinking it had little choice, moved away from what has been called "pluralistic decision making in wages and prices" toward formulation of a national policy set by government. Businessmen, believing as they did that prices were and should be set in the market place *by businessmen,* could not regard this move with equanimity. Blough, therefore, moved to increase prices. What was extraordinary was his rationale for so doing. "Even though costs have risen," he said, "there has been no increase in prices since 1958 because of competitive pressures from domestic and foreign producers. If the products of U. S. Steel are to compete successfully, the plants and facilities must be as modern and efficient as the low-cost mills. Only by generating the funds necessary can our company continue to compete." He then admitted that "price increases will add to the competitive difficulties. But this will only be temporary." It seemed to classical students that nothing could be less in harmony with their theory than an increase in prices in the midst of intense competition and at a time when demand was falling off. If Steel had been successful in maintaining the price increase ordained by its Board, it would have written an ignominious obituary to the "law of supply and demand." As things turned out, the price increase could not be sustained, for competitors did not go along with it. Unfortunately, however, this denouement was blamed on President Kennedy, who seemed certain that in the absence of government pressure, Steel was capable of raising prices for the whole industry. He was wrong, but this is beside the point. In one way or another, both parties in the dispute seemed to believe that supply and demand were as dead as Cicero's Latin. Blough believed that prices were administered by businessmen; the President believed that the government should have the power to veto the administered prices of businessmen.

Both sides, and the public as well, regarded the steel incident as a piece of economic *realpolitik*. Kennedy later mused, "If I had failed to get a recision that would have been an awful setback to the office of the Presidency." In defense of his policies, Blough told United States Steel stockholders:

> There was no doubt that a price increase was necessary. . . . We did not know whether other major steel producers would also raise their prices*. . . . We could assume that they [also] needed the profits necessary to pay for the replacement and modernization of worn-out and obsolete facilities. . . . Competition with substitute materials and foreign sources might add temporarily to our competitive difficulties. But the continued improvement in the economy as well as some improvement in the demand indicated that a moderate price increase might be competitively possible. . . . It was our judgment that we should delay no further in testing the market. . . . I do not see how anyone could fail to understand clearly three things: first, that we had declined to enter into any commitment . . . regarding future price actions; second, that we believed a substantial improvement in our cost-price relationships to be necessary not only in the interests of the company, its owners, and its employees, but in the interest of the entire nation; and third, that any price decision we might make would be . . . controlled by competitive forces.

In April 1963, when the economy was about to launch a boom, an epilogue was added to the incident. Wheeling Steel, a small producer that was experiencing great trouble, announced an increase in some steel prices. Nothing happened. The government did not cry aloud; it made no public statement; Wheeling's competitors did not go along; and Wheeling rescinded the price increase much more quietly than it had announced it.

BUSINESS OPINION ON THE NATURE OF PROFITS

The whole bag of tricks encompassed in the theories of competition, price making, and such was closely related to the problem of who got what and how much from what was produced by the total economy. As has been duly noted, the businessman's theory of prices consisted of a concept of supply and demand with great emphasis on costs and demand inelasticity, together with a varying belief that free competition was the order of the day. When prices were set

---

* The government strongly intimated that the whole business was an example of collusion.

and goods were produced, costs had to be met. Payments were made to the sellers of raw materials and to tax collectors. Then came the wages of labor and perhaps interest payments to banks and to bond and noteholders. What was left was profit or loss—the residual after all other costs had been deducted from total receipts. "Profit," Enders Voorhees of U. S. Steel told a Senate committee, "is the arithmetic result of subtracting from one's receipts from customers the cost of producing and selling the goods sold." But this did not justify profits. It did not explain why they were paid or the nature of their economic function.

Professional economists, interested in impeccably logical models, have almost always worked from the premise that businessmen try to maximize profits in the kind of pleasure-maximizing, pain-minimizing world that was so close to the minds of the classical school. Admittedly, no one is ever sure what this means. No one is sure whether it means in the short or the long run, or whether it is exclusively in terms of money or in terms of total satisfactions, psychic as well as the more mundane. Whatever it means, the concept is indispensable for the construction of an economist's model, because without an assumption of the objectives of the entrepreneur, there would be no taking-off place or any landing place for the theorist's musings. But businessmen have never been that tolerant of the games that economists play. If economic theorists knew and taught that the businessman's objective was to maximize profits, that was more than most businessmen knew. Indeed, only a few were sure what their primary objective was; but most were quite sure that it was not to maximize profits. One of the most thoughtful students of profits in the business world, Donaldson Brown, thought GM's economic objective was to produce not necessarily the highest attainable rate of return on capital employed, but the highest return consistent with attainable volume in the market. The long-term rate of return was to be the highest expectation consistent with a sound growth of business. Paul Litchfield of Goodyear believed this meant in the long run. "A company may be tempted to seize the immediate return. . . . But such a policy is short-sighted. . . . Competition will rush in whenever profits are large and will soon destroy its advantage."[38]

Management always resisted, sometimes more passionately than at other times, what contemporary economists refer to as the principle of maximization and what past economists called the felicific calculus. Just exactly what is wrong in a moral or ethical sense with maximizing profits is as much a puzzle as what is meant by maximization. But businessmen have always associated the practice with the behavior of the robber barons in medieval Germany or in the United States of "years ago," a vague slice of time that can be defined as one chooses to define it. Each new generation of business leaders thinks that Father may have been and often was a robber baron, groveling for the last one eighth and exploiting widows, orphans, workers, and the weak in general. But all that, they are quick to assert, has changed.

Perhaps there is some truth to the contention that the objective of maximization was once much more in the forefront than it is now. Some of the changes that have occurred in business organization and in the external environment, such as the switch from the owner-entrepreneur to the career executive, the pressures from labor and government, and so forth, tended to reduce the urge to get as much as one could out of each ounce of effort. But, on the other hand, there were also factors that made profit maximization less urgent for the closely owned company than for the modern collectively owned large corporation. For one thing, it was always true that beyond a certain point the desire for more money—the marginal utility of money in the dialect of economics—diminished very rapidly. This point was much more quickly reached by those who had a large stake in ownership than by those with a small equity and a high salary. For another thing, it was psychologically easier to run risks with one's own empire than with a fief held in escrow for a heterogeneous group of stockholders. When someone told Lammot du Pont that the hired manager was likely to spend the company's money without exercising due caution, Lammot quickly informed him that the reverse was true. "That's not the point. The danger is that he'll spend it with too much caution."

Yet the contemporary business leader, who, according to many authorities, is not paid according to the profits he makes, holds profits in far higher repute than did the business leader of thirty or forty years ago. In the years after World War I, businessmen seemed to go out of their way to avoid talking about profits. One gets the impression after plowing through a mass of material that it was crude and unmannerly to talk about the nature and function of profits. Thus, C. R. Hook, in the early 1930s when the disappearance of profits had become a major concern, spoke of profits as "a much abused term which should be avoided wherever possible; profits are nothing but the remainder interest left over and used to pay for the hire of tools."[39] Occasionally, a business leader went so far as to speak of the possibility of profits being too high. Said Ernest T. Weir in 1932, "If the producer expects his goods [to be] consumed, he must do his share in having the consumer's income on an equitable basis. If the producer's profit is excessive, it must be taken from the consumer, and slowly but surely the power of consumption declines and production is not absorbed. Also the trouble is intensified by the producer from his excess share of earnings, using them to increase his plant and equipment, and his production. Thus there results a chasm between the requisites of prosperity—production and consumption—that eventually brings the collapse." Later, Weir added a wistful note: "If there had been some power which could have, by a stroke of the pen, taken some per cent from capital and given it to labor ten years ago, we might have had no depression. The overexpansion of industry would have been curtailed by this mythical reduction in the return to capital, and the purchasing power of wage earners would have been greater by reason of this increase to labor."[40]

If such opinions existed in the years after World War II, they were not being uttered aloud. Profit was still being regarded as a residual; in the words of Clarence Francis of General Foods, it was "what is left after conducting business during a specific time." But it was now thought to be immensely important—the vitamins and the proteins that made the economic mare go. Said Charles Mortimer of General Foods, "The number of jobs and the rate of profit are inseparably connected." For the bankers, S. Sloan Colt added, "If we are to have an expanding economy, I believe the all important role of business profits must be more generally understood."

In the opinion of those who worked in the executive suites during the twenty years after World War II, profits were never high enough. Measured as a per cent of sales, the profits of some industries, such as food retailing, were considered abysmally low; measured as a per cent of net worth, some other profits seemed equally scrawny; and in comparison with the rise in GNP and in labor's wage, what had happened to profits was downright ludicrous. Profits, according to Leslie Worthington in a 1962 talk entitled "How to Succeed by Really Trying," had not kept pace because of rising costs, especially the cost of labor. His colleague Roger Blough, speaking on "The Unprofitable Puzzlement," commented unequivocally, "Profits are not high enough." Lamar Fearing of International Paper put it the other way, "Profits are too low."[41]

It "had to be agreed," according to business spokesmen, that business was "entitled to a fair profit on every item." A favorite argument was that "profits were losing their purchasing power" because in dollars of constant purchasing power they were not increasing fast enough in relation to total production or in relation to the depreciation of property. Reese Taylor of Union Oil pointed out that "formerly a mile of pipeline could be built for $12,000, now it takes $30,000." But critics of this argument wasted no time in pointing out its many fallacies. To begin with, they did not understand why consumers should pay the cost of investment. They interpreted management's view to be that prices should be high enough to provide the capital necessary for expansion *plus* a "fair" return to the owners. But, they pointed out, profits were not confined to dividend payments; there was a matter of capital gain on the equity in a business, and in the years after World War II, stock prices leaped and bounded and jumped ahead at a rate that was considered downright scandalous by those who did not own common stocks and by some of those who did.[42]

The critics in any event always questioned the legitimacy of profit. "Why should profits be paid?" they kept asking, and business leaders went to immense pains to try to answer the question. In the 1920s, two reasons were stressed and restressed: profit was a payment for taking risk and profit was a payment for investment money. S. Z. Mitchell, the utility tycoon, spoke for a multitude of businessmen when he said, "To secure investment money, the return must be reasonable. 'Reasonable,' in this case, means the return which will induce the man with the money to invest in the particular enterprise. What this return must be in any particular case necessarily varies according to the investor's idea of the risk in such case. The infallible rule is, the greater the risk the greater must be the yield."[43]

Following the great transformation in business opinion that came with the depression and war, business leaders explained profits not much differently from the way they had been explained in Neanderthal times. Here and there, some business leader was realistic enough to say that profits were the reward for good decision making. Roger M. Blough came as close as most when in answer to the question: "What does the black ink on a company's profit and loss statement mean?" he replied, "First, that the firm produces a good or service which is in demand by the customer. Second, that it turns out a good product. Third, that it produces with reasonable efficiency. Profits, in brief, are proof that the company is rendering a valued service, and rendering it reasonably well."

Businessmen perhaps did not believe that profits were the wages of management. Instead they emphasized that profits had a three-fold function. They were a payment to savers and investors, an incentive to invest in tools and equipment, and a trigger of economic change. According to Roger Blough, "Part of the profit will be paid to those whose savings and investment made possible the acquisition of the tools with which the group succeeded. The balance of it will be used to provide new tools to increase productivity further. Without profits there will, sooner or later, not only be no new tools but no tools at all."

Profits, as every student of economics knew, were a cost, but business leaders carried this a little further. "Profits are a cost of doing business," said Bert S. Cross of Minnesota Mining and Manufacturing Company. "For it is through profits, and profits alone, that money is immediately available for reinvestment." To management it was an easily explainable set of links in an obvious chain. First, the prospect of profits offered an incentive to save and invest. "The hope of profits," said Charles E. Wilson of GM, "is the incentive that encourages people to save, to invest their savings in productive enterprise, and to develop new businesses." S. Sloan Colt and many more agreed. Said Colt, "Business profits provide the incentive and the means for making the investments in new plant and equipment which we must have if we are to make economic progress." The second link in the chain was profit's role in persuading the saver to turn his money into *risk* capital, not into any old capital. Thus, a firm made money. It split the profits with the stockholder, paying him dividends and plowing the rest back. Profits' final role was to trigger economic change. The whole linkage was admirably summed up by Robert G. Dunlop of Sun Oil: "Profits serve as the wages or rental that the company pays for the rental of plant and tools. . . . Profits are at once the inducement to risk savings in the face of uncertainty, and the reward for having succeeded. Profits measure the performance of the managers of the capital invested and at the same time they regulate the allocation of capital among businesses. Rising profits signal the need for expansion and attract capital. Declining profits signal the need for contraction and repel capital."[44]

The Dunlop argument illustrated how businessmen mired themselves in trouble when they discussed economic theory. If profits were

paid as a reward to those who supplied investment funds, they were
no different from payments of interest on borrowed funds. Moreover, if profits belonged to the stockholder and were paid to him to
induce him to lend to or buy stock in a venture capital situation,
there really was no justification for the common corporate practice
of paying less than half of earnings in dividends and plowing the
rest back into the business. To the critics of modern corporate policy,
it seemed logical that to the owner belonged the profits. The dilemma
was illustrated by the following discussion between Dunlop and Senator Flanders:

FLANDERS: You spoke of profits as a stimulant to the investment of
savings. I take it that is a general observation because later on you said
it is the policy of the Sun Oil Co. to make its new investment by plowing back profits. . . .

DUNLOP: The last time we sought equity capital was in 1925.

Intolerant critics or perfectionists in economic theory might think
that the businessman's theory and explanation of profit left much
to be desired. Academically, the critics were right, but that was really
everybody's fault, for the run-of-the-mill theorist had no different
theories about the nature and function of profits than the businessman had. In both cases, profit was a residual, and its function was
lost in fuzziness.

THE EXPLANATION FOR LABOR'S SHARE IN THE
TOTAL PRODUCT

The same could not be said about wages, the price of labor. Here,
business opinion changed greatly and became sharper and more concise as the economy changed from the period between two wars to
the period after World War II. Among businessmen in the 1920s,
there were many different schools of thought about what made wages
what they were. To some executives, like Charles M. Schwab, wages
should be "fair," and in the absence of non-interfering forces, like
unions and the government, wages would be fair. But what did
"fair" mean? No one bothered to answer, for it was assumed that
everyone knew the answer. It was not until many years later that

Tom Girdler of Republic Steel explained what fair wages were. "When wages are too low," Girdler explained, "the best men look for work in other industries. Wages should never be so high as to force prices to the point that the customer is lost. Prices should never be so low as to prevent fair wages."

In explaining why wages were paid in the first place, business opinion shuttled back and forth between a cost-of-living theory and a purchasing power argument. In the first couple of years after the Armistice of 1918, inflation continued to alarm the public which believed among other things that wage rates were much too high. Businessmen shared this belief, but they also felt a sympathy for workers because the cost of living was so high. This naturally set in motion a process of circular reasoning; the cost of living was high because wages were high and wages were high because the cost of living was high, but the cost of living was high because wages were high. "The high wages of the war," said Thomas Lamont at the 1922 convention of the Bankers Association, "had a somewhat 'spoiling' effect upon labor. They gave labor the feeling that it must always share in the prosperity—never in the adversity of business. I deplore that feeling; yet I beg to remind you that that feeling of labor, in so far as it was directed to the improvement of living conditions . . . was wholly right." And Gary had this to say, "Labor . . . is paid very large rates, but with exceptions, is not paid more than is proper because compelled to pay high prices for living costs."

What could be done to resolve the dilemma? Some businessmen thought there was nothing else to do, but cut the circle in the middle by reducing wages. But Gary and others objected, ineffectually to be sure. Said Gary during the recession of 1924, "The air is filled with suggestions that other [wage reductions] be made. . . . The costs of living are high, and so far as we can, let us keep the wages high enough to give the man a good and reasonable support." The *Times* reported that the Iron and Steel Institute, to which these remarks were directed, responded with loud applause. Still later in 1927, Owen D. Young expressed the opinion that "business, if it is to fulfill its ideal, owes men an opportunity to earn a living."

Enough has already been said in another context about the "high wage philosophy" of the 1920s to make it unnecessary to go into it in detail here. Ford and Filene were its most articulate champions. But others joined the chorus. It seems likely, however, that businessmen didn't really believe in the purchasing power theory.* What they really appeared to think was that the wages they paid were based on what George down the street was paying. Typical was the wage policy of F. C. Dumaine, textile tycoon, head of Waltham Watch, and later of the New York, New Haven & Hartford Railroad, who operated on the "theory that wages at the plant should be the same as those paid by domestic competitors."[45]

In this early period, little attention was paid to productivity as an explanation for wages, although among economic theorists this was the heyday of marginal productivity theory, that is, the theory that wage rates would be set at a point equal to the output of the last added worker. To be sure, here and there, some business leaders occasionally referred to the relationship between wages and product. For example, C. N. Piez of the Link Belt Company in 1920 thought: "We have lost sight of the relationship between production and wages. Personally, I have always felt that production was the only basis for wages." Gary regretted that output per worker had declined, but this was worse than nothing, for Gary was wrong; productivity had not declined. Some, like Paul W. Litchfield, combined productivity with purchasing power, "The amount of wages which can be paid is always measured by the amount of goods made by high-wage labor which the public can absorb, but there is a constant stimulus to pay as good wages as possible . . . because of its effect on the market." But these were minority views.[46]

The question of hours was closely allied with wages, and here again little attention was paid to productivity. In October 1926, Henry Ford recommended that industry adopt a five-day week. He thought it would increase productivity. But he did not propose to raise wages commensurately. "I never said," he protested, "that I would pay six days' wages for five days' work and I never will do such an uneconomic and impossible thing." Nevertheless, his suggestion was rejected with as much hostility as had greeted his 1914, $5 day. Gary reacted by saying, "I shall require further proof before I am satis-

---

* In an analysis of "Changing Opinion about Business Prosperity" (*American Journal of Sociology*, March 1933), Hornell Hart found that in 1929 in the huge circulation magazines that were sympathetic to the business view, 5.3 per cent of the indicators examined favored high wages; none were opposed. In the so-called "liberal" magazines, 1.9 per cent of the indicators were favorable to high wages; 1.2 per cent were not. In 1932, among the business magazines, 1.4 per cent were in favor, 1.5 per cent were opposed to high wages. Among the liberals, it was 3.6 per cent for and 0.1 per cent against.

fied that any man or any number of men can do as much work in
five days of eight hours each as in six days of eight hours each."
Iron Age was less kind, "Ford is not the first producer to go on a
five-day period. . . . The simple interpretation is that the sale of
Ford cars has been declining." Small businessmen joined in with remarks that included "Idle hours breed mischief" and "The work
of the world cannot be done in five eight-hour days per week." After
a Chamber of Commerce referendum showed 1676 to 3 against the
Ford philosophy, John E. Edgerton of the NAM had the last word:
"Six days shalt thou labor. . . . These constant attempts to amend
the Decalogue and to adapt by alterations the moral law to the
appetites developed by easy and loose living constitute the outstanding peril of our unprecedented prosperity."[47]

THE STRESS ON PRODUCTIVITY

The depression changed all this. What had not been possible in
good times became absolutely necessary in bad times. Hours of work
were cut back sharply, and business leaders found, as Myron C.
Taylor put it, "Men working three days a week do more work than
on six days." The productivity concept made equally impressive gains
on the question of wages and emerged far ahead in the list of explanations of why wages were what they were. The changing opinions of
Alfred Sloan told the story. Before the depression, Sloan had been
relatively quiet, but there were indications that he subscribed essentially to the high-wage doctrine. The depression and the following
recovery saw him emerge as one of the most articulate business
leaders. In almost every speech he dwelled on the distinct connection between wages and productivity. "High wages," he said, "do not
create prosperity. . . . An inflexible wage scale freezes the process
of recovery. The best wage scale is that which permits the fullest
productivity; a fundamental point, almost universally overlooked, is
that the price at which a worker can sell his labor is limited to the
price that some employer can afford to pay." When a bill was introduced in Congress to place a minimum on wages and a maximum on
hours, Sloan insisted that the only possible way in which this could
be accomplished would be by a concurrent increase in productivity.
Yet clear as it seemed to them, those who supported the productivity
line were convinced that they were very much in the minority. James

W. Hook, a thoughtful executive of a machine tool company, explained that management's wage depends on supply and demand; capital may refuse to invest if the risk is too great or the opportunity for gain too small; but labor must produce, and is paid for productivity. "One may perhaps wonder," he added, "why the belief persists so stubbornly that it is possible to raise appreciably the real income of labor as a whole except as its total productivity is increased."[48]

Those who did not buy the productivity analysis felt just as lonely with their opinions as did Hook and Sloan. Robert Johnson of Johnson and Johnson clung to the belief that unemployment could be solved by higher wages and fewer hours. He added, however, that he had been unable to find a sympathetic group in organized business. Yet he had hopes, for "some of his colleagues were being converted and the influx of younger men would play a part."[49]

Johnson's hopes were doomed to frustration, for the next generation of business leaders were altogether devoted to the "productivity determines wages" opinion. To be sure, in the immediate postwar years, there were throwbacks to the cost-of-living approach. Robert Wason, head of the NAM in 1946, thought it "proper that wages should rise and fall with the cost of living," and Millard D. Brown, the perennial small business spokesman, thought that there were two ways of setting wages—one by the cost-of-living index; the other, "according to the market price of the commodity, say, for example, 50 per cent." But with the passing years, these views faded away. Immediately after the war, Sloan labeled the cost-of-living explanation of wage rates "an economic absurdity." He argued that "such a policy can only result in an unending spiral of increasing wages and prices. . . . The only sound attack is more and more production with increased efficiency." By the 1950s, the overwhelming majority followed his productivity approach. "Unless prices are to keep on climbing," said Charles E. Wilson of General Electric in a typical opinion, "higher wages can be paid only out of increased productivity of labor."

Business leaders regarded wage increases in excess of productivity not only as the cause of inflation, but as the cause of unemployment and recession, and as an unfair usurpation on the part of labor. A whole array of the most prominent business leaders was solidly for this opinion, but three quotations will be sufficient to illustrate the typical point of view. Said E. Hazard of Continental Can, "There is a myth that labor's effort alone increases productivity. According to this myth, if productivity increases 3 per cent, then wages ought to be increased 3 per cent as well. This reasoning leaves virtually nothing for the consumer or the investor."[50] It availed little to point out that the reasoning in this typical business opinion led to a false conclusion. If both productivity and wage rates rose by the same per cent, labor would not gobble up the whole increase; investors and management would also be sure to reap some of the gain, since the increase in wage rates would not swallow the total gain in product even though the percentage rise in both cases was the same. It availed equally little to point out that income in these years rose faster than price and that profits including capital gains were at levels undreamed of by the greediest entrepreneurs of the previous generation.

Business leaders went on insisting that "from here on, increases in productivity, through lower prices, must be shared with consumers and owners of capital as well as with labor." Most business leaders did not think this was occurring. Like many others, Ernest Breech thought that industry was getting the short end of the stick. He pointed out that in the ten years after the war, profits had declined $600 million, but taxes were up $9.5 billion and wages, $60 billion. "Clearly," he argued, "the stockholders as a group got no return on their added investment." Of course, it did not take long for critics to point out that Breech conveniently omitted what had happened to capital gains as evidenced by price rises on the stock exchange. But once again, it did not much matter, for businessmen were convinced, as they were convinced of nothing else, that wages were rising faster than productivity and at the expense of the consumer and the entrepreneur.

10. BUSINESS ATTITUDES TOWARD LABOR UNIONS

"Unions are simply more or less complete monopolies and possess
the same ability to raise prices as does any sellers' monopoly."

Sumner H. Slichter, 1931.

According to Roger Blough, wages in steel in one particular phase
after World War II rose 7 per cent while productivity went up 2
per cent.* How was this possible? How could wages keep rising faster
than productivity? To business leaders, there was a simple answer to
the riddle. They reasoned that real wages—the purchasing power of
what labor received—could not go up faster than productivity. Admittedly, money wages could keep rising, but if such increases exceeded the increment in man-hour output, they had to be compensated for by equivalent price increases. Fundamentally, it was the
power of labor unions and their leaders that made possible this so-
called "wage-price" spiral. Roger Blough spoke for almost all businessmen when he wrote: "Their [the unions] strength and influence
in America today can hardly be overestimated. Union leadership . . .
establishes national wage patterns which in recent years have increased
labor costs to a point where such actions now seem to be recognized, at least by many thoughtful people, as major contributors to
inflation. . . . We shall have to face up squarely to one undeniable
fact . . . that America is costing itself out of many markets. This,
too, is part of the price we pay for the multiple-company unions."[1]

Businessmen have never looked with affection upon labor unions.
Indeed, it is a moot question whether the government or the labor
union, the government bureaucrat or the labor boss has stood higher

* Naturally, labor denied this.

on the list of those on whom the business world wasted no love. Management's favorite unions, in the words of Mr. Dooley, were those that had "no strikes, no rules, no contracts, hardly any wages, an' dam few members." There have been, to be sure, consistent attempts to deny this. It has been said on more than a few occasions that the businessmen's opinions and attitudes toward labor unions have changed radically. In 1960, for example, a literary magazine described an evening out with a steel tycoon and a labor leader. According to the story, Benjamin Fairless during the 1959 steel strike took his wife and daughter to dinner at a New York luxury restaurant. By coincidence, David McDonald, president of the Steel Workers, was entertaining Zsa Zsa Gabor and a few other friends at an adjoining table. "And what happened?" asked the review, "Mr. Fairless sent over a bottle of champagne; Mr. McDonald unhesitatingly accepted it."[2]

CHANGES IN ATTITUDE

One of the morals drawn from this ancedote was that the management lion was lying down with the union lamb, or *vice versa*. It was closer to the truth to say that management had resigned itself to the inevitable. During the early part of the era, employers thought they had little to fear from the unions. Unions, they thought, were like "bad" children. They could be ignored, or their actions could be resisted as a piece of impertinence on the part of a group that had nothing of advantage to offer to anyone. True to the classical view, businessmen did not think that unions could raise labor's real wages; to the contrary, union efforts to raise wages could only result in inflation or unemployment or both. Businessmen of the 1920s never tired of pointing this out. Judge Gary, for example, always argued that labor unions existed either because an employer was foolish enough to recognize them, so that "the men cannot get employment except by joining the unions," or because the workers felt abused. "Make it certain all the time," he advised, "that the men in your employ are treated as well, if not a little better, than other men who are working for people who deal and contract with unions . . . and, so far as you can, cultivate a feeling of friendship, and influence your men to the conclusion that it is for their interests in every respect to be in your employ." Henry Ford said much the same thing when he blamed the existence of the unions on the international bankers and added: "Let the manufacturers and owners treat their men like men; let them pay a living wage and give them working conditions conducive to self expression. . . . There isn't a union in the country formed primarily by the men themselves or run for their benefit."

Banker Waddill Catchings of Goldman, Sachs & Co. and of the then-famous writing team of Foster and Catchings objected, as did businessmen and bankers generally, to jurisdictional and sympathy strikes, "featherbedding," interference with management's right to hire and fire, and bargaining between the employer and union leaders who "did not work in his company and were not concerned with its success or failure." "In defiance of the fundamental facts that the world can enjoy only what is produced," wrote Catchings, "the labor union has always proceeded as if there was only so much work to be done." According to Catchings, "The most serious obstacle to sound constructive effort in solving this great industrial problem is that college professors, college men (and some less thoughtful but equally well-intentioned men within industry) favor the labor union in a struggle the underlying causes of which they do not yet understand."[3]

Evidently, there was still a great deal of paternalism in management's attitude toward the workers, and it kept cropping up in the expressed opinions of old-style entrepreneurs. Thus, Charles M. Schwab, in recalling the Homestead strike, told reporters: "I said, 'Boys, this won't do. There never was a strike in the world that paid anybody. . . . We must get together, and if you place your confidence in me . . . you will get a square deal.' Well, I settled that strike." Forty years later, another entrepreneur, M. G. O'Neil of General Tire, looked back nostalgically to these carefree and *gemütlich* days: "Many is the time our rubber workers won measures from management. . . . Although the measures cost him money, my father would provide the beer to help the workers celebrate." According to Schwab, labor-management relations were always compatible, an illusion that haunted business leaders all through the twenty years after World War I. Said Schwab, "The capacity of America to progress is not altogether due to the great economic advantages we enjoy or to the marvellous improvements in machine and technical science. It is, I believe, due in great part to the good will which has come about between labor and capital."[4]

By the years after World War II, paternalism had evidently died and been buried. Management had come to accept labor unions, not eagerly, or enthusiastically, or joyfully, but resignedly just as it had come to accept ulcers, back trouble, and the attaché case as necessary accouterments in the march of time. They only hoped that the unions would learn to live responsibly. John E. Rovensky, banker turned industrialist, thought, "All sound-thinking businessmen today recognize the right of labor to collective bargaining. Unions are an absolute necessity. . . . But what labor needs today is wiser and more far-sighted leadership to avoid making the mistakes employers made when they were in the saddle."[5]

LABOR-MANAGEMENT RELATIONS IN THE EARLY 1920s

The transition from a period when labor unions were regarded paternalistically and patronizingly to a period when they came to be regarded as ruthless, anti-social monopolies, like all transitions, did not take place overnight. There was some evidence of it even before 1920. It was still hardly evident in 1929, but had become a reality by 1946.

The first inkling of things to come occurred right after World War I. With the Armistice, business leaders prepared to move back to the *status quo ante bellum,* to normalcy as Warren G. Harding was about to call it. Much to their surprise and consternation, they learned that labor sincerely believed that it had been treated harshly during the war. Unions pointed to what they thought were the swollen profits of business, and charged that the workers had been shortchanged. They announced that under no circumstances would they agree to an abandonment of the wartime collective bargaining that it had taken so long to achieve. Business, for its part, feared that any concessions it might make would be regarded as a sign of weakness leading to further demands. The government attempted to bridge the gap by holding a Labor-Management Conference, but since neither side appeared to be willing or able to unravel the maze of cross purposes or to make concessions, the conference failed, and a wave of strikes swept over the country in 1919. All major industries were affected, but the steel strike was easily the most prominent. As a contest in public relations, the conflict was one-sided with industry easily the victor. Judge Gary, speaking for the Steel Corporation, immediately branded the strike a Bolshevist-inspired threat to the entire American system. There were many who disagreed. Sociologists, writing about the strike, denied that it was a Communist plot. A few business leaders and bankers, as Otto Kahn expressed it, did not "look upon the attitude of labor as being actuated to any serious extent by Bolshevist or kindred motives."[6]

But public opinion was clearly on the side of business. Dealing from strength, Gary refused to have any dealings with the strike leaders. Under no circumstances would he recognize the union or the principle of collective bargaining as union leaders defined and interpreted it. In decrying the labor movement, Gary predicted the worst. According to him, "The end sought by union labor leaders, that at least to which their efforts tend, means disaster and destruction. It is noticeable that often times they seek to control politics. . . . Worse than everything else, they would dominate the Supreme Court, our citadel of defense to person and property—to civilization itself."[7]

It was clear that what was fundamentally involved was the problem of collective bargaining by labor unions. What was at issue was the extent that business was prepared to deal with unions. And on this, business leaders were adamant. Most of them were willing to go along with Otto Kahn when he pressed employers "to recognize the dignity and status of the worker." They agreed with him in wanting "the closest possible relations between employer and employee." Some even approved of giving the worker "an effective voice in determining jointly with the employer the conditions under which he works." But this was to be a privilege granted by the employer, not a right to be turned over to a labor union. In explaining his company's labor relations, Schwab said, "We discuss matters, but we never vote. I will not permit myself to be in a position of having labor dictate to management." But Schwab added, "The remarkable thing is that in all the sifting of complaints and in all the adjustment of grievances, we find that in 70 per cent of the cases the workmen are right." Schwab's remarks demonstrated that in addition to believing that everyone had his place, management lived in suspicious fear of unions. In the midst of the labor strife of 1920, Secretary of Commerce Hoover called a meeting of key industrialists who had "advanced views toward employee relations." Present among others were A. C. Bedford of Standard Oil, C. B. Seger of U. S. Rubber, and C. A. Coffin of General Electric. Hoover proposed that they establish more cordial relations with AFL's Samuel Gompers. The audience was cold to the suggestion.[8]

THE TACTICS USED IN RESISTING THE UNIONS

During the decade after the war, business leaders and business organizations resisted unionization with many different tools. But various as they were, they could be summed up under three main headings: the anti-union trade association, the open-shop drive, and welfare capitalism.

As labor strived to accomplish its objectives through trade unions, business in turn organized employers' associations. Among the most important anti-unionist organizations were the National Founders Association, the National Metal Trades Association, and the National Association of Manufacturers. Few business leaders openly expressed their opinions about this movement, but the officials of the associations were more loquacious. At the 1920 annual convention of the NAM, President Kirby put together a set of typical remarks. "Organized labor," he charged, "is just the same today as it was in 1884. . . . There is no difference. They [union leaders] claim that the Reds have gotten in and impregnated the organization with Bolshevism. . . . Why there has never been anything but Reds at the head of that organization."[9]

Trade associations were the chief media through which business leaders carried on their drive for the "open shop" in the early years of the 1920s. This drive, which was to blossom forth once again in the 1950s under the term "the right to work," stipulated that "No person shall be refused employment or in any way discriminated against on account of membership or non-membership in any labor organization, and there should be no discriminating against or interference with any employee who is not a member of a labor organization by members of such organization."[10]

Businessmen were prepared to pay a heavy price to protect the worker's freedom. When Judge Gary announced that the open shop was "for the best interest of the employer, the employee and the general public," his board of directors supported him with the following resolution:

We are prepared to accept, regardless of the sacrifices necessary thereto, whatever losses may be sustained in maintaining the right of each American citizen to enter into his individual contract.

Ostensibly, the open shop, like the right to work, was designed to protect and encourage the worker's freedom, but to most observers outside of business, it was more negative than positive; it was according to their lights more anti-union than pro-freedom. And businessmen in their expressed opinion and by their behavior gave the skeptics much evidence to support their view. Gary, after expressing the opinion that the "natural and certain effects of labor unionism are expressed by inefficiency and high costs," recommended as a way of avoiding the plague, "publicity, regulation, and reasonable control through Government agencies" applying to "both organized capital and organized labor." Backing their words with action, industrialists enforced the open shop by the use of the blacklist, strike breakers, constabulary, the hiring of labor spies and *agents provocateurs* as well as by influencing the press and applying community pressure.[11]

There was still a third method—the encouragement of welfare capitalism and industrial democracy—by which businessmen intentionally or unintentionally thwarted unionism. The wave of strikes which engulfed the economy in 1919 and to a lesser extent in the three following years signified to some of those who were interested in the problems of modern industrialism that something was basically amiss in labor relations. To most businessmen and bankers, the things that were out of gear were the laborer and the labor union; strikes were simply the result of the temperamental caprice of willful, selfish men. To a smaller number, such an explanation seemed overly simple. Many in this group sought the answer to the difficulties in "industrial democracy." This rather loose term included all plans which envisaged the inclusion in one form or another of labor in management. Before the war, John D. Rockefeller, Jr., had preached some form of employee representation, the Filene Brothers had adopted a system for their department store, and a few others had made equally important contributions. But at best the movement made slow progress. Then, in the hectic days after the war, industrial democracy had a short, but memorable day in the sun. In the *Readers' Guide to Periodical Literature* for 1919–21, eight times as much space was devoted to "Employee Representation" as in the period 1925–28.

Industrial democracy, in short, was a postwar phenomenon. E. A. Filene, its most articulate champion, thought the pendulum swung sharply from industrial democracy to industrial autocracy after 1924. By that time, the labor movement had ceased to be a threat to management, and by then too, the prevalent tone of business had shifted subtly from a degree of idealism to a resurgence of realism. The tone of the NAM convention of 1925 illustrated the first. The presidential address of that year commended the AFL for "keeping subdued the more radical elements." Illustrative of the second was an interchange between Henry Ford and George Johnson of Endicott-Johnson shoe manufacturers. "It is not necessary," said Ford, "for the employer to love the employee, or for the employee to love the employer. What is necessary is for each to try to do justice to the other according to his deserts." In contrast, Johnson thought, "Such a thing as democracy in industry, love in industry is possible, and it's good business. It's got to be made possible. It's the only answer for human beings."[12]

Welfare capitalism had more staying power than industrial democracy. All through the 1920s, businessmen used profit sharing, employee stock ownership, pension plans, bonus arrangements, unemployment insurance, guaranteed wages, company unions, and other types of welfare capitalism to help the worker or to convince him that his best interests were in harmony with the best interests of management. The idea of welfare capitalism really began just before the war. As early as 1898, Filene's department store had established a "works council." The Dennison Manufacturing Company in 1916 established the first employer plan for unemployment insurance; the first group insurance was written in 1913; and Sears, Roebuck began its profit-sharing plan in 1916.

Many of the components of welfare capitalism enjoyed an accelerated growth after the war, but at no time were they nearly as important as they became after World War II when the term "fringe benefit" became an accepted part of the language. The famous profit-sharing plan set up by Endicott-Johnson, the shoe company, distributed $1,000,000 in 1923. Thereafter it ran downhill rapidly and faded out altogether in 1930. Stock purchase plans became more popular in the latter part of the decade and were viewed as the beginning of the millenium. The National Industrial Conference Board estimated in late 1927 that employees owned or were buying considerably more than $1 billion of securities. Unfortunately, however, many of these new investors lost heavily when the market crashed.

The most enthusiastic proponents of employee stock ownership included George Eastman, Julius Rosenwald, and Colonel Harley Proctor. Before the war, Eastman had been skeptical about such plans, but soon after the Armistice he urged the board of directors to set aside $20 million of common stock to be sold to employees with two years of service. The Sears, Roebuck plan was even more famous, and Proctor and Gamble, beside selling stock to employees, had representatives of labor on the board of directors.

Proctor and Gamble also began, in 1923, a plan to guarantee forty-eight weeks of annual employment. Hart, Schaffner and Marks attempted to alleviate the effects of technological unemployment by contributing to a reserve fund $50,000 which was augmented by a $25,000 contribution from the Amalgamated Clothing Workers and distributed among 150 cutters who had lost their jobs to the machine. Other companies that adopted noted plans to relieve the effects of unemployment included Dennison Manufacturing, the Walworth Company, Fels Soap, and Hills Brothers, food packers. The businessmen who installed these plans were untiring in their efforts to convert other leaders to their opinion. Filene, in challenging the business world to solve the unemployment problem, said, "The ideal solution would be for business leaders to get together and publicly accept the responsibility for unemployment, pledging themselves that hereafter whatever else happens they will guarantee to organize employment for all who are willing to work."

Most businessmen insisted that they could not adopt anything like a guaranteed wage or guaranteed employment because of the cyclical nature of their business. To which Colonel Proctor replied: "I do not think there is anything peculiar in the soap business that makes a plan more adaptable to it than to any other industry."*[13]

Most businessmen approached welfare capitalism from the point of view of dollars and cents and profit and loss. John J. Raskob, for example, believed that the experience at General Motors proved that "money paid in benefits is returned in the lower cost of production." A study by J. David Houser found that most employers who favored welfare capitalism believed that it was profitable to do so. But there were additional motives. Cyrus McCormick, Jr., of the Harvester Company saw in employee stock ownership "a very practical step

---

* In 1929, it was estimated that 364 firms, employing about one ninth of private non-agricultural labor or 3¾ million employees (many of whom were managers), had old-age pension plans. A slightly larger number of firms had company unions; there were about 385 of them with 690,000 employees in 1922, and 399 with 1,547,766 workers in 1928. A few of these were really employee-representing, but most of them were clearly devices to prevent the invasion of a trade union.

toward removing any possible danger of Bolshevism." Other businessmen said their motive was a "desire for approval," and in a few cases,
welfare capitalism was pursued for frankly sentimental reasons.[14]

THE DEPRESSION AND THE FEAR OF REVOLUTION

By 1929, optimists about management-labor relations had good
cause to be optimistic. Business had reached a pinnacle of prestige,
the strike wave of the post-Armistice years was a matter of unrecol-
lected history; business leaders were throwing bouquets at the hierarchy of the AFL in one of the labor-capital honeymoons that
occurred intermittently in industrial relations; and academic economists were announcing a new day of "people's capitalism" in which
workers were sharing as never before in the great affluence that had
come upon the country.

Harmony came to an abrupt halt when prosperity collapsed in
1929. To be sure, bloody and violent disputes did not accompany
the outbreak of the depression, but businessmen lived in anxious fear
of the revolutionary potentials of "hard times." When unemployment
absorbed as much as 25 per cent of the labor force and reached eight
digits, such fears did not seem without some foundation in fact. Like
other groups of citizens, businessmen did not understand that strikes
and industrial unrest occur more frequently in periods of rising and
prosperous business than in times of deep depression. During the
twenty years after World War I there were three great waves of
strikes: In 1919 when labor endeavored to maintain the gains that
it had achieved during the war; in 1933 when enterprising labor leaders used the beginnings of recovery and the newly enacted National
Industrial Recovery Act as levers to increase the membership of their
unions; and in 1936–37 at the height of a recovery period and just
prior to the recession of 1937. In all three of these difficult periods,
management insisted that it was "right" or, more accurately, that labor was "wrong."

This attitude on the part of businessmen did not, however, mean
that they were inhumane, unsympathetic, or deliberately cruel. Pigheaded they might be, but they did not think that the palliatives offered by liberals were the answer to labor's or business' troubles.

R. R. Deupree of Proctor and Gamble dismissed all of them as not dealing with fundamentals, saying:

> The normal desire and the outstanding goal for every self-respecting man is the opportunity to work, with the assurance that if he works well he will continue to hold his job. Advancement, increases in pay are today incidental to that ever-present, dark shadow of involuntary unemployment. . . . Pension plans, profit sharing plans, sick benefit plans, Christmas Baskets—all have their place, but that place is secondary to the provision of regular jobs.

Tragically, however, businessmen had nothing really constructive or plausible to suggest. Many of them did join in the public outcry for far-reaching reforms, but when specific reform measures were proposed, they reacted in a confused and contradictory fashion. This was demonstrated clearly by the business reaction to proposals for unemployment insurance and old-age pensions. In the previous period of prosperity, business leaders and business spokesmen had had no time for such matters, but now a change occurred. As John E. Edgerton, small businessman and president of the NAM in 1930, said, "Unemployment insurance, old-age relief . . . are receiving consideration from manufacturers who would not have thought of them a few short years ago." Myron C. Taylor, Walter Gifford, and Alfred P. Sloan were among the many who supported share-the-work plans and some sort of payments to relieve unemployment. In June 1932, a large number of Chicago's leading businessmen, including executives of Armour, International Harvester, Santa Fe, Marshall Field, Inland Steel, urged President Hoover to support federal relief. But when it came to specific proposals, businessmen floundered around between humanitarianism and fear of government. The NAM did not deny that unemployment existed, nor did it oppose private unemployment insurance, but it did oppose government insurance because that would break down the worker's moral fiber. Alvin Macauley, president of Packard Motors and of the Automobile Chamber of Commerce, did "not like any plan that would force employers and employees to contribute to a fund."[15]

OPPOSITION TO LABOR UNIONS AND THE CLOSED SHOP

One thing business leaders were sure of was that labor unionism was not the answer to any problem. In the latter part of the period between two wars, a *Fortune* survey of executive opinion found that almost 50 per cent (48.4) believed that labor unions had hurt the country, and only 31.8 per cent believed that they had helped. It was probable that this vote would have been more anti-union at the beginning of the period.[16]

Two episodes in the depressed thirties shed light on what business thought of unions—the events surrounding the enactment of the National Industrial Recovery Act and those associated with the Wagner Act.

Section 7 (a) of the NIRA was designed to secure to employees the right to organize and bargain collectively through representatives of their own choosing. The pattern that emerged recalled what had happened during the war when the government had first taken steps to encourage collective bargaining. In order to provide a mechanism for such bargaining and at the same time to prevent labor unions from flourishing, companies had set up industrial relations plans or company unions. The same behavior began with the NRA. During the debate on the bill, friends of business introduced an amendment specifically stating that company unions were legal for purposes of Section 7 (a). Much to their disappointment, the amendment failed. What business was trying to do was to solidify the open shop. Henry I. Harriman of the Chamber of Commerce, who was enthusiastic about the NRA, had only one objection, "the principle of the open shop was not in the bill." When the company union amendment failed, the more pessimistic businessmen anticipated the worst. J. A. Emery, NAM spokesman, warned that "the bill means the virtually immediate and complete unionization of all labor in all industry." But most business leaders did not share this gloomy view. Trade associations immediately began instructing their members in the art of forming company unions. Identical methods were used: standardized forms, a standard constitution, and an identical letter announcing the plan. By the time NRA code making had begun, many firms were ready with a company sponsored vehicle for collective bargaining that met the requirements of Section 7 (a).[17]

Most industry leaders would have nothing to do with "outside" unions. Concentrating on the potential power which the new law gave to these unions, the business attitude was a mixture of fear, suspicion, and hostility, born of a conviction that unions were essentially anti-social and anti-economic. But many businessmen were far more realistic about unions than were some of the sentimental liberals, for they recognized the objectives that union leaders had to pursue. Alfred Sloan analyzed these objectives accurately when he said, "It is axiomatic in employer-employee relationships that organized labor, as such, can never be satisfied. It cannot afford to be satisfied, for being dissatisfied is the very foundation of its continued existence." And Henry S. Dennison, one of the most "liberal" of businessmen, regarded trade unionism with the same skepticism: "Much as I look forward to and favor the wider range of classical unionism in this country, I cannot overlook the flat fact that it is not unionism but the abilities of union leaders which determines whether unionism shall be of net service or disservice to workers and to the country." The automobile industry included in its code (with the consent of the President, it was said) a provision that "employers may exercise their right to select, retain, or advance employees on the basis of their individual merit without regard to affiliation or non-affiliation with any labor or other organization."

As one would expect, steel men were also in the forefront of those who objected to the new opportunities for unionism. Before the NRA became law, Robert P. Lamont, head of the American Iron and Steel Institute, emphasized that "the industry stands positively for the open shop; it is unalterably opposed to the closed shop. For many years it has been and is now prepared to deal directly with its employees collectively on all matters relating to their employment. . . . It is unwilling to conduct negotiations with outside organizations of labor." The passage of the Act did nothing to change the minds of the steel leaders. Madam Perkins recalled that at the meeting on the steel code, she attempted to introduce a group of them, including Grace, Weir, Taylor, and Girdler, to AFL's William Green. "Most of them," she wrote, "backed away like frightened boys. . . . Only William Irvin [of U. S. Steel] did not join the huddle."[18]

Since there was no agreement on the legality of company unions, the NRA set off a multitude of strikes, the most publicized being the strike against Ernest T. Weir's Weirton Steel Company at Weirton, West Virginia. The company had formed a company union and refused to bargain with the Amalgamated Iron and Steel Workers. The union claimed that the Weirton employee representation plan did not fulfill the requirements of "representatives of their own choosing." Weir in turn insisted that management did not interfere with the company union and that it was free to pursue its own policies. The Amalgamated argued that it had the support of the majority of employees in the company, and when Weir refused to negotiate, a strike was called, ostensibly to assist in the enforcement of Section 7 (a). An appeal was made to the Labor Board, which had been appointed by the President to facilitate the enforcement of the labor section of the Recovery Act. Weir expressed his dissatisfaction with this process as follows: "This Board should not encourage such unfounded strikes and irresponsible leadership by dignifying their complaints with a hearing." He further stated that the National Steel Company, of which Weirton Steel was a part, would maintain its policy of refusing to deal with the Amalgamated. The strike in his opinion had been caused by "three or four foreigners." During the strike Weir was charged with having said to the sheriff at Weirton, "We may have to shoot a few" steel strikers. As industrial relations at Weirton progressively became worse, Weir emerged as a national figure. He lost the sympathy of the public, but he gained the good will of his colleagues in the steel industry.* The Amalgamated's action dragged through the Labor Board and eventually the United States brought suit charging the company with seven violations of the code. At the trial, Weirton's counsel declared that his client regarded the Act as unconstitutional, illegal, unethical, unnecessary and communistic, socialistic legislation passed by a group who had no sympathy for the right of a private entrepreneur to manage and control his own business as he wished to control it.

The eventual decision of the Wilmington Federal Court held that the Weirton company union was legal and that Section 7 (a) was unconstitutional. Weir had won a sweeping victory, not only for his own opinions, but also for the opinions of the mass of industrialists. At the 1935 meeting of the American Iron and Steel Institute, Weir, who had previously been cited as the man who by his incessant price cutting had foiled the efforts to "stabilize" the steel business, was

---

* Weir got much the worst of it in congressional hearings. And no one of any influence attempted to defend him at the time. But later, in 1963, a novel by William Hoffman, *The Dark Mountain,* sympathetically presented the case of a man whose career strongly resembled that of Weir.

wildly cheered when Schwab introduced him as the "star of the industry."

Following the judicial victory, the magazine *Steel* editorialized: "The Nields decision apparently withdraws from the steel industry the necessity for collective bargaining." Thus, the decision of the federal court returned matters to the status quo ante NRA, and industrialists were elated. Labor unions, on the other hand, were considerably dejected, and labor spokesmen in Congress prepared to replace the NRA's Labor Board with a new law which would create an independent labor board together with new rules for collective bargaining. In short, out of the profusion of controversies, of which the Weirton case was the most famous, came the Wagner Act to establish a National Labor Board, which would be designed to enforce collective bargaining by representatives of labor's own choosing.

Henry Dennison was one of the few businessmen who expressed any kind words for the Wagner Act, but he too objected to the cavalier rejection of all company unions. Much more typically, J. A. Emery said, "The Wagner bill will excite irritation, resentment, and bitterness in employment relations. . . . It will stimulate complaints, promote the interruption of employment. . . . It will secure, through the union, monopolistic control; assuring the unrestricted use of the strike, and thus confer the power to assess the public with the cost of sustaining a labor monopoly, maintained with Federal aid, relieved of appropriate legal control, and without corresponding responsibility for the acts of its agents."

Businessmen objected to the Wagner Act because it placed no restrictions on labor. In addition, they viewed it as unconstitutional and unfair in that it deprived minorities of their rights. They denied that in bargaining an individual had less power than a group. They also insisted that the Act would delay recovery and create an unbridgeable chasm between labor and capital. Small businessmen joined in with a set of complaints of their own. They stressed the basic differences between the "big" and the "little," and argued that the Act should apply, if at all, only to big business. Said the lawyer for the National Lock Company,

Small industries located in small communities and employing not over 2,000 persons should not be handled in the same manner and subjected to the same treatment as those engaged in mass production, requiring mass labor, such as the coal mines and the steel mills. . . . I want to say that I regard this bill of Senator Wagner's as a primer from Moscow, and I think that this committee and the Senate . . . should turn their backs on it; pick up the American flag and walk in the other direction.

The United States Chamber of Commerce believed much as had those who espoused the open shop in a previous decade: "In the exercise of the right to organize and bargain collectively through representatives of their own choosing, employees should be free from coercion or restraint from any source. There should be no attempt to lessen through legislative restrictions . . . the freedom of employes in determining the form of any organization created voluntarily."

It was eminently fair to assert that the individual must be free to choose membership or non-membership in any organization, but as in every such statement, ample room had to be allowed for different interpretations. Employers professed to favor the open shop, one in which the worker could choose to join or not to join a union as he saw fit; but in reality the open shop was one in which employment was open only to non-union members. Many of these plants had no grievance procedure and refused to recognize any outside employee representation, but ironically they often paid higher wages than did union shops. Such in any event was the case in two of the most strongly anti-union firms, the Ford Motor Company and the Weirton Steel Company, and in one of these no labor union was ever able to establish itself.

Liberals regarded the labor opinions of business leaders as at best myopic and at worst evil. But businessmen always thought their labor relations best for all concerned. They were especially proud of their welfare work. Typically, chairman Taylor of U. S. Steel reported, in 1934, to the stockholders that he "didn't believe there was a brighter page in the history of a company than the one which your corporation wrote with respect to the treatment of its employees during the entire depression." Taylor was well aware of Steel's sad picture during the depression. Under the pressing load of continuous reductions in production, the average wage of steel workers dropped from $33 a week in 1929 to $13 a week in 1932. As a palliative for the unemployment and the low incomes that had become the rule, Steel resorted to share-the-work plans and distributed boxes of food that were charged to the future earnings of the recipients. Between

1925 and 1935, Steel spent approximately $140 million for welfare. Meanwhile, too, it had capped its welfare program by forming a company union, which, ironically enough, turned against the corporation in 1935.[19]

Eventually, the Wagner Act became law, although it had no easy road to enactment. A group of eminent attorneys, members of the Liberty League, advised one and all that the Act was unconstitutional. John L. Lewis, who had already taken steps toward divorce from the AFL, expressed almost as much dissatisfaction with the new law. But this was really neither here nor there. As the CIO undertook to organize the mass-production industries, business leaders prepared to defend their position. To them it seemed that Armageddon had finally been reached. A. H. Young, vice-president in charge of industrial relations of the United States Steel Corporation, said he "would rather go to jail and yet be true to the principles of peaceful cooperation in industry." He declared that he "would never accept any formula in industry which is an unpalatable and unrighteous and unjust technique imposed on us by demagogues." But others were more pragmatic and opportunistic. A small independent steel executive explained to a professor who was studying the industry, "I'm an industrial politician. I never had any labor trouble and I don't want any. . . . I'll go along with the union as long as it's top dog here. My idea is to keep out of trouble."

STEEL'S 1937 AGREEMENT WITH THE UNION

Then suddenly in 1937 came a sensational development. The United States Steel Corporation broke away from its competitors and signed a contract with the CIO. A variety of reasons have been presented for this development, but regardless of the causes—whether it was Mrs. Myron Taylor's personal admiration for John L. Lewis, the tense diplomatic situation in Europe with its resultant demand for increased armaments, or whether it was simply a surrender by Gary's successors—the fact was that Myron Taylor and John L. Lewis signed a contract by which the United Steel Workers of the CIO became sole collective bargaining agent for the steel workers of the corporation. The managements of the "Little Steel" corporations were shocked by what they considered the treachery of "Big Steel." Tom M. Girdler, head of Republic Steel, was said to have greeted the news with language not suitable to the dignity of a great steel executive. Even after considerable time had passed, Girdler remained unreconciled. "Many thousands of workers," he wrote in retrospect, "were shocked, even horrified by the news that United States Steel had settled with the union. . . . I was bitter about this. So were the vast majority of the steel men of the nation. . . . Why did we not all sign? Simply because we were convinced that a surrender to CIO was a bad thing for our companies, our employees, indeed for the United States of America."[20]

The leaders of Youngstown, Republic, National, and Bethlehem were so incensed by the action of the Steel Corporation that at the next meeting of the Iron and Steel Institute, they moved into a position of control. Girdler and Weir became the new bulwarks against the spread of advancing unionism. In the spring of 1937, the CIO moved against Republic and Youngstown. In 1936, an attempt had been made through strikes at Johnstown to influence Bethlehem to sign with the union, but that had failed as the businessmen of Johnstown organized "back-to-work" movements against the novel tactics of the union, and a Citizens' Committee distributed pamphlets calling upon the townspeople to "Join the CIO and help build a Soviet America."

Finesse was lost on Weir and Girdler. Weir had successfully fought the budding union movement in 1933 with tactics which were neither novel nor subtle, but which had proved successful through years of industrial warfare. The CIO never managed to unionize the Weirton Steel Company. Girdler, steel executive with experience in many far-flung steel mills, was not nearly as successful. The labor strife which resulted in the so-called "Memorial Day Massacre" at South Chicago in 1937 ended with Republic also signing with the CIO. Girdler never reconciled himself to this turn of events. At the height of the difficulties, he went to Washington to defend his point of view. He told the investigating committee that he would never sign a written contract with "an irresponsible, racketeering, violent, Communist body like the CIO" unless the Supreme Court upheld such a ruling. He would not, he continued, be influenced by the rulings of the National Labor Relations Board. In this, he had the support of the business community which thought, as William S. Knudsen of GM later expressed it, "The National Labor Relations Board makes no pretense even of paying any attention to the employer's side of the case. . . . There is no record of a single decision where he had a ghost-of-a-show." Girdler went on to say that it would hardly matter if the great majority of his employees voted for the CIO as its bargaining agent. Spectators in Washington were said to have cheered when the colorful Republic executive expressed his opinion that he had considered the "CIO irresponsible ever since he first heard of it."

In the later investigation by the La Follette Committee into the activities of Republic during this period, much was unveiled that did serious damage to Girdler's reputation. Girdler, however, never doubted that he had been right. He thought the La Follette Committee had engaged in "a strangely conducted inquiry" which was "unable to keep the truth from getting into the records." In Girdler's opinion, most of the Republic workers were against the CIO; the CIO engaged in violence; there were Communists in the midst of the workers; and most of the agitators who engaged in violence were from out of town. Years after the Memorial Day tragedy, Girdler wrote, "The news reached me at my Cleveland home. From that moment until now I have been unable to see how I could have prevented the clash. It happened only because the Communist leaders wanted it to happen."

Girdler believed that there had never been a time that he could "remember, boy and man, when collective bargaining did not exist in the steel industry." To him it was inconceivable that the CIO was agitating for collective bargaining. The real issue, he thought, was not collective bargaining, but the closed shop and the check off. Perhaps one of the difficulties was that Girdler had the businessman's definition of collective bargaining. In his opinion, questions of wages, hours, working conditions, industrial injustice, and seniority rights were all includable as subjects open to bargaining, but not the right to hire and fire, the right to install equipment leading to improvements in quality and competitive position, nor the right of men to work who did not belong to a particular organization.[21]

CONTINUED OPPOSITION TO THE WAGNER ACT

Sitdown strikes eventually persuaded the automobile producers to enter into contracts with the CIO. The same sequence of events occurred in the rubber industry, and finally "Little Steel," with the exception of Weir, surrendered. Adding to the defeat, the Supreme Court, in the Jones and Laughlin case, held the Wagner Act constitutional. Nevertheless, business leaders continued to object. In every poll of business opinion, the Wagner Labor Relations Act led all the rest in the list of the laws that businessmen opposed. Social Security had been accepted, the agitation against the public utility holding bill had petered out, and the SEC was accepted, but year after year business groups agitated for relief from the Wagner Act. At every convention of the United States Chamber of Commerce, there were demands that the Act be made to apply to labor as well as capital. Up to 1939, the Chamber went on record as favoring outright repeal of the Act, but subsequently it supported "structural amendments." The National Association of Manufacturers adopted a program called "Fundamentals of Satisfactory Employment Relations," which called for amendment of the National Labor Relations Act, the outlawing of sitdown, secondary, sympathetic, and general strikes as well as the strike for the check off. It asked for a restoration of the labor injunction and the prohibition of interstate movement of paid pickets.

Individual businessmen also continued to make the Wagner Act their chief target. At a meeting of the United States Chamber of Commerce, silence greeted C. S. Ching, director of industrial and public relations for the United States Rubber Products Company, when he asked for "a realistic approach to the Act." One of the delegates was quoted as characterizing the speech as "pouring soap grease on the crowd out of an old gourd dipper." At the same meeting, the delegates rose and cheered when Senator Burke of Nebraska called the Act "America's Public Enemy No. 1."[22]

LABOR-MANAGEMENT RELATIONS AFTER WORLD WAR II

During the war, management and labor continued to snipe at each other, but whatever sniping was done was insignificant in terms of the real objective of attaining V-E and V-J Day. But as soon as the war ended, the war between business and the unions resumed. The strategy and tactics were, however, different from those followed in the thirty years before the war. Business could not ignore or patronize the unions as it had done in the 1920s. And paternalism toward workers was certainly a thing of the past. The anti-unionism of the 1930s was also gone; management had come to realize that unions were here to stay. In the new atmosphere of wary, distrustful, and sometimes hostile coexistence, the best that management thought it could achieve was an effective means of containing union power. It, therefore, subtly changed its strategy. In arguing against the unions and in presenting its case to the public, management differed from the past by putting more emphasis on the importance of productivity and more stress on the monopolistic nature of labor unions. This, of course, is a generalization that applied to the majority of business opinion, but not all. More businessmen seemed to subscribe to the modal point of view on this issue than on any other issue. Yet as with all economic problems, there was still some divergence from the consensus.

Any power group that is confronted with real or threatened revolt will contain splinter groups that react differently from the majority. In labor-management relations as in the movement for civil rights and in the controversy between big business and big government, there were many who regretted reality, many who recognized the irrationality of warfare and yearned for peace and harmony without knowing how to achieve either. Henry Ford II, in 1964, spoke for this group when he said: "It seems to me, we have made a great deal of progress in many aspects of our relationship with the UAW, but little progress in reducing the atmosphere of militancy and crisis that surrounds the negotiation of a new agreement. I believe that this atmosphere is a dangerous anachronism, an obsolete carry over from the bitter labor-management conflicts of a generation and more ago."

There were hawks as well as doves in the management group. The more "hard-nosed" industrialists, who were especially prominent in steel and motors, urged business to draw a specific line and to hold this line without any thought of compromise or retreat regardless of union demands, attacks, or pleas. In the 1930s, Tom Girdler had said, "Before I sign a CIO contract, I'll go back on the farm and dig potatoes." In 1947, Charles E. Wilson of GM told a Senate committee that he would never sign a contract for a closed shop. "When it gets around to that," he said, "they can make a farmer out of me." When the country faced one of its intermittent steel strikes in 1959, some steel managers resolved not to budge from the last offer made to the union, but there was a general fear that if confronted by another labor-management imbroglio the government would intervene. In order to dissuade the Eisenhower administration from any such action, Charles M. White of Republic held a press conference at which he said that the country could stand a three-month strike without "depriving anyone of real necessities." Having resolved to fight it out even if it took all summer, the steel industry proceeded to demonstrate that it was determined to do just that. A steel strike began in July 1959, continued for 116 days, and was finally settled, it has been said, through the intervention of Vice-President Nixon.[23]

The less determined in the struggle could hardly be expected to go along with the more determined leaders of steel, motors, and others of a past generation. At about the same time that Wilson talked about going to the farm, a survey showed that only 15 per cent of 1000 companies thought that union security clauses had resulted in a further deterioration in labor-management relations. Most employers, it is true, opposed the closed shop and industry-wide bargaining, but here again, there was one association, the clothing manufacturers, which supported both.

The "doves" readily admitted that anti-social behavior was often caused by "unscrupulous leadership," but they felt that more often society and the business managers themselves, not the workers or the union rank and file, were responsible for the difficulties with unions. Dudley W. Figgis of the American Can Company called for mutual respect among consumers, workers, and owners. "There are some cases," he said, "in which labor is the victim of unscrupulous leadership. On the other hand, industrial leadership must take its share of the blame also, because for many years, management was more concerned with placing value behind its securities than with the interests of the workers and the consuming public." In similar vein, Louis Kirstein explained that "like all groups that suddenly achieve power, labor is showing certain excesses. That is to be expected." Kirstein blamed manufacturers for part of this because their attitude toward unions had been "pathetically shortsighted." Gerard Swope, now at the end of his long career, told his fellow industrialists that whether they liked it or not, unionization might be the justification for management's job, for it made the manager's job more difficult, and "therefore, he has to do better if he is to continue to hold it."[24]

LABOR UNION MONOPOLIES AND COST-PUSH INFLATION

Whatever their diagnosis, business leaders regarded the behavior of labor unions as an advanced form of juvenile delinquency. Whether they attributed the problem to irresponsible leadership, to society's indifference, or to the insensitive behavior of past management, at the heart of the whole hostility were the twin complaints of wages rising faster than productivity and inflation-inducing monopoly.

Immediately after the end of the war, business leaders, "liberals" as well as "reactionaries," bankers as well as steel men, began to publicize the argument that labor unions were responsible for "cost-push" inflation. All through the 1950s and early 1960s, they argued that wages were rising faster than output per man-hour, and that the consequence of this state of affairs was price inflation with all the tragedy that it brought to the economy in general, to business investment in particular, and to the unfortunates who were on a fixed income. Joseph L. Block of Inland Steel, who was often cited as a spokesman for liberal business opinion, devoted much of his talks in the late 1950s and early 1960s to explaining that "the unrestricted power of labor unions is obviously responsible for much of the inflation we have had and unless this inflationary trend is curbed, we could be faced with a very disastrous situation." Block often pointed out that "the real objectives of labor and management are the same," but, nevertheless, the country seemed to be faced annually with the "dubious choice of a nation-wide strike or a dose of inflation."[25]

Many other business leaders thought it equally obvious that wage increases, that is, cost-push, were the root cause of price inflation. Thus, George Champion to a 1964 Chamber of Commerce dinner: "How can we criticize others when some of our own labor unions insist upon inflationary wage increases that far outstrip gains in productivity? Other elements, of course, contribute . . . but union demands have been a major causal factor." Henry Ford II claimed that the AFL-CIO was not using its power to "increase the growth of the American pie but to cut a larger share for its constituents . . . unquestionably thwarting the very improvement in productivity and growth that it wants."

In general, business leaders thought it so self-evident that unions through their pressure on wages pushed prices up that they did not bother to elucidate any further on the subject. In the 1958 hearings on the condition of the country, more than half of the businessmen and bankers who testified casually mentioned wage "increases in excess of productivity" as a root cause of inflation and then went on to something else.

How could wages continue to outstrip productivity? Well, as Roger Blough said at the beginning of this chapter, it was a matter of monopoly power on the part of the unions and their leaders. J. L. Block referred to "the monopoly power which enables a single union . . . to call a strike that brings to a halt all or the preponderance of production." Charles E. Wilson followed a typical theme in expressing an opinion that combined hostility toward unions with the new realization that unions were here to stay. "Unions can have a sound and constructive place in American economic life," said Wilson. "On the other hand, the majority recognize that they must be protected against predatory abuse of monopoly power under the guise of unionism."[26]

FEAR OF UNION POLITICAL POWER

Business leaders certainly feared union economic power, but their fears went much further than this. They feared the political and social power of the unions as well. And some feared that the unions would demolish the whole fabric of the American culture. During the railroad strike in May 1946, the president of the Chamber of Commerce, William K. Jackson, suggested that "new consideration be given to compulsory arbitration" because "today the Lewises, the Murrays, and the Petrillos, and their kind are infinitely more powerful as monopolists, than the capitalists and promoters of yesteryear." Twelve years later, in hearings on the economic situation, a utility executive, R. G. Rincliffe of Philadelphia Electric Company said almost the same thing: "The power of the unions is now far beyond that of any corporation." In the same hearings, George Romney, then of the American Motors Corp., quoted "somebody" as having said:

Today the greatest concentration of political and economic power in the United States of America are not found in the overregulated, overcriticized, overinvestigated, overtaxed business corporations and certainly not in their hag-ridden, brow-beaten, publicity-fearful managers.

The greatest concentration of political and economic power are
found in the underregulated, undercritized, underinvestigated, tax-
exempt and specially privileged labor organizations and in their aggressive publicity seeking and far too often lawless managers.

Romney then went on to say, "Why, the railroad trust and Standard
Oil and the Bank of the United States, and things of that type, were
picayune compared to the concentrations of power today in unions
and some corporate enterprises."[27]

Long before Romney's statement, it had become possible for a
man as thoughtful and as lacking in impetuosity as John M. Hancock,
partner in Lehman Brothers, to say: "For some time it has seemed
obvious that the top union group in Washington has had the one
major objective of increasing greatly the union movement's power and
not just *economic* power . . . but *national level political* power."[28]

Apparently, what business leaders really feared was that unions
would achieve political power and exercise that power to turn the
country sharply in the direction of collectivism. And what was more,
many business leaders thought that nothing could be done to prevent this. In 1959, Henry Ford characterised the merger of the AFL
and CIO that had taken place in 1955 as "the most aggressive ascend-
ant force in politics . . . a bulwark of an extreme left wing economic
viewpoint." Ralph Cordiner, viewing the American scene in despair
and calling the AFL-CIO the most aggressive and successful force in
politics, thought the congressional election in 1958 would probably
give labor a clear majority to pass or repeal legislation at will and
nothing could be done about it. Of course, both views were wrong.
Labor union leaders are not collectively minded, for the first victims
of the liquidation that would inevitably come with the dawn of collective utopia would be the labor-union leaders. Similarly, the political
power of the labor-union leader has been demonstrated in election
after election to be not much stronger than a wall of gossamer. As
W. G. Caples, president of Inland Steel, once told his colleagues,
"Labor unions don't control votes. Studies have shown that inside the
shop the worker considers himself a worker, but outside he thinks of
himself as a member of the middle class. The pressure of social
groups . . . is what determines his vote."[29]

The picture of the union leader as a dictator unaffected or undaunted by what his members thought or felt was also considerably
exaggerated. Just how much was illustrated by Ernest Breech of the

Ford Motor Company. In the midst of union-management negotia-tions in 1958, Breech spoke out about labor union leaders in what he characterized as a very courageous if foolhardy way. He disposed of Walter Reuther, the head of the UAW, as a "union leader with monopolistic power who apparently feels he must always be out to get everything he possibly can." But Breech was astute enough to know that Reuther was not the master of all he surveyed; he too had a problem. "I don't think," said Breech, "most of us can appreciate the tremendous pressures upon a union leader seeking to maintain and increase his position of power. He must constantly defend him-self against the natural drives of ambitious and power-hungry rivals to supplant and surpass him. He must constantly try to achieve for his followers greater gains than his rivals." Breech warned his fellow businessmen not to think that they would do any differently. They too, in Reuther's position, would blame all their troubles and the country's troubles as well on the greed and gluttony of industry. They too would find a scapegoat in "administered prices." They too would act "without regard to economic consequences."[30]

WHAT TO DO ABOUT THE UNIONS

Businessmen had much to say about how to solve the problem of recalcitrant unions. Some, like Herman Steinkraus of Bridgeport Brass and the Chamber of Commerce, thought that the problem would go away in the course of simple economics. "Consumer de-mand," said Steinkraus, "will bring labor peace." Most of his peers were far less sanguine. They saw no possibility that appeasement would bring the labor-union lions to sup with the management lambs. During the recession of 1957, Milton C. Lightner, president of Singer Manufacturing and the NAM, impatiently exploded: "The American people can expect little or no cooperation from these leaders of organized labor [AFL-CIO] in solving two of the most urgent prob-lems—resuming economic progress without a renewal of wage-price inflation and curbing abuses of power by autocratic union leaders."[31]

Few businessmen proposed to meet what they considered a most unjust and uneconomic labor situation with force. At least, none openly espoused this tactic. As J. D. Zellerbach summed up what seemed to be typical business opinion, "the most stupid tactic in labor relations is a show of force." And as they shrank from this once popular method of meeting the threats of unionism, there seemed to remain only one other alternative. In the well-established American tradition of meeting crucial problems with the phrase, "there ought to be a law," business turned to Congress and the state legislatures to redress their grievances. As Lightner put it in an impassioned speech in 1958, "We have seen collective bargaining turned into a brutal farce. . . . The assumption that unions could do no wrong has bemused those charged with enforcing the law. . . . In virtually every walk of life, there is increasing concern and a rising demand to bring union monopoly power under control. . . . Industrial leadership must support that demand. This is not to 'bust' unions. . . ."[32]

The appeal to law followed two main routes: the amendment or repeal of the Wagner Act and the adoption of state right-to-work laws. The general philosophy followed closely the principles that had been advanced by the veteran anti-union warrior Tom Girdler in 1937: 1) employees should have the free right to bargain collectively without coercion from *any* source, 2) no employee should be forced to pay dues to a union, 3) a secret ballot before a strike, 4) the responsibility of a union in any controversy should be equal to the responsibility of the employer.

In 1946, as the country returned to the relative calm of a peacetime economy, businessmen argued among themselves over the relative merits of outright repeal or extensive revision of the Wagner Act. Ernest T. Weir denied that he had ever asked for repeal of the Wagner Act; he had, he insisted, favored nothing more than its modification. The Chamber of Commerce, after considerable wrangling, resolved in favor of revision rather than repeal. In the NAM, the same argument occurred with the majority supporting revision and "a powerful minority" holding out for repeal.

Well in the forefront of the debate that was going in business circles were such articulate leaders as Charles M. White of Republic, Charles E. Wilson and Alfred P. Sloan of General Motors, and William K. Jackson, the small businessman president of the Chamber of Commerce. As strikes and labor troubles became routine news items,* Jackson came out in favor of compulsory arbitration, revealing more

---

* Among others, the strike against the oil industry and the 113-day strike against GM in late 1945–46, the steel strike in January–February 1946, the seven-month strike against Allis Chalmers in 1945–46, the coal and railroad strikes in the spring of 1946, and a general strike in Stamford, Connecticut, in January 1946.

about the opinion of small business than about the opinion of the members of the Chamber of Commerce. Certainly, none of the articulate spokesmen for big business, in their extensive proposals for legislation, supported compulsory arbitration. Indeed, Charles M. White, successor to Tom Girdler, specifically rejected compulsory arbitration, because it "deprived management of its right and duty to exercise its own judgment." What White proposed was the amendment or replacement of the Wagner Act to "impose responsibilities and penalties upon labor for wrongful conduct, preserve the right of free speech, penalize both unions and strikers for felonies or mass picketing." He also proposed the amendment of the anti-trust laws "so that unions and their members would be subject to ordinary criminal law." White believed that "there should be an end to compulsory unionization and that an employee should be permitted to join or not join a union as he might see fit." Most of his fellow executives felt the same way. Wilson called for prohibiting industry-wide collective bargaining and compulsory unionism, outlawing strikes over jurisdictional disputes, and subjecting unions to "equality of the law." Shortly afterward, Sloan urged Congress to put a legal limitation on the right to strike. "Labor," Sloan held, "has become a monopoly and monopoly leads to dictatorship." He recommended subjecting unions to the Sherman Act, outlawing the closed shop, and amending the Wagner Act's "curtailment of free speech."[33]

For once, business had apparently struck a responsive chord with the public. The Republicans made considerable inroads on the Democratic majority and eventually took over control of Congress in the elections of 1946. Meanwhile, however, Congress and even President Truman, sensitive to public pressure, had initiated measures to reduce labor-union power or to check the wave of strikes. In late May, the government seized the country's struck railroads and the President introduced a bill which among other things would have given the government the power to draft striking workers and send them back to work under the jurisdiction of the armed forces. Meanwhile Representative Case of South Dakota had introduced an anti-strike bill which was designed "to make" both labor and management "responsible." It would have made unions as well as management liable for breaches of contract. It would also have outlawed secondary boycotts, unionization of foremen, and employer contributions to union-administered welfare funds, and would have provided for fact-finding boards in disputes involving public utilities. Industry was enthusiastically in favor of the bill, but President Truman vetoed it, and Congress was not able to pass it over his veto.

The struggle did not end with the impasse over the Case bill, which industry supported, and the Truman bill, which industry opposed. In 1947, a Republican-controlled House passed the Taft-Hartley Act, which sought in the words of one of its authors to make labor as "responsible" in labor-management relations as the Wagner Act had made capital "responsible." Even though labor leaders condemned the new law as "slave legislation," it did not slow down unionization. Nor did it effectively curb business' twin *bêtes noires* in labor relations, union monopoly power and wage increases in excess of productivity gains.

Business leaders, chagrined because the Taft-Hartley Act had not removed their bugbears, suddenly lost what had been at best only a halfhearted faith in federal legislation. They abandoned their campaign in Congress. To be sure, here and there, some business leaders continued to urge Congress to extend the Sherman Act to cover labor unions. But these were exceptions to the general rule. Most businessmen who did anything at all about legislation to curb union power did it through the executive branch of the federal government and through so-called "right-to-work" laws on the state level.

As early as 1946, three states (Nebraska, South Dakota, and Arizona) had already passed constitutional amendments designed to guarantee the right to work regardless of membership or non-membership in a labor union. But with the disenchantment that came after Taft-Hartley failed to fulfill business hopes, the right-to-work campaign moved into high gear. Probably its most articulate and persistent advocates were the officials of the Sante Fe Railway led by its dynamic chief executive Fred Gurley. Much more *sotto voce,* Donald Richberg, onetime New Dealer and disillusioned railway labor lawyer, also carried on a patient campaign. The letters in his papers from Walter Geist, president of Allis-Chalmers and Cecil B. De Mille, the movie producer, seem to indicate a cautious approval of right to work. De Mille was enthusiastic, but the others, while agreeing in principle, thought it would be "sounder to adopt the position enunciated in the Taft-Hartley Law." One business leader, Gerard Swope, scolded Richberg for his efforts. "I am afraid," wrote Swope, "you are losing some of your youth and vigor and your radical ideas —which I am still trying to hold on to."

But both Richberg and Swope were out of harmony with the general tenor of business opinion. Most businessmen, on the other hand, had come to accept the reality of unions. They weren't very happy about their feelings, for they certainly did not like unions, but they had resigned themselves to the fact that unions were here to stay, and there was nothing they could do but grin and bear it.

11. BUSINESS OPINION IN RETROSPECT

One of the least equivocal opinions that businessmen hold about themselves is that they are entirely different from the businessmen of yesterday in the way they conduct business and in the way they think about economic issues. This is nothing new. In every era, as the young succeed the old, they do so with the conviction that they are living in a time of mammoth change. Businessmen are no different. Each new generation believes it is living in the midst of a revolution in behavior and in thinking.

Undoubtedly, business behavior today is different from what it was in the 1920s, for no world stands still. Certainly, today's entrepreneur looks, thinks, and acts differently from the way the entrepreneur of the 1920s thought and acted. But the much-publicized revolution in business opinion that is supposed to have taken place in the last twenty years is, like the equally publicized revolution in sex, greatly exaggerated. According to the sociologists who are assumed to know about such things, the post-World War II *"revolution"* in the sex habits of the American male and female is a godchild of someone's romantic imagination. If ever a *revolution* occurred in this important aspect of life, it occurred in the 1920s or even before then in the Progressive Era. The same is true of the highly heralded change in business thinking.

In 1945, a respected financial columnist wrote: "A fundamental change has come over the American businessman since 1929. Elmer Gantry has gone and so has the stuffed shirt with the dollar sign and Colonel Blimp sitting in the club window. The typical businessman and industrialist whom one meets when traveling around the country today is a keen specialist in management, production, engineering, or one or the other technical professions. With some exceptions, of course, he is not out to smash the unions, to break down wage scales.

He has accepted the idea that unions are here to stay and so is a good part of the New Deal. In fact, although he would not admit it publicly, in many cases he has accepted a good part of the New Deal philosophy. He wants sustained high levels of production and employment at good productive wages, in an atmosphere of industrial peace at home and world peace abroad because he figures that means a beneficial circle instead of the vicious circles of the past. He thinks it is better business to provide jobs and wages that will sustain buying power of consumers at reasonable prices to himself than to enforce extortionate prices and profits at the risk of driving the customers of all industry out of their jobs and out of the market."

Much of this is true and much is untrue. The businessman has changed his views on labor unions and what determines wages. His opinions about his objectives and about government fiscal policy and the causes of business cycles are also different from what they were forty years ago. But he has never been a Colonel Blimp, and the truth is that yesterday's business leader was the specialist; today's is more the generalist. Similarly, the power to "enforce extortionate prices," always much exaggerated, has existed more in the printed page than in the realities of economic life. What is, however, of greater importance is that most of the truth in the above quote was true of businessmen before 1945. All businessmen, except those who were irrational, wanted prosperity, peace, and high levels of production, rather than depression, war, and low levels of production. It isn't that business philosophy has undergone a radical change, but that the old wine is more attractive in new bottles and more palatable with the change of temperature at a time when tastes in general have changed.

Once again, it should be emphasized that at no time has there been a complete body of opinion to which all businessmen subscribed. The variety of differences in occupation, in function, in mental capacity, in personality, and in social background among businessmen made for massive differences in opinions on economic issues as well as on the general philosophy of life, differences incidentally that were greater among business leaders than among most other groups, including farmers, workers, doctors, teachers, and bookmakers. Only among the intellectuals could one find a set of more diversified opinions.

There are half a dozen ways of cataloguing business leaders. They may be divided according to age, education, profession, type of business, and the ownership stake they hold in the firms they manage.

The professions in which executives spent most of their careers had much to do with their economic philosophy and economic opinions. Lawyers thought differently about economic issues than did the company heads who came up through the marketing department, finance, or general administration.

Sharp differences also existed between the professional managers and the businessmen who owned their own firms. Hired executives had to subordinate themselves to the organization. They had to be more tactful and more literate. They were generalists more often than they were specialists, and they tended to be people manipulators rather than thing manipulators. The owner-manager could at the expense of public relations be an intellectual barbarian with poor human relations, because he was directly responsible only to himself.

Just as there were differences between professional managers and owners, so the opinions of bankers and financiers were significantly different from those of their counterparts in manufacturing and retailing, a fact that was instinctively known to industrialists and those in trade. The publicly expressed opinions of financiers were much more influenced by professional economists than were the opinions of other businessmen. In the 1920s, for example, orthodox Wall Street opinion bore the distinctive stamp of classical economic theorists. Bankers like Albert H. Wiggin, Winthrop Aldrich, Charles Mitchell, and George Davison were stanch advocates of sound money, free trade, laissez-faire, and the escalator approach to the business cycle with its emphasis on the evils of unsustainable growth. Bankers always feared the threat of inflation whether the economy was in the trough of a depression or at the peak of an "unsustainable boom." Industrialists, on the other hand, were never very happy about sound money and they preferred to compromise with laissez-faire.

Some industries and some firms perpetuated their own distinctive type of leadership and their own body of opinion. Corporations which, it has been said, had neither a body to be kicked or a soul to be damned nevertheless took on a spirit of their own that persisted despite the death or resignation of individual executives. United States Steel is a classic example. From Gary on, chairmen tended to be lawyers with an interest in public relations and decided, if archaic, opinions about economic problems.

Businessmen in industries whose nature led them to believe that the demand for their product was inelastic—textile manufacturers, retailers, steel men, and so forth—were obsessed by the specter of overproduction. On the contrary, producers who were not overly concerned with price elasticity, such as automobile and machine tool makers, emphasized productivity and rejected policies that stemmed from overproduction theories.

Business leaders could also be divided according to objective. Henry Dennison once differentiated among four different types. First there was the "manorial," who believed that the purpose of a business organization was to gratify the will of those in control. Among these individuals, non-economic motives loomed large. Dennison called the second type the "classical economic theory group" who believed the goal was to make the most money. Third came the school that wanted to maximize production, and last were those who believed that business organizations existed for the purpose of providing not only a satisfactory living but a satisfactory life for the men and women involved.

Most business leaders were anonymous and inarticulate. But even here there were different ways of classification. There were highly articulate "conservatives" who expressed far-out opinions in an individualistic, paternalistic, father-knows-best manner.* There were the "liberal" mavericks who early began to talk about social responsibility, who had an empathy for labor and labor unions, and who approved with varying degrees of enthusiasm government intervention through "planning" and deficit financing.† There were also the low-key thoughtful entrepreneurs among both liberals and conservatives who emphasized a reasoned approach to economic issues and were more restrained than sensational in their conservatism or liberalism.‡

With all these differences and more in outlook and approach, it was impossible to discern a concise ideology. Nevertheless, it is possible to generalize about modal opinions and how they changed over time. There has always been a body of opinion in which the majority of businessmen believed. Among businessmen, there was little question but that the American capitalistic system produced maximum freedom and maximum individual welfare. Nor was there much doubt that businessmen were the chief contributors to the maintenance of the system. As most businessmen viewed economic growth, profits were the source of capital, and capital was the most essential ingredient in the recipe for economic growth. Yet businessmen, it was often

---

* As, for example, Ernest T. Weir and Edward V. Rickenbacker.
† Particularly, E. A. Filene.
‡ Alfred P. Sloan and Henry S. Dennison, for example.

said, were just as much, if not more, interested in service as in profit.

Businessmen were in much less agreement in the way they evaluated the other participants in economic and social life, that is, the intellectuals, the government, labor unions, and farm spokesmen. Businessmen, with some exceptions to be sure, did not understand intellectuals. They regarded them with uneasy suspicion, sometimes tinged with awe and sometimes tinged with hostility.

No such ambivalence characterized business attitudes toward government. So-called "liberal" opinion ranged from E. A. Filene's enthusiasm for governmental intervention to the sympathetic approval of Owen D. Young. But liberal opinion was always the minority opinion. Most businessmen resisted government intervention with word and deed. For them, the best politicians were the statesmen who acknowledged the prestige of business and put no unreasonable obstacles in the way of business decision making. To them, Harding, Coolidge, and Eisenhower were the best Presidents in post-1920 America; Roosevelt, Truman, Kennedy, and Johnson were the worst, in that order.

There was also something close to a consensus in the opinion about labor unions. Except for a few mavericks, businessmen believed, with varying degrees of vehemence, that labor unions were anti-democratic monopolistic institutions with vast powers over costs and prices.

Business opinion ebbed and flowed around this basic core, reflecting the ups and downs, the booms and busts in economic activity and the changes that occurred in the education and advice that businessmen received.

Business opinion in the 1920s was to a significant degree the victim of the prosperity of the era and the exalted stature and prestige of the businessman. Carried away by the latter into delusions of grandeur, business leaders paid lip service at least to a set of opinions that were far removed from the beliefs and objectives that had always been considered traditional to the business way of life. It became fashionable to de-emphasize the profit motive and to make much of the role of stewardship and the objective of service. Businessmen were urged to prefer cooperation to competition, and to follow the widely discussed high-wage doctrine. What was retained from the heritage of the past was a weakened belief that prosperity would eventually give way to depression and a conviction that government's role in the economy was always negative never positive.

The confidence that businessmen felt in themselves and in the future evaporated in the depression. The prevalent attitude was one of frustration, helplessness, and bewilderment. The executives who had seemed so competent and world-conquering a few years before abandoned most of their prior opinions as they sought to find a way out of the sea of economic confusion into which the depression had thrown them. For the moment, business forgot its involvement with service as it struggled to maintain a few dollars of profits. In labor relations, businessmen forsook the high-wage doctrine and settled down to do battle with the unions. In businessmen's eyes the market place had also changed its form; it had lost its attractiveness and turned into a place of gloom. Competition, which in prosperity had seemed so barbaric and so tiresome, now appeared to be an albatross that hampered businessmen's efforts to remain solvent. Most of the business leaders, conservatives and liberals, vied with each other in thinking up plans for eliminating the brutal effects of competition. All the steel leaders and most of the oil producers bemoaned the overproduction caused by competition. Textile manufacturers and retailers talked to each other about unfair competition. The Chamber of Commerce and other business organizations, spurred on by liberals Gerard Swope and E. A. Filene, led a movement to relax the anti-trust laws in order to permit businessmen to cooperate about prices and production. Only the largest automobile manufacturers, the big bankers, and a few non-conformist retailers objected to the current trend in the direction of a planned society in a mature economy. For their part the bankers continued to warn against easy money, government spending, and inflation.

As the depression deepened, many lost faith in democracy and yearned for a leader "who could bring order out of chaos." They welcomed Roosevelt in his first hundred days, but they quickly lost their allegiance as he failed to balance the budget, an objective which at least 90 per cent of businessmen considered a *sine qua non* for economic recovery. Toward the end of the depression, business and government became involved in a feckless struggle over which group was to control the seats of power. Both the Administration and the businessmen insisted that they were arguing over the way to economic recovery, but in reality the contest was over matters of principle that had little to do with self-interest. Most of the New Dealers had an opportunity to vocalize their antagonism toward business, and they made the most of it by punishing business for its past, present, and future sins. For their part, businessmen spent their time in worrying over the future of the "American Way of Life" and the "Free Enterprise System," and in expressing their justifiable indignation with the uncertainties created by bureaucracy.

The wrestling with the Roosevelt administration came to an end at the outbreak of World War II, for it was then that the New Deal died and was quietly buried. With the end of the war, there emerged a new group of businessmen and a more realistic business opinion. Gary, Filene, Kahn, Wiggin, Durant, Mitchell, and Schwab died or were hardly heard from after the late 1920s or the early years of the New Deal. In the middle period, Sloan, the Du Ponts, Brown, Weir, Hook, Girdler, and Ford were among the more articulate. But these too are gone and the stage now belongs to Ford the Second, David Rockefeller, Cook, Thornton, Heineman, Townsend, etc.

There is no question that the present generation of businessmen is more sophisticated than its parents were. It is a natural law of life that each new generation must be taller and stronger and capable of greater accomplishment. It would be astonishing, perhaps even astounding, if Junior weren't smarter than Dad, if for no other reason than that Junior stands on the shoulders of the past. He began in the middle of the paragraph that his parents started to write.

How did the differences between the generations affect business opinion? How is today different from fifty years ago? For one thing, there is less disparity of opinion than there was in the 1920s and especially during the 1930s. The spectrum from the most "conservative" to the most "liberal" is much narrower than it was then. There are successors to Swope and Sloan, but there are no counterparts to Filene and Girdler.

The strategy and tactics, the structure and organization of business have changed greatly, but not so much the objectives. It is no longer fashionable to downgrade the profit motive, but on the other hand, there is no headlong flight from the concept of service. Since World War II, most businessmen—bankers, manufacturers, retailers, and those in transportation—have been engaged in seeking an equilibrium between profits and an elusive, undefinable something known as social responsibility. Only a minority—those who were the products of the 1920s—persist in taking a wary view of the profit motive. An even smaller minority regard the objective of social responsibility as a pious ambiguity. This is not to say, however, that business inevitably and inexorably follows its own self-interest measured in dollars and cents. Businessmen have probably never done so, and there were many instances in the fifty years after 1920 when they did not do so. One clear lesson emerged from the often petty quarrel between the New Deal and business. That was that most businessmen would strenuously resist behavior and action that threatened to jeopardize their freedom, even though such behavior might be conducive to economic growth and higher profits. "On questions of principle," Thurman Arnold once wrote, "great masses of people will always take sides. Which side they take depends not on self-interest, but on the chance of association of temperament which makes them emotionally responsible to one set of symbols or another."

The most significant difference between yesterday's and today's views lies in the way that businessmen look at government and the unions. Most business leaders know that both have come to stay. A few find nothing wrong in this, but most regret it intensely, reconciling themselves to the bitter taste of the inevitable. The relationship between business and the labor unions is one of tepid coexistence. To the modal businessman, labor unionism is an adult form of juvenile delinquency, much to be regretted, but, nevertheless, a part of reality. The paternalism toward labor that was so characteristic of the 1920s is gone and so is the bitterly emotional hostility of the later period. In the new accommodation with the unions, business leaders make much of productivity which was hardly mentioned a generation ago.

Relations between business and government are much better than the interplay with the unions. In contrast to twenty years ago a number of business leaders are willing to agree that government can exert a positive and beneficial influence on economic life. Many have abandoned their faith in annually balanced federal budgets and are not at all terrified by the prospect of frequent federal deficits. To be sure, they are still in the minority of business opinion, but they are articulate enough to convince observers that they actually represent the majority.

Critics of business are the first to agree that some major changes have occurred in the business system, but they think that these changes have redounded to society's disadvantage rather than to its advantage. They charge that businessmen are no longer producers, but sellers of goods that no one really wants. In one of the popular phrases of the day, they have switched from being manipulators of things to being manipulators of people. For their part, businessmen acknowledge that marketing and human relations have become more important than production and finance. The challenge a generation ago, it is said, was mastery over the physical environment; in the modern era, the challenge is mastery over men. Thus, they are not in essential disagreement with this part of the critics' brief, but they couch their agreement in a way that suggests approbation rather than disapproval.

Critics also charge that the separation of ownership from control that characterizes the collective nature of modern business has made management a self-perpetuating oligarchy with responsibility to no one and with powers that are not legitimate. Most businessmen do not understand the indictment and those who do understand it are equally mystified. They insist that professional management, with or without a large ownership interest, has become a part of modern corporate life like big business and small stockholders. They choose to explain their legitimacy by arguing that professional management acts just as the owner-entrepreneur did, that is, in the best interests of the owners. The great difference is that now the owners are a broad and diverse group, instead of a small and homogeneous one.

Regardless of what the critics say, the mid-century executive has far more hostages to fortune than his predecessors dreamed of having. He is responsible not only to himself, but to government, labor, the consumer, and sometimes even to the stockholders. He, therefore, has to be more sophisticated and, as the modern word would have it, more knowledgeable than the executive at the beginning of the century. His level of executive education is much higher and he depends much more on his advisers and his ancillaries to give him their thoughts which he has to weigh carefully because the necessity of "keeping in touch with the field" is much more intense.*

Whatever the extent of the change in business opinion, it was less than that of other groups. Labor union leaders, whether they liked it or not, had to change. Following a conservative line that got them nowhere, they had no power or influence in the 1920s. Their strategy became more adventuresome during the depression. But once they had achieved a more secure place in the sun, they again became steadfast in holding to their opinions. Farmers, having learned that most people found unpalatable the Bryanesque prescription for prosperity through governmental manipulation of the currency and coinage, de-emphasized inflation and easy money and adopted a new tactic of

* One management service estimates that an executive in 1900 could keep informed by reading forty-five minutes a day, but that it took two hours in 1920, three in 1940, and four in 1960.

having the government restrict production. Academic economic theorists were the most flexible of all, concocting a "new economics" every ten or twenty years. In forty years they swung from neo-classical equilibrium theory to disillusion, to Keynesianism, and then took off with equal self-confidence in hot pursuit of a neo-Keynesian general equilibrium model.

Businessmen experienced their greatest change in coming to accept the reality of labor unionism and the mixed economy. This was hardly a revolution, but the fact that business opinion did not change as much as that of other groups is no proof that it was wrong. Nor for that matter is it any proof that it was right. In retrospect, however, there is not much value in arguing about the right or wrong, the truth or falsity of any opinion. Such matters are much too subjective. It is more rewarding to consider how much influence business opinion had and how it compared with the opinions of other blocs in the economic world.

Nonsense and naïveté are not the monopoly of any one group. Businessmen were certainly not innocent of expressing their share of absurdities. But it is questionable whether they were any more guilty than the general mix of society. Some of the more popular themes among businessmen in the 1920s—the de-emphasized profit motive, the high-wage doctrine, and the notion of eternal, uninterrupted economic prosperity—were ingenuous and unreal. But they were no more so than the opinions that prevailed among statesmen and academic economists. It was a popular myth that with the newly formed Federal Reserve System we had found the key to perpetual prosperity. One and all apparently approved the denigration of the profit motive and the sanctification of "service," although no one was sure what the word meant.

During the depression and the struggle with the New Deal, business opinion became more and more sprinkled with platitudes. The "tax burden" was always "confiscatory"; government spending was "all right if necessary"; the incompatible twins "growth and stability" were never separated. But banality was a universal malady during the depression. Calvin Coolidge's "The future may be better or worse," was only topped when Bernarr MacFadden told the city unemployed to go to the country. People who should have known better uttered nonsense about overproduction and "poverty amid plenty" when the national income was less than $50 billion. It was the thirties not the twenties that was the era of wonderful nonsense when Hoover was castigated as a profligate, and Roosevelt promised to balance the budget by reducing government spending.

Businessmen had a less clear view of their objectives than other groups. Labor union leaders wanted, in the words of Samuel Gompers, "more and more, now and now." Farmers wanted their "fair share of the national income." Politicians wanted to get elected. Academic economists were ostensibly interested in finding out how man used his scarce resources for maximum want satisfaction. But businessmen were not sure whether their objective was to maximize profits, or to act as stewards, or to be socially responsible, or to hold the organization together. Other members of society were not nearly so mixed up about business objectives. They knew, whether it was true or not, that businessmen were out to make as much money as possible, or as the economist expresses it, to maximize profits.

The businessmen's confusion about their objectives was one reason why business opinion had indifferent influence over society. Most businessmen believed firmly in the bourgeois values of industry, thrift, profit making, economic freedom, the superiority of the market place, and law and order. But they were at times just as much confused about the exact meaning of these virtues as they were about their objectives.

During the prosperity years of the 1920s, there is no doubt that most Americans shared business' respect for the middle-class values. Whether this was because of business or because of the appeal of the middle-class values is another question. But in any event, the depression put the faith to a severe test. It was no longer so plain that industry and thrift paid off. Unemployment made a mockery of economic freedom, and it seemed to more than a handful of Americans that the automatic market place had stripped its gears. Even among businessmen, there was much questioning and backsliding. Old words lost their meaning as new philosophies came to the fore. Conservatism, which had meant a distrust of change, a belief that when it was not necessary to change, it was necessary not to change, came to mean the philosophy in which businessmen and business spokesmen were assumed to believe. Liberalism, which had meant laissez-faire and individualism, came to mean just the opposite. Liberals were now defined to include those who favored more government intervention, those who empathized with labor and warmly supported labor unions, and those who spoke more about the cost of living and overproduction than about scarce resources and productivity.

Once the reality of the depression was accepted, conservatism fell out of fashion and liberalism with its emphasis on sociology rather than economics took its place. A philosophy that appealed to the young usurped the philosophy that still appealed to most of their elders. In the process, business lost most of the influence it had once possessed, and its position of power was assumed by government.

In recent years, there has been some return to the older faith. It is no longer so self-evident that there is something inherently "good" about liberalism and something inherently "bad" about conservatism. Judgments made on the basis of such criteria seem in retrospect to have been just as often wrong as they were right. Time has not corroded the opinions of such liberal businessmen as Dennison and Flanders, but the opinions of Swope, Baruch, and Filene do not read as well as they once did. On the other hand, the conservative views of Sloan and Weir no longer seem so wrong and so horrible as they were once regarded. More people in positions of authority talk about the sickness of government* and the tyranny of labor unions and seek business' help to meet the crises of the day. Among academic economists, there has been a return to the belief that the market determines everything. Ironically enough, one of the effects of this has been to eliminate the entrepreneur altogether, so that he is treated as nothing more than a robot.

The much-discussed "turn to the right" is symptomatic of the renaissance of middle-class ideals. But a full turn to the right does not seem to be in the cards in the near future. The foundations of the conservative structure were too shaken by the trauma of the depression. Business as the chief repository of the old middle-class values, is, therefore, in an ambivalent position. It has regained some of its lost prestige, but judged by the prevalent trends in politics, the course of legislation, the success of the labor unions, and the general indifference to "free enterprise" (whatever that phrase may mean), the majority of business opinion has little influence over general opinion or over the general course of events. Moreover, businessmen have not made an unqualified return to the faith themselves and are therefore hampered in increasing their prestige, for as the late Professor Schumpeter was at great pains to point out, the prestige of American

---

* See the brilliant article by Peter Drucker, "The Sickness of Government," in *The Public Interest*, Winter, 1969.

capitalism and the American businessman varies directly with the prestige of middle-class values.

Commentators and critics of business have contended that American business opinion (invariably referred to as an ideology and creed) has not and does not conform to the "Democratic Tradition." One critic has expressed this stratospherically abstract proposition by asking whether the business ideology fulfills its function, and whether it is resourceful and flexible enough and morally inspiring enough to bring capitalism through this age of strain. His answer, as one could expect, is no. But just what is meant by the "Democratic Tradition" and by "morally inspiring" remains as mysterious as the definition of "social responsibility." It should not be the purpose of business to reform society. Social responsibility and the democratic tradition, assuming they have a definition, are the concern of all citizens as individual citizens. The objective of the businessman as a businessman should be to run a business as efficiently as possible, in short to make a profit. When they depart from that objective, businessmen get into trouble as they got into trouble in the 1920s and again in the 1930s. Businessmen are human, not superhuman, but much of the criticism leveled at them is based on a superhuman premise. To repeat what Edgar Queeny said in his defense of his colleagues:

> The majority of the friends I had made in the business world were taking what I thought was an unjustified beating. Some were rich, but they were not wicked. Most were selfish, but so were many workers of my acquaintance. . . . My businessmen friends were not saints, nor were they ogres feeding upon unfortunate fellow-beings, as some high priests of the social sciences were intimating. . . . Business did not have clean hands; but the critics and detractors were not fair nor honest toward it, either.

APPENDICES

Business Leaders Cited in Readers' Guide, 1925–1961

	1925				1935				1948				1961			
	1	2	3	4	1	2	3	4	1	2	3	4	1	2	3	4
Manufacturing	130	42	274	67	169	33	140	42	139	60	131	19	197	72	204	39
Transportation	21	10	23	9	25	10	15	4	35	17	70	2	36	19	63	20
Banking	43	11	31	6	35	7	34	6	40	6	18	2	53	14	24	7
Trade	19	8	16	8	24	6	7	0	20	8	22	0	26	10	15	5
Utilities & Insurance								5								
Utilities	20	6	25	6	32	12	33		13	0	0	0	17	6	14	5
Insurance									13	5	8	2	14	4	5	0
Total	233	77	369	96	285	68	229	57	260	96	249	25	343	125	325	76

(1) Total number of business leaders in the sample.
(2) Number of the sampled business leaders cited in *Readers' Guide.*
(3) Number of times business leaders cited.
(4) Number of articles, speeches, etc., *by* business leaders.

APPENDIX B

Men holding five or more directorships among 250
great corporations in 1935

DAVISON, G. W., Greenwich, Conn., chairman, Central Hanover Bank & Trust Co.

AVERY, S. L., Chicago, chairman, Montgomery, Ward & Co.

MELLON, R. K., Pittsburgh, president, Mellon National Bank.

WIGGIN, A. H., New York City, formerly chairman, Chase Bank.

BAKER, G. F., New York City, chairman, First National Bank (N.Y.).

ECKER, F. H., New York City, president, Metropolitan Life Ins. Co.

MC LENNAN, D. R., Lake Forest, Ill., Continental Illinois National Bank & Trust Co.

PERKINS, T. N., Westwood, Mass., member executive committee, Stone & Webster, Inc.

REYNOLDS, J. E., New York City, president, First National Bank (N.Y.).

ADAMS, C. F., Boston, capitalist.

LOOMIS, E. E., New York City, president, Lehigh Valley R. R. Co.

POTTER, W. C., New York City, chairman, Guaranty Trust Co.

TAYLOR, M. C., New York City, chairman, U. S. Steel Corporation.

WEINBERG, S. J., Scarsdale, N.Y., Goldman, Sachs & Co.

WOOLEY, C. M., Greenwich, Conn., chairman, American Radiator & Standard Sanitary Co.

BUCKNER, M. N., Fishers Island, N.Y., chairman, New York Trust Co.

CARLTON, NEWCOMB, New York City, chairman, Western Union Telegraph Co.

COUNTY, A. J., St. Davids, Pa., Chemical Bank & Trust Co.

CRAWFORD, D. A., Golf, Ill., president, Pullman, Inc.

GRAY, W. S., JR., Greenwich, Conn., president, Central Hanover Bank & Trust Co.

HAYDEN, CHARLES, New York City, Hayden, Stone & Co.

HERRICK, R. F., Boston, capitalist.

LAMONT, T. W., New York City, J. P. Morgan Co., Drexel & Co.

MC INNERNY, T. H., New York City, president, National Dairy Products Corporation.

PROSSER, SEWARD, Englewood, N.J., chairman, Bankers Trust Co.

ROBINSON, H. M., Pasadena, Calif., Security-First National Bank, vice-chairman executive committee.

SIMPSON, JAMES, Chicago, chairman, Commonwealth Edison Co.

SPRAGUE, A. A., Chicago, Chicago & North Western Rwy. Co., member finance committee and director.

STOCKTON, PHILLIP, Boston, president, First National Bank (Boston).

SUNNY, B. E., Chicago, chairman, Chicago Great Western Railroad Co.

VANDERBILT, CORNELIUS, New York City, capitalist.

WADSWORTH, ELIOT, Boston, capitalist.

WARRINER, S. D., Philadelphia, president, Lehigh Coal & Navigation Co.

WING, D. G., Brookline, Mass., chairman, First National Bank (Boston).

APPENDIX C

Forbes's Fifty Men Making America, 1917

Archbold, John D.

Armour, J. Ogden

Baker, George F.

Bedford, A. C.

Bell, Alexander Graham

Carnegie, Andrew

Davison, H. P.

Dollar, Robert

Douglas, W. L.

Duke, James B.

DuPont, T. Coleman

Eastman, George

Edison, Thomas A.

Farrell, James A.

Ford, Henry

Forgan, James B.

Frick, Henry C.

Gary, Elbert H.

Gaston, William A.

Goethals, George W.

Guggenheim, Daniel

Hammond, John Hays

Heckscher, August

Hepburn, A. Barton

Insull, Samuel

Kahn, Otto H.

Keith, Minor C.

Kingsley, Darwin P.

McCormick, Cyrus H.

Morgan, J. P.

Nichols, Wm. H.

Patterson, John H.

Perkins, George W.

Reynolds, George M.

Rockefeller, John D.

Rosenwald, Julius

Ryan, John D.

Schiff, Jacob H.

Schwab, Charles M.

Shedd, John G.

Simmons, E. C.

Speyer, James

Stillman, James

Vail, Theodore N.

Vanderbilt, Cornelius

Vanderlip, Frank A.

Warburg, Paul M.

Willys, John N.

Wilson, Thomas E.

Woolworth, F. W.

APPENDIX D

Forbes's *Fifty Foremost Business Leaders of 1947*

Aldrich, Winthrop W.
Allyn, S. C.
Biggers, John D.
Brown, Lewis H.
Carpenter, W. S., Jr.
Clement, M. W.
Collyer, John L.
Dallas, C. Donald
Deupree, Richard R.
Douglas, Donald W.
Dow, Willard H.
Fairless, Benjamin F.
Firestone, H. S., Jr.
Ford, Henry, II
Francis, Clarence
Giannini, L. M.
Gifford, Walter S.
Gimbel, Bernard S.
Goldwyn, Samuel
Grace, Eugene G.
Hoffman, Paul G.
Holman, Eugene
Hook, Charles R.
Johnston, Eric A.
Jones, W. Alton

Kaiser, Henry J.
Keller, K. T.
Lincoln, James F.
Lincoln, Leroy A.
Luce, Henry R.
Luckman, Charles
Martin, Glenn L.
Martin, Thomas W.
McCormick, Fowler
Mellon, Richard K.
Merrill, Charles E.
Norris, Ernest E.
Queeny, Edgar M.
Rand, James H.
Rentscheler, Gordon S.
Rickenbacker, E. V.
Rockefeller, Nelson A.
Sarnoff, David
Schram, Emil
Watson, Thomas J.
Wilson, C. E. (GE)
Wilson, C. E. (GM)
Wood, Robert E.
Woodruff, Robert W.
Young, Robert R.

APPENDIX E

The "Twenty-Five Greatest Living Businessmen," as decided by the University of Michigan poll of 500 executives, 1967.

Robert S. McNamara
George Romney
James C. Penney
J. Paul Getty
Henry Ford II
Henry J. Kaiser
Roger M. Blough
David Sarnoff
Conrad N. Hilton
Howard Hughes
Ernest R. Breech
Thomas J. Watson, Jr.
Frederic G. Donner
Joseph Kennedy
Senator Charles H. Percy
Cyrus Eaton
William R. Hearst, Jr.
Crawford H. Greenewalt
Frederick R. Kappel
Lee A. Iacocca
Eli Lilly
Lynn A. Townsend
Clint Murchison
Juan A. Trippe
William P. Lear

APPENDIX F

The "Twenty-Five Greatest Businessmen" named in a poll of 500 business executives taken by David L. Lewis, associate professor of Business History, University of Michigan.

Henry Ford
Andrew Carnegie
Thomas A. Edison
John D. Rockefeller
Alfred P. Sloan, Jr.
Bernard M. Baruch
Alexander G. Bell
E. I. du Pont
Walter P. Chrysler
Harvey S. Firestone
George Eastman
Marshall Field
Walt Disney
J. Pierpont Morgan
Andrew W. Mellon
Thomas J. Watson, Sr.
Frank W. Woolworth
Cyrus H. McCormick
W. R. Hearst
Sebastian S. Kresge
Richard W. Sears
Charles Goodyear
George Westinghouse
Eli Whitney
Cornelius Vanderbilt

Source: *The MBA,* April 1968.

APPENDIX G

The "64 Rulers of America" named by James W. Gerard
in August 1930.

John D. Rockefeller, Jr.
Andrew W. Mellon
J. P. Morgan
George F. Baker
John D. Ryan
Walter C. Teagle
Henry Ford
Frederick K. Weyerhaeuser
Myron C. Taylor
James A. Farrell
Charles M. Schwab
Eugene G. Grace
H. M. Warner
Adolph Zukor
William H. Crocker
O. P. Van Sweringen
M. J. Van Sweringen
W. W. Atterbury
Arthur Curtiss James
Charles Hayden
Daniel C. Jackling
Arthur V. Davis
P. G. Gossler
R. C. Holmes
John J. Raskob
P. S. du Pont
Irenee du Pont
Lammot du Pont
H. F. du Pont

Eugene du Pont
A. Felix du Pont
Eugene E. du Pont
Edward J. Berwind
Daniel Willard
Sosthenes Behn
Walter S. Gifford
Owen D. Young
Gerard Swope
Thomas W. Lamont
Albert H. Wiggin
Charles E. Mitchell
Samuel Insull
Fred J. Fisher
Charles T. Fisher
Lawrence P. Fisher
William A. Fisher
Edward F. Fisher
Albert J. Fisher
Howard Fisher
Daniel Guggenheim
William Loeb
G. W. Hill
Adolph S. Ochs
W. R. Hearst
Robert R. McCormick
Joseph Medill Patterson
Julius Rosenwald
Cyrus H. K. Curtis

Roy W. Howard
Sidney Z. Mitchell
Walter Edwin Frew

Amadeo P. Giannini
William Green
Matthew Woll

APPENDIX H

A breakdown of the subjects treated in the speeches and articles of the executives of 130 of the country's largest firms, 1960–65.

1. General economic issues (international economic problems, prices, profits, competition, taxes, debt, etc.) 176
2. Management, marketing, technical (designed for the trade) 50
3. Reports to annual meetings, security analysts, and such 26
4. Talks on the function of free enterprise, etc. (sometimes referred to as Rotary-Chamber of Commerce pieces) 14
5. Expository, historical, scientific 14
6. Special pleading (for example, railroads for mergers or against featherbedding; steel for higher prices, etc.) 12
7. On the business image and business responsibility 11
8. Forecasts for the whole economy or for specific industries 10
9. Commencement addresses 10

NOTES

FOOTNOTES

Chapter 1, pp. 3–35

1. Frederic Lewis Allen, *Only Yesterday*, New York, 1931, p. 177.
2. Ernest E. Calkins, *Business the Civilizer*, Boston, 1928, p. 232; Strassburger, quoted in the *New York Times*, March 28, 1927.
3. In a brilliant book (*The Dream of Success*), Kenneth Lynn very plausibly argued that the novels of Dreiser, London, Lewis, and others demonstrated just what the businessman said they demonstrated.
4. For Penrose's view, see James E. Watson, *As I Knew Them*, Indianapolis, Ind., p. 294; *New York Times*, Oct. 23, 1924.
5. *Nation's Business*, May 1927; William Allen White, *Puritan in Babylon*, New York, 1938.
6. Robert R. R. Brooks, *As Steel Goes . . .* , New Haven, Conn., 1940, p. 199.
7. For example, Garet Garrett, Samuel Crowther, and Merle Thorpe. More recently, Henry Taylor, David Lawrence, etc.
8. See John H. Stalker, Jr., *The National Association of Manufacturers: A Study in Ideology*, an unpublished Ph.D. dissertation in the library of the University of Wisconsin; William H. Whyte, *Is Anybody Listening?*, New York, 1952, p. 5; Elliott Osborne, *Men at the Top*, New York, 1959; Alfred S. Cleveland, "NAM: Spokesman for Industry?," *Harvard Business Review*, May 1948.
9. *New York Times*, March 22, 1923.
10. Clarence W. Barron, *They Told Barron*, New York, 1930, p. 120; E. A. Filene, *The Way Out*, Garden City, N.Y., 1934, p. 271.
11. George Harrison Papers, Special Collections, Butler Library, Columbia University.
12. *Commercial and Financial Chronicle*, Aug. 12, 1922.
13. P. W. Litchfield, *Industrial Voyage*, Garden City, N.Y., 1954.
14. "What Little Business Really Thinks About Big Business," *Factory Management and Maintenance*, March 1950; *New York Times*, Oct. 22, 1965.
15. Paul M. Mazur, *American Prosperity*, New York, 1928, p. 267.
16. A. C. Bedford, "What is a Captain of Industry?," *Nation's Business*, Nov. 1925.
17. C. A. Heiss, *Accounting in the Administration of Large Business Enterprise*, Cambridge, Mass., 1943, p. 57.
18. W. T. Grant, "We Prosper in Spite of Ourselves," *Nation's Business*, April 1930.
19. Edward Angly, *Oh Yeah?*, New York, 1931, p. 34.

20. W. L. Clayton, "The Future of Capitalism," *Vital Speeches,* Oct. 1, 1936; Daniel Willard, "The Challenge to Capitalism," *Review of Reviews,* March 1931.

21. Fred I. Kent Papers, Manuscript Collection, Firestone Library, Princeton University.

22. Barron, *op. cit.,* pp. 13–14.

23. U. S. Congress, Senate, Committee on Education and Labor, *Report on Violations of Free Speech and Rights of Labor* (La Follette Report) 1942, No. 6, Part 4, p. 51; *New York Times,* May 1, 1935; July 8, 1934.

24. Elmer Davis, "Roosevelt: The Rich Man's Alibi," *Harper's Magazine,* Oct. 1939.

25. Bronson Batchelor, ed., *The New Outlook in Business,* New York, 1940, p. 96; Adolph C. Babenroth and Howard T. Viets, *Readings in Modern Business Literature,* New York, 1928, p. 256.

26. Strother H. Walker and Paul Sklar, *Business Finds Its Voice,* New York, 1938, p. 6; Testimony of Charles R. Hook of American Rolling Mills to the La Follette Committee, No. 6, Part 6, p. 44.

27. Edgar Queeny, *Spirit of Enterprise,* New York, 1943, pp. VI, IX.

28. Adolf A. Berle, Jr., *The Twentieth Century Capitalist Revolution,* New York, 1954.

29. La Follette Report, *op. cit.,* p. 176; *New York Times,* Dec. 8, 1937; *Nation's Business,* June 1939.

30. *New York Herald Tribune,* Jan. 8, 1938.

31. Lynn A. Townsend, "Just How Unfavorable Is the Climate for Business?," unpublished speech, May 3, 1963; Charles G. Mortimer, *The Purposeful Pursuit of Profits and Growth in Business,* New York, 1966; Crawford H. Greenewalt, *The Uncommon Man,* New York, 1959.

32. John Tebbel, *The Inheritors,* New York, 1962, p. 7; Edwin P. Hoyt, *The Guggenheims and the American Dream,* New York, 1967, p. 234.

33. *Wall Street Journal,* Sept. 9, 1968. A survey of intellectual and businessmen in *Business Week,* Jan. 27, 1962.

34. Unpublished speech by Logan T. Johnston, 1961; *Proceedings of the Golden Anniversary Convocation of the School of Commerce, Accounts and Finance,* New York University, 1950; Townsend, *op. cit.*

35. George Howard Allen, *Individual Initiative in Business,* Cambridge, Mass., 1950, pp. 68–69.

36. Townsend, *op. cit.; Commercial and Financial Chronicle,* Nov. 29, 1945.

37. James C. Worthy, *Big Business and Free Men,* New York, 1959, pp. 3–4.

38. Theodore Houser, quoted in Herrymon Maurer, *Great Enterprise,* New York, 1955, p. 195; Johnston, *op. cit.*

39. Theodore Houser, *Big Business and Human Values,* New York, 1957, pp. IX; See also P. W. Litchfield, *Autumn Leaves,* Cleveland, Ohio, 1945, p. 81; Robert Wood Johnson, *People Must Live and Work Together or Forfeit Freedom,* Garden City, N.Y., 1947, p. 20.

Chapter 2, pp. 36–58

1. *New York Times,* Dec. 23, 1926; June 13, 1928.

2. *Recent Economic Changes,* New York, 1929, p. 496.

3. Elbert H. Gary, "Change in Business Attitudes," *Current History*, March 1926.

4. Quoted in Charles A. Beard, ed., *Whither Mankind?*, New York, 1928, p. 95.

5. Otto H. Kahn, *Reflections of a Financier*, London, 1921, p. 68.

6. *Review of Reviews*, March 1929; "Modern Ideas of Big Business," *World's Work*, Oct. 1926.

7. David G. Loth, *Swope of GE*, New York, 1958; Litchfield, *Autumn Leaves*, p. 83; *Current History*, July 1965.

8. N. R. Danielian, *A.T. and T.*, New York, 1929, p. 404.

9. *New York Times*, March 3, 1923; B. C. Forbes, *Men Who Are Making America*, New York, 1926, p. X.

10. *Commercial and Financial Chronicle*, Nov. 12, 1927.

11. *New York Times*, Feb. 9, 1926; E. A. Filene, *The Way Out;* Gerard Swope, "What Big Business Owes the Public," *World's Work*, March 1927; Walter Gifford in *World's Work*, June 1926.

12. *Nation's Business*, July 1926.

13. *Fortune*, March 1928; Allen Nevins, *Study in Power: John D. Rockefeller*, New York, 1953, Vol. I, p. 19. Lever quoted in Roy Lewis and Rosemary Steward, *The Managers*, New York, 1961, p. 114; *New York Times*, Feb. 15, 1924.

14. Vanderlip Papers, Special Collections, Butler Library, Columbia University.

15. *Nation's Business*, Feb. 1930.

16. Quoted in Gilbert Seldes, *Years of the Locust*, Boston, 1932, p. 267.

17. Harvey O'Connor, *Steel-Dictator*, New York, 1935, p. 344.

18. Queeny, *Spirit of Enterprise*, p. 39.

19. E. A. Filene, *Successful Living in This Machine Age*, New York, 1932, p. 37.

20. John D. Rockefeller, Jr., *The Personal Relation in Industry*, New York, 1930, p. 31; Alfred P. Sloan, *Adventures of a White Collar Man*, Garden City, N.Y., p. 145; Batchelor, *The New Outlook in Business*.

21. *American* magazine, April 1945; Johnson, *People Must Live and Work Together*, p. 20.

22. Greenewalt, *The Uncommon Man*, p. 84.

23. Johnson, *op. cit.*, p. 11.

24. La Follette Committee, No. 6, Part 6, p. 146; Tom Girdler, *Boot Straps*, New York, 1943, pp. 129, ff.; Arthur Pound, *The Turning Wheel*, Garden City, N.Y., 1934, p. 415; *Fortune*, March 1938, *Commercial and Financial Chronicle*, Oct. 1927.

25. *New York Times*, July 3, 1966.

26. *Commercial and Financial Chronicle*, May 5, 1955.

27. Clarence Francis, "Answering Opportunity's Knocks," *Dun's Review*, April 1953.

28. *Commercial and Financial Chronicle*, July 18, 1957.

29. Frank W. Abrams, "Management's Responsibilities in a Complex World," *Harvard Business Review*, May 1951; Annual Conference of Harvard Business School Alumni Association, 1948.

30. *Commercial and Financial Chronicle*, April 22, 1948, Nov. 15, 1945; *New York Times*, July 3, 1966; *National Industrial Conference Board Record*, April 1964.

31. Robin Marris, *The Economic Theory of Managerial Capitalism*,

New York, 1964, p. 57; Robert Wood Johnson, *Robert Johnson Talks It Over,* privately printed, 1949, p. 167.

32. George R. Vila, "The Bridge of Understanding," unpublished speech, 1964.

33. Frederick R. Kappell, *Business Purpose and Performance,* New York, 1964, p. 11.

34. *New York Times,* July 3, 1966; John E. Swearingen, "The Executive Decision," *Vital Speeches,* June 1, 1964; J. P. Levis, "Remarks to the California Manufacturers' Association," unpublished speech, 1964; O. P. Thomas, "Economic Planning," unpublished speech, 1965.

35. Daniel J. Haughton, "Remarks to Theta Chi," unpublished talk, May 2, 1964; Ralph Cordiner in *Saturday Review,* Jan. 17, 1959; Ralph Cordiner, *New Frontiers for Professional Managers,* New York, 1956.

36. Worthy, *Big Business and Free Men,* p. 37.

37. Greenewalt, *The Uncommon Man,* p. 38.

38. *Business Week,* April 29, 1961; *New York Times,* July 3, 1966.

39. Houser, *Big Business and Human Values,* p. 28.

40. *The Conference Board Record,* Feb. 1965.

Chapter 3, pp. 61–74

1. *New York Times,* Jan. 2, 1921; *Commercial and Financial Chronicle,* Jan. 1921; Donaldson Brown, *Reminiscences of an Industrialist,* Port Deposit, Md., 1957, p. 41.

2. *New York Times,* April 29, Jan. 17, Oct. 5, 1921.

3. *Ibid.,* Jan. 9, 1921; Dec. 19, 1920.

4. *Ibid.,* Jan. 2, 1921; *New York Evening Post,* Dec. 30, 1920.

5. Otto H. Kahn, "The Road to Prosperity," *Forum,* Oct. 1921; *New York Evening Post,* Dec. 30, 1920; *Recent Economic Changes,* New York, 1929, p. 524; *Journal of Commerce,* Aug. 20, 1921; C. A. Gulick, *Labor Policies of the United States Steel Company,* New York, 1924, p. 58.

6. *New York Times,* Oct. 23, 1921; Kahn, *Reflections of a Financier,* pp. 321 ff.

7. *New York Times,* Oct. 4, 1921.

8. *Ibid.,* May 14, 20, 1922; Oct. 7, 1921; Dec. 18, 1920; *Commercial and Financial Chronicle,* Nov. 12, 1921; Feb. 10, 1922; Otto H. Kahn, "Prosperity and Taxation," *Forum,* June 1922; Barron, *They Told Barron,* p. 52; Kahn, *Reflections of a Financier,* pp. 42, 75.

9. *New York Times,* May 11, 1921.

10. *New York Times,* Jan. 2, 1921; *New York Evening Post,* Dec. 31, 1920.

11. *New York Times,* Aug. 20–23, 1921; *Commercial and Financial Chronicle,* July 16, 1921.

12. *New York Evening Post,* Dec. 31, 1920; *New York Times,* Oct. 2, Aug. 20, 1921.

13. *New York Times,* Jan. 13, 1921; *Commercial and Financial Chronicle,* Jan. 1922.

14. *New York Evening Post,* Dec. 30, 1922.

15. Alfred D. Chandler, *Strategy and Structure,* Cambridge, Mass., 1962; Alfred P. Sloan, *My Years with General Motors,* Garden City, N.Y., 1964.

Chapter 4, pp. 75–114

1.   In his fascinating study of the 1920s, Frederick Lewis Allen carefully qualified his judgment: "So cogent were the arguments that at last the great majority of even the sober financial leaders were won over in some degree." *Only Yesterday*, p. 310. In *The Great Boom and Panic*, Chicago, 1965, Robert T. Patterson reports that the views of John J. Raskob (at least a colonel in the ranks of the bulls) were "typical of the outlook of many business leaders." In his classic, *The Great Crash*, Boston, 1955, John Kenneth Galbraith wrote, "The bankers were also a source of encouragement to those who wished to believe in the permanence of the boom." See also Robert Sobel, *The Big Board*, New York, 1965, and Edwin P. Hoyt, *The Tempering Years*, New York, 1963.

2.   *New York Times*, Dec. 28, 1925.

3.   *New York Times*, Nov. 20, 1925; Jan. 12, 1928; *New York Evening Post*, Jan. 2, 1926; Seligman Papers, Special Collections, Butler Library, Columbia University.

4.   "Business Men and the Business Cycle," *Annals*, Vol. 109, Sept. 1923.

5.   *New York Times*, May 30, June 28, 1924.

6.   *New York Times*, Jan. 10, 11, 15, 18, Feb. 15, March 11, May 18, 1924; *Commercial and Financial Chronicle*, Jan. 5, 26, March 22, 1924; Andrew W. Mellon, *Taxation: The People's Business*, New York 1924, *passim*; *Wall Street Journal*, Nov. 21, 1923.

7.   *New York Times*, May 9, 1924; *Commercial and Financial Chronicle*, July 1924.

8.   *New York Times*, Feb. 21, April 6, 29, 1924; *Commercial and Financial Chronicle*, Aug. 1924.

9.   Fred I. Kent Papers; *Trade Winds*, quoted in W. T. Foster and Waddill Catchings, *Profits*, Boston 1925, p. 243.

10.   *New York Evening Post*, Dec. 30, 1923.

11.   David F. Jordan, *Managing Personal Finances*, New York, 1945, p. 294; *Commercial and Financial Chronicle*, Sept. 8, 1923; *New York Times*, Jan. 1, Aug. 9, June 20, 1924.

12.   *New York Times*, Jan. 1, 1925; Jan. 1, 1926.

13.   E. H. Gary, "The Business Situation," *Saturday Evening Post*, Feb. 6, 1926; *New York Times*, Sept. 26, Sept. 23, Feb. 26, 1926.

14.   *New York Times*, Oct. 25, Nov. 6, 1924; Jan. 1, 1925; Jan. 1, 1926; Thomas N. McCarter, *One Phase of a Jerseyman's Activities*, Garden City, N.Y., 1933, p. 395; *New York Evening Post*, Jan. 2, 1925; *Saturday Evening Post*, Feb. 6, 1926.

15.   R. D. Grant, "What Governs the Ups and Downs of Business," *System*, Jan. 1925; E. H. Gary, "Business Cycles Versus Common Sense," *Saturday Evening Post*, Dec. 18, 1926; C. C. Chapman, *The Development of American Business and Banking Thought*, New York, 1936, p. 69; S. M. Vauclain, "Speeding Up for Prosperity," *Nation's Business*, May 1928; Edgar Heermance, *The Ethics of Business*, New York, 1926, p. 164; D. D. Lescohier, *History of Labor in the United States*, New York, 1935, p. 90.

16.   *New York Times*, Feb. 9, April 23, 1926. For views on the course of the economy, see *New York Times*, Jan. 1, 1926; *New York Evening Post*, Jan. 2, 1925; *New York Herald Tribune*, Jan. 1–2, 1926.

17. *Nation's Business*, May, 1925; *New York Herald Tribune*, Jan. 2, 1926.

18. *New York Times*, Oct. 26, 1926; May 20, Oct. 10, 17, 1927; M. W. Alexander, "America's New Era of Economic Power," *Current History*, Oct. 1925.

19. *Commercial and Financial Chronicle*, Jan. 1927; *New York Times*, Jan. 1, 20, 1927; Victor M. Cutter, "Our Greatest Economic Problem," *Current History*, Oct. 1927.

20. Warburg Papers, Yale University Library; *New York Times*, Sept. 11, Oct. 5, 1926.

21. *New York Times*, March 11, 1921; Senate Committee on Banking and Currency, "Investigation of Stock Market Practices" (1934); Ferdinand Pecora, *Wall Street Under Oath*, New York, 1939, p. 51.

22. *New York Herald Tribune*, Jan. 2, 1929; *New York Times*, Jan. 1, 1928; Thomas Nixon Carver, *The Present Economic Revolution in the United States*, Boston, 1928, pp. 9, 27, 90, 261.

23. Clarence Wooley, "The Business Cycle—Myth or Reality," *World's Work*, Dec. 1927; *New York Evening Post*, Jan. 3, 1928; *New York Times*, Jan. 2, 1928.

24. *New York Herald Tribune*, Jan. 2, 1928; *Brooklyn Daily Times*, Jan. 12, 1928.

25. *Commercial and Financial Chronicle*, March 1928.

26. *New York Times*, April 21, 1928.

27. *Literary Digest*, May 12, 1928.

28. *New York Times*, June 17, July 15, 1928.

29. *Literary Digest*, June 9, 1928; *American Bankers Association Journal*, July 1928.

30. *Review of Reviews*, Sept. 1928; *New York Times*, Sept. 20–Oct. 3, Nov. 11, 1928; *New York Sun*, Oct. 13, 1928.

31. *New York Evening Post*, Jan. 2, 1929; *New York Times*, Jan. 1, 1929; *New York Herald Tribune*, Jan. 2, 1929; *Commercial and Financial Chronicle*, Jan. 12, 1929; *National City Bank Review*, Jan. 1, 1929.

32. *New York Times*, Feb. 13, March 6, 1929; *Commercial and Financial Chronicle*, March 30, 1929.

33. Alexander Dana Noyes, *The Market Place*, Boston, 1938, p. 323; Warburg Papers; also reprinted in *Commercial and Financial Chronicle*, March 7, 1929.

34. *New York Evening Post*, Feb. 27, 1929; *Commercial and Financial Chronicle*, March 2, April 1, 14, 1929; *The Bankers Magazine*, April 1929; *New York Times*, April 2, 1929.

35. *Commercial and Financial Chronicle*, March 23, April 6, May 18, 1929.

36. Kent Papers; *Commercial and Financial Chronicle*, July, Aug. 1929.

37. John J. Raskob, "Everybody Ought To Be Rich," *Ladies' Home Journal*, Aug. 1929.

38. Paul Mazur, *American Prosperity*, p. 250; Charles A. Dice, *The Stock Market*, New York, 1929.

39. *Commercial and Financial Chronicle*, Sept. 1929; *New York Times*, Sept. 20, Oct. 15, 21–24, 1929; *New York Herald Tribune*, Oct. 21, 1929.

40. *New York Evening Post*, Oct. 24, 1929; *New York Times*, Oct. 30, 1929; *Business Week*, Nov. 2, 1929.

41. *Business Week*, Dec. 11, 1929; Jan. 29, 1930.

Chapter 5, pp. 115–58

1. *New York Times,* Jan. 1, 1930.
2. *Ibid.*
3. *Ibid.,* Nov. 11–27, 1929.
4. Allen, *Only Yesterday,* p. 30; Thurman W. Arnold, *The Folklore of Capitalism,* New Haven, 1937, p. 17; Bruce Bliven, "Let's Buy America," *New Republic,* Aug. 3, 1932.
5. *New York Times,* June 22, Aug. 19, Sept. 14, Oct. 21, Nov. 25, Dec. 23, 1930; Jan. 2, 14, 18, 1931; Jan. 1, Feb. 10, 1932.
6. Senate Finance Committee, "Investigation of Economic Problems" (1933). Business leaders were overwhelmingly in favor of the RFC. See Senate Banking and Currency Committee, "Creation of RFC" (1931).
7. *New York Times,* Jan. 25, 1932; Arthur M. Schlesinger, Jr., *The Crisis of the Old Order,* Boston, 1957, p. 180.
8. O'Connor, *Steel-Dictator,* p. 360; *New York Times,* Jan. 24, May 29, 1936; Harvey O'Connor, *Mellon's Millions,* New York, 1933, p. 338; Fred I. Kent Papers; "Investigation of Economic Problems"; Senate Committee on Education and Labor, "Hearings to Create a National Labor Board" (1935), p. 526; *Literary Digest,* June 9, 1923; John P. Diggins, "Flirtations with Fascism," *American Historical Review,* Vol. 71, No. 2, Jan. 1966.
9. Senate Banking and Currency Committee, "Operation of the National and Federal Reserve Banking Systems." Part 1 (1931). Mary Jane Matz, *The Many Lives of Otto Kahn,* New York, 1930; "Investigation of Economic Problems."
10. Kent Papers.
11. *New York Times,* Oct. 21, 1930; Charles A. Beard, ed., *America Faces the Future,* Boston, 1932, p. 44; *Scribner's* magazine, Sept. 1935; *Saturday Evening Post,* Nov. 8, 1930; March 28, 1931.
12. Senate Banking and Currency Committee, "Hearings on the Banking Act of 1935."
13. *New York Times,* Jan. 1, 1932; Kent Papers; *Commercial and Financial Chronicle,* Jan. 1931; "Operation of the National and Federal Reserve Banking Systems."
14. *New York Times,* Jan. 30, 1931.
15. *New York Times,* Jan. 1, 24, 1932; Jan. 27, 1933; George L. Harrison Papers; Kent Papers.
16. "Investigation of Economic Problems."
17. *Ibid.;* Senate Banking and Currency Committee, "Creation of RFC" (1931).
18. House Banking and Currency Committee, Hearings, "To Provide a Guaranty Fund for Depositors in Banks" (1932).
19. *New York Times,* Jan. 2, 1931.
20. Marriner S. Eccles, *Beckoning Frontiers,* New York, 1951; Marriner S. Eccles, *Economic Balance and a Balanced Budget,* ed., by Rudolph L. Weissman, New York, 1940.
21. "Investigation of Economic Problems."
22. J. George Frederick, ed., *A Philosophy of Production,* New York, 1930, chap. 6; "Investigation of Economic Problems."
23. Litchfield, *Industrial Voyage,* 1954.

24. Beard, ed., *America Faces the Future*, chap. V; *New York Times*, Jan. 17, 1931.

25. Henry Ford, *Moving Forward*, Garden City, N.Y., 1930, p. 2; Paul Mazur, *New Roads to Prosperity*, New York, 1931, pp. 25, 26, 54; Mazur, *America Looks Abroad*, New York, 1930, p. 32.

26. Filene, *Successful Living in This Machine Age;* E. A. Filene, *Speaking of Change*, New York, 1939, chap. 4.

27. *The Golden Book* magazine, June 1932.

28. House Committee on Labor, "Hearings on Thirty-Hour Week Bill" (1933), p. 787.

29. *New York Times*, Aug. 31, 1930; Jan. 27, 1933; George Seldes, *Freedom of the Press*, Indianapolis, Ind., 1935, p. 159.

30. *New York Times*, Feb. 14, Oct. 13, 1932; Ernest T. Weir, "Men and Machines," *American* magazine, Aug. 1933; James D. Mooney, *Wages and the Road Ahead*, New York, 1931; Samuel Crowther, ed., *A Basis for Stability*, Boston, 1932, p. 66; Proctor W. Hansl, *Years of Plunder*, New York, 1935, p. 280.

31. *New York Times*, March 11, 1931; Kirstein Papers, Baker Library, Harvard University.

32. *New York Times*, Aug. 24, 1932.

33. J. George Frederick, ed., *The Swope Plan*, New York, 1932, pp. 19, 66; J. George Frederick, ed., *Readings in Economic Planning*, New York, 1933, p. 333; A. Reppy, ed., *National Conference on The Relation of Law and Business*, New York, 1931, p. 109; *New York Times*, Nov. 8, 1931; April 15, 1932; "Investigation of Economic Problems."

34. *Nation's Business*, June 1933; Senate Hearings on the Thirty-Hour Bill.

35. Crowther, *A Basis for Stability*, p. 59.

36. *New York Times*, May 2, 13, 27, June 7, 23, 1932; "Investigation of Economic Problems"; *Nation's Business*, June 1932.

37. *New York Times*, Jan. 15, 19, Dec. 4, 1932.

38. Seligman Papers.

39. *New York Herald Tribune*, Jan. 5, 1932.

Chapter 6, pp. 159–209

1. *New York Times*, Oct. 19, 20, 25, 1932.

2. *New York Sun*, Dec. 19, 1939; Loth, *Swope of GE*, p. 253.

3. A. A. Berle, Jr., "Private Business and Public Opinion," *Scribner's* magazine, Feb. 1934.

4. Vanderlip Papers.

5. Quoted in O'Connor, *Steel-Dictator*, p. 355.

6. Arthur M. Schlesinger, Jr., *The Coming of the New Deal*, Boston, 1958, p. 502.

7. Ernest K. Lindley, *The Roosevelt Revolution, First Phase*, New York, 1933, pp. 74 ff.

8. John T. Flynn, "Other People's Money," *New Republic*, Dec. 3, 1933; *New York Times*, May 18, March 5, April 27, 1933.

9. Quoted in Ferdinand Pecora, *Wall Street Under Oath*, p. 52; House Committee on Labor, "Hearings on Thirty-Hour Week Bill" (1933), p. 649; *New York Times*, June 13, 22, 1933.

10. Schlesinger, *The Coming of the New Deal;* John Morton Blum, *From the Morgenthau Diaries,* Boston, 1959, p. 64.

11. *New York Times,* April 12, 27, May 27, June 23, 1933; Senate Committee on Banking and Currency, "Report on Investigation of Stock Exchange Practices" (1934).

12. Watson, *As I Knew Them,* p. 254; *New York Times,* June 3, 1933.

13. *New York Times,* May 10, 1933; "Hearings on Thirty-Hour Week Bill."

14. *New York Times,* June 14, 1933.

15. H. P. Kendall, "Cotton Textiles First," *Survey Graphic,* Sept. 1933; *New York Times,* Feb. 23, 1934; Eugene G. Grace, "Industry and the Recovery Act," *Scribner's* magazine, Feb. 1934; *New York Times,* May 26, 1933; Ralph E. Flanders, "Business Looks at the NRA," *Atlantic Monthly,* Nov. 1933.

16. *New York Times,* May 21, 1933; Nov. 8, 1933; *New York Herald Tribune,* June 29, 1933; Marquis James, *Alfred I. duPont,* Indianapolis, Ind., 1941, p 502.

17. *Steel,* Aug. 20, 1933.

18. Brown, *Reminiscences of an Industrialist.*

19. *New York Times,* Jan. 11, 1934; May 1, Nov. 7, 1935; "Human Rights and Property Rights," *Vital Speeches,* Dec. 3, 1934.

20. T. I. Parkinson, "A Call to Action," *Vital Speeches,* Nov. 1, 1938; Kirstein Papers.

21. *New York Times,* Feb. 28, 1934; Nov. 8, 1933; *Commercial and Financial Chronicle,* March 3, 1934.

22. *Ibid.,* Nov. 4, 1933, *New York Times,* Nov. 20, Dec. 7, 1933; Senate Finance Committee, "Hearings on Investigation of the NIRA," part I and II, 1934.

23. *New York Times,* May 28, 1935; "A Great Spiritual Victory," *Steel,* June 3, 1935.

24. *Steel,* June 3, 1935; *New York Times,* June 7, 1935.

25. *New York Times,* Nov. 16, 19, 24, 1933.

26. Vanderlip Papers; *New York Times,* Nov. 30, 1938; H. W. Prentis, Jr., "The Catalyzers of Liberty."

27. *New York Times,* March 14, 1934; Alpheus Mason, *Harlan Fiske Stone,* New York, p. 371; *Fortune,* April 1934.

28. Kent Papers.

29. *New York Times,* March 8, 1935; Brown, *Reminiscences.*

30. Vanderlip Papers; George Wolfskill, *The Revolt of the Conservatives: A History of the American Liberty League, 1934–40,* Boston, 1962.

31. *Nation's Business,* June 1935; *New York Times,* May 3, June 27, Sept. 7, 1935.

32. *New York Times,* Oct. 10, Dec. 4, Dec. 17, 1935.

33. *New York Times,* Jan. 7, May 20, 29, 1936.

34. Charles A. and Mary R. Beard, *America in Midpassage,* p. 331; Richberg Papers, Library of Congress; Albert Shaw Papers, New York Public Library; G. E. Edwards, *Evolution of Finance Capitalism,* New York, 1938, p. 331; *New York Times,* Oct. 28, 1936.

35. *New York Times,* Jan. 15, May 3, 1937; Jan. 3, 1938; Arthur M. Schlesinger, *New Deal in Action,* New York, 1940, p. 5.

36. *The Secret Diary of Harold L. Ickes,* New York, 1954, Vol. II, pp. 240–42.

37. *New York Times,* Jan. 15, 8, 9, Feb. 2, April 28, Nov. 18, 1938.

38. Harrison Papers.

39. *Emporia Gazette*, May 1, 1936; Elliott V. Bell, *New York Times*, Aug. 16, 1936.

40. For typical comments, see Kent Papers; *Vital Speeches*, Dec. 30, 1935; Schlesinger, *Coming of the New Deal*, p. 311; *New York Times*, June 10, 1935; May 6, 1938.

41. *Commercial and Financial Chronicle*, Feb. 5, 1938; Senate Banking and Currency Committee, "Hearings on the Banking Act of 1935"; Senate Finance Committee, "Hearings on the Economic Security Act (1935)"; *New York Times*, April 25, 1931.

42. "What Business Thinks," *Fortune*, Oct. 1939; "Third Survey of Executive Opinion," *Fortune*, Dec. 1940.

43. Mason, *Harlan Fiske Stone*, p. 370; *New York Times*, May 20, 1938; April 21, 1936.

44. La Follette Report, No. 6, Part 6, p. 121; A. W. Robertson, "The Rule of Minorities," *Vital Speeches*, April 15, 1939.

45. *New York Times*, April 8, 1936; Nov. 16, 1938; Sept. 26, 1935; Alfred P. Sloan, Jr., "Industry's Responsibilities Broaden," *Vital Speeches*, Dec. 30, 1935.

46. Litchfield, *Industrial Voyage;* Kent Papers; *The Basic Papers of George Humphrey*, Cleveland, Ohio, 1965.

47. *New York Times*, May 29, 1936; May 20, 1934; May 22, 1936; Alfred P. Sloan, "Important Questions of National Policy," *Vital Speeches*, Dec. 17, 1934.

48. Hearings on the Black-Connery bill, p. 761; *New York Sun*, Jan. 4, 1936; *New York Times*, Dec. 8, 15, 1937.

49. *Ibid.*, June 16, 1934.

50. Harrison Papers; *New York Times*, Sept. 16, 1933; Jan. 26, May 23, 1934; Henry S. Dennison, *et al.*, *Toward Full Employment*, New York, 1938.

51. Percy H. Johnston, "Our Overwhelming Tax Problems," *Vital Speeches*, Oct. 22, 1934; Philip Benson, "The Budget, Inflation, and Saving," *Vital Speeches*, March 25, 1935; Winthrop Aldrich, "The Financing of Unemployment Relief," *Vital Speeches*, Dec. 17, 1934; Coolidge estimate in the Harrison Papers.

52. *New York Times*, Dec. 11, 1935; Jan. 13, 1937.

53. *New York Times*, Jan. 13, 14, 1937; Eccles, *Economic Balance and a Balanced Budget*, p. 5.

54. *Vital Speeches*, July 29, 1935; Kent Papers; *New York Sun*, Jan. 4, 1936; Economists National Committee on Monetary Policy; *Vital Speeches*, Nov. 5, 1934.

55. *New York Times*, March 21, 1939; Jan. 18, 1934; Harrison Papers; *New York Times*, Nov. 19, 1933; Kent Papers; *New York Times*, May 4, 1938; Senate Committee on Banking and Currency, "Hearings on the Banking Act of 1935"; *New York Times*, Jan. 13, 21, July 3, 1937. For a criticism of the orthodox position, see George Morrison, *Liquidity Preferences of Commercial Banks*, Chicago, 1966.

Chapter 7, pp. 210–47

1. House Committee on the Judiciary, "Study of Monopoly Power" (1950).

2. C. C. Rohlfing, *et al.*, *Business and Government*, Chicago, 1938, p. 1.

3. Robert R. Wason, "Our Domestic Policy," *Vital Speeches*, March 13, 1966; *New York Times*, May 21, 1952.

4. *Commercial and Financial Chronicle*, July 18, 1949.

5. *Ibid.*, May 25, 1950.

6. *Ibid.*, Oct. 11, 1951.

7. C. E. Wilson, "The Camel's Nose Is Under the Tent," *Vital Speeches*, Oct. 15, 1951; H. W. Prentis, Jr., "America Tomorrow," *Ibid.*, Feb. 15, 1947; Wason, *op. cit.; New York Times*, April 16, 1952; *Commercial and Financial Chronicle*, Sept. 18, 1952.

8. Walter Linn, "Dangers to Our American Way of Life," *Vital Speeches*, March 15, 1947; *Commercial and Financial Chronicle*, April 29, 1948; Nov. 9, 1950; *New York Times*, Dec. 14, 1949.

9. *New York Times*, Nov. 12, 1952; *Commercial and Financial Chronicle*, Jan. 7, 1952; Oct. 14, 1948; Sept. 20, 1951.

10. *Ibid.*, June 7, 1951; *New York Times*, Oct. 1, 15, 1952.

11. Russell Leffingwell, "Outlook and Prospects of End of War," *Yale Review*, June 1945; Charles E. Wilson, "Problems Industry Faces," *Vital Speeches*, Jan. 1, 1947.

12. *Commercial and Financial Chronicle*, July 31, 1947; *New York Times*, Oct. 2, 1947.

13. *Commercial and Financial Chronicle*, Feb. 14, 1947; *New York Times*, March 15, 1946; Sept. 4, 1947.

14. *New York Times*, Aug. 14, 28, 1947; *Commercial and Financial Chronicle*, Oct. 2, 1947.

15. Joint Committee on the Economic Report, "Current Price Developments" (1947), p. 212; *New York Times*, Jan. 2, Feb. 4, 14, May 21, 1948; *Commercial and Financial Chronicle*, Jan.–Feb. 1948; Joint Committee on the Economic Report (Flanders Report), "Corporate Profits" (1948).

16. *New York Times*, April 24, May 24, 1946.

17. *Ibid.*, Jan. 3, 9, March 8, April 29, 1949; *Commercial and Financial Chronicle*, Jan. 9, 1949; Nov. 1950; May 31, 1951.

18. *Commercial and Financial Chronicle*, Feb. 9, March 1, Oct.–Nov. 1950; Feb. 1951; Nov. 12, 1952; Sept. 24, 1953; *New York Times*, Jan. 6, 7, 8, 23, Feb. 2, 1954.

19. *Commercial and Financial Chronicle*, March 4, Aug. 5, 1948; Aug. 17, Dec. 21, 1950; Oct. 23, 1947; May 1, 1952; *New York Times*, Nov. 27, 1950; Humphrey, *The Basic Papers of George Humphrey*, p. 40.

20. *Commercial and Financial Chronicle*, Nov. 18, 1945; *New York Times*, Jan. 29, 1948.

21. *New York Times*, March 5, 1946; Jan. 19, 1952; *Commercial and Financial Chronicle*, Jan. 24, 1952.

22. *Commercial and Financial Chronicle*, Jan. 29, 1948; Dec. 21, 1950; Sept. 15, 1949; Feb. 26, 1948; Nov. 22, 1951; Feb. 21, 1952; Joint Committee, "Current Price Developments" (1947); Flanders Report (1948).

23. *New York Times*, July 5, 1948.

24. *Commercial and Financial Chronicle*, March 4, Jan. 15, 1948; *New York Times*, Jan. 5, 1948.

25. *Commercial and Financial Chronicle*, Aug. 17, 1950; Jan. 11, Feb. 8, 1951.

26. *Ibid.*, Dec. 11, 1947; Earl Bunting, "Industry's Answer to the Police State," *Vital Speeches*, Dec. 15, 1947; *New York Times*, Dec. 5, 1949; Jan. 23, 1948.

27. *New York Times,* Jan. 14, Aug. 24, 1947; April 20–22, July 2–9, 1948.

28. *Commercial and Financial Chronicle,* May 27, 1948; Nov. 30, 1950; April 19, July 5, 1951.

29. *New York Times,* May 8, 1952; *Commercial and Financial Chronicle,* Jan. 29, Oct. 7, Dec. 9, 1948; Bunting, *op. cit.;* Lewis H. Brown, "Fighting Inflation," *Vital Speeches,* Jan. 1, 1948.

30. *New York Times,* Jan. 13, Sept. 15, Nov. 23, 1949.

31. *New York Times,* March 1–3, 14, April 5, 8, 24, 1946; Lewis H. Brown, "How to Get the Country Back to Work," *Vital Speeches,* March 15, 1946; *New York Times,* Oct. 16, 1946.

32. *New York Times,* May 4, 1947; *Commercial and Financial Chronicle,* June 3, 1948.

33. *New York Times,* Jan. 26, 1952; *Commercial and Financial Chronicle,* Oct. 1950; Jan. 1951; May 1, June 19, 1952.

34. *New York Times,* May 4, 1946; Feb. 17, 1948; Feb. 16, 1949; Osborne, *Men at the Top,* p. 203.

35. *New York Times,* May 8, 1952; Bunting, *op. cit.; Commercial and Financial Chronicle,* Aug. 18, 1948; Wason, *Vital Speeches,* March 13, 1946; Kent Papers.

36. *Commercial and Financial Chronicle,* Feb. 5, 1948.

37. *New York Times,* March 8, 1947; Bunting, *Vital Speeches,* Dec. 15, 1947.

38. Joint Economic Committee, "Current Price Developments" (1947); Kent Papers.

39. *New York Times,* Aug. 1, 1949; Wason, *Vital Speeches,* March 13, 1946; *Commercial and Financial Chronicle,* Jan. 23, 1948; Allen, *Individual Initiative in Business,* p. 14; Clifford Hood in *Advanced Management,* Oct. 1950; *New York Times,* March 5, 1948; June 4, July 15, 1947.

40. Humphrey, *The Basic Papers of George Humphrey.*

41. John L. Collyer and H. P. Liversidge in *Commercial and Financial Chronicle,* Oct. 11, 18, 1951; See also Gwilym Price in *Coronet,* Jan. 1950; Don G. Mitchell, "Call to Action on Taxes," *Vital Speeches,* Dec. 4, 1947; Henry J. Kaiser, *New York Times,* Nov. 18, 1948; Winthrop W. Aldrich, *Commercial and Financial Chronicle,* Nov. 22, 25, 1951; *New York Times,* April 1951.

42. *Commercial and Financial Chronicle,* Jan. 15, 1953; *Mill and Factory,* Oct. 1952; *New York Times,* Nov. 12, 13, 1952.

43. *Commercial and Financial Chronicle,* Feb. 10, 1955.

Chapter 8, pp. 248–97

1. *Vital Speeches,* May 15, 1955.

2. *Rubber World,* April 1957; *Commercial and Financial Chronicle,* March 14, 1957; *New York Times,* March 7, 1957.

3. "Government of Men and Money," an address by Henry C. Alexander, Nov. 28, 1960.

4. Unpublished speech by Paul Gorman, 1964; Osborne, *Men at the Top,* p. 187; unpublished speech by Logan T. Johnston, 1962.

5. John E. Swearingen, "Government and the Corporation in the Mid-1960's," unpublished speech, 1964; *Commercial and Financial Chronicle,* March 14, 1957.

6. Theodore Sorensen, *Kennedy,* New York, 1965, p. 45; Hobart

Rowen, *The Free Enterprisers,* New York, 1964; *New York Times,* Jan. 7, 1965.

7. Hearings before the ICC, June 1955; unpublished speech by Daniel J. Haughton, May 2, 1964; Clarence A. Randall, "A Creed for Free Enterprise," *Commercial and Financial Chronicle,* Oct. 6, 1955.

8. M. J. Rathbone, unpublished speech, 1961; *New York Times,* April 27, 1956; *Commercial and Financial Chronicle,* July 5, 1956.

9. *Commercial and Financial Chronicle,* Nov. 2, 1961; Dec. 5, 1957; *New York Times,* Feb. 2, 1967.

10. *New York Times,* May 3, 1966.

11. L. B. Worthington, "The Business of America," unpublished speech, 1964; B. F. Biaggini, "The Management of Change," unpublished talk, 1965; Eugene Holman in "Investigation of the Financial Condition of the U.S." (1958); Benjamin Fairless, "Private Enterprise in the Public Interest."

12. *Commercial and Financial Chronicle,* Jan. 11, 1964.

13. James F. Oates, unpublished talk, 1962; Herbert V. Prochnow, 1962; *Commercial and Financial Chronicle,* May 16, 1962.

14. *United States News and World Report,* Dec. 25, 1961.

15. J. Edward Warren, "Toward a Progressive Future," unpublished speech, 1964.

16. *Commercial and Financial Chronicle,* April 5, 1956.

17. *Ibid.,* May 19, 1962.

18. *Ibid.,* May 22, 1962; Jan. 17, 1963.

19. *Ibid.,* June 2, 1965; *New York Times,* May 25, 1965.

20. Edward A. O'Neil, "Investment in America," unpublished talk, April 1965.

21. *Wall Street Journal,* Nov. 10, 1965; *New York Times,* Jan. 10, 1966.

22. *New York Times,* Feb. 7, 1961; Aug. 17, Dec. 2, 1965; *Wall Street Journal,* Nov. 10, 1965; Lawrence Litchfield, Jr., "New Dimensions in International Business;" James F. Oates "How Can We Improve Our Unfavorable Balance of Payments," unpublished speech, 1963.

23. *Commercial and Financial Chronicle,* Dec. 1, 1955; *New York Times,* Oct. 24, 1955.

24. *New York Times,* April 5, May 11, 1957.

25. *Ibid.,* Jan. 8, April 13, 1958.

26. *Ibid.,* Oct. 19, Dec. 4, 1962.

27. *Commercial and Financial Chronicle,* Jan.–June 1962; March–Sept. 1966; "Abreast of the Market," *Wall Street Journal,* Jan.–June 1962; March–Sept. 1966.

28. See the estimates offered by Herbert V. Prochnow, Devereux C. Josephs, Ralph Cordiner, and Leo Cherne in the *Commercial and Financial Chronicle,* 1955, 1956, and 1958.

29. *Commercial and Financial Chronicle,* March 15, 1956; May 22, 1958; Donald C. Cook, "The Economic Outlook," Nov. 4, 1965.

30. *Commercial and Financial Chronicle,* Feb. 6, 1957; Jan. 1, 1959.

31. "Investigation of the Financial Condition of the U.S." (1958); *Commercial and Financial Chronicle,* March 7, May 7, 1957.

32. *Ibid.,* July 8, 1957.

33. R. C. Gerhan, "The Case of the Vanishing Dollar," *Vital Speeches,* Jan. 15, 1960; *Commercial and Financial Chronicle,* April 2, 1958; July 21, 1955; July 4, 1957; H. Bruce Palmer, "Inflation Control," *Vital Speeches,* April 15, 1960; Hutton to Richberg, July 30, 1956.

34. Harold Quinton, "A History of Inflation," *Vital Speeches,* Nov. 15, 1960.

35. *Commercial and Financial Chronicle,* Oct. 11, 1956; Nov. 7, 1957; May 14, 1959; *New York Times,* May 12, 1959; "Investigation of the Financial Condition of the U.S." (1958).

36. *Commercial and Financial Chronicle,* Nov. 15, 1956.

37. *Ibid.,* June 6, Oct. 3, 1957; House Committee on the Judiciary, Subcommittee on Anti-trust and Monopoly, "Administered Prices" (1957); U. S. Steel, "Annual Report," March 20, 1957; Roger Blough, "Inflation as a Way of Life," *Vital Speeches,* Feb. 1, 1957; *Free Man and the Corporation,* New York, 1959; "The Bread of Tomorrow," an unpublished address, Nov. 1966.

38. "Investigation of the Financial Condition of the U.S." (1958); Ernest Breech, "Unions," *Vital Speeches,* April 1, 1958.

39. *Commercial and Financial Chronicle,* Nov. 28, 1957; April 7, 1959.

40. "Investigation of the Financial Condition of the U.S." (1958); Carl R. Megowan, "The Economy of the Future and Its Roadblocks," unpublished speech, 1959; *Wall Street Journal,* Dec. 13, 1965.

41. *Commercial and Financial Chronicle,* Dec. 6, 1956; "Investigation of the Financial Condition of the U.S." (1958).

42. *Commercial and Financial Chronicle,* April 14, 1955; Jan. 24, 1957; *New York Times,* Dec. 5, 1965.

43. *Ibid.,* Dec. 13, 1956; Oct. 29, 1959; David Rockefeller, "Are We Growing Too Fast?" *Vital Speeches,* Dec. 1, 1956; *New York Times,* Nov. 21, 1957; Nov. 2, 1965.

44. Emmet G. Solomon, "The Quality of Credit," unpublished address, 1965.

45. Lewis W. Douglas, "Some Open Questions on Inflation," *Vital Speeches,* July 1, 1957; S. Clark Beise, "Are Our Money Controls Outmoded?", *Commercial and Financial Chronicle,* Nov. 22, 1956.

46. *Ibid.,* May 17, 1956; *New York Times,* May 14, Oct. 25, 1956; Robert R. Young, "Whose Inflation?," *Vital Speeches,* Dec. 15, 1956; Senate Judiciary Committee, "Administered Prices" (1957).

47. "Investigation of the Financial Condition of the U.S." (1958); *New York Times,* July 1, 1965.

48. "Investigation of the Financial Condition of the U.S." (1958); *Commercial and Financial Chronicle,* May 7, 16, 1957; Sept. 4, Dec. 25, 1958; May 14, 1959.

49. National Small Business Association, "Bulletin," Washington, D. C., Aug. 1964.

50. Thomas Graham Belden and Marva Robbins Belden, *The Lengthening Shadow; The Life of Thomas J. Watson,* Boston, 1962, p. 282.

51. Donald C. Cook, "The Economic Outlook," unpublished talk, Nov. 1965; *Commercial and Financial Chronicle,* April 3, 1958; *American Banker,* Aug. 10, 1965; Rudolph A. Peterson, "Debt in a New Environment," New York University Graduate School of Business Administration, 1964.

52. *Commercial and Financial Chronicle,* Nov. 10, 1955; July 28, 1959; Oct. 3, 1963; James F. Oates, Jr., "Thinking Ahead in Federal Tax Policy," unpublished talk, Nov. 1965; *General Electric Forum,* Vol. VI, No. 3, July–Sept. 1963; George Moore, "Domestic Growth and Our Role as a World Banker," unpublished speech, 1963.

53. "Investigation of the Financial Condition of the U.S." (1958); *Banking,* Feb. 1963; Roger Blough, "Government—A Wonderful Cash Business," unpublished address, Oct. 1962; George Champion, "Our Growing Responsibilities in a Changing World"; "Let's Stop Apologizing for Free Enterprise," unpublished talks, 1964 and 1965.

54. Blough, *op. cit.; Commercial and Financial Chronicle,* Oct. 6, 1955; Feb. 22, 1962; Jan. 17, 1963; "Investigation of the Financial Condition of the U.S." (1958); Logan T. Johnston, "Candy Canes and Sugar Plums," 1962.

55. *New York Times,* June 8, 1961; Nov. 30, 1962; "Investigation of the Financial Condition of the U.S." (1958).

56. *New York Times,* March 8, April 3, May 17, 22, 1958; "Investigation of the Financial Condition of the U.S." (1958).

57. *Commercial and Financial Chronicle,* Oct. 26, 1961; *Business Week,* April 29, 1961; *Steel,* May 5, 1961.

58. *New York Times,* June 29, 1962; J. Doyle DeWitt, unpublished talk, March 27, 1963.

59. Arjay Miller, unpublished talk, Sept. 1963; *General Electric Forum,* Vol. VI, No. 3, July–Sept. 1963; *Commercial and Financial Chronicle,* May 7, 1963; *New York Times,* Dec. 1, 1966.

Chapter 9, pp. 301–43

1. C. H. Crennan, "Business Men and the Business Cycle," *Annals,* Vol. 109, Sept. 1923.

2. O'Connor, *Mellon's Millions,* p. 339; *Commercial and Financial Chronicle,* Nov. 9, 1950.

3. *Ibid.,* Nov. 9, 1950; unpublished address by M. G. O'Neil, "Free Enterprise—the Right to Go Broke," 1965.

4. *New York Times,* April 27, 1921; *Wall Street Journal,* Feb. 17, 1967.

5. J. P. Seiberling, "Humbug and Double Talk," *Vital Speeches,* June 20, 1946; Winthrop W. Aldrich, *Vital Speeches,* Dec. 17, 1934.

6. Batchelor, ed., *The New Outlook in Business,* p. 56; J. Howard Pew, *What the Future Holds for the American System of Free Enterprise,* New York, 1939, p. 13; *Commercial and Financial Chronicle,* Feb. 13, 1947.

7. *New York Times,* Nov. 12, 1924.

8. *Commercial and Financial Chronicle,* May 21, 1927; J. H. Williams, "The Sherman Act Today," *Atlantic Monthly,* March 1928.

9. Chapman, *The Development of American Business and Banking Thought,* p. 68; Heermance, *The Ethics of Business,* pp. 149–50; Arthur R. Burns, *The Decline of Competition,* New York, 1936, p. 153.

10. *Journal of Commerce,* Oct. 29, 1921; Beard, ed., *Whither Mankind?,* p. 104; *New York Times,* May 21, 1927.

11. Bernard Baruch, *My Own Story,* New York, 1957, p. 116.

12. David Sarnoff, "Science Will Destroy the Laggard," *Nation's Business,* Jan. 1930.

13. Blough, *Free Man and the Corporation,* p. 11; House Committee on the Judiciary, Subcommittee on Anti-trust, "Administered Prices" (1957).

14. *New York Times,* Aug. 13, 1957; Mortimer, *The Purposeful Pursuit of Profits and Growth in Business.*

15. Benjamin Fairless, "Detour Ahead," unpublished speech, 1950; Robert E. Wilson, "Oil Competition in the Midwest," *Vital Speeches,* Oct. 15, 1950.

16. "Administered Prices" (1957); Lammot du Pont Copeland, "Building a Strong Economy," unpublished talk, 1962; *Commercial and Financial Chronicle,* Nov. 13, 1950; M. J. Rathbone, "A Businessman's View of Some Antitrust Problems," unpublished speech, 1965; *New York Times,* Sept. 9, 1966.

17. *Commercial and Financial Chronicle,* Dec. 16, 1953; *New York Times,* May 31, 1964.

18. Thomas W. Lamont, "Problems of the Incoming Administration," *Harper's Magazine,* March 1921; Otto H. Kahn, "The Road to Prosperity," *Forum,* Oct. 1921.

19. *Nation's Business,* May 1937, quoting the Chamber, Jan. 21, 1922; *New York Times,* May 14, 1922.

20. *New York Post,* July 5, 1923; Jan. 2, 1925; W. L. Clause, "Shall We Be the World's Bankers?" *Nation's Business,* Sept. 1925; *New York Times,* Sept. 23, 1926.

21. *New York Times,* Oct. 20–21, 1926.

22. *Ibid.,* Feb. 8, 1929; House Ways and Means Committee, "Hearings on Tariff Readjustment," 1929, Vol. III; *New York Herald Tribune,* Jan. 2, 1929.

23. *New York Times,* May 30, June 20, Nov. 15, 1930; McCarter, *One Phase of a Jerseyman's Activities,* p. 578; Arthur D. H. Smith, *Men Who Run America,* Indianapolis, Ind., 1936, p. 289.

24. Crowther, ed., *A Basis for Stability,* p. 54; *New York Times,* April 27, Oct. 28, 1933; Senate Committee on Finance, "Hearings on Renewal of Reciprocal Trade Agreements Act," 1940, p. 605.

25. Senate Investigation of Economic Problems, 1933; Senate Committee on Finance, "Hearings on Reciprocal Trade Agreements," 1934; *New York Times,* May 29, 1936.

26. *New York Times,* May 22, 1936.

27. *New York Herald Tribune,* Nov. 30, 1945; *New York Times,* Jan. 12, 1947; Feb. 6, 1961; May 31, 1964; Feb. 8, 1967; *Wall Street Journal,* Feb. 17, 1967; Roger M. Blough, "Time for a New Look at Foreign Trade," unpublished speech, 1967.

28. Elbert H. Gary, "Remarks at Annual Meeting of the United States Steel Corporation," April 16, 1923; "Address at Semi-Annual Meeting of the American Iron and Steel Institute," Oct. 27, 1922.

29. Investigation of Economic Problems (1933); E. G. Nourse, *Price Making in a Democracy,* Washington, D.C., 1944, p. 329; TNEC, *Investigation of Concentration of Economic Power,* Part 19 (1939), pp. 10,651, 10,652, 10,657, 10,737.

30. *New York Times,* Jan. 28, 1921; Barron, *They Told Barron,* p. 55; C. Ackerman, *George Eastman,* Boston, 1930, pp. 253 ff.

31. *New York Times,* Feb. 6, 1926; July 28, 1927.

32. *Ibid.,* Oct. 25, 1930; Oct. 21, 1932; *"Fortune* Looks at Steel," *Fortune,* April 1936.

33. Seligman Papers.

34. Alfred P. Sloan, Jr., "Important Questions of National Policy," *Vital Speeches,* Dec. 17, 1934; "Shall We Have More or Less?," *Vital Speeches,* June 1, 1936; P. G. Hoffman, "Free Enterprise—Can It Survive?" *Vital Speeches,* Jan. 15, 1939; TNEC, *Investigation,* Part 21, p. 11,199.

35. National Bureau of Economic Research, *Recent Economic Changes,* New York, 1932, p. 615; Ida M. Tarbell, *Life of Elbert H. Gary,* New York, 1925, p. 343; *"Fortune* Looks at Steel," *Fortune,* April 1936; Eugene G. Grace, "Industry and the Recovery Act," *Scribner's,* Feb. 1934.

36. *Commercial and Financial Chronicle,* Sept. 30, 1954; Ben Heineman, "Economics of Railroading Today," unpublished talk, 1959.

37. *Commercial and Financial Chronicle,* Oct. 27, 1955; House Committee on the Judiciary, Subcommittee on Antitrust, "Administered Prices"

(1957); "Price Development and Economic Stabilization," 1947; TNEC, *Investigation*, Part 19, p. 10,526.

38. Brown, *Reminiscences of an Industrialist;* Litchfield, *Autumn Leaves*, p. 88.

39. Batchelor, ed., *The New Outlook in Business*, p. 133.

40. Ernest Dale, *Great Organizers*, New York, 1960.

41. Flanders Committee; Charles Mortimer, "The Power of Free Choice," unpublished talk, 1963; "Current Price Developments," 1947; Lamar Fearing, "America in a Challenging World," unpublished speech, 1962.

42. Robert E. Williams, "Is Anybody Interested?" unpublished speech, 1965; *United States News and World Report*, Oct. 10, 1947.

43. Sidney Alexander Mitchell, *S. Z. Mitchell and the Electrical Industry*, New York, 1960, p. 79.

44. Roger M. Blough, "Private Enterprise in the Public Interest"; Bert S. Cross, 1964; Flanders Committee; Robert G. Dunlop, "Profits and a Free Society," unpublished speech, 1962.

45. William P. Sandford and Willard H. Yeager, *Business Speeches by Businessmen*, New York, 1930, p. 488; Tom Girdler, "Industry and Labor," *Fortune*, Jan. 1938; *Commercial and Financial Chronicle*, Oct. 28, 1922; *New York Times*, May 23, 1924; Tarbell, *Owen D. Young*, New York, 1932, p. 157; C. W. Moore, *Timing a Century*, Cambridge, Mass., 1945, p. 187.

46. Litchfield, *Autumn Leaves*, p. 85; NAM, *Open Shop Encyclopedia*, New York, 1921, p. 112.

47. *New York Times*, Oct. 6, 17, 25, 1926; Robert W. Dunn, *Labor and Automobiles*, New York, 1927, p. 96; *Iron Age*, Oct. 14, 1926; Marion C. Cahill, *Shorter Hours*, New York, 1932, p. 250.

48. Alfred P. Sloan, "Important Questions of National Policy," *Vital Speeches*, Dec. 17, 1934; Batchelor, *The New Outlook in Business*, p. 145.

49. Senate Committee on Education and Labor, "Hearings on Fair Labor Standards Act of 1937," p. 105.

50. *New York Times*, Oct. 21, 1946; Flanders Committee; E. Hazard, "The Real Danger in Automation," unpublished talk, 1964; James Oates, "The Challenge of Big Government to a Free Enterprise Economy," unpublished talk, 1962; see also Ernest Breech in *Vital Speeches*, April 1, 1958.

Chapter 10, pp. 344–73

1. Blough, *Free Man and the Corporation*, pp. 60 ff.

2. *Saturday Review*, Aug. 27, 1960.

3. Robert H. Wiebe, *Businessmen and Reform*, Cambridge, Mass., 1962, p. 166; *Commercial and Financial Chronicle*, Aug. 12, 1922; Waddill Catchings, "Our Common Enterprise," *Atlantic Monthly*, Feb. 1922.

4. *Nation's Business*, Feb., 1930.

5. *Commercial and Financial Chronicle*, Jan. 24, 1952.

6. Kahn, *Reflections of a Financier*, p. 19.

7. Quoted in O'Connor, *Steel-Dictator*, p. 299.

8. Barron, *They Told Barron*, p. 82; Irving Bernstein, *The Lean Years*, Boston, Mass., 1961, p. 147.

9. Albion G. Taylor, *Labor Policies of the National Association of Manufacturers*, Champaign, Ill., 1928, p. 42.

10. La Follette Committee, Report, No. 6, Part 5, p. 10; National

Association of Manufacturers, *Open Shop Encyclopedia*, New York, 1921, pp. 17, 61.

    11. *New York Times*, April 19, 1921; *Journal of Commerce*, May 19, 1921.

    12. *New York Times*, July 16, 1924; J. David Houser, *What the Employer Thinks*, Cambridge, Mass., 1927, p. 24.

    13. E. A. Filene, *Successful Living in This Machine Age*, p. 67; Sam A. Lewisohn, *et al.*, *Can Business Prevent Unemployment?*, New York, 1925, pp. 16 ff.

    14. Houser, *op. cit.*, p. 67; Robert W. Dunn, *Americanization of Labor*, New York, 1927, p. 157. But see Robert Ozanne, *Wages in Practice and Theory*, Madison, Wis., 1968 and same author, *A Century of Labor-Management Relations at McCormick and International Harvester*, Madison, Wis., 1967.

    15. Batchelor, ed., *The New Outlook in Business*, p. 119; *New York Times*, Dec. 29, 1929; Oct. 12, 1930; Aug. 30, 1931; Bernstein, *op. cit.*, p. 467.

    16. "What Business Thinks," *Fortune*, Oct. 1939.

    17. *New York Times*, May 29, June 14, 1933.

    18. Alfred P. Sloan, "Important Questions of National Policy," *Vital Speeches*, Dec. 17, 1934; Senate Committee on Education and Labor, "Hearings to Create a National Labor Board" (1934); Frances Perkins, *The Roosevelt I Knew*, New York, 1946, pp. 221–22; Senate Committee on Finance, "Hearings on National Industrial Recovery" (1933); *New York Times*, Aug. 28, 1933.

    19. "The United States Steel Corporation," *Fortune*, April, May, June 1936.

    20. *New York Times*, May 25, 1935; Brooks, *As Steel Goes . . .* p. 199; Girdler, *Boot Straps*, p. 226.

    21. *New York Times*, June 25, 1937; Girdler, *op. cit.*, pp. 228, 329, 266; *Nation's Business*, June 1938; Tom M. Girdler, "Industry and Labor," *Fortune*, Jan. 1938.

    22. *Nation's Business*, June 1936; *New York Times*, Dec. 10, 1937.

    23. *New York Times*, May 28, 1959; June 21, 1955; Jan. 29, 1947.

    24. Dudley W. Figgis, address delivered at Stevens Institute, June 5, 1948; Kirstein Papers; Loth, *Swope of GE*, p. 256.

    25. Joseph L. Block, "The Joint Responsibility of Labor and Management," "The Role of Government in the Economy," unpublished speeches 1956 and 1957; see also *U.S. News and World Report*, June 8, 1956.

    26. *New York Times*, Dec. 10, 1946; Feb. 20, 1959.

    27. *Ibid.*, May 24, 1946; "Investigation of the Financial Condition of the U.S." (1958).

    28. *Commercial and Financial Chronicle*, April 19, 1951.

    29. *New York Times*, Feb. 20, 1959; Oct. 19, 1958; Sept. 28, 1951.

    30. Ernest Breech, "Unions," *Vital Speeches*, April 1, 1958.

    31. Herman Steinkraus, "The Future of American Labor-Management Relations," *Vital Speeches*, Feb. 15, 1956; *New York Times*, Dec. 13, 1957.

    32. J. D. Zellerbach, "What Does Labor Really Want?," *American* magazine, May 1947; *Commercial and Financial Chronicle*, April 10, 1958.

    33. *New York Times*, Dec. 15, 1937; Nov. 8, Jan. 16, Dec. 10, 20, 1946.

INDICES

NAME INDEX

SUBJECT INDEX